GREEKS AND BARBARIANS

EDINBURGH READINGS ON THE ANCIENT WORLD

GENERAL EDITORS
Michele George, *McMaster University*
Thomas Harrison, *University of St Andrews*

ADVISORY EDITORS
Paul Cartledge, *University of Cambridge*
Richard Saller, *University of Chicago*

This series introduces English-speaking students to central themes
in the history of the ancient world and to the range of scholarly
approaches to those themes, within and across disciplines. Each
volume, edited and introduced by a leading specialist, contains a
selection of the most important work, including a significant
proportion of translated material. The editor also provides a guide
to the history of modern scholarship on the subject. Passages in
ancient languages are translated; technical terms, ancient and
modern, are explained.

PUBLISHED
Sparta
Edited by Michael Whitby

Greeks and Barbarians
Edited by Thomas Harrison

IN PREPARATION
Ancient Slavery
Edited by Keith Bradley

Sexuality in Ancient Greece and Rome
Edited by Mark Golden and Peter Toohey

Ancient Myth
Edited by Richard Gordon

Alexander the Great
Edited by Simon Hornblower

The 'Dark Ages' of Greece
Edited by Ian Morris

The Ancient Economy: Recent Approaches
Edited by Walter Scheidel and Sitta von Reden

Roman Religion
Edited by Clifford Ando

Augustus
Edited by Jonathan Edmonson

GREEKS AND BARBARIANS

Edited by
Thomas Harrison

EDINBURGH UNIVERSITY PRESS

© Editorial matter and selection Thomas Harrison, 2002

Edinburgh University Press Ltd
22 George Square, Edinburgh

Typeset in Sabon
by Norman Tilley Graphics, Northampton
and printed and bound in Great Britain
by MPG Books Ltd, Bodmin, Cornwall

A CIP Record for this book is available from the British Library

ISBN 0 7486 1270 X (hardback)
ISBN 0 7486 1271 8 (paperback)

Contents

Acknowledgements

For permission to reprint the articles included in this volume, I should like to thank the following: Professor James Redfield and the University of Chicago Press (Ch. 1), Dr Simon Goldhill and the Hellenic Society (Ch. 2), Professor Suzanne Saïd, Professor Edmond Lévy and the journal *Ktema* (Ch. 3), Giulio Einaudi editore (Chs 4, 12), Professor Anna Morpurgo Davies and Presses Universitaires de Nancy (Ch. 6), Presses Universitaires de France (Ch. 7), the University of North Carolina Press (Ch. 5), Annales littéraires de l'Université de France-Comté (Ch. 8), the journal *Annales* (ch. 9), Professor Frank Walbank and the journal *Phoenix* (Ch. 10); I have been unsuccessful in tracing the holder of the rights to Ch. 11 by the late Professor Robert Browning. Details of the original place of publication of articles are given at the head of each chapter.

For permission to reproduce the photographic images in Chapter 4, I am grateful to the Antikensammlung der Universität, Erlangen (fig. 3), the Staatliche Kunstsammlungen Dresden (fig. 4), the Museum of Fine Arts, Boston (fig. 5), the Archaeological Institute of the Dodecanese, Rhodes (fig. 6), the British Museum, London (fig. 7), the Staatliche Antikensammlungen und Glyptothek, Munich (fig. 8), the Réunion des Musées Nationaux, Paris (fig. 9), DAI Athen (fig. 10, from *AM* 107 [1992], p. 174 f.), the Antikenmuseum Basel und Sammlung Ludwig (fig. 13), the National Archaeological Museum, Athens (fig. 14).

Thanks are also due to the many who have offered their advice and help in the preparation of this volume: to Pierre Briant, Anna Morpurgo Davies, Suzanne Saïd and Frank Walbank for their kind co-operation, and to Stefan Brenne, Helen and Sebastian Brock, Philip Burton, Emma Dench, Andrew Erskine, Jo Goddard, Nino Luraghi, Lynette Mitchell, Robin Osborne, Catherine Pickstock and Mary Whitby for a variety of advice, bibliography and practical help. Above all, I am grateful to Antonia Nevill for her translations of Chs

3, 4, 7, 8, 9 and 12, to Paul Cartledge for his wise advice and his meticulous editing, to the copy-editor, Fiona Sewell, and to John Davey of Edinburgh University Press, both for allowing me to undertake the volume and for his guidance throughout its production.

T.H.

Note to the Reader

The articles and excerpts included in this book were originally published in a range of different journals and books. A degree of uniformity has been imposed (for example, in the abbreviations used), but many of the conventions of the original pieces have been preserved. This applies to spelling and punctuation (UK or US) and to different modes of referencing: chapters using the Harvard (i.e. name and date) system are followed by individual bibliographies; those using 'short titles' usually have footnotes and no bibliography.

The final bibliography contains works referred to by the editor.

Editorial notes and translations of ancient texts are introduced either within square brackets [ ] or in daggered footnotes †. Some Greek terms, especially those in use in English, have been transliterated.

All abbreviations of ancient texts, modern collections, books and journals, used either in the chapters or in the editorial material, are listed and explained on pp. x–xiii.

Other abbreviations have, in general, been avoided. The following abbreviations are contained within the republished articles: ap. (quoted by), op. cit. (the same work as cited earlier), id. (the same author), ibid. (in the same work), *pace* (with due respect, i.e. contradicting), s.v. (under the word, i.e. used of dictionaries), conj. (correction to manuscript reading proposed by), per litt. (in private correspondence).

Abbreviations

1 ABBREVIATIONS OF REFERENCES TO PRIMARY SOURCES

Aelian	*V[aria] H[istoria]*
Aesch[ylus]	*Ag[amemnon], Eum[enides], Pers[ians], P[rometheus] V[inctus]* = *Prometheus Bound, Suppl[iants]*
And[ocides]	
A[nthologia] P[alatina]	= Palatine (or *Greek*) Anthology
Archil[ochus]	
Ar[istophanes]	*Thesm[ophoriazousae]*
Arist[otle]	*Ath[enaion] Pol[iteia]* = *Constitution of the Athenians, Rhet[oric]*
Arr[ian]	*Anab[asis]*
Athen[aeus]	
Cic[ero]	*Verr[ines]*
Dem[osthenes]	
Din[archus]	
Dio Chrysostom	*Or[ations]*
Diod[orus Siculus]	
Diog[enes] Laert[ius]	
Dion[ysius of] Hal[icarnassus]	
Eur[ipides]	*Alc[estis], And[romache] El[ectra], Hec[uba], Her[acles], Med[ea], Or[estes], Phoen[icians], Supplices* = *Suppliants, Tro[iades]* = *Trojan Women*
Flav[ius] Jos[ephus]	
H[ero]d[o]t[us] = Her[odotus]	
Hes[iod]	*Th[eogony], Op[era]*=*Works and Days*
H[omer]	*Il[iad], Od[yssey]*
Hyper[ides]	

x

Isoc[rates]
Lys[ias]
Paus[anias]
Pl[ato]   *Crat[ylus], Leg. = Laws, Ph[ae]dr[us],*
                   Prot[agoras], Resp. = Republic, Th[aeate]t[us]
Plin[y]   *N[atural] H[istory]*
Plut[arch]   *Apopth[egmata] Reg[um], Art[axerxes],*
                   Mor[alia], Per[icles]
Soph[ocles]   *Aj[ax], Ant[igone]*
Thuc[ydides]
Xen[ophon]   *Anab[asis], Cyr[opaedia], Hell[enica]*

2 ABBREVIATIONS OF JOURNALS
AND MODERN EDITIONS

ABV	*Athenian Black-figure Vases*
AHR	*American Historical Review*
AJP	*American Journal of Philology*
AM	*Mitteilungen des Deutschen Archäologischen Instituts. Athenische Abteilung*
ARV	*Athenian Red-figure Vases*
ASNP	*Annali della Scuola Normale Superiore di Pisa*
BCH	*Bulletin de correspondance hellénique*
Bond	G. W. Bond, *Euripides* Hypsipyle
C&M	*Classica et Mediaevalia*
CAH	*Cambridge Ancient History*
ClAnt	*Classical Antiquity*
CPh or *CP*	*Classical Philology*
CQ	*Classical Quarterly*
CR	*Classical Review*
CRAI	*Comptes-rendus de l'Académie des Inscriptions et Belles-Lettres*
Diehl	*Anthologia Lyrica Graeca*
DK	H. Diels and W. Kranz, *Die Fragmente der Vorsokratiker*
FGrHist or *FGH*	F. Jacoby, *Die Fragmente der griechischen Historiker*
GR	*Greece and Rome*
GRBS	*Greek, Roman and Byzantine Studies*
HSCP	*Harvard Studies in Classical Philology*
IG	*Inscriptiones Graecae*

JHS	*Journal of Hellenic Studies*
KA	R. Kassel and C. F .L. Austin, *Poetae Comici Graeci*
LEC	*Les Études Classiques*
LIMC	*Lexicon Iconographicum Mythologiae Classicae*
MH	*Museum Helveticum*
ML	R. Meiggs and D. M. Lewis, *Greek Historical Inscriptions*
MW	R. Merkelbach and M. L. West, *Hesiodi Theogonia, Opera et Dies*
N	A. Nauck, *Tragicorum Graecorum Fragmenta*
NJbb	*Neue Jahrbücher für Antike und Deutsche Bildung*
OCD	*Oxford Classical Dictionary*
PCPS	*Proceedings of the Cambridge Philological Society*
PG	J. P. Migne (ed.), *Patrologiae Cursus, Series Graeca*
PL	*Patrologia Latina*
PP	*Parola del Passato*
P.Tebt.	*Papyri from Tebtunis*
PWRE	See *RE* below
QUCC	*Quaderni urbinati di cultura classica*
RA	*Revue archéologique*
RAC	*Rivista di archeologia cristiana*
RE, PWRE	A. Pauly and G. Wissowa, *Real-Enclopädie der classischen Altertumswissenschaft*
REA	*Revue des études anciennes*
REG	*Revue des études grecques*
RHR	*Revue de l'histoire des religions*
RPh	*Revue de philologie*
RSC	*Rivista di Studi Classici*
SBBerlin	*Sitzungsberichte Berlin*
SIFC	*Studi di Filologia Classica*
Snell	B. Snell, *Bacchylidis Carmina cum Fragmentis*
SO	*Symbolae Osloenses*
TAPA	*Transactions of the American Philological Association*
TPS	*Transactions of the American Philolosophical Society*
Viz Vrem	*Vizantiiski Vremennik*

West	M. L. West, *Iambi et Elegi Graeci*
WS	*Wiener Studien*
YCS	*Yale Classical Studies*

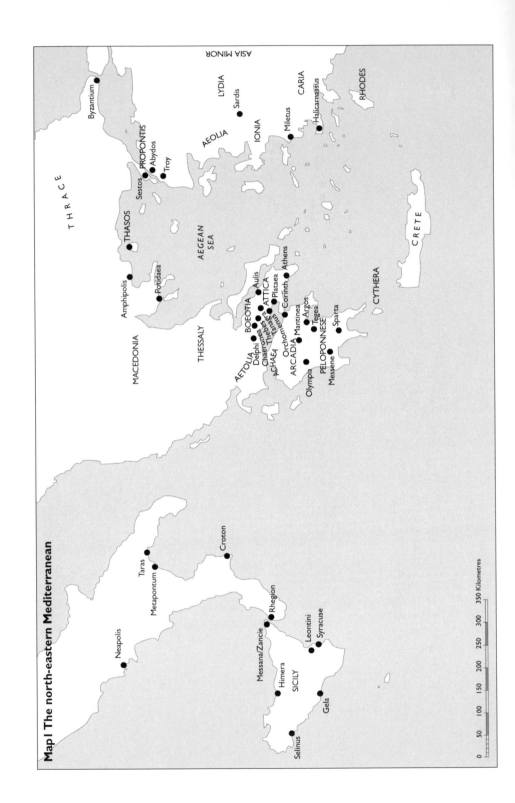

Map I The north-eastern Mediterranean

THRACE

MACEDONIA

THESSALY

AETOLIA
ACHAEA
ARCADIA
PELOPONNESE

Delphi
Chaeronea
Orchomenus
Thebes
Tanagra
BOEOTIA
Aulis
ATTICA
Plataea
Corinth
Athens
Mantinea
Argos
Tegea
Sparta
Olympia
Messene

Amphipolis
Potidaea
THASOS

Byzantium
Sestos
Abydos
Troy
PROPONTIS

AEGEAN
SEA

AEOLIA
LYDIA
Sardis
IONIA
Miletus
CARIA
Halicarnassus
RHODES

CRETE

CYTHERA

ASIA MINOR

Neapolis
Taras
Metapontum
Croton
Rhegion
Messana/Zancle
Himera
SICILY
Leontini
Syracuse
Gela
Selinus

0   50   100   150   200   250   300   350 Kilometres

Map 2 The Mediterranean and Near East

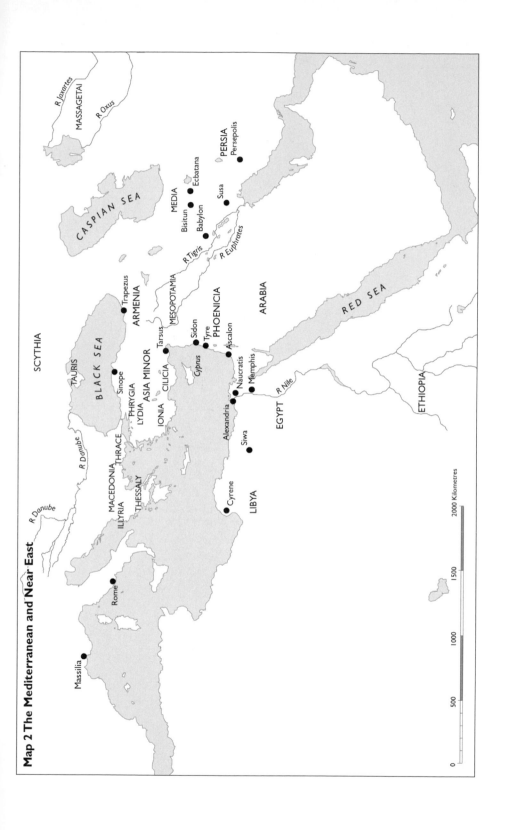

General Introduction

How one group of people views or 'constructs' others – and how, by doing so, it constructs its own identity – is one of the central themes of history. It is a theme that can be traced in any number of historical contexts: the Chinese Han dynasty's image of foreign peoples as illiterate nomads,[1] the sexual stereotypes of the French (promiscuous, irresponsible) nursed by the English, of the English (with their allegedly cold, functional view of lovemaking) nursed by the French;[2] or, more preposterously, the medieval French tradition, which survived even to the nineteenth century, that Englishmen had tails 'which they cunningly concealed'.[3]

In the study of the representation of foreign peoples, however, the Greeks occupy a special place. For just as the Greeks are often seen as the originators of many of the key features which distinguish 'western' civilisation, so many of the less attractive intellectual movements of western history have seen their justifications in Greek antiquity. To be a European, Edward Said wrote in his enormously influential essay *Orientalism*, means to belong 'to a part of the earth with a definite history of involvement in the Orient almost since the time of Homer'.[4] Aeschylus' play the *Persians* has been described (by Edith Hall) as 'the first unmistakable file in the archive of Orientalism, the discourse by which the European imagination has dominated Asia ... by conceptualising its inhabitants as defeated, luxurious, emotional, cruel, and always as dangerous'.[5] Aristotle's idea of 'natural slavery' (a theory, as we will see, rooted in earlier,

---

[1] See Hall, *Inventing the Barbarian*, pp. 61–2.

[2] See Pryke, 'Nationalism and sexuality'; for the invention of a British identity in opposition especially to the French, see Colley, *Britons*; see also McDonald, 'We Are Not French!'.

[3] Southern, 'England's first entry into Europe', at p. 141.

[4] *Orientalism*, p. 78.

[5] Hall, *Inventing the Barbarian*, p. 99; for this and other such structural polarities as characteristic of Greek thought, see Lloyd, *Polarity and Analogy*; more accessibly Cartledge, *The Greeks*.

I

less theoretically self-conscious, representations of the societies of the Near East), provided, as Wilfried Nippel recounts later in this volume (Ch. 12), the foundation for later justifications of Spanish colonialism.

To observe such continuities is not simply, however, to indict classical culture, to suggest that it is retrospectively 'tainted'; nor is it to deny or obliterate the more positive aspects of the Greeks' legacy. Acknowledging these less attractive aspects of the classical tradition is vital, not only to free ourselves from their grip, but also in order better to understand the reality of the *ancient* past, to prevent the retrospective projection of monolithic, modern categories onto the ancient world.[6] The purpose of this volume is to bring to a wider audience material which emphasises the difference and the *complexity* of Greek representations of foreign peoples – or barbarians, as they termed them.

HISTORICAL OVERVIEW

To begin with, it is important to emphasise the very different historical circumstances that pertained in the case of ancient 'orientalism'. Though the Greeks (from the late eighth century) established a large number of colonies in the Mediterranean and Black Sea – a movement which contributed in great part to the Greeks' reflections on their own identity and social organisation[7] – these were small-scale ventures initiated by individual, autonomous city-states (or *poleis*), motivated by droughts and political tensions at home as well as by the desire for trade, co-ordinated, if at all, only by the oracular shrine of Delphi.[8] Only in the Hellenistic period (following Alexander's conquests of Egypt and the Near East) was the relationship of Greeks and native peoples unequivocally that of ruler and ruled. Greek colonies, moreover, were by no means the exclusive, or even primary, context for the interaction of Greeks and foreign peoples: in the archaic period, Greeks served in Egypt or the kingdoms of the Near East as craftsmen, administrators and mercenaries. Though, until recently, scholars of classical art ascribed all that was best in Persian art to *Greek* craftsmanship,[9] it is clear that the position of such

---

[6] See my observations on the discontinuities in the history of European identity, *Emptiness of Asia*, pp. 41–2.

[7] See Murray, 'History and reason', Nippel (below, Ch. 12).

[8] See the important corrective of Osborne, 'Early Greek colonisation?' (e.g. on the misleadingly 'statist' overtones of the term 'colony').

[9] See below, introduction to Part I.

Greeks abroad was more often than not a subordinate one. Other forms of contact, of course, were more likely to feed a negative stereotype of the barbarian – not least the institution of slavery, increasingly identified by the Greeks as the natural status of barbarians.[10] We are a long way here, however, from modern imperialism, with its systematic drive to demarcate and control languages, landscapes and peoples.[11]

The representation of foreign peoples also varied significantly over time. Just as the emancipation of slaves in Britain's Caribbean colonies gave rise to a change in perception of black men (from pretty and effeminate to archetypally masculine),[12] or just as the Napoleonic wars gave added impetus to the British stereotype of the French as unreliable and promiscuous,[13] so similarly Greek images of foreign peoples can be seen to respond – though not in any simple or direct fashion – to the history of events.

The first major such event was the repulse of the Persian invasions of Greece, known collectively as the Persian Wars (490–479). The Persian Wars were not the single cause of the pejorative portrayal of the Persians and the rise of the 'barbarian'. Many of the ingredients of that portrayal – the image of barbarians as an untidy horde of countless peoples, the association of foreign peoples with incomprehensible speech (and the 'orientalising' technique of portraying foreign languages by a spattering of foreign vocabulary interspersed in Greek),[14] and the impression of the immense wealth of the monarchies of the Near East (an impression associated in particular with the Lydian King Croesus) all long predate the Persian Wars.[15] Other aspects of the later Greek–barbarian antithesis, however – in particular, the contrast between Greek democracy and oriental despotism – were very much less marked in the period before the Persian Wars: tyranny was a feature of many archaic Greek *poleis*, the aspiration of many aristocratic youths.[16] Homer's Trojans in most respects are portrayed as sharing in the same culture and way of life as their

---

[10] For a survey of forms of contact (e.g. diplomacy, trade and war) between Greece and Persia (and the Near East in general) in the classical period, see Miller, *Athens and Persia*, Chs 2–5; for slavery, pp. 85–7. See further below, p. 10.

[11] See e.g. the excellent Benedict Anderson, *Imagined Communities*.

[12] Hall, *White, Male and Middle Class*, pp. 205–54.

[13] Pryke, 'Nationalism and sexuality.'

[14] Hall, *Inventing the Barbarian*, p. 18.

[15] Untidy horde: H. *Il*. 2.803–4, 4.436–8; cf. Aesch. *Pers*. 399–407. For language, see below, introduction to Part II. For the representation of barbarians in the archaic period, see esp. Hall, *Inventing the Barbarian*, Ch. 1; Schwabl, 'Das Bild der fremden Welt'; Weiler, 'The Greek and non-Greek world'; Lévy, 'Naissance du concept de barbare'; see further below, n. 18.

[16] See e.g. Drews, 'The first tyrants in Greece'.

Greek enemies – unlike the Trojans of fifth-century tragedy, who, in the light of the Persian Wars, were painted in barbarian colours.[17] A number of recent studies have emphasised the extent of Near Eastern influences on the Greek world, and of contact between the Greek world and the Near East, influences and contact that took place not – as in the post-Persian War period – against the backdrop of an ideology of contempt for oriental decadence but in a spirit of apparent openness.[18]

The Persian Wars organised such stereotypes of the east, sharpening the focus, for example, of the contrasts between eastern luxury and Greek simplicity, despotism and democracy, and emphasising (if not initiating) an assumption of Greek superiority.[19] Aeschylus' celebration of Athenian and Greek victory in his *Persians* (472) contains many of the contrasts between Asia and Greece that were to be developed by later authors: between the unaccountable monarchy of the Persians and the effective, accountable democracy of Athens, between the slavish masses of the king's vast flotilla and the small band of Greeks, each 'the lord of his oar', between the empty pomp of the Persian court (with its deference to god-like kings and the excessive authority of royal women) and the masculine simplicity of the Athenians.[20]

This Persian–Greek polarity clearly has specifically Athenian characteristics. The Persians who came to Marathon in 490 BC had as their guide the expelled Athenian tyrant Hippias. The subsequent rise of the barbarian in the Athenian imagination occurred in tandem with the demonisation of Athens' sixth-century tyrants, the Peisistratids, and the development of a self-conscious democratic ideology.[21] Athens' part in the Persian Wars also served as a justification of the rule Athens exercised over its fifth-century empire.[22] There is good reason to suppose, however, that the Persian–Greek

[17] Hall, *Inventing the Barbarians*, pp. 21–47; contrast, however, pp. 19–21 on foreign names, and now Mackie, *Talking Trojan*.
[18] For the 'orientalising age' in Greek history, see esp. Burkert, *The Orientalizing Revolution*; West, *The East Face of Helicon*, esp. Ch. 12; Kopce and Tokumaru, *Greece between East and West*. For Near Eastern influences on Homer, see now Morris, 'Homer and the Near East'. For contacts, see further below, n. 48.
[19] Contrast Jonathan Hall's over-simplistic distinction, *Ethnic Identity*, p. 47, of an 'aggregative' Greek identity before the Persian Wars (i.e. built up on the basis of similarities with peers) and an 'oppositional' identity after the Persian Wars. For the transition marked by the Persian Wars see also Hall, *Inventing the Barbarian*; Diller, 'Die Hellenen–Barbaren-Antithese'; Pugliese Carratelli, 'Le guerre mediche'.
[20] See esp. Hall, *Inventing the Barbarian*, Ch. 2; Harrison, *Emptiness of Asia*; see further below, introduction to Part I.
[21] See Lavelle, *The Sorrow and the Pity*.
[22] See Harrison, *Emptiness of Asia*, Chs 5–6, 9; for the use of the Persian Wars in Athenian rhetoric, see esp. Loraux, *L'invention d'Athènes*.

polarity was not restricted to Athens.[23] Other cities fought retrospectively over their parts in the Persian Wars.[24] The association of
Persia with Greek tyranny was also widespread elsewhere, in those
cities in which the Persians had sponsored tyrannies until the beginning of the fifth century.[25] Most importantly perhaps, the *Histories*
of Herodotus, written under the shadow of the first part of the
Peloponnesian War (431–404), clearly had a broader currency than
in Athens. The *Histories* are increasingly (and rightly) seen as comparing the Persian empire with the Athenian empire that developed
in the light of the Persian Wars, and as offering an implicit critique
of Athenian imperialism (rather than simply a glorification of
Athens).[26] Herodotus in many ways undercuts the assumption
of Greek cultural superiority, mocking the Greeks, for example, as
children in their knowledge of the gods by comparison with the
Egyptians;[27] his account of the Persian Wars envisages Greek victory
as in large part the result of consistent Persian mistakes. Nevertheless, he also reflects a much more celebratory tradition of the
Persian Wars, one which sees the Greeks' victory as due to their
innate freedom, the pattern of Persian error as the result of their
monarchy, and their lack of proper reverence for the gods.[28]

The end of the Persian Wars (possibly formalised in a treaty of
449), and the end of a series of subsequent conflicts with the Persians
in the eastern Mediterranean and in Egypt, did not lead to the disappearance of the Persians. Other enmities, of course, came to the
fore in this period. It is not an accident that it was against the backdrop of the Peloponnesian War that Euripides ascribed barbarian
traits to the Greeks themselves.[29] It is sometimes claimed also that the
comic poet Aristophanes, writing in the same period, reserved real
hostility for the Peloponnesians, while the Persians were the butt
only of humour.[30] Nevertheless, the Persians remained central, both

[23] Contrast Hall, *Inventing the Barbarian*, pp. 16–17.
[24] See now Harrison, *The Emptiness of Asia*, Ch. 5; also West, 'Saviors of Greece'.
[25] Austin, 'Greek tyrants and the Persians'.
[26] See esp. Fornara, *Herodotus*; Stadter, 'Herodotus and the Athenian *arche*'; Moles,
'Herodotus warns the Athenians'; the same comparison between Athenian and Persian imperialism can be seen implicitly in Thucydides' account of the Athenian expedition to Sicily with
its echoes of Xerxes' expedition to Greece: see Rood, 'Thucydides' Persian Wars'; Harrison,
'Sicily in the Athenian imagination'.
[27] See below, Ch. 7; see also Harrison, *Divinity and History*, Chs 7–8, App. 2.
[28] See now Harrison, 'The Persian invasions'; contrast Hall, *Ethnic Identity* p. 45 (citing
Nippel, *Griechen, Barbaren und 'Wilde'*, pp. 14–16), asserting simplistically that no adverse
comparison between Greeks and barbarians is made by Herodotus (by comparison with
Aeschylus).
[29] For Euripides, see below, Ch. 3 (Saïd); Hall, *Inventing the Barbarian*, Ch. 5 ('The polarity deconstructed'). For a late fifth-century 'crisis', see Reverdin, 'Crise spirituelle et évasion'.
[30] Miller, *Athens and Persia*, p. 28.

(as the vanquished enemies of the Persian wars) to the self-image
of Athens, and as the single most significant off-stage presence in
relations between the Greek cities.[31] Notoriously under-represented
in Thucydides' account of the Peloponnesian War,[32] the financial
support of the Persians was crucial in deciding the war's outcome in
the Spartans' favour. The Persian king continued to serve as the
guarantor of a series of settlements between the cities of Greece in
the fourth century.

Ideology, however, has a life of its own, and does not merely
respond to the history of events. The representation of foreign
peoples in the late fifth and fourth centuries undergoes a number of
contradictory movements: Euripides' problematisation and refraction of the Greek–barbarian polarity; the use of Persia as a model
of the ideal monarchy by Xenophon in the *Cyropaedia*;[33] the identification (associated with Isocrates) of Greek identity with culture
rather than birth;[34] the continuation and elaboration of a stereotyped
portrayal of the wealth and decadence of the eastern barbarian in
Xenophon, Plato, and fragmentary historians such as Ctesias;[35]
the development of an ideal of Panhellenic unity (through the Panhellenic orations of Gorgias and Lysias and the work of Isocrates).[36]

This final dimension of fourth-century thought on the barbarian
also had an aggressive aspect in its rallying call for a campaign of
revenge against Persia; this call was answered in the campaign
planned by the Macedonian king Philip and subsequently executed
by his son Alexander. Alexander's conquest of the Persian empire
in many ways left the stereotyped image of the eastern barbarian
unscathed. Unquestionably, however, it had drastic and sudden consequences on relations between the Greeks and non-Greek peoples.
Alexander's conquests led not only to the establishment of a series of
'successor kingdoms' and to the foundation of Greek settlements as
far afield as modern Afghanistan,[37] but also to the political margin-
alisation of the old Greek world. Old clichés had also to adapt to new
circumstances: the displacement of Persian by Graeco-Macedonian

---

[31] See Miller, *Athens and Persia*, Ch. 1, but especially Lewis, *Sparta and Persia*; Hornblower,
'Persia', pp. 64–96.

[32] See Andrewes, 'Thucydides and the Persians'.

[33] See further below, introduction to Part III, and Ch. 8 (Briant).

[34] This was not necessarily a change that entailed a greater inclusiveness: see Walbank below
(Ch. 10).

[35] See further below, introduction to Part I.

[36] See further Walbank below (Ch. 10).

[37] For Alexander's conquests see Bosworth, *Conquest and Empire*; for an excellent and up-
to-date introduction to Hellenistic history, see Shipley, *The Greek World*.

kings inevitably gave impetus to a positive Greek ideal of monarchy.[38]

Such a narrative of events fails, however, to bring out the full complexity of Greek representations of foreign peoples. To begin with, it gives a disproportionate weight to the Persians, obscuring the diversity of different barbarian peoples in Greek thought. Though the Greeks on occasion spoke as if barbarians constituted a single homogeneous group[39] – or as if they spoke the same 'barbarian language'[40] – even at the most stereotyped level there were significant differences in the representation of foreign peoples: the nomadic Scythians, whose resistance of Persian invasion through flight provided an analogy for the Athenian evacuation of Attica during the Persian Wars;[41] the Thracians, archetypally ferocious and venial;[42] the Egyptians, proverbial for their religious scruples, and for the depth of their knowledge of human history;[43] the Persians, once (like the Greeks themselves) poor but free, before their kings became frozen in the atavistic desire to expand their empire, and their subjects ruined by its spoils.[44] The Greeks themselves, moreover, were far from being a homogeneous group. Though the projection of a barbarian 'other' may often have served to reinforce the unity of the 'Greek', it may often also shed light on the fragility of the Greek–barbarian antithesis, and on the differences between Greeks: differences in religious cult, in language, in myth, and in political and social organisation.[45]

We have also to allow for the differing imagination, curiosity and blinkered vision of individual authors. Herodotus, for example, as James Redfield's piece ('Herodotus the Tourist', Ch. 1) demonstrates, employs a whole range of different models for making sense of the many peoples he describes. Egyptian customs often present a mirror image of those of the Greeks: Egyptian women, for instance, urinate standing, men sitting (2.35). At the same time, however, he compares the funerals of Spartan and Persian kings (6.58), and details how knowledge of the gods came from Egypt to Greece (e.g. 2.49–50)

---

[38] See esp. Walbank, 'Monarchies and monarchic ideas'.

[39] Aesch. *Pers.* 434; Soph. fr. 587; Eur. *And.* 173.

[40] See e.g. Soph. *Aj.* 1262–3; Ar. fr. 81 KA; Xen. *Anab.* 1.8.1; Pl. *Tht.* 163b; Diod. 5.6.5; Arr. *Anab.* 3.6.6.

[41] See esp. Hartog, *Mirror of Herodotus*, e.g. pp. 51, 203; for the Scythians, see further below, Ch. 1 (Redfield), Ch. 4 (Lissarrague).

[42] Thuc. 7.29; Hdt. 5.6; see further Asheri, 'Thrace and Thracian society'; Archibald, *Odrysian Kingdom*, pp. 94–102.

[43] See further below, Ch. 1 (Redfield), Ch. 9 (Hartog).

[44] See further below, Ch. 1 (Redfield), Ch. 8 (Briant).

[45] See further below, introduction to Part III.

8 *General Introduction*

or homosexuality from Greece to Persia (1.135). He also ascribes a Greek-style ethnocentrism to both Persians and Egyptians: the Egyptians, he claims, call all those who do not speak their language 'barbarians' (2.158; cf. 1.134).[46] Other authors similarly confound any simple Greek–barbarian antithesis. How are we to understand the contradictions within Xenophon, between his lifelike account of the expedition of the 'Ten Thousand' Greek mercenaries into Persia in the *Anabasis*, the positive idealisation of Persia in the *Cyropaedia*, and the Panhellenism and negative stereotypes of barbarians of the *Agesilaus*? How characteristic of his time was the ironic subversion of a simple Greek–barbarian antithesis performed by Euripides? Can we indeed be certain that Euripides did intend to undermine this antithesis?

THE ORGANISATION OF THIS VOLUME

The purpose of this volume is to survey as wide a range as possible of the Greeks' responses to foreign peoples; it is also to examine the influence of the Greeks' ideas and images in later Greek and European history, and to represent the richness and diversity of modern scholarship on these themes.

Part I examines some of the major sources for the Greek conception of the barbarian: the fifth-century historian Herodotus (Ch. 1: Redfield), the Athenian tragedians Aeschylus and Euripides (Chs 2–3: Goldhill, Saïd), and, finally, classical Athenian art (Ch. 4: Lissarrague).

Part II then looks in more detail at a number of themes across a broader range of sources: the Greeks' myths of their own descent from the Egyptians and Phoenicians (Ch. 5: Hall), the issue of the diversity of the Greek language and of Greek representations of foreign languages (Ch. 6: Morpurgo Davies), and finally the Greek conception of foreign religions and the consequences of this for our understanding of Greek religion (Ch. 7: Rudhardt).

Part III considers more closely the range of foreign peoples with whom the Greeks were in contact. Two pieces examine, in turn, the persistent Greek idea of 'Persian decadence' (Ch. 8: Briant) and the special status accorded to Egypt by the Greeks as a source of, in particular religious, wisdom (Ch. 9: Hartog).

---

[46] For Egyptian attitudes to foreign languages, see Donadoni, 'Gli Egiziani e le lingue degli altri'. For language as a criterion of 'barbarism', see further below, introduction to Part II and Ch. 6 (Morpurgo Davies).

Finally, Part IV offers a variety of historical overviews. F. W. Walbank's classic article 'The Problem of Greek nationality' (Ch. 10), first published in 1951, looks back over the history of scholarship at the ways in which the history of Greece has been written as the failure of the Greek states to unify into a single 'nation-state'. The Byzantinist Robert Browning (Ch. 11) surveys the continuing potency of the Greek–barbarian antithesis in later Greek history. Finally, with Wilfried Nippel's 'The Construction of the "other"', we turn to a still broader history, to the use of Greek categories in modern European thought, in justification of colonialism or in modern scholarship on the ancient world.

The aim in selecting these pieces has been to satisfy a number of (sometimes conflicting) criteria: to cover a wide chronological span, to present a range of ancient sources and of sub-themes, to display a broad spectrum of foreign peoples, and to give some sense of the variety of modern approaches.

With the exception in particular of the overviews of Browning and Nippel, of Hall's treatment of archaic myth, or of the chronologically wide-ranging survey of attitudes to Egypt by Hartog, the volume centres on the classical period, from the Persian Wars to Alexander's conquest of the Persian empire. Part I concentrates on the evidence of the fifth century. For the more theoretical perspective of fourth-century authors – Xenophon, Isocrates, Plato, Aristotle – the reader is referred to other chapters (Hartog, Briant, Nippel, Walbank). Almost all the sources (including the artistic material examined by Lissarrague) derive from Athens. The extent to which the pejorative attitudes represented, say, in Aeschylus' *Persians* reflect a broader Greek perception of the Persians or of the 'barbarian' is, as we have seen, one of the central (and most problematic) questions which overhang this topic.

As for the range of themes covered, there is no dedicated discussion included of the 'gendering' of foreign peoples, of the representation of foreign women, or of the political contrast pointed between Greek democracy and eastern despotism. Discussion of these themes is spread across the different contributions.[47] The introductions to parts attempt to supplement, as well as to introduce, the articles included here.

Two other questions receive no systematic discussion here: the

---

[47] For gender and foreign women, see Rosellini and Saïd, 'Usages de femmes', and below, Ch. 8 (Briant), Ch. 1 (Redfield) and the introduction to Part III; for politics, see esp. Ch. 2 (Goldhill), Ch. 10 (Walbank).

extent of *actual contact* between Greeks and 'barbarians' and the degree of *reality* of Greek representations of foreign peoples. In an important recent work, *Athens and Persia in the Fifth Century*, Margaret Miller has collated a mass of fragments of evidence to suggest that 'over the later sixth and fifth centuries a comparatively large proportion of Athenian adult males ... had some personal experience of the peoples of the Persian empire'.[48] This experience occurred in a variety of forms: through the service of Greeks in the Persian court of Persepolis;[49] through the settlement of non-Greeks in Greek communities, or the interaction of the Greek cities of Asia Minor with their neighbours;[50] through warfare, trade or embassies;[51] or through aristocratic 'guest-friendship'.[52] Such contacts, of course, became more everyday still in the light of Alexander's conquests. The extent to which the native peoples of the successor states were excluded from contact with ruling Greek elites is a matter of debate.[53] Recent discussions, however, have moved away from a simplistic (and often crudely Hellenocentric) emphasis on 'Hellenisation' towards a more complex model of two-way cultural interaction.[54]

The decision to omit any dedicated discussion of Greek–barbarian contact is one that has been made partly out of necessity and partly on academic grounds. Conclusions as to the degree and type of contacts between Greeks and foreign peoples are often, of course, implicit in the history of representations. The stereotyped characterisation of a people, the blurring of a historical people with mythical

---

[48] Miller, *Athens and Persia*, p. 3. For contact between Greeks and foreign peoples, see also e.g. Austin, *Greece and Egypt in the Archaic Age*; Burstein, 'Greek contact with Egypt and the Levant'; Hall, *Ethnic Identity*, pp. 46–7; Lewis, *Sparta and Persia*; Starr, 'Greeks and Persians'; West, *The East Face of Helicon*, Ch. 12; Ridgway, *The First Western Greeks*; Arafat and Morgan, 'Athens, Etruria and the Heuneburg'; Coleman and Walz, *Greeks and Barbarians*; Haider, 'Griechen im Vorderen Orient'; Weiler, 'Soziogenese'; Descoeudres, *Greek Colonists and Native Populations*; Tsetskhladze and de Angelis, *The Archaeology of Greek Colonisation*; Tsetskhladze, *The Greek Colonization of the Black Sea Area*; see also Chs 8–9 of *CAH* VI² (1994).

[49] See also Nylander, *Ionians in Pasagardae*; Lewis, 'Persians in Herodotus'.

[50] See also e.g. Hornblower, *Mausolus*, pp. 11–14; Asheri, 'Fra Ellenismo e Iranismo' (and other essays in the same volume); Balcer, 'The Greeks and the Persians', 'Fifth century BC Ionia'; Baslez, 'Présence et traditions iraniennes', 'Les communautés d'Orientaux'; Vickers, 'Interactions between Greeks and Persians'.

[51] See also, on embassies, Mosley, 'Greeks, barbarians, language and contact', *Envoys and Diplomacy in Ancient Greece*.

[52] See esp. Mitchell, *Greeks Bearing Gifts*, Chs 6–7.

[53] See the survey of Burstein, 'The Hellenistic age', at pp. 50–2; for Greek/non-Greek relations in the Hellenistic age, see further e.g. Peremans, 'Egyptiens et étrangers dans l'Egypte ptolémaïque'; Fraser, *Ptolemaic Alexandria*, esp. Ch. 2; Thompson, *Memphis under the Ptolemies*, Ch. 3 on 'ethnic minorities'.

[54] See pre-eminently Kuhrt and Sherwin-White, *Hellenism in the East*; Sherwin-White and Kuhrt, *From Samarkand to Sardis*; also Momigliano's classic *Alien Wisdom*.

analogues,[55] the deformation of the native traditions of a foreign people for Greek ideological ends: all these may be taken to suggest a relative ignorance of, and indifference towards, the people in question. In another sense, however, contact and representations can be distinguished. In compiling her archive, Miller sets out to 'disprove' the 'commonplace of modern scholarship that the Athenians hated and despised the Persians'.[56] Arguably, however, this is too simplistic. The evidence of 'cultural borrowings' (of parasols and peacocks, architectural forms and iconographic motifs) that Miller adduces does not necessarily disprove, or work against, the pejorative prejudices against Persia that are found in Greek sources.[57] Borrowings do not simply suggest a 'readiness to adopt foreign culture traits' (p. 243). To carry a parasol is not necessarily to advertise your pro-Persian sympathies; indeed the fact that parasols were used by men in Persia but by women in Athens suggests that the borrowing of forms of dress may have fitted seamlessly both with the prevalent image of barbarians as decadent and effeminate and with the Athenian ideal of austerity in dress.[58]

Another approach would be to argue that the images of foreign peoples contained in literary sources operate on a different level from 'real life'. There may have been many Greeks – tradesmen, mercenaries, courtiers of the Persian king – whose actual experience of foreign peoples led them to eschew the prejudices of their fellow Greeks, even, like the Athenian Themistocles, to learn a foreign language.[59] One such Greek – of whom we hear from a piece of graffiti in Abu Simbel in Egypt – describes himself, in Greek, as an *alloglossos*, a 'foreign-language speaker', so adopting the linguistic ethnocentrism of the Egyptians and turning on its head the Greek idea of the *barbaros* (a term which seems originally to have desig-

---

[55] See e.g. Hall, *Inventing the Barbarian*, pp. 66–9; see further below, Ch. 4 (Lissarrague), introduction to Part II.

[56] Miller, *Athens and Persia*, p. 1. Cf. Morris, *Daidalos and the Origins of Greek Art*, describing the Persian Wars as (p. 371) introducing 'a double standard of Medism among the people of Athens, who condemned Persians, or heard them, condemned in public rhetoric, while admiring Persian institutions (including kingship) and enjoying Oriental luxuries in dress and household property'. See here my comments on Griffith, 'The King and Eye', *The Emptiness of Asia*, pp. 105–8.

[57] Miller acknowledges (fleetingly) the existence of such pejorative portrayals (pp. 257–8), but observes revealingly that Hall (in her *Inventing the Barbarian*) 'overstates the case' (p. 257 n. 62).

[58] See here, Geddes, 'Rags and riches'; Kurke, 'The politics of *habrosyne*'; Lombardo, '*Habrosyne e Habra*'.

[59] Plut. *Themistocles* 29.5. Themistocles' achievement seems to have been seen as a sign of his unique intelligence; see further Harrison, 'Herodotus' conception of foreign languages'.

nated those who could not speak Greek).[60] Contact, however, may
equally result in the confirmation of stereotypes – as the case of
Xenophon, if not also of Herodotus,[61] may suggest. We must surely
begin, moreover, from what evidence we have – in great part, that of
representation[62] – rather than use scarce proof of contact to impose
an order on that evidence.

To discuss the veracity of Greek representations of foreign peoples
would require a whole series of volumes. It might also provide a
distraction: critics and historians have often confused the two objects
of Greek representation and foreign reality, supposing that Athenian
potters intended to distinguish accurately the differing characteristics
of various foreign peoples, or that Aeschylus felt obliged to give an
accurate portrayal of the Persian court.[63] It should be stated at the
outset that the Greek representation of foreign peoples is driven by
a set of imperatives other than those of historical accuracy: the need
to convey a recognisable image of a barbarian people led potter or
poet to conflate the characteristics of different peoples – of Medes
and Persians, for example[64] – and to rely on a limited repertoire of
stereotypes. Some ancient authors – notably Herodotus – may have
taken pride in the setting straight of their contemporaries' conceptions of foreign peoples (notwithstanding the schematic nature of
their own accounts). In general, however, there was likely to have
been little impetus to distinguish between 'genuine' and false knowledge.[65]

There is another reason for initially distinguishing between these
two objectives – representation and reality. The task of writing
the history of barbarian peoples – of the ancient Persians, say, or
Thracians – is an immensely complex one. In large part, we must rely
in doing so on non-Greek evidence, in so far as it exists – in the case
of Persia, for example, on the archaeology of the royal palaces, on a
small number of royal inscriptions, and on the administrative records

[60] ML 7a.4; see further above, n. 46. For the term *barbaros*, see esp. Lévy, 'Naissance du
concept de barbare'; see further below, Ch. 6 (Morpurgo Davies) and introduction to Part II.
[61] My caution is due to the controversy over the extent of Herodotus' travels: see my
comments, *Divinity and History*, pp. 23–4 (with a summary of bibliography).
[62] Miller is also often forced into speculative reconstructions of the means by which cultural
borrowings took place: so, e.g., (of the failed Athenian expedition to Egypt) she comments that
'Every squadron relieved must have taken back to Greece their share of booty and stories' (p.
18).
[63] See further Harrison, *The Emptiness of Asia*, pp. 41–7.
[64] See Graf, 'Medism'; Tuplin, 'Persians as Medes'. For the conflation of different peoples
in iconography, see below, Ch. 4 (Lissarrague); Bovon, 'La représentation des guerriers perses'.
[65] Harrison, *Emptiness of Asia*, pp. 44–7. For Greek knowledge of Persia, see also Tuplin,
Achaemenid Studies, Ch. 3.

known as the 'Persepolis tablets'.[66] But the construction of a history of Persia depends also upon the reading of *Greek* texts, and on the attempt to re-read those texts in a way that bypasses pejorative Greek attitudes to Persia. Often though, as we will see later in discussing Persian women,[67] there is a danger that this alchemy – the reuse of Greek texts for Persian history – is performed in too simplistic and convenient a fashion: facts that reflect well on Persia are believed, those that do not are dismissed as motivated by Greek bias. It is vital that the rewriting of Persian history (and similarly of the history of other peoples for whom we are reliant on Greek sources) should depend upon the prior reading of Greek representations *in their own terms*.

To attempt to summarise the full range of modern scholarly approaches is similarly an impossible undertaking. Many aspects of the subject – the interest in the term *barbaros* or in the ethnic origins of the Greeks – are the same now as they were for Julius Jüthner[68] and others in the first half of the twentieth century. None the less, it would have been impossible to compile a book resembling this one even in the early 1980s. In talking of 'ethnic origins' historians now have in mind the *imagined* origins of a people, the way in which the Greeks or others express their sense of a common identity through a 'real or pretended' kinship or common ancestor.[69] A book title such as *Race Mixture among the Greeks before Alexander* (1937)[70] clearly speaks of the preoccupations, or at least of the language, of a time removed from our own. The greater emphasis on representations rather than on the history of relations between Greeks and foreign peoples is again a recent change.

The credit (or blame) for this shift must be spread widely. These changes are related to a number of others within, and outside, classical studies: the increasing influence of social anthropology,[71] and of structuralism and post-structuralism;[72] the rise of social and cultural

---

[66] For which see Lewis, 'The Persepolis tablets'.

[67] See below, introduction to Part III.

[68] Jüthner, *Hellenen und Barbaren* (1923), citing much older works. For a more recent German survey, see Dihle, *Die Griechen und die Fremden*.

[69] See now esp. Hall, *Ethnic Identity*; much of this modern emphasis, however, is foreshadowed in the article of Walbank below (Ch. 10).

[70] Diller, *Race Mixture among the Greeks*. See also Thomson, *Greeks and Barbarians* (1921), with such sentences as 'The Scythians were not all savages' (p. 21), with its apparent evocation of Hellenism and barbarism as eternal categories, but with a hint of self-consciousness ('We lovers of Greece are put very much on our defence nowadays,' p. 10).

[71] Nippel, *Griechen, Barbaren und 'Wilde'*; Redfield (Ch. 1, below).

[72] See esp. Hartog's *Mirror of Herodotus*.

history, and of a more political style of reading Greek tragedy;[73] a more critical attitude to the later 'reception' of classical culture;[74] and an increasing self-consciousness within the discipline of classics; the revolutionary rewriting of Persian history since the early 1980s,[75] and an increasing concentration on Herodotus, his subtlety as a historian,[76] and the affinity between his own broad conception of 'history' and that of modern historians. Two works in particular have given impetus to the modern study of ancient 'barbarians': François Hartog's *The Mirror of Herodotus* (originally published in French in 1980) and Edith Hall's study of the barbarian in tragedy, *Inventing the Barbarian* (1989).

Nevertheless, it would be misleading to give an impression of an established sub-discipline or of a consensus between scholars. Most of the authors whose work is contained in this volume arrive there as specialists in very disparate fields: Greek tragedy (Goldhill, Saïd), Athenian art (Lissarrague), philology (Morpurgo Davies), the history of religion (Rudhardt), Persian, Greek or Byzantine history (Briant, Walbank, Browning). Moreover, the work of Hartog and Hall is viewed by many with suspicion. Hartog's *Mirror* has frequently been overlooked in the Anglo-Saxon world, and criticised for its schematic (and in some eyes fanciful) construction of the polarities in Herodotus' work.[77] A number of scholars, especially those who lay stress on the degree of contact between Greeks and barbarians, or who nurse a particularly romantic image of classical literature, view Hall's emphasis on the chauvinism of Greek culture with disquiet or contempt. In conclusion, then, it should be insisted: to observe the chauvinism and ethnocentrism implicit in Greek literature and art, or to trace the legacy of such attitudes, is not to condemn such works wholesale, to suggest that they are any less interesting or valuable as literature or art;[78] nor is it to single out their creators as uniquely chauvinist. It is rather to attempt to understand them in the context of a broader Greek culture, and to see the Greeks – and ourselves – warts and all.

[73] See e.g. Goldhill's *Reading Greek Tragedy*, 'The Great Dionysia and civic ideology'.
[74] See esp. Nippel, below, Ch. 12.
[75] Pierre Briant, *Histoire de l'Empire Perse*; Wiesehöfer, *Ancient Persia*; and the volumes of the *Achemenid History Workshop* edited by Sancisi-Weerdenburg, Kuhrt and others.
[76] See Harrison, *Divinity and History*, Ch. 1.
[77] See the excellent review article of Hartog, *Mirror of Herodotus*, by Dewald ('the final effect, I think, is much more fluid and complicated than H[artog] realizes').
[78] See here Said, *Culture and Imperialism*, p. 225.

PART I

Sources

Introduction to Part I

Herodotus' *Histories*, his account of the Persian invasions of Greece and their background, are not the earliest of the works discussed in this part on sources. That privilege goes to Aeschylus' play the *Persians*, performed in 472 BC within a decade of Xerxes' expedition to Greece. In another sense, however, they provide a natural starting point. As James Redfield's 'Herodotus the Tourist' (Ch. 1) demonstrates, the *Histories* reveal a whole range of different models (relativism, polarity, diffusionism) for the understanding of foreign peoples. Herodotus' accounts of foreign peoples also cover a wide variety of topics – Herodotus finds symmetries, for example, in nature, in climate, in geography, and in a whole range of human customs or *nomoi* – and introduce an enormous range of 'barbarians'. Redfield's distinction of 'hard' and 'soft' peoples, and his demonstration of how the Persians, initially hard, become soft through their conquests of the soft peoples of Asia, also show how Herodotus' ethnography is vital to his presentation of historical causation.[1] Perhaps the most important contribution of Redfield's piece, however, is to bring out the way in which Herodotus' accounts of foreign peoples are structured by Greek categories and assumptions,[2] the way in which 'cultural relativism becomes ethnocentric'. This emphasis provides a useful antidote to a modern tendency to ascribe an excessive cultural relativism to Herodotus.[3]

Redfield's emphasis on polarity in Herodotus' representation of foreign peoples needs to be read in conjunction with François Hartog's study, *The Mirror of Herodotus*, and alongside both other

---

[1] See further Harrison, 'The Persian invasions'.
[2] See also Ch. 7 (Rudhardt), below.
[3] See e.g. Gould, *Herodotus*; against Herodotus as liberal, see Harrison, 'Herodotus and the ancient Greek idea of rape'; for (foreign) women in Herodotus, see esp. Rosellini and Saïd, 'Usages de femmes', and now Gray, 'The rhetoric of otherness'.

recent work on 'mythical geography'[4] and on polarity in Greek thought,[5] and general works on Herodotus' treatment of foreign peoples.[6] Herodotus must also be seen in the context of other fifth-century writers on barbarian peoples, such as Hecataeus of Miletus, Xanthus of Lydia, or Hellanicus of Lesbos,[7] of Hippocratic medical texts such as *Airs, Waters, Places*,[8] and of the fourth-century doctor in the court of the Persian king Artaxerxes, Ctesias of Cnidus.[9] Much heat but little light has been produced by controversy over the actual extent of Herodotus' travels: Herodotus has been seen alternatively – and equally implausibly – as a pseudo-historian, carefully constructing a false history before history existed, or as a studious (and again strikingly anachronistic), sifter of his sources.[10] What is beyond question is that Herodotus had access, however indirectly, to native traditions of a number of foreign peoples, and sometimes also to the written sources of the Near East, but that such material underwent a complex process of 'deformation' before it found its way to the pages of his *Histories*.[11] What is also beyond question is that he frequently retold stories the truth of which he knew to be suspect.[12]

In the case of Aeschylus' *Persians*, written and performed for the stage of the Athenian festival of the Dionysia, such questions of sources or of historical intentions might be thought to be irrelevant. As the only surviving 'historical tragedy' from classical Athens, however, it has often been interpreted on the erroneous assumption that Aeschylus intended to give an accurate impression of the setting of his play – the court of the Persian king Xerxes at Susa – or that, when

[4] See e.g. Romm, 'Herodotus and mythic geography', *The Edges of the Earth*; Gianotti, 'Ordine e simmetria'.

[5] Lloyd, *Polarity and Analogy*; Cartledge, *The Greeks*.

[6] See e.g. Burkert et al., *Hérodote et les peuples non-Grecs*; Cartledge, 'Herodotus and the "Other"'; Laurot, 'Idéaux grecs et barbarie'; Lévy, 'Hérodote *philobarbaros*'; Payen, *Les Îles Nomades*.

[7] See the survey of Drews, *Greek Accounts of Eastern History*, and now the excellent article of Fowler, 'Herodotos and his contemporaries'.

[8] See e.g. Backhaus, 'Der Hellenen-Barbaren-Gegensatz'; Jouanna, 'Les causes de la défaite des Barbares'; 'Collaboration ou résistance au barbare'; and now Thomas, *Herodotus in Context*. For medical writers, see also below, Chs 1, 12.

[9] See Bigwood, 'Ctesias as historian of the Persian wars'; Lenfant, 'Ctésias et Hérodote'; Momigliano, 'Tradizione e invenzione'; Sancisi-Weerdenburg, 'Decadence in the empire'. See now also Clarke, *Between Geography and History*, on Hellenistic geography.

[10] For further bibliography, see Harrison, *Divinity and History*, pp. 23–4.

[11] For the 'deformation' of oral tradition, see esp. Murray, 'Herodotus and oral history'; less satisfactorily Sancisi-Weerdenburg, 'The orality of Herodotus' *Medikos Logos*'. For Near Eastern written sources, see e.g. Armayor, 'Herodotus' catalogue of the Persian empire'; Martorelli, 'Storia persiana in Erodoto'. See further my comments, 'The Persian invasions'.

[12] For such questions, see my comments, *Divinity and History*, pp. 23–30.

the news of the Persian defeat at Salamis is brought back to Susa by a distraught messenger, he felt bound (by historical duty or by the presence of veterans in his audience) to put an accurate account of the events of Salamis and the flight of the Persians into the mouth of his character.[13] In his 'Battle Narrative and Politics in Aeschylus' *Persae*' (Ch. 2), Simon Goldhill – following on from his earlier work emphasising the essentially *civic* nature of Greek drama[14] – instead places the play's representation of the Persians in its ideological context: that of the Athenian democratic ideals of submission to collective action and of accountability, ideals underlined by the anonymity of the Greeks in the play by contrast to the elaborately listed Persian commanders.

In another sense, however, Goldhill's reading of the play is more conventional. Like many of the play's modern interpreters, he sees it as strikingly sympathetic to the plight of the defeated Persians: for Aeschylus to have composed a *kommos* (or lament) for a defeated enemy is a 'remarkable event'; Aeschylus is questioning rather than affirming the Athenians' response to their victory in the Persian Wars. Like Gilbert Murray before him, Goldhill compares this Greek response favourably with the British responses to Germany and Germans in the years following the First and Second World Wars.[15] Arguably, however, there is a tension between the sympathy for the Persians ascribed to Aeschylus and the stress laid by Goldhill on oppositions between Athens and Persia. The same tension lies at the heart of the interpretation of Edith Hall[16] (the author, more than any other, who has emphasised the chauvinism implicit in the play and Aeschylus' contrast of Greek virtues and Persian vices) and in the readings of most other modern critics.[17] I have argued elsewhere for an interpretation of the play as more unequivocally *unsympathetic* to the Persians, and that modern scholars have projected onto Aeschylus and the Athenians the freedom from xenophobia and humility in victory to which they aspire.[18]

---

[13] See Harrison, *Emptiness of Asia*, Chs 1, 4.

[14] See esp. his 'The Great Dionysia and civic ideology', also his *Reading Greek Tragedy*.

[15] Murray, *Aeschylus*, pp. 127–8.

[16] In her *Inventing the Barbarian* (for the *Persians*, see esp. Ch. 2), and in her subsequent edition of the play. Comparison with Hall's main predecessor, Bacon's *Barbarians in Greek Tragedy*, with its concentration (as the author herself acknowledged) on the *facts* about barbarian peoples contained in tragic texts, makes clear how interpretation of the theme has advanced; nevertheless, Hall is sometimes distracted by questions of the veracity of the play irrelevant to her theme of Greek representation: see Harrison, *Emptiness of Asia*, Ch. 3.

[17] See e.g. the vague remarks of Pelling, 'Aeschylus' *Persae* and history' (though with excellent observations on the play's historical value).

[18] Harrison, *Emptiness of Asia*.

Where Hall's work is strongest, and supplements Goldhill's piece most clearly, is in its analysis of the techniques by which Aeschylus (and later playwrights) evokes the exotic barbarism of the Persians – the technique, for example, by which he suggests foreign speech by a spattering of foreign words. This concentration on the play's visual and aural dimensions, however, can obscure other aspects: how, for example, are we to understand Aeschylus' unrealistic elevation of Xerxes' father Darius into a positive model of kingship?[19] The play can also be usefully approached through comparison with Herodotus' account of the Persian Wars, not simply of their respective versions of the battle of Salamis, but of the ideological motifs common to both authors: Herodotus and Aeschylus both appear to draw from a common pool of 'knowledge' of the Persian court.[20]

With Suzanne Saïd (Ch. 3), we turn then to the later problematisation of the Greek–barbarian antithesis by Euripides. Saïd shows how Greek conceptions of the imagined wealth, the innate slavishness and the barbarity of barbarian peoples are repeatedly undermined by the context in which they are introduced by the playwright: how, for example, the Phrygian slave of the *Orestes* reflects the faults of the play's Greek hero, how the *Bacchae* dissolves altogether the distinction between Greek and barbarian, or the contradiction implicit in the sacrifice of Iphigenia (in the *Iphigenia in Aulis*) to punish the Phrygian (Trojan) abuse of Helen.

Saïd's reading must be seen alongside that of Edith Hall, who emphasises again Euripides' refraction of a simple barbarian antithesis ('the polarity deconstructed') and the emergence of the types of the 'barbaric Greek' and the 'noble barbarian'.[21] We should also see it in the light of recent readings of Herodotus which find in his work a similar ironic subversion of the simplistic polarity of Greek and barbarian. The story, for example, of the Spartan regent Pausanias refraining from a barbaric revenge on the corpse of the Persian commander Mardonius (9.78), a story cited by Saïd, and other anecdotes of Pausanias after the battle of Plataea – his ostentatious respect for a female Greek prisoner, or his dramatic comparison of a simple Spartan meal with the banquet laid out for the Persians (9.82) – can be seen as signs of Pausanias' later degeneration into tyrannical

---

[19] For the play's contrast between Darius and Xerxes, see Saïd, 'Darius et Xerxes'; for my explanation in terms of the Chorus's failed emancipation from the habit of monarchy, see *Emptiness of Asia*, Ch. 8.

[20] Harrison, *Emptiness of Asia*, Ch. 3.

[21] *Inventing the Barbarian*, Ch. 5.

excess. Thucydides completes the story, telling of how Pausanias dressed in Persian clothes and kept a 'Persian table' (1.130). Similarly, the conclusion of Herodotus' *Histories* shows – through the barbaric punishment of a Persian at the hands of the father of Pericles (and through an ironic flashback to the height of the 'hardness' of the Persians) – the Athenians taking on the mantle of empire from the Persians, and also adopting their excesses.[22] Aeschylus, by contrast, can be shown in the *Persians* to be shielding the Athenians from implicit comparison with the Persians: the Athenians' democracy and their proper reverence towards the gods prevent their indulging in comparable excesses.[23]

A similar tendency towards experimentation and the refraction of the Greek–barbarian antithesis can be seen in late fifth-century Attic comedies. In the surviving plays of Aristophanes foreign peoples do not feature centrally. Rather they appear in brief cameos such as the Scythian archer scene in the *Thesmophoriazousae*[24] or the long-awaited return of ambassadors from Persia in the *Acharnians*, in the characterisation of Athenian politicians as barbarian slaves,[25] or in a wealth of details (inevitably exploited for comic effect) of foreign religion, wealth, food, clothing, language or customs.[26]

Finally in this part, François Lissarrague (Ch. 4), like Suzanne Saïd, collapses the Greek–barbarian antithesis in his examination of the images of foreign peoples on Attic pottery. Lissarrague explains these scenes in terms of the context in which the pottery was used – the formalised drinking of the symposium. Greek drinkers, he argues, themselves become 'other' through the consumption of wine. He shows how imaginary peoples, such as the pygmies or the Amazons, are conflated with 'real' barbarians such as the Scythians.[27] His discussion of the Amazons also brings out the overlayering of different 'others': the Amazons are at once feminine and foreign. Like James Redfield in Chapter 1, Lissarrague shows how it is Greek categories

---

[22] See esp. Boedeker, 'Protesilaus'; Dewald, 'Wanton kings, pickled heroes'. Such ironic readings in many ways originate in Charles Fornara's masterpiece, *Herodotus*.

[23] Harrison, *The Emptiness of Asia*, pp. 104–10. For an argument, however, that Herodotus conceives the Persians' defeat as in large part caused by their lack of reverence for the gods, see Harrison, 'The Persian invasions'.

[24] See further Hall, 'The archer scene'.

[25] For such accusations of false citizenship, see Halliwell, *The Laughter of Dionysus*.

[26] See esp. Long, *Barbarians in Greek comedy*; Tuplin, *Achaemenid Studies*, p. 141 ff.; Daumas, 'Aristophane et les Perses'; Pretagostini, 'Aristofane "etnologo"'. For foreign languages in comedy, see below, introduction to Part II.

[27] See also here Lissarrague's 'Être Scythe à Athènes'.

and assumptions (rather than any duty of accuracy in depiction) which dictate the 'description' of foreign peoples.

Lissarrague's piece needs again to be read alongside François Hartog's treatment of the use of the Scythians in Herodotus. A curious sidelight is provided by the Athenians' purchase, following the Persian wars, of a body of Scythian archers (or slaves dressed as Scythians) to serve as a proto-police force in Athens.[28] Lissarrague's argument that the Scythian archer is succeeded in the period after the Persian Wars by the Persian archer should be seen first against the backdrop of recent work that examines the use of the Amazons as an analogue for the Persians,[29] and secondly alongside Ann Bovon's discussion of the representation of Persian warriors: Attic images of the Persians, she emphasises, combine personal observation and traditional stereotype.[30]

Finally, Lissarrague's proposed interpretation of the Eurymedon vase – that the impending penetration of the Persian 'Eurymedon' (the name of a battle between the Athenians and Persians) by a Greek suggests the moral that, in Kenneth Dover's words, 'we've buggered the Persians!'[31] – has been challenged by Gloria Ferrari Pinney and James Davidson.[32] They question why, if this reading is correct, the Greek is not a soldier, why the vase is a wine jug, why national characteristics are not more pronounced and why the act of penetration is not actually shown: 'If this is a triumph, why not show the moment of penetration, the triumphant act? As it is, the most the vase can claim is, "We have high hopes of buggering the Persians."'[33]

Many other questions relating to artistic evidence remain uncovered – in particular, that of the interaction between Greek and foreign (especially Near Eastern) art. As I mentioned above in the general introduction, scholars of earlier generations held (on few

[28] For a survey of evidence, see Hunter, *Policing Athens*, pp. 145–9; see further Hall, 'The archer scene'.

[29] See e.g. Castriota, *Myth, Ethos and Actuality*; Tyrrell, *Amazons*; duBois, *Centaurs and Amazons*; Henderson, 'Timeo Danaos'; for critical comment and further bibliography, see Mills, *Theseus*; Harrison, *The Emptiness of Asia*, pp. 31–9. For a rather over-tidy survey of Athenian and Hellenic identity through art, see also Harrison, 'Hellenic identity'.

[30] Bovon, 'La représentation des guerriers perses'. For the representation of the Persians (or the analogy of the king with the legendary Midas), see Miller, 'Persians', 'Midas'. More broadly, see Raeck, *Zum Barbarenbild in der Kunst Athens*; see also now Cohen, *Not the Classical Ideal*, Pt III ('External others').

[31] Dover, *Greek Homosexuality*, p. 105 (the exclamation mark is Dover's); Hall, 'Asia unmanned', p. 111. For the alleged sexual dimension of the Greeks' defeat of the Persians, see below, introduction to Part II.

[32] Ferrari Pinney, 'For the heroes are at hand'; Davidson, *Courtesans and Fishcakes*, pp. 170–1, 180–2.

[33] Davidson, *Courtesans and Fishcakes*, p. 171.

grounds other than prejudice) that the sculptures of the Persian capital of Persepolis were the work of Greek craftsmen. The Swedish scholar Carl Nylander, followed by Margaret Cool Root and others, have effected a revolution in the study of Persian art, highlighting the difficulty of distinguishing between 'national' styles, and suggesting a much more complex picture of cultural interaction.[34] As Root has demonstrated, in the past 'hybrid' or 'Graeco-Persian' art on the western fringes of the Achaemenid empire has been interpreted as evidence of the meagreness of Persian cultural influence. The same evidence, by the slightest 'rhetorical redirection', could just as easily be seen as suggestive of significant cultural interplay.[35] This line of work has been continued in the recent study of Margaret C. Miller, which catalogues in intricate detail the cultural borrowings – both those which are incontestable and others which are more tenuous – of the Greeks *from* the Persians.[36] As argued above, however (in the general introduction), Miller's interpretation of such contacts – that they necessarily contradict, or work against, Greek prejudices against the Persians – may be contested.

[34] Nylander, *Ionians*; Root, *The King and Kingship*.
[35] Root, 'From the heart'. See also Vickers, 'Interactions between Greeks and Persians'; Francis, 'Greeks and Persians'; Starr, 'Greeks and Persians'; for the Hellenistic period, Colledge, 'Greek and non-Greek interaction'.
[36] Miller, *Athens and Persia*.

1 *Herodotus the Tourist*†

JAMES REDFIELD

"Let me think—we don't see the other side of the moon out here, no."
"Come, India's not as bad as all that," said a pleasant voice. "Other side of the earth if you like, but we stick to the same old moon." Neither of them knew the speaker nor did they ever see him again.

—E. M. Forster, *A Passage to India*

Herodotus, as we know, is both Father of History and Father of Anthropology. Sir John Myres wrote: "so far as Herodotus presents us ... with a science of anthropology ... he is little, if at all, behind the best thought of our own day."[1] Even as of 1908 this seems extravagant. Herodotus lacks a principle which Tylor, in the generation before Myres, had already put at the head of cultural anthropology, namely, that every culture is a "complex whole"—or, as we would say, a system. Herodotus merely notes particular traits; he is not concerned with the functional, structural or stylistic coherence of the cultures he describes.

Here, for instance, is his account of the Adurmachidae, the people who inhabit the border between Egypt and Libya (4. 168):

> They observe most Egyptian customs but the clothes they wear are rather those of the rest of the Libyans. Their women wear a bangle on each shin, made of bronze. They let the hair on their head grow long, and when a woman catches lice on herself she bites them in retaliation and then throws them away. These are the only Libyans who do this, and they are the only ones who before setting up a household display their virgins to the king. When the king finds one of them pleasing he himself takes her maidenhood.

Herodotus notes points which distinguish this people from others, and especially points which a Greek finds odd, and therefore repel-

† Originally published in *Classical Philology* 80 (1985), 97–118.
I am thankful for helpful comments on various drafts of this paper by D. Lateiner, A. Momigliano, G. Walsh, and P. White. All translations are my own.
    [1] "Herodotus and Anthropology," in *Anthropology and the Classics*, ed. R. R. Marett (Oxford, 1908), p. 135.

lently interesting. Oddity is an ethnocentric principle; other people, from this point of view, are interesting because they wear odd clothes, eat odd foods, have odd customs and odd ideas of the proper and the shameful—odd, that is, by the standard of one's own culture. Woman bites louse is news. Herodotus seems thus not so much the precursor of Malinowski and Boas, as of *Strange as It Seems* and *Believe It or Not*.

My inquiry into Herodotus' anthropology thus begins with an antipathy to it. I was raised among ethnographers, for whom such unsystematic travelers' reports were the opposite of science. Nevertheless, the ethnographic perspective does provide an entry to Herodotus, for if every culture is a system, every artifact within the culture is characteristic of it—Herodotus' *Histories* included. The more ethnocentric his interests, the better they define his culture.

To travel and observe is a thing characteristically Greek; the prototype is Odysseus, who "wandered much, ... who saw the cities of many men and knew their mind." For a Greek there are three great reasons for travel: commerce, war, and seeing the sights (Hdt. 3. 139; cf. Pl. *Resp.* 556C, Isoc. 17. 4); the Greek word for the last is *theoria*. *Theoria* has a particular meaning of going to see the great spectacles, the international games and festivals of the Greeks, sometimes as a member of an official party—but the word also is used in the general sense of going to see another country. Thus we learn from Thucydides (6. 24) that one of the motives which drew the great Athenian expedition to Sicily was the desire of the young men "for sights and *theoria*." The love of *theoria* is there presented as a weakness, but in Herodotus it is characteristic of the sage—of the Scythian Anacharsis, who "saw a great part of the earth" (4. 76 γῆν πολλὴν θεωρήσας) and in the process became partly Hellenized, and of Solon, who made *theoria* his reason for leaving Athens (1. 29; Arist. *Ath. Pol.* 11. 1 adds commerce as an additional motive). Herodotus was neither the first nor the last Greek to spend some part of his life improving himself by visiting foreign parts.

Herodotus was interested in natural wonders and imposing monuments, but he had a special interest in the life of the peoples, in what we would call their culture. For this concept he has at least three different words: *diaita*, *ēthea*, and *nomoi*.

Diaita has to do with material culture, with what people eat and drink (3. 23) and otherwise consume (1. 202), and with their livelihood (1. 157, 4. 109). The word also simply means "residence"—human (1. 36, etc.) or animal (2. 68). *Ēthea* are more subjective, relating culture to personality; according to their *ēthea* people are more or less savage (4. 106 vs. 2. 30). More sophisticated *ēthea* (which may accompany a more luxurious *diaita*) are said to be "deeper" (4. 95); such people are, as we say, "more cultivated." *Ēthea* have to do with the cultural tone or ambiance of a community; one can feel a longing for the *ēthea* of one's home (1. 165). *Ēthea* also simply means the customary dwelling-places or "haunts"—of men (1. 15, etc.) or of animals (2. 93, 7. 125).

Nomos means something more explicit than *ēthea*, something more definite as command or prohibition. Very often a *nomos* is a written law (and that may be the original meaning of the word);[2] when used for a custom it means something which can be put into words and stated as a rule. *Nomoi* are specifically human; the word has no relevance to animals. Furthermore, *nomoi* are the sign of a certain level of culture; every people has its *ēthea*, but the most savage people have no *nomoi* at all (4. 106); they are incapable of stating rules for themselves. In the one place where *diaita* and *nomoi* are contrasted (4. 78), the former refers to clothing, the latter to religious observance.

Diaita, *ēthea*, and *nomoi* all vary from place to place and change over time. All three concepts carry with them a certain relativism; it is assumed that the *diaita*, *ēthea*, and *nomoi* of each people seem right to them. *Nomoi*, however, are special in that they are often accompanied by an explanation. The Egyptians ease themselves in their houses but eat in the street "saying that shameful necessities ought to be done in secret, things not shameful, openly" (2. 35). The Persians do not build temples or make images "and they charge with folly those who do such things, because, I think, they do not hold the gods anthropomorphic, as the Greeks (obviously) [κατά περ] do" (1. 131). It is through the discussion and comparison of diverse *nomoi* that the observing traveler becomes explicitly conscious of the relativism of culture; each people has its own *nomoi* and makes sense of them in its own terms.

Often, however, the discussion is over before it has properly begun. We may compare the traveler evoked in Plato's *Laws* (637C) who arrives in Taras during the feast of Dionysus to find the whole population drunk in the street. Initially the traveler is disapproving, but then:

> There is one answer which seems to resolve the question, so that the behav-
> ior is not wrong but right. For anyone will say in answer to the wondering
> stranger who looks upon something contrary to his own habits: "Do not

---

[2] G. P. Shipp, *NOMOS "Law"* (Sydney, 1978).

wonder, stranger. This is our *nomos;* perhaps you in such matters have a different one."

Herodotus often appears as just such a "wondering stranger" or, as we would say, *tourist* (one gloss for *theoria* is "tourism"), and his relativism seems just such a tourist's relativism. The tourist, after all, goes abroad to see people different from himself; it is wonderful that they are different, but there is nothing to wonder about in this, since people simply do differ and it is enjoyable that they do.

If *nomoi* are unmotivated, merely different, then they signify mere difference, as different countries have different flags and postage stamps. Such things cannot be studied, except very superficially; they can only be collected. The tourist then becomes a collector of *nomoi* which are the emblems of the various countries he visits in fact or in thought. Holland: wooden shoes and windmills. Paris: cafés and the Eiffel Tower. Similarly Herodotus likes to tell us: "These people all paint themselves red and eat monkeys" (4. 194). Like any collector, Herodotus likes his *nomoi* rare, gaudy, and curious.

The tourist makes no attempt to fit in; he rather accepts a specific social role: that of foreigner. In so doing he shows himself comfortable with his own culture, which is strong enough to sustain him even in his temporary position as an outsider. I am at home elsewhere, he says; therefore you will accept the fact that I am different, as I enjoy the fact that you are different. The greater the difference, the more the journey is worth the trip and the more worth collecting are the images, memories, and souvenirs that the tourist takes home with him.

The tourist, in fact, travels in order to be a foreigner, which is to say, he travels in order to come home. He discovers his own culture by taking it with him to places where it is out of place, discovers its specific contours by taking it to places where it does not fit. Tourism is thus both a proof and a source of cultural morale. Herodotus is glad to notice that the Egyptians (like the Greeks) "call all those who do not speak their language barbarians" (2. 158). Insofar as this attitude is reasonable in the Egyptians, so also is it reasonable in the Greeks. The tourist comes home with a new knowledge that he is at home, with a new appreciation of the only place where he is not a foreigner. Thus cultural relativism becomes ethnocentric and serves to reinforce the tourist's own norms; since he is Greek it is proper that he continue to be Greek.

I can now make more precise my initial antipathy to Herodotus' anthropology. I was brought up to despise tourists. For the ethnographers who raised me, the tourists were intruders in a world we wished kept inviolate. We classed them with missionaries, capitalists, government administrators—with all those modern intruders who wished to appropriate and transform the natives. The tourists were a special problem in that they were uncomfortably like us; we ethnographers had come to this place to observe, and so had they. We, however, had come to work and respected the native culture; they were on vacation and merely enjoyed it. They deprived the natives of dignity by treating their culture as a spectacle; in the process they themselves became ridiculous. We worked hard to fit in; we were prepared to share the hardships of the natives, learn their language, conform to their customs, value their values. The tourists were cheerfully out of place, taking photographs without asking, demanding the comforts of home, patronizing the natives for being different. They were a blot on the landscape. People we might have liked on their own ground in Omaha or Stuttgart appeared, when met in the field, loud, stupid, and coarse. They made us ashamed of our own culture.

Ethnographers, at least while in the field, characteristically align themselves with the natives against their own people. This is an odd thing to do, and is the practical result of ethnographic relativism, which holds that there are no superior societies. Every culture is worthy of respect as a functioning system; every culture in its own way makes full use of human capacities. It is true that ethnography itself might seem evidence of superiority; we study them, while they do not study us. But this (thinks the ethnographer) is not different from the fact that the tourists visit the natives while the natives do not visit the tourists. The superiority is in power, not real value. The tourist accepts and enjoys this superiority; the ethnographer tries to overcome it by participant observation, which means abandoning power and throwing oneself on the mercy of the natives. Only in this way can the ethnographer begin to see the culture as the native sees it, from the inside, not as a collection of oddities but as a meaningful, livable, complex whole.

Participant observation does not mean active participation, which would change the culture; ethnographers rather try to efface themselves, to become invisible, in order, as far as possible, to observe the culture in its inviolate condition, as if they were not there. The professional concern of the ethnographer (as opposed to a merely personal response) is not for the natives as people, but as a culture; to the extent that ethnographers make friends and acquire local obligations these in fact become an obstacle to their work.

The ethnography, further, is not for the natives but for us; the native has no need of the relativism which makes ethnography possible. For the native, the local culture is simply "the way"; if others have other ways, that is, so to speak, their problem. That we are interested in the ways of others is characteristically our problem. We may not be superior to them, but we are, in this crucial respect, different.

The ethnographer, driven from home by certain modern concerns, has come into the field in order to think, and he (or she, obviously) thinks about certain problems he has brought with him—even if he often does not know what they are until he gets there. He is not content when the native says to him: "This is our *nomos;* perhaps in such matters you have a different one." The ethnographer seeks to discern the underlying cultural system, and he brings it home with him. Ethnography is in its own way also a form of appropriation, signaled when the ethnographer speaks to his colleagues of "my people."

Ethnography reflects a hunger for cultural system, a hunger which seems to characterize us. It is no accident that we became theoretically interested in these cultures just as we began, practically, to appropriate and destroy them. Modernism is an unprecedented historical experience; for the first time one cultural system is taking over the world. A society of such power must inspire anxiety in its members; are we sure that our culture is so superior that the species benefits by the transformation of mankind in our image? We are not sure that modernism coheres as a culture should cohere; we seem to ourselves sometimes out of control. Our interest in cultural systems may then be interpreted as a search for the sources of cultural coherence, of control. We are interested in *nomoi* because we experience *anomie* [the absence of *nomoi*]. Ethnography, from this point of view, is an effort intellectually to rescue ourselves from our own history, and the ethnographer is never more modern than when he leaves this modern scene to immerse himself in another culture. (The classic meditation on this paradox is Lévi-Strauss' *Tristes tropiques*.)

This concludes my dialectical introduction. My initial antipathy to Herodotus' anthropology, it turns out, was based on my own ethnocentric expectations. The Greeks were great tourists, but not participant observers; it seems that this is a sign of their higher cultural morale. They had a culture and relied on it; this does not mean that they were unobservant travelers, or without anxieties, or that their principles of observation were trivial. If we are to understand Herodotus' inquiry into culture we must see the problem as it presented itself to him.

It may be relevant that *theoria* was a term adopted by the philosophers for their own activity—the *locus classicus* is the anecdote of
Pythagoras and Leon of Phlius (Diog. Laert. *Life of Pythagoras* 8;
further citations in A. Delatte, *La vie de Pythagore de Diogène
Laërce* [Brussels, 1922], ad loc.). Asked to explain the meaning of
philosophos, Pythagoras compared life to the great games: some
come to compete, some to buy and sell, but the better sort come as
spectators. This triad is paralleled in Herodotus 3. 139, already cited,
and a link between philosophy and *theoria* is explicit in the story
of Solon, who traveled φιλοσοφέων γῆν πολλὴν θεωρίης εἵνεκεν
[over much of the earth as a philosopher for the sake of observation]
(1. 30). The tourist, it seems, can also travel in order to think.

   Solon's moralism is thematic in the *Histories*: Solon transmits it to
Croesus, and Croesus, once he has understood it in adversity (1. 86.
3), transmits it to Cyrus (1. 207) and Cambyses (3. 36). Its later heir
is Artabanus, counselor to the next two Persian kings (note the verbal
echo: 1. 32. 4, 7. 49. 3). It is a moralism founded on experience of
the wide world—Croesus, asking Solon to approve his prosperity,
expressly links Solon's πλάνη and σοφίη, his "wandering" and
"wisdom." It is also a moralism critical of barbarian values—if some
barbarians have it, they become the ineffective "warners" of those
who lead the barbarians.† Solon thus displays the wisdom derived
from *theoria* as something peculiarly Greek and something more
than mere experience; the thoughtful Greek traveler comes to his
experience confident that he can give a definitive interpretation of
the non-Greek world he visits. He travels not so much to learn as to
teach.

   Solon, I would suggest, appears in Herodotus' narrative as a kind
of alter ego of the narrator himself. Herodotus did not so much
derive his interpretations from his inquiries; rather he brought to his
inquiries value and categories wherewith to interpret them. His book
does more than tell us what is in the world; it teaches us how to think
about it.

   The primary categorization is in the first sentence: the distinction
between Greeks and barbarians. Although this categorization appears
at times to be overcome by a secondary relativism, it remains primary; the *Histories* is a Greek book for Greeks about Greeks and
others—and it makes Greek sense of the others. As Herodotus, a

---

   † For the pattern whereby the warnings of 'wise advisers' are inevitably rejected by the
kings or tyrants to whom the advice is addressed, see esp. the classic article of Richmond
Lattimore, 'The wise adviser in Herodotus'. For the role of Solon in the *Histories*, see now
Harrison, *Divinity and History*, Ch. 2.

culturally self-confident Greek spectator, traveled in fact and in thought among the others, he collected wonders and oddities, and as his collection formed he arranged it in his mind. He has an eye for the exceptional, and also for regularities, patterns. Nowhere does he discuss the principles whereby he arranged and selected his collection. He does not discuss his interests; he pursues them. Nevertheless, there are some principles, characteristic of him and of Greek ways of interpreting experience.

Let us begin with a relatively simple (and frequently observed) point: Herodotus' taste for symmetry. Symmetry is pervasive in Herodotus, most subtly in the narrative, where it often takes the form of *tisis*—for which one gloss might be "poetic justice." In the greatest case "of all those we know," *tisis* took the form of a retribution with the symmetry of the *lex talionis*† (8. 105–6; cf. 6. 72. 1). Often symmetry asserts itself without subtlety, as in Herodotus' assertion (denounced by Eratosthenes ap. Strabo 1. 3. 22) that if there were men at the back of the North Wind there would have to be men at the back of the South Wind, too (4. 36. 1). Herodotus seeks out symmetry in his geography, as when he makes the Danube symmetrical to the Nile (2. 33–34). He finds symmetry in nature, as in the case of the Nile fish: the males swim before the females, dropping their milt which the females swallow; the females swim back before the males, dropping their eggs which the males swallow (2. 93). Such natural symmetry can also be called *tisis*, as in the case of the Arabian snakes: the females eat the males, and then the offspring eat the females (3. 109). Herodotus also finds symmetry in cultural arrangements, as in the Babylonian river trade, where the boats carry the donkeys downstream and the donkeys carry the boats upstream (1. 194—"This I find the greatest wonder of all things there, except for the city itself.").

Wonder is the beginning of wisdom when it leads to further thought. In Herodotus' case this takes the form of a taste for system, which is a philosophical tendency. Herodotus' thoughtful love of wonders leads him to prefer those wonders which because of their inner structure, the symmetry of their elements, are "good to think." (We shall see more examples below.)

A related tendency leads him to arrange the oddities he has collected in a frame of systematic oppositions. The most striking example occurs in the account of Egypt; just as the Egyptian sky and

† The principle of the extraction of retribution in kind.

river are different from those elsewhere so also the Egyptians are
opposite (ἔμπαλιν) in their *ēthea and nomoi*.

He then develops the point in no fewer than eighteen oppositions
(2. 35–36), of which I quote only the first four:

> Among them the women shop and sell in the markets; the men stay home
> and weave. Others weave pushing the wool upward; the Egyptians down-
> ward. Men carry burdens on their heads, women on their shoulders. The
> women urinate standing, the men sitting down.

In Egypt both nature and culture are upside down—that is, opposite
to what a Greek would expect. I am reminded of Lévi-Strauss'
description in *Tristes tropiques* of Fire Island, where, according to
him, the inversion of sea and land is echoed by the sexual inversion
of the inhabitants; the sterile male couples push their groceries about
in baby carriages. Both descriptions are systematic, in that a pattern
of difference is found to pervade more than one realm; both are
somewhat comic—because, I think, of their excessive lucidity;
such elegant mirror-oppositions must seem partly the work of the
observer, by a sort of verbal sleight-of-hand.

This brings us to the most famous of all the Herodotean passages
on *nomos*; it is in the form of a comment on the madness of
Cambyses, whose most dangerous symptom was that he laughed
at the *nomoi* of the Egyptians (3. 38):

> If one should make the offer to all mankind and tell them to select the finest
> *nomoi* from all *nomoi*, after review each would take his own. Nor is it likely
> that anyone but a madman would think this ridiculous. There is plenty of
> evidence that all men have this relation to their *nomoi*, in particular this:
> Darius, calling the Greeks who were at his court, asked them how much
> money they would take to eat their dead fathers. They said they wouldn't
> do it at any price. Darius then called some Indians, the so-called Callatiae,
> who eat their parents, and asked them, while the Greeks were present and
> informed by interpreters of what was said, how much money they would
> take to burn their fathers with fire. They gave a great cry and asked him not
> to blaspheme. That is the way it is with *nomos*, and Pindar seems to me to
> have put it right, saying that *nomos* is king of all.

I wish to set this passage next to another superb example of
Herodotus' taste for system (3. 108. 2–4):

> Somehow divine forethought is, as you might expect, wise, and has made
> those creatures that are cowardly in spirit and edible also numerous in their
> progeny, so that some may be left over when they are eaten, whereas all that
> are harsh and dangerous have few progeny. Take the hare: it is hunted by
> every beast and bird and by mankind; so also it is numerous in progeny. It
> alone of all beasts becomes pregnant while pregnant; some of the young
> in its belly have hair, some are hairless, some are just being formed by the

mother, some are being conceived. That's the sort of thing it is, while the lioness, the strongest and boldest, conceives once in her life. When she gives birth she ejects the womb along with her offspring. The cause is as follows. When the cub in the mother first quickens, having by far the sharpest claws of any animal, it scrabbles at the womb, and the more it grows the more it moves about scratching. Then delivery is near and there is nothing left of the womb that's sound.

The part about the hares is of course (as stated) wrong;[3] five minutes' reflection would have shown Herodotus that the part about the lions is worse than wrong; it is obvious nonsense. If lions bred in this way, there would be no lions. Herodotus is not uncritical; if we ask why this point got by him, we are compelled, I think, to reply that it answered his hunger for symmetry. Having made an extravagant statement about rabbits, he felt the need to balance it with an equally extravagant statement about lions. The passage, I would argue, is in its very absurdity a key to Herodotus' *mentalité*.

Similarly with the Callatiae. I am myself doubtful that any Indians or other people have ever piously eaten their dead (except in a highly reduced, largely symbolic sense), even though such customs are reported a number of times in Herodotus (cf. 1. 216, 3. 99. 1, 4. 26) and have been reported many times from various parts of the world;[4] the reports never seem to come accompanied by very much in the way of evidence. However, the reality of the custom is not at issue here; I am suggesting a different point: the custom, whether actual or mythical, interests Herodotus (and us) because it fills out a systematic opposition.

Cremation, the heroic funeral, was never the universal Greek custom, but the epics wrote it into Greek consciousness as the ideal type. By cremation the dead body, the natural man, was annihilated, leaving nothing behind but *kleos* and *sema*, memory and monument—that is, the dead person was converted into a meaning, a culturally preserved identity. The dead were thus purified by being completely acculturated. From the *Iliad* onward the eating of the dead appears as the ultimate impurity.

From the point of view of the Callatiae, however, their own solution is equally a purification—working in the opposite direction. To treat the dead person as meat is to return the natural man to nature, classified as mere matter appropriate to cultural exploitation—and

---

[3] The hare, my zoological friends tell me, can be pregnant by several sires at once, since its period of fertility is unusually long. The implantation of all eggs, however, takes place at the same time, and all the young develop and are born together.

[4] See "Affectionate Cannibalism," chap. 5 of E. Sagan, *Cannibalism* (New York, 1974).

this may also be thought of as an honorable disposal of the remains. The modern equivalent, I suppose, is to give one's body to science. In any case the symmetry of the two solutions draws our attention to the fact that each succeeds only partially, by asserting half of the paradox of death—which is that when life ceases, cultural existence continues, so that a corpse both is and is not a person. *In comparison with each other*, therefore, both solutions are revealed as arbitrary.

At this point I enter in evidence another meditation on cannibalism, that in *Tristes tropiques:*[5]

> Confining ourselves to the forms of anthropophagy which rely on mysticism, magic, or religion ... we can recognize ... that the moral condemnation of such customs implies either a belief in the bodily resurrection of the dead which will be compromised by the material destruction of the corpse, or else affirms a link between body and soul; ... that is to say, implies beliefs which are of the same nature as those in the name of which the ritual feeding is practiced; we have no particular reason to prefer one to the other. Furthermore, the disengagement from the memory of the deceased, of which we complain in cannibalism, is certainly no greater ... than that which we tolerate in the display of dissection.
>
> In any case we ought to understand that certain of our own customs, from the point of view of an observer from another society, would seem to him to be of the same nature as that anthropophagy which seems to us alien to the notion of civilization. I am thinking of ... our penitentiaries. Taking an overview, one would be tempted to oppose two types of societies: those which practice anthropophagy, that is, who when confronted by certain individuals possessing potent forces see in their absorption of them the sole means of neutralizing them, and even of profiting from them, and those societies which, like ours, practice *anthropoemy* (from the Greek *emein*, vomit); confronted by the same problem, they have chosen the opposite solution; which consists of expelling these potent beings from the social body, holding them temporarily or permanently isolated, without human contact, in establishments designed for the purpose. For the greater part of the societies which we call primitive, such a custom would inspire profound horror; it would display to their eyes the same barbarism which we are inclined to impute to them owing to their symmetrical customs.

The parallel with Herodotus is so good that I am inclined at this point to acknowledge that my initial distaste for Herodotus' ethnography was based on a misunderstanding, and on my own intellectual provincialism. I should have understood that Herodotus' interests are not micro-systemic, in the internal coherence of particular cultures, but macro-systemic, in the patterned display provided by the range of cultures. Those two great tourists, Herodotus and Lévi-Strauss, have made their science by setting culture against culture in a pattern of symmetrical oppositions.

[5] (Paris 1955), pp. 348–49.

The parallel should not, however, be pushed too far. Lévi-Strauss is characteristically modern. He is attempting (if I understand him) to give a general account of man, of human nature as expressed in the general categories of culture—and intends thereby to bring before us a vision of that Golden Age which (as Rousseau had told him) is neither behind us nor before us, but within us. Lévi-Strauss, in fact, aims to achieve a kind of scientific consciousness proper to the universal man. Herodotus remains a Greek, and a historian. His oppositions are firmly located in time and space; he is attempting to describe, not all possible worlds, but the particular world he found before him. That is why Herodotus does not write about his categories, but simply employs them—because he is not trying to state the a priori conditions of all experience, but rather to bring some order into the chaos of his actual experience. In his cultural geography he employs categorical oppositions in an attempt to discern the ordered structure of the inhabited world.

The central opposition, from this point of view, is that between Egypt and Scythia. The Egyptians and the Scythians are the two peoples most thoroughly described by Herodotus; they are alike, also, in that neither people borrows from the customs of others (2. 79. 1, 2. 91. 1, 4. 76. 1). Placed toward the northern and the southern edges of Herodotus' world, these two peoples display self-contained, self-created—and contrasted— cultural systems.

Nature is wonderful (that is, different from Greece) in both places, but differently. In Egypt the sky is wonderful because it never rains (2. 14. 1), while the river is wonderful because it varies inversely from rivers in other places, rising when others fall (2. 19. 3). In Scythia the sky is wonderful because it rains inversely from other places, in summer, not in winter (4. 28. 2); the great river, the Danube, is wonderful because it never varies. The core of the comparison is the rivers; the Dneiper is called the most productive river except for the Nile (4. 53. 2). The Nile, however, holds the country together; it is a means of communication (2. 96), while the Scythian rivers divide Scythia into districts, and serve as barriers to travel and invasion (4. 47).

The Scythian rivers are plural, and this plurality of rivers is the most notable fact about the country (4. 82). The Nile is single, although broken up into channels—which are explicitly compared to the Scythian rivers (4. 47. 1). The Scythian rivers, however, are natural, while the Nile channels are artificial; the latter were cut by King Sesostris (2. 108. 2)—and the result is a country in a crucial respect opposite to Scythia: whereas the Scythians ride horses and live in wagons, Egypt is a country where horses and chariots are useless (2. 108. 3).[6]

Sesostris divided the country into equal lots (2. 109. 1) and invented geometry in order to take account of changes produced by shifts in the river (2. 109. 2). In Egypt nature is under cultural control. Egyptian history begins before Sesostris with King Minas, who first directed and controlled the Nile (2. 99). Before him lower Egypt was marsh (2. 4. 3); by controlling the river the people brought into existence the greater part of usable Egyptian territory (2. 15). In Scythia, by contrast, the territory was there before the people; all three origin stories (4. 5–11) specify that before the Scythians the land was empty (ἐρήμη). Scythia is a natural landscape which came to be inhabited; Egypt is a landscape radically reconstructed by habitation. The relation between man and nature in Egypt is also reciprocal, since their soil and water made them a people; the oracle proclaimed that all those watered by the Nile are Egyptians (2. 18. 3). The Scythians have no proper soil, and wander; on one occasion, pursuing the Cimmerians, they missed their way and ended in Media (4. 12), where they spent twenty-eight years (4. 1).

The Egyptians stay put while their power expands and contracts; at the point of their furthest advance they got as far as Scythia (2. 103). The Scythians, at the furthest limit of their wandering, were induced by the Egyptian pharaoh to turn back (1. 105). Each people marks the limit of the other's history.

The Egyptians excel all others in their memory of the past (2. 77. 1, 145. 3) and believe themselves the eldest of the peoples (2. 2. 1—but experiment proved them wrong). The Scythians claim to be the youngest of the peoples (4. 5. 1—but the stories told about this are various and doubtful). The history of Egypt is told in terms of the succession of their kings; stories are told of them, and their monuments are admired. Power is centralized in Egypt; the attempt of the Egyptians to have many kings was a failure, "since they were not able to manage their lives for any length of time without a king" (2. 147. 2). The Scythians also have kings, but these are plural; there is a foundation-legend of Scythian kingship (4. 5) but no continuous history of their kings. The funerals of the Scythian kings are elaborate and characteristically involve the wandering of the funeral cortege through all the peoples of the district (2. 71–72), but the royal tombs,

---

[6] On this and other points of contrast between Egypt and Scythia, see F. Hartog, "Les Scythes imaginaires: Espace et nomadisme," *Annales (ESC)* 34 (1979): 1137–54. [See further Hartog, *The Mirror of Herodotus*.]

so far from being famous monuments, cannot be located by outsiders (4. 127). The death of a Scythian king is a collective experience which is intense, extensive—and ephemeral.

Egypt is fullest of wonders (2. 35. 1), whereas in Scythia there is (besides the rivers) only one wonder: the footprint of Heracles (4. 82). Similarly the Egyptians have invented more things than any other people—including altars, divine images, and temples (2. 4. 2), which are unknown in Scythia (4. 59. 2—except in the cult of Ares). The Scythians by contrast have invented only ἕν τὸ μέγιστον [one very great thing], the one great art of not being conquered (4. 46. 2). In terms of Archilochus' fable, to which Herodotus surely alludes, the Egyptians are cultural foxes, the Scythians cultural hedgehogs.†

Egypt is politically and economically unified, but culturally diverse; different gods are worshipped differently in different places (2. 42. 2). The Scythians differ in their livelihood (4. 17–19) and are loosely organized politically, but all worship the same gods (except that the Royal Scythians have a special cult of Ares) and these few in number (4. 59. 1). Scythia is characteristically simple. In Egypt, for instance, the pig is unclean and swineherds are outcasts, but once a year the Egyptians eat pork (2. 47. 2) and explain this by a story which is not suitable for circulation. (Pigs also work their fields: 2. 14. 2.) In Scythia, where pigs are also unclean, no pigs are raised at all (4. 63). The Scythians refused to accept the Dionysiac rites, originated by the Egyptians (2. 49. 1), on the ground that "it makes no sense to seek out a god who sends men mad" (4. 79. 3). The idea was, as it were, too fancy for them. Egyptian manners are delicate; the Egyptians, especially the priests, bathe and change their clothes constantly and "carry out, so to speak, myriads of ceremonies" (2. 37. 3). There is no mention of Scythian priests (although they have numerous soothsayers, 4. 67. 1); the Scythians in general never wash their bodies with water at all (4. 75. 2).

Egypt is tightly held together as a tense synthesis of diverse elements; Scythia is an open field of cultural tendencies. The Scythians are surrounded by other peoples, whose customs sometimes appear to be more extreme versions of their own. These include the Anthropophagi, who wear Scythian clothes but are cannibals (4. 106). The Scythians themselves do not eat human flesh, although they taste human blood in their oath-taking (4. 70) and drink the blood of their

---

† The allusion is to Archilochus fr. 201 West ('The fox knows many things, but the hedgehog knows one big one'), famously the starting point for Isaiah Berlin's *The Hedgehog and the Fox*.

enemies (4. 64. 1). They also rejoice in human sacrifice (4. 62. 3, 73)—which is absolutely unknown in Egypt (2. 45. 2). Such customs may be thought of as modified cannibalism.

A more distant people in the same district are the Issedones. These (like the Indians) piously eat the flesh of their dead relations, and also gild their skulls (4. 26). The Scythians gild the skulls of their enemies and use them as drinking cups; they also make garments of their skins (4. 64–65). The similarity between the two sets of customs lies in the use of the dead body as a natural resource, capable of transformation into food or an implement. The opposite solution is Egyptian embalming, whereby the body is fully acculturated into a monument. Since there are three grades of embalming, according to price (2. 86. 2), the class structure continues to classify even corpses, who remain in this sense members of society.

These contrasts also play a role in the historical narrative, since Egypt and Scythia are the scenes of the two great Persian projects which come between Cyrus' creation of the Persian empire and Xerxes' invasion of Greece: the expeditions of Cambyses and Darius. Egypt is vulnerable only at one point, through the Arabian desert (3. 5. 1), yet once entered it is easily conquered. It has, so to speak, a hard shell, but is soft at the core. Once inside, however, Cambyses runs mad and kills himself. Scythia, by contrast, is wide open; one needs only to cross the rivers. Yet Darius, while himself unharmed, never makes contact with the Scythians. Scythia withdraws like a mirage; Egypt (to shift the metaphor) is a quicksand which swallows the invader. You cannot get into Scythia; you cannot get out of Egypt.

These contrasts, however, are not explicit in Herodotus' text; only rarely does he explicitly compare cultures. I believe that they nevertheless latently shape his understanding of the world and of the events which take place in it. The contrast between Egypt and Scythia, after all, is not peculiar to Herodotus. For the Hippocratic *Airs, Waters, Places* (18) the Scythians and the Egyptians are the extreme types of mankind: "they are *sui generis* and not at all like others" because they are subject to the extremes, respectively, of cold and of heat. A century later Plato has adapted this contrast to his tripartite division of the soul (including the Greeks as a mediating term):

> It would be absurd to think that the spirited part could exist in cities except by derivation from individuals who possess this principle, as, for example, in Thrace and Scythia and generally up that way, or the love of learning, which is chiefly attributed to our part of the world, or the love of money, which one

might say has a particular existence among the Phoenicians and down in Egypt.

(*Republic* 435E–36A)

Egypt and Scythia are here classed with other peoples; the contrast between them is a specific case of a generic contrast, of great import-ance in Herodotus: the contrast between soft peoples and hard peoples. (These are my terms, not Herodotus', but cf. 9. 122.) Soft peoples are characterized by luxury, the division of labor, and com-plexity of *nomoi*, especially in the sphere of religion; hard peoples are simple, harsh, and fierce. Among soft peoples market-exchange proliferates; hard peoples rely on gift and theft, the heroic modes of exchange. Soft peoples centralize resources through taxation, build monuments, are literate and organized; their politics tend toward tyranny. Hard peoples have relatively weak political organizations and tend toward anarchy. Soft peoples tend to acculturate their dead, hard peoples to naturalize them; among hard peoples women are treated as an abundant natural resource, more or less freely available, whereas among soft peoples women tend to become a commodity, disposed of by sale, through prostitution, or otherwise.[7] Hard cultures fall short of civility; they are unwelcoming and difficult to visit. Soft cultures are confusing and seductive, difficult to leave once visited. The contrast is already partially realized in the wanderings of Odysseus, in the contrast between the cannibalistic giants, Laestrygonians and Cyclopes, who fail to treat the traveler as a guest, and the seductive charmers, Calypso and Circe, who entertain the traveler so successfully that they threaten to transform him and make it impossible for him to leave.[8]

In Herodotus the hard and soft peoples of the world are located on a real map, and carefully differentiated within each category. The Scythians and the Egyptians are the prototypical cases, partly because they lie at the edges of the historical world. Beyond them is the mythical: beyond the Scythians, the Issedones, who tell of the one-eyed Arimaspoi and the griffins (4. 16. 1); beyond the Egyptians, empty space, crossable only by the Ichthyphagoi, and then the Ethiopians "of long life" (3. 17. 1), like the Arimaspoi known only by hearsay. These mythical outer neighbors remind us of the mythi-cal sources of the contrast: the Ethiopians, with their Table of the Sun

---

[7] See M. Rosellini and S. Saïd, "Usages de femmes et autres nomoi chez les 'sauvages' d'Hérodote," *ASNP* ser. 3, 8 (1978): 949–1005.

[8] For a fuller discussion of this categorical contrast in the *Odyssey*, see my "Odysseus: The Economic Man," in *Approaches to Homer*, ed. C. Rubino and C. Shelmerdine (Austin, 1983), pp. 218–47.

(3. 18), live in a world which appears to be, like the houses of Circe and Calypso, one of magical abundance; the one-eyed Arimaspoi remind us of the Cyclopes.

Herodotus says (3. 116):

> I do not believe this notion that there are one-eyed people in nature, having the rest of their nature like that of other people. But the ends of the earth, as they surround the rest of the world, are likely to have in them those things which seem to us finest and most rare.

We place the fabulous beyond the edges of the known world, he suggests, not only because they are beyond our knowledge, but because, as we move toward the edges, we encounter more extreme conditions and therefore atypical forms, both natural and cultural. The ends of the earth, for Herodotus, are districts full of oddities, monsters, and rare valuable substances. The center, by contrast, is a sphere of mixtures. "The ends of the earth must have got as their share all that is finest, in precisely the way [κατά περ] Greece got as its share the most finely blended seasons" (3. 106. 1). The edges, as they are extreme, are also stable. The mythical peoples are unchanging, and being unreachable are immune to outside influence. The Egyptians and the Scythians also borrrow nothing from their neighbors. The center, by contrast, as it is a sphere of natural mixture, is also a sphere of cultural mixture, where the peoples are transformed by contact with each other. (Note that the verb used in 3. 106. 1 for the mixture of the seasons is elsewhere used for the relations of friendship [4. 152. 5, 7. 151] or enmity [5. 124. 1, conjectured at 7. 145. 1, 9. 37. 4] arising from contact between states.) The center of Herodotus' historical map is Ionia, where the natural mixture is most delicately balanced (1. 141. 1); the Ionians are also mixed with other peoples (1. 146. 1). Ionia is also the zone of contact between the two central peoples whose enmity is the theme of the *Histories*: the Greeks and the Persians.

The Persians "most of mankind adopt foreign *nomaia*" (1. 135). In this they are like the Greeks, and like Herodotus, who is always alert, not only for what *nomoi* have been borrowed by his people, but for others which might be worth borrowing. Herodotus also notes Persian borrowings, and displays the Persians to us as a people in the process of cultural change. The Persians begin as a hard people, but their conquest of the Medes brings them, in Cyrus' metaphor, from the thistle to the feast (1. 126. 3). They change further by conquering the Lydians; previously they had nothing ἁβρόν or ἀγαθόν, luxurious or good (1. 74. 1). The Lydians in turn are reduced to insignificance and evicted from history when they are induced to give up arms in favor of womanish clothes, "lyre-playing, and retail trade" (1. 155. 4 καπηλεύειν). (Herodotus elsewhere records that the Lydians themselves invented (along with games) coined money and retail traders, κάπηλοι (1. 94).) Trade is a "soft" institution, since it requires bargaining, which is devious, as opposed to the forceful courage required in war. Cyrus is contemptuous of trade (1. 153), but the Persians are moving in that direction, as is seen in the contrast between Father Cyrus and Trader (κάπηλος) Darius (3. 89. 3). In the process their *nomoi* are changing: "when they find out about any sort of enjoyment they take it up; most notably they have learned from the Greeks to copulate with boys" (1. 135). Having become more sexual, they break their own rule against anthropomorphic gods by borrowing Aphrodite "from the Assyrians and the Arabs" (1. 131). Their religious institutions are becoming more complex.

At the center the relation between hard and soft becomes dynamic. The contrast is in play in the four generations of the Persian monarchy, which provide the *Histories* with an integrating chronology. Cyrus led a hard people against soft peoples, and transformed the Persians in the process. Cambyses then invaded the prototypical soft people, the Egyptians; the invasion was a success, but the result was the internal collapse of the Persian monarchy. The monarchy was then reconstituted by Darius on a new basis; Persians were traditionally taught before all else to tell the truth (1. 136. 2; cf. 138. 1), but Darius is a partisan of the convenient lie (3. 72. 4). Darius in his turn attacked the prototypical hard peoples, the Scythians and their neighbors; the expedition was a failure and had as its main practical result the further entanglement of the Ionians with the Persians: the Ionians showed themselves, according to the Scythians, the worst and most cowardly of free men, but the best, and most faithful of slaves (4. 142). The softening of the Ionians, however, had not affected all the Greeks; when Xerxes invaded Greece he led a soft people against a hard people, and was doomed to failure.

The contrast between hard and soft thus provides a way of reading the dynamic of history, of interpreting the general character of events. The pattern is foreshadowed in the personal history of Cyrus. After Cyrus has fulfilled his historical role (in relation to the Greeks) by establishing Persian power over Asia Minor, Herodotus completes his account of the conquerer by telling of two further expeditions—only two out of many (1. 177): against Babylon and the Massagetae. These two anticipate the contrast between Egypt and Scythia.

Babylon has some points in common with Egypt. The god is said to sleep in the temple there "just as in Egyptian Thebes" (1. 182. 1). Most of the arts of civilization originated in Egypt, but a few important items originate in Babylon (2. 109. 3). Babylonian lamentations are also "pretty much like those in Egypt" (1. 198). In both places married couples bathe after intercourse. More significant: Babylon, like Egypt, is extremely fertile, watered not by rain but by irrigation; neither country raises grapes or olives, the two crops which, as Homer and Hesiod tell us, require the greatest κομιδή, close care and attention. In both countries, then, the acculturation of nature is relatively complete and effortless. Babylon, like Egypt, has one weak point (where the river enters the city, 1. 191), and once entered is easily conquered.

The Massagetae, says Herodotus, are much like the Scythians (1. 215. 1), and some people think they actually are Scythians (1. 201). One of their customs is wrongly attributed to the Scythians (1. 216. 1). Like the Scythians, they intoxicate themselves on vapor (1. 202. 2). Some of them eat wild food and raw fish; their copulation is impersonal or even open, like that of cattle (1. 202). They are loose in unacculturated nature. Their country is easily entered, but like the Scythians they turn out to be unconquerable.

The counselor Croesus, made wise by misfortune, provides Cyrus with a strategy, which is exactly that of Odysseus with the Cyclops. Cyrus is to allow the Massagetae to defeat him, and then provide them with a feast and unmixed wine to make them drunk (1. 207). The strategy is successful (1. 221). Cyrus, however, fails to imitate Odysseus completely; he does not take his opportunity for retreat, and is killed. The Queen of the Massagetae then puts Cyrus' head in a bag of blood, carrying out her threat: "although you can never have enough of it, I shall glut you [κορέσω] with blood" (1. 212. 3).

The savage queen, by employing the concept of *koros*, invokes the Greek tragic vocabulary. *Koros* is the appetite which gains increase by what it feeds on; those who prosper too much, or in the wrong way, become insatiable, ἀκόρητος. *Koros* is linked with *atē*, violence which overrides proper limits, and also with *hybris*, a confusion of the mind evidenced by moral and practical error. All this is familiar, and told in a hundred Greek stories. The story of Cyrus is in Herodotus another such. He no sooner conquers Babylon than he is filled with a passion (ἐπεθύμησε) to subdue the Massagetae (1. 201). "Many and weighty the forces that excited him and urged him on: his birth, which seemed to have something more than human about it, and the good fortune he had had in the wars" (1. 204. 2). Unbroken success is here linked to the illusion of godlike powers, and to the neglect of the lesson Solon taught Croesus: that all mortals are thrall to circumstance (cf. 1. 207. 2). Cyrus' attack on the Massagetae is an act of *hybris* (1. 213. 3). Any Greek would recognize him as ripe for destruction.

Herodotus' particular contribution seems to be the link between this tragic scenario and the (also traditional) contrast between cultures I have here labeled "soft" and "hard." This link is not explicit, but evidently underlies patterned repetitions in the narrative. There are in the *Histories* no conquests of hard peoples by soft peoples; evidently such conquests have occurred, but Herodotus does not tell their stories. The hard, simple peoples cannot be conquered (although they can be temporarily fuddled by the arts of complex culture). The best one can do is to inflict some damage on them and withdraw (cf. also the Libyan expedition, 4. 203). In any case the simple peoples are not worth conquering, since they have nothing. Those who invade them do so out of sheer love of invasion—which is irrational. Cyrus makes the same mistake with respect to the Massagetae that Croesus had made with respect to Cyrus (cf. 1. 71. 2–4).

The soft, complex peoples, on the other hand, can be conquered, but in defeat they take their revenge by transforming the conquerer. They soften him, and at the same time fill him with just that irrational insatiability which will lead him into destruction. Cambyses' successful invasion of Egypt leads him to attempt the invasion of Ethiopia. This appears to break the pattern, since the Ethiopians are properly classed as soft, like the Egyptians—but Cambyses never reaches them. He is defeated by the ultimate hard environment, the open space between Egypt and Ethiopia. He does not encounter cannibals; instead his soldiers become cannibals to one another (3. 25. 4–7).

There is thus in the *Histories* an alternation between corruption through excessive assimilation and destruction through irrational expansion into the void. *Koros* leads to *atē* and *hybris* on a world-historical scale. The first six books establish the pattern; in the last three Herodotus interprets the Great Persian War within the frame of this pattern. He has Artabanus tell Xerxes that those who advise the invasion are "letting *hybris* develop"; it is wrong "to teach the soul to seek always to have more than is before it" (7. 16. 2). The Delphic oracle spoke of the Persian army as the embodiment of *Koros*, child of *Hybris*, dreadfully raging" (8. 77. 1). Xerxes, in fact, is portrayed as one who goes beyond a neglect of limits and aspires to the *abolition* of limits, who dreams of an empire "bounded by the *aither* of Zeus," where "the sun shall see no country bounding ours, but I will put them all with you in one country" (7. 8. 1–2).

The rule of Xerxes (like all Oriental monarchies) is a *tyrannis* [tyranny], and *hybris* is characteristic of the *tyrannos*, the tyrant, who becomes "sated' with crimes" (ὕβρι κεκορημένος) and does "reckless wrong" (3. 80. 3 ἀτασθάλα; cf. 81. 2). Herodotus never portrays the Near Eastern monarchies as fully legitimate; from tyrant Gyges (1. 14. 1) onward they are haunted by tragic moral instability. Artabanus would prefer caution, "remembering the expedition of Cyrus against the Massagetae and how it fared, remembering that of Cambyses against the Ethiopians, and myself having joined the army of Darius against the Scythians" (7. 18. 2). But even Artabanus has to give in; the expedition is evidently urged on by a higher power. Thus at Salamis and Plataea the Persian army met its destiny, and evolving national character became fate; softened by their success, the Persians were led to attack those hard people the Greeks.

With this moral Herodotus actually concluded his *Histories*. The very last paragraph (9. 122) looks at first glance to be one more free-associative digression. Herodotus has just been telling of the punishment of Artauctes, an *atasthalos* [wicked man] who had been guilty of sacrilege against the hero Protesilaus:

> The ancestor of the Artauctes who was thus crucified was the Artembares who suggested to the Persians the position which they adopted in their application to Cyrus, saying as follows: "Since Zeus gives the Persians the leadership, and to you among men, Cyrus, by your conquest of Astyages, come, let us leave this land we hold, which is after all small and a rough one, and let us take a better. There are many near us; and many yet further off; if we take one we shall be impressive in a variety of ways. It is fitting that men who rule should do this. And what moment could be finer than this, when we rule many men and all Asia?"
>
> Cyrus listened and was unimpressed; he told them to go ahead, but while he told them to do it also advised them to get ready to be no longer rulers but rather among the ruled—since from soft countries soft men generally spring. It does not belong to the same soil to produce impressive fruits and also men who are good at war. The result was that the Persians took their leave, yielding to the judgment of Cyrus: they chose to rule living in difficult country, rather than to sow the plain and be slaves to others.

This bit of Persian wisdom is in fact an ironic criticism of the Persians: if the Persians had been true to this judgment, the Great Persian War would not have happened; if Cyrus himself had been true to it, he would not have attacked Babylon and then the Massagetae.†

---

† For the close of the *Histories*, see now Boedeker, 'Protesilaos'; Dewald, 'Wanton kings,

While this irony is Herodotus' last word, it is not the moral of the *Histories*. His book, after all, is not written for the Persians, but for the Greeks, and its meaning must be applicable to them. It is true that at the time of the Great Persian War the Greeks are a relatively hard people, the Persians relatively soft; but this is a somewhat superficial reading. The Greeks are unlike the Massagetae, Ethiopians, and Scythians; they are a historical people, and are changing. The *Histories* is indirectly about that change, and is a contribution to it.

The Greeks in important respects are like the Persians. The Persians are ὑβρισταί [hybristic] by nature" (1. 89. 2), but *hybris* is also endemic in Greece (cf. 2. 152. 3, 3. 48. 1, 3. 137. 2, 4. 159. 4, 5. 74. 1, 6. 85. 2, 6. 87, 6. 91. 2). The inherited *nomos* of the Persians is a constant restlessness (7. 8. 1), but the Greeks are equally restless (7. 11. 2). The Great Persian War is the end of a story for the Persians, but for the Greeks it is the middle phase: as their moment of greatest success, it is also a moment of danger. They also may become soft and reckless. After all, we know from Thucydides (1. 128–34) that Pausanias, the victorious commander at Plataea, was transformed by his success, that he was led into luxury and folly, into an attempt to collaborate with Xerxes, and eventually into madness and literal self-destruction. Herodotus does not tell this story, but he probably expects his audience to know it, and he certainly knows it himself; at one point he rather casually remarks that "the *hybris* of Pausanias gave [the Athenians] their excuse to seize the leadership from the Lacedaemonians" (8. 3. 2). It seems that when Herodotus tells how Pausanias, on the battlefield after Plataea, laughingly mocked the luxurious Persians for being so foolish as to attack a poor people like the Greeks (9. 82), he tells the story in ironic criticism of Pausanias, and as a warning to the Greeks. (Laughter is always a bad sign in Herodotus.)[9]

It is tempting to go beyond this point, and to think that for Herodotus and his audience in the mid-fifth century the tyrannical Athenian empire was the moral heir of the Persians, threatened with the same moral collapse. In any case the *Histories* must propose to its Greek audience the question: Is the tragic story ineluctable, or can the outcome be altered by human choice? Is there anything about the Greeks which might make it possible for them to escape from the cycle of *koros, hybris, atē*?

pickled heroes'. For Herodotus' account of the Persian wars, see Harrison, 'The Persian invasions'.

[9] Cf. D. Lateiner, "No Laughing Matter: A Literary Tactic in Herodotus," *TAPA* 107 (1977): 173–82.

At this point it becomes appropriate to consider one more passage on *nomos*: the conversation between Xerxes and Demaratus in Book 7 (101–5). Xerxes asks if the Greeks will resist the huge army he is bringing against them; Demaratus asks in response if Xerxes wants a pleasant answer or a true one. Reassured, Demaratus goes on to say that the Greeks will resist:

> "In Greece poverty is a constant companion from infancy, excellence is a thing acquired, crafted by wisdom and a powerful *nomos*. That is the instrument whereby Greece defends itself against poverty—and slavery as well … I speak about … the Lacedaemonians in particular, and tell you that they will never come to terms with you while you are bringing slavery to Greece, and further that they will meet you in battle even if all the other Greeks give way to you. Don't ask me with what numbers they will be able to do this. If a thousand are in the field, these will fight you, and if they are less, and if they are more."†

Xerxes (like Cambyses and Pausanias) laughs and mocks Demaratus:

> "How could a thousand or ten thousand or fifty thousand, free men as they are, all on a level and not ruled by any single individual, stand up against such an army? … If they were ruled by an individual in our way they might through their fear of him become better than their nature; they might under the compulsion of the whip go against those who outnumber them. But since they have been let go into freedom they could not do either of these things."

Demaratus says in his reply:

> "The Lacedaemonians … although they are free are not entirely free. They have a master, their *nomos*, and they fear it far more than your subjects fear you. And so they do whatever it commands. And it always gives the same command: it does not allow them to flee from any mass of people in battle; they must stay in the ranks and conquer or perish."

These proud words of Demaratus were proved on the field of Thermopylae (cf. 7. 234. 1); they were proved in a more interesting way at Plataea. That battle broke out while Pausanias was arguing with a subordinate who had refused to obey an order—refused, not out of cowardice, but because the order seemed to him dishonorable (9. 55–57). The Greeks were thus initially in disarray; nevertheless they fought well. The Persians also fought well until their commander was killed; then they ran away (9. 63). The Greeks thus displayed the danger and also the power of their characteristic *nomos*. They are sometimes bad subordinates because each thinks himself entitled to his own ideas; they are not loyal to an overlord, but to an idea. But since each has made this idea his own, each is

---

† For the motif of Persian numbers, see now Harrison, *The Emptiness of Asia*, Ch. 7.

ready to die for it; they do not require an overlord to keep them in the ranks.

The hereditary *nomos* of the Persians is monarchy (3. 82. 5), whereas the Greeks enjoy free institutions; these have "the fairest of names, *isonomia* (3. 80. 6). *Isonomia*, equality before the law, is the opposite of tyranny (5. 37. 2), as is *isokratia*, equal distribution of power (5. 92. 1). Both imply open debate, *isagoria* (5. 78). Matters to be determined are referred *es to koinon* (3. 80. 6) or *es meson* (3. 142. 3)—that is, to the community at large. A tyrant cannot be talked to (3. 80. 5); free institutions, by contrast, proceed by talking. As a result, everyone has a personal stake in the community and becomes bold in its defense (5. 78).

The Great Persian War was fought between an empire and an alliance. The unexpected victory of the alliance demonstrated the power of free institutions. The Greek alliance barely held together; at every step their common strategy was debated, and their continual disagreements threatened their unity. But when brought to the proof, they had the courage which belongs only to the consenting citizen, in contrast to the fearful subject.

Everywhere "*nomos* is king," but only among the Greeks is *nomos* political rather than cultural. The barbarians merely have their *nomoi* ("use" them, in the Greek expression)—and since political power among them is typically in the hands of tyrants, power is typically a threat to their *nomoi*. It is characteristic of the tyrant to "interfere with inherited *nomaia*" (3. 80. 5). The mad Persian Cambyses, for instance, burned Egyptian Amasis' body; in so doing he (accidentally) conformed to the *nomos* of the Greeks, but succeeded in violating the *nomoi* of both Egyptians and Persians. The Persians worship fire (1. 131. 2) and therefore consider corpses improper to it (3. 16. 3); they rather give their corpses to predatory animals (1. 140). The Egyptians, by contrast, think that fire *is* an animal; they do not allow their corpses to be eaten by animals or by fire either (3. 16. 4). Persians and Egyptians therefore do (or rather refrain from doing) the same thing for opposite reasons. This may stand as a last example of Herodotus' taste for symmetry.

To return to Cambyses (who, we remember, proved his madness by scoffing at *nomoi*): he went so far as to conceive a desire to marry his sister. His jurisconsults told him that they found no *nomos* which told a man to marry his sister, but they did find a *nomos* which said that the King of the Persians could do whatever he liked (3. 31). By this sophistic answer they set royal authority against *nomos*; the tyrant may even be said to *prove* his authority by defying the *nomoi*.

In the free Greek cities, however, authority is legitimate, that is, constituted by *nomoi*. Lycurgus brought the Lacedaemonians to *eunomie*, stable lawfulness, by instituting the ephors and the *gerousia* [the Spartan council of elders]; he "changed around all the *nomima* and took precautions that they not be transgressed"(1. 65. 5). Among the Greeks a change in *nomoi* can strengthen *nomos*; this is because *nomoi* are not merely traditional but are a matter of conscious design, just as they are founded on debate and consent.

Before Lycurgus the Lacedaemonians were *kakonomotatoi*—most lacking in stable lawfulness—and also "incapable of mixing with strangers (1. 65. 2). Some said Lycurgus got his laws from Apollo, but the Lacedaemonians themselves said that he borrowed them from Crete (1. 65. 4). He thus made his people capable of mixing with strangers by himself mixing with strangers.

The separation of the warriors from the rest of the people is something the Lacedaemonians learned from Egypt (2. 167. 2). Similarly Solon borrowed a *nomos* from Amasis of Egypt and enacted it in Athens—"and they use it still, for no fault is found with it" (1. 177. 2). Solon was both tourist and lawgiver; the two roles are evidently not unconnected.

The Persians, as we have seen, borrowed *nomoi* in their quest for enjoyment; Greek eclecticism was more critical. When Herodotus recommends a foreign *nomos*, as is the case with the Egyptian calendar, it is because it is more intelligent (2. 4. 1; cf. 1. 196). In this he is typically Greek, since intelligence (what Plato called "love of learning") is the special cultural trait of the Greeks (1. 60. 3). From this point of view the Great Persian War is to be seen not so much as a conflict between soft and hard, as a contest between a relatively weak, thoughtless solution to the problem of the center, and a relatively strong, thoughtful solution. This is not good ethnography; Herodotus does not get inside the Persian mind enough to see that their policies were, from their own point of view, thoughtful. But it is good Greek patriotism, and it gives the Greeks good advice. Herodotus calls upon the Greeks to be critical assimilators, to experience cultural change not as mere diffusion but as a thoughtful choice between options.

It follows that Herodotus presents the critical comparison of cultures as itself a crucial element of Greek culture. Herodotus toured the world in fact and in thought in order to explore the system of the world; this, as we have seen, is a way of thinking about being Greek, and is also (for him) a peculiarly Greek way of being in the world. If, further, the tragic cycle is to be broken, if Greece, having secured her frontier and having reassimilated the softened and partly barbarized Ionians, is not to become soft at the center, the solution must be found in this peculiarity of the Greeks. To be aware of the system of mankind, of the laws which govern the transformations of *nomoi*, is in some degree to be free of systematic necessity. Herodotus, in the mid-fifth century, still holds to the hope that the Greeks can take charge of their culture and make it work, not only culturally, but politically. Herodotus thus does more than exemplify the Greek form of civilization; he makes a practical contribution to it. His book is a contribution to the continuing cultural debate of the Greeks—and, implicitly, a praise of the civilization which made that debate possible. Hitherto (to paraphrase Marx) the peoples had only attempted to change the world; the Greeks, however, also found it necessary to interpret it.

2 Battle Narrative and Politics in Aeschylus' Persae[†]

SIMON GOLDHILL

In 'The Great Dionysia and civic ideology', I argued that the Festival of the Great Dionysia needed to be seen in the context of fifth-century Athenian culture and that the plays which make up a major part of this festival could be seen as offering a profoundly questioning attitude towards what might be called fifth-century Athenian democratic *polis* ideology. One play which seems to fit uneasily into that description of Athenian tragedy—as indeed it fits uneasily into many general arguments about Athenian theatre—is Aeschylus' *Persae*. In this brief paper I want to suggest some ways in which the social and political context I outlined in my earlier paper may help us to understand certain elements of the *Persae* which have worried critics.

Although the *Persae* is, of course, the only extant tragedy whose plot is concerned with contemporary events,[1] there are elements that make 'history play' a misleading term to apply.[2] It is, like most other tragedies, set in and largely concerned with a place that is not Athens,

---

[†] Originally published in *Journal of Hellenic Studies* 108 (1988), 128–93.

[1] We know little of Phrynichus' *Sack of Miletus*, or of his *Phoenissae*, on which the *Persae* is said to be based (by the Hypothesis). Other 'historical tragedies' (e.g. Moschion's *Themistocles*, Philicus' *Themistocles*) are fourth-century or later.

[2] Much criticism has focused on the nature of this 'historical writing'. In general, see e.g. R. Winnington-Ingram, *Studies in Aeschylus* (Cambridge 1983) 1–15; H. Kitto, *Greek tragedy*[2] (London 1961) 33–45, 'Political thought in Aeschylus', *Dioniso* xliii (1969) 160–5 and, in particular, *Poiesis* (Berkeley 1966) 74–115; M. Gagarin, *Aeschylean drama* (Berkeley 1976) 46–50; H. Broadhead, *The Persae of Aeschylus* (Cambridge 1960) xv ff.; D. Conacher, 'Aeschylus' *Persae*: a literary commentary', in *Serta Turyniana* (Urbana, Chicago, London 1974) 143–68; R. Lattimore, 'Aeschylus on the defeat of Xerxes', in *Classical Studies in Honor of W. A. Oldfather* (Urbana 1943) 82–93; H. Lloyd-Jones, *The justice of Zeus*[2] (Berkeley 1983) 88–9. For attempts to tie the play closely to a specific political situation, see F. Stoessl, 'Aeschylus as a political thinker', *AJP* lxxiii (1952) 113–39; A. Podlecki, *The political background of Aeschylean tragedy* (Michigan 1966), who both see the play as written expressly to support Themistocles. For more general attempts to relate the play to a political background, see V. di Benedetto, *L'Ideologia del potere e la tragedia Greca* (Turin 1978) 3–43; G. Paduano, *Sui Persiani di Eschilo: problemi di focalizzazione drammatica* (Rome 1978) *passim*, especially 1–27, 71–84.

and it involves characters who are other than Athenian citizens—
females, barbarians, kings etc.[3] The narrative, moreover, as various
critics have pointed out, is specifically 'theological', that is, the events
of the recent past are seen in terms of divine causation, a divine
punishment.[4] The Persians provide for the Athenian audience an
exemplum, so critics have argued, of the need to avoid *hubris*. As
often in Athenian culture, the East constitutes a privileged locus of
what is different from Athenian society,[5] which is used to articulate
concerns and positive values about the Athenians' own selves—the
logic of the negative *exemplum*. The extensive *kommos* [lament] for
such a defeated enemy is less easy to fit into such a description of the
play, however, and critics have been led to describe it as 'satire' or
even *Schadenfreude* [malicious joy].[6] The sympathy—not to mention
'pity' and 'fear'—that one would normally associate with mourning
might be seen rather as part of Aeschylus' turning the narrative away
from a simple extolling of Athens' victory over the Persians towards
the wider concerns of the theological or moral drama. It is not so
much the fact of triumph as the factors that have led to triumph that
interest Aeschylus.

One of these factors that has been too rarely discussed is the theme
of power and its correct use particularly in a political context—a
typically Aeschylean concern. The *Oresteia* leads from the question
of *dikē* [justice] in the house of Atreus to its conclusion in the *dikē*
of the *polis*—the 'just city' of Plato's search. The *Seven against
Thebes* dramatizes the leader of the city, a man who fights for the city,
being ruined in part by the curse of his *oikos* [household]. The
Suppliants not only focuses on the tensions and ambiguities of the
terms κράτος and κύριος ['power' and 'sovereign' or 'master'], but
also has one of the most explicit and most discussed exchanges on
political system and power (*Supp.* 365 ff.). The *Prometheus Bound*,
if perhaps not by Aeschylus, is Aeschylean at least in its concern with

[3] For discussion and bibliography on Athenian self-definition and its importance in tragedy,
see S. Goldhill, *Reading Greek tragedy* (Cambridge 1986), especially 57–78, and now
F. Zeitlin, 'Playing the Other: theater, theatricality and the feminine in Greek drama',
Representations xi (1985) 63–94.

[4] See, for example, Winnington-Ingram (n. 2) 1–15; H. Kitto, *Greek tragedy*[2] (London
1961) 33–43; Paduano (n. 2) 71–84; Benedetto (n. 2) 3–43; Gagarin (n. 2) 46–50; Conacher
(n. 2) 163–8; E. Holtsmark, 'Ring composition and the *Persae* of Aeschylus', *SO* xlv (1970)
23; M. Anderson, 'The imagery of the *Persians*', *GR* xix (1972) 166–74.

[5] See in particular F. Hartog, *Le miroir d'Hérodote* (Paris 1980); S. Pembroke, 'Women in
charge: the function of alternatives in early Greek tradition and the ancient idea of matriarchy',
Journal of Warburg and Courtauld Institutes xxx (1967) 1–35.

[6] So, for example, Blomfield, quoted by Broadhead (n. 2) xv; A. Sidgwick, *Aeschylus' Persae*
(Oxford 1903) on 847; A. Prickard, *The Persae of Aeschylus* (London 1928) xxviii. For a more
balanced view, see Gagarin (n. 2) 84–6.

the corrupt and corrupting power system of tyranny and its effect on the various characters of the drama. Indeed, such an interest in political constitutions and the effect of different political constitutions is a topic essential to fifth-century intellectual endeavour, as well as fifth-century political life (especially with the growth of democracy). Herodotus, as has been extensively discussed, develops the oppositions between rule by a single ruler, rule by a few, and rule by the people not merely in the famous debate of the Persian nobles.[7] Evidence on the sophists suggests an active as well as intellectual interest in the development of constitutions.[8] Indeed, as Finley sums up, from the middle of the fifth century onwards such 'conscious political analysis and reflection ... was continuous, intense, and *public*'.[9] The *Persae* also contains a series of remarks that are directly linked to such concerns, which will also, I hope, indicate an important but often ignored aspect of the opposition of Greeks and Persians.[10]

Immediately before the entrance of the messenger, the queen begins to question the chorus about Athens. The apparent lack of dramatic motivation for such questioning has worried many critics,[11] who have seen Aeschylus looking to exploit a patriotic audience reaction (230–45):[12]

κεῖνο δ' ἐκμαθεῖν θέλω,   230
ὦ φίλοι, ποῦ τὰς Ἀθήνας φασὶν ἱδρῦσθαι χθονός;

Xo.   τῆλε πρὸς δυσμὰς ἄνακτος Ἡλίου φθινασμάτων.
Ba.   ἀλλὰ μὴν ἵμειρ' ἐμὸς παῖς τήνδε θηρᾶσαι πόλιν;
Xo.   πᾶσα γὰρ γένοιτ' ἂν Ἑλλὰς βασιλέως ὑπήκοος.
Ba.   ὧδέ τις πάρεστιν αὐτοῖς ἀνδροπλήθεια στρατοῦ;   235
⟨*Xo.*   *   *   *   ⟩
⟨*Ba.*   *   *   *   ⟩
Xo.   καὶ στρατὸς τοιοῦτος, ἔρξας πολλὰ δὴ Μήδους κακά.

---

[7] iii 80–2. See e.g. M. Giraudeau, *Les notions juridiques et sociales chez Hérodote* (Paris 1984) 101–11; F. Lasserre, 'Hérodore et Protagoras: le débat sur les constitutions', *MH* xxxiii (1976) 65–84; A. Ferrill, 'Herodotus on tyranny', *Historia* xxvii (1978) 385–98; K. Waters, *Herodotus on Tyrants and Despots, Historia Einzelschriften* xv (1971); J. de Romilly 'Le classement des constitutions d'Hérodote à Aristote', *REG* lxxii (1959) 81–99, and, in particular, D. Lanza, *Il tiranno e il suo pubblico* (Turin 1977) esp. 39–41, 226–32.

[8] A sophistic interest in *nomoi* need hardly be stressed (the standard work remains F. Heinimann, *Nomos und Phusis* [Basel 1945]). Protagoras was involved in drawing up the constitution of Thurii, see V. Ehrenberg, 'The foundation of Thurii', *AJP* lix (1948) 149–70.

[9] M. Finley, *Politics in the ancient world* (Cambridge 1983) 123.

[10] The *Persae* was produced in 472 BC. I take it as an early indication of Finley's 'intense and public' analysis and reflection.

[11] E.g. Flickinger, as discussed by Broadhead (n. 2) xix. For a more interesting discussion and extensive bibliography, see Paduano (n. 2) 15–27; see also n. 13 below.

[12] Page's text.

Ba.   πότερα γὰρ τοξουλκὸς αἰχμὴ διὰ χεροῖν αὐτοῖς πρέπει;   [239]
Xo.   οὐδαμῶς· ἔγχη σταδαῖα καὶ φεράσπιδες σαγαί.   [240]
Ba.   καὶ τί πρὸς τούτοισιν ἄλλο; πλοῦτος ἐξαρκὴς δόμοις;   [237]
Xo.   ἀργύρου πηγή τις αὐτοῖς ἐστι, θησαυρὸς χθονός.   [238] 240
Ba.   τίς δὲ ποιμάνωρ ἔπεστι κἀπιδεσπόζει στρατῶι;
Xo.   οὔτινος δοῦλοι κέκληνται φωτὸς οὐδ᾽ ὑπήκοοι.
Ba.   πῶς ἂν οὖν μένοιεν ἄνδρας πολεμίους ἐπήλυδας;
Xo.   ὥστε Δαρείου πολύν τε καὶ καλὸν φθεῖραι στρατόν.
Ba.   δεινά τοι λέγεις κιόντων τοῖς τεκοῦσι φροντίσαι.   245

[But I wish to learn this,   230
My friends: where on earth do they say that Athens is founded?
Chorus: Far towards the setting of the waning Lord sun.
Queen: Was this the city my son desired to make to make his prey?
Ch.   Yes, for all Greece would become subject to the king.
Qu: Do they have such a mass of men for their army?   235
⟨Ch.   *   *   *   ⟩
⟨Qu.   *   *   *   ⟩
Ch.   And their army is large enough; it did many injuries to the Medes.
Qu: Do they use bows and arrows in their hands?   [239]
Ch: Not at all. They have spears for close combat and shields for
       armour.   [240]
Qu: And do they have anything else? Do they have ample wealth
       in their palace?   [237]
Ch: They have a spring of silver, a treasury in the earth.   [238] 240
Qu: And who is shepherd over them and is master to their army?
Ch: They are called neither the slaves nor subjects of any man.
Qu: How then can they withstand enemy invaders?
Ch: So as to destroy the great and excellent army of Darius.
Qu: What you say is terrible for the parents of those on campaign to
       think on.]   245

The exchange may seem poorly motivated, but I hope to show
that it does not arise merely out of 'jingoism',[13] but rather is a way
for Aeschylus of underlining an important element in the drama. The
terms of the eulogy need to be specified. The queen first wonders at
her son's desire to hunt down *this* city. The chorus answers that all
Greece would then be subservient (ὑπήκοος) to the king. Athens
holds the key to Greece. The queen assumes that this is because of
the sheer numbers of its army (ἀνδροπλήθεια στρατοῦ 235)—but the
chorus is taken to correct such an assumption; either by the addition
of the army's *quality* (so Broadhead glosses 236 in the MS. reading,
as he himself prints with reservations); or, if Page's text is printed, as

[13] The description of P. Walcot, *Greek drama in its theatrical and social context* (Cardiff
1976) 96. Benedetto (n. 2) links these lines to Athenian claims of hegemony; *cf.* Gagarin (n. 2)
33 for the emphasis on Athens in this play. It is not by chance that Athens is the only Greek
force mentioned, as I discuss below.

above, by the supplement of some such qualification as 'No, but
their sailors are specially famous for their bravery' (Page, reported
in Broadhead),[14] or, less negatively, *naves habent satis validas* [they
have sufficient strong ships] (Page, *OCT*). In either case, the military
prowess of the Athenians is being linked to something other than
weight of numbers. The specific sense of this Athenian military force
is further specified in the next couplet. The queen wonders if their
strength stems from archery, a question which seems to be asked
merely to be denied by the chorus' assertion that the Athenians are
hoplites with heavy shield and close contact spear: ἔγχη σταδαῖα καὶ
φεράσπιδες σαγαί [they have spears for close combat and shields for
armour]. The old debate between bowmen and hoplites has quite a
different tone in the fifth-century city, with its citizen hoplite army
(especially when opposed to the fighters of Persia).[15] Indeed, within
the context of the militarism central to fifth-century Athenian ideology (as discussed in 'The Great Dionysia and civic ideology'), it is
clear that the exchange is constructing an opposition between the
Athenian hoplite warrior (and the values associated with it) and the
Eastern fighter.[16] This opposition is continued and further specified
in the next three couplets. First, the queen asks about wealth. This is
an important theme in the *Persae* in particular,[17] where the Persians'
riches are regularly emphasized from the *parodos* [opening chorus]
onwards (*cf.* e.g. the repetitions of πολύχρυσος [gold-laden] 3, 9, 45,
53)—the excessive luxury of the East is a *topos* of Greek views of
the barbarians (*cf.* the queen's remarks 159–72). But the chorus'
response adds a further important point. For the 'spring of silver,
treasure of the soil' (240) has been taken at least since the scholia
[ancient commentaries] to refer to the mines at Laurium and
Thoricus.[18] Herodotus vii 144 states that Themistocles persuaded
the Athenians to spend this new wealth on ships rather than themselves.[19] It was, he comments, the saving of Greece to have turned

---

[14] (n. 2) 90 n. 1.

[15] *Cf.* Soph. *Ajax* 1120 ff., which is discussed by Goldhill (n. 3) 157–8; also Eur. *Her.* 157
ff., and Eur. *El.* 377, which I have commented on in *GRBS* xxvii (1986) 168.

[16] *Cf.* 85 ἐπάγει δουρικλύτοις ἄνδρασι τοξόδαμνον Ἄρη [Ξέρξης] [he [Xerxes] thrusts
against men famed for the spear, an Ares who fights with the bow] for a similar opposition
of Persian bowmen and Athenian spearsmen. At 460–1, however, the Greeks use bows, but
J. Labarbe, *La loi navale de Themistocle* (Paris 1957) 180 comments that these are unlikely to
be Athenians. G. Bond's extensive note (on Eur. *Her.* 161) underestimates the *continuing* and
developing importance of traditional military values in fifth-century writing.

[17] See e.g. Gagarin (n. 2) 44–5; Anderson (n. 4) 170–2.

[18] See e.g. Podlecki (n. 2) 15, and Winnington-Ingram, *Gnomon* xxxix (1967) 641–3.
Verrall sees a similar reference at *Eum.* 945–6 γόνος ... πλουτόχθων [the rich child of the
earth].

[19] See Labarbe (n. 16) *passim*. Even if evidence for 'Themistocles' law' is not conclusive, it

Athens into a maritime power (ἀναγκάσας θαλασσίους γένεσθαι Ἀθηναίους [having compelled the Athenians to become a people of the sea]). Before the narrative of the sea-battle which saves Greece, the text hints at the income—and its distribution—which made such a victory possible. The opposition between the personal luxury of the Persians and the common expenditure of the Athenians on their fleet adds another element to the constructed opposition of Athenian and barbarian.

The queen's next question specifies still further the relation between Athenian power and its system: who rules their army?[20] If ποιμάνωρ [shepherd] echoes the Homeric ruler's relation to his men (e.g. ποιμένα λαῶν [shepherd of men]), the *hapax* [unique occurrence of the term] ἐπιδεσπόζειν [is master to] slants the enquiry towards a suggestion of a more tyrannical rule (*cf. Eum.* 527, 696, where δεσποτεῖσθαι [to be subject to tyranny] is one of the extremes of political system to be avoided). The chorus' stirring response does not merely mean that the Athenians are slaves to no external man (ὑπήκοοι [subjects] 242 significantly echoes ὑπήκοος [subject] 234), but also implies the democratic system of joint decision making, collective authority, as the queen's following remark makes clear. For her assumption that men without a single ruler cannot fight well points to the regular opposition of monarchy (tyranny) and democracy as alternative systems of power (so important also in Herodotus; *cf.* e.g. Her. vii 103 for the same point that a single ruler is necessary for military and political order—made there by Xerxes).[21] The chorus' final assertion of the sufficiency of the Athenian force and the queen's apt expression of worry add a suitably pessimistic note to herald the arrival of the messenger.

This exchange, then, does not merely praise the Athenians but, more importantly, praises them through a series of oppositions that

is difficult to account for the rapid and great rise in Athenian naval power without assuming a conscious diversion of state funds.

[20] Broadhead asks pertinently if στράτῳ here means 'people' (as at e.g. *Eum.* 569); certainly the overlap of citizen and soldier makes such a rendering easy.

[21] Winnington-Ingram (n. 2) 7 writes 'Herodotus is the best commentator on the first half of the *Persae*, giving us the range of ideas within which the Aeschylean characters are moving.' The opposition of tyranny and democracy is particularly evident in later fifth-century writing, but the early and continued importance of the tyrannicides as founders of democracy—a patently untrue assertion—demonstrates the role of tyranny from the earliest days of democracy as the always-to-be-rejected alternative. See M. Taylor, *The Tyrant slayers: the heroic image in fifth-century B.C. Athenian art* (New York 1981), who sees a cult of Aristogeiton and Harmodius as stemming from 'a need to reverence the city state' 193. On tyrants and tragedy, see D. Lanza (n. 7) 1–32, 95–159; H. Berve, *Die Tyrannis bei den Griechen* (Munich 1967) 190–4; G. Cerri, 'Antigone, Creonte e l'idea della tirannide nell'Atene del V secolo', *QUCC* x (1982) 137–55; and in particulat G. Cerri, *Il linguaggio politico nel Prometeo di Eschilo: Saggio di semantica* (Rome 1975).

relate closely to the sense of Athenian ideology I discussed in 'The Great Dionysia and civic ideology'. It is as a hoplite citizen army and navy, state-funded, and in its collective values essentially linked to the practice and principles of the democratic *polis*, that the Athenians' military sufficiency is discussed here, immediately before the narrative which demonstrates the results of such sufficiency.[22]

The emphasis on the difference between Persians and Greeks has been already prepared for in the development of the scene towards this exchange. Atossa's dream (176 ff.) articulates the disjunction between Greek and Persian, of course, how they cannot be yoked together (an image picked up in the yoking of the Hellespont).[23] But the queen's conclusion puts this difference in interesting terms (211–14):

> εὖ γὰρ ἴστε παῖς ἐμὸς
> πράξας μὲν εὖ θαυμαστὸς ἂν γένοιτ' ἀνήρ,
> κακῶς δὲ πράξας οὐχ ὑπεύθυνος πόλει,
> σωθεὶς δ' ὁμοίως τῆσδε κοιρανεῖ χθονός.

> [For be sure of this: my son,
> should he succeed, would be a man to wonder at,
> but if he fails, he will not be accountable to the city;
> but if he is saved will still be sovereign of this land.]

Here, too, critics (e.g. Schütz, who is rejected by Broadhead) have suggested that the connection between this conclusion and the queen's earlier remarks is weak. Again, however, her language points to the underlying political dimension of the opposition of Greek and Persian. The Persian king is οὐχ ὑπεύθυνος πόλει [not accountable to the city]. To be ὑπεύθυνος [accountable] and specifically ὑπεύθυνος πόλει [accountable to the city] is the mark of the Athenian political system.[24] It is the mark of monarchy to be with-

---

[22] Each element of this exchange is picked up, however briefly, in the messenger's words. The number of the Persians before the battle and then dead is repeatedly stressed (e.g. 272, 432, and the repetition of πλῆθος [mass] and related words at 272, 334, 337, 342, 352, 429, 432; *cf.* H. Avery, 'Dramatic devices in Aeschylus' *Persians*', *AJP* lxxxv (1964) 174–7); and the contrast in numbers between Greeks and Persians is forcibly made (337 ff., 352). The insufficiency of the bow is declared (278), and the role of wealth is hinted at in the language of 250–2. The single leader apart from his troops is perhaps picked up at 465 ff. in the picture of Xerxes watching the disaster from the high bank (467) near the sea. That the Athenians are called slaves to no man is perhaps echoed in their cry of ἐλευθεροῦτε πατρίδ', ἐλευθεροῦτε ... [liberate your fatherland, liberate ...] (403).

[23] On the imagery of yoking, see O. Taplin, *The stagecraft of Aeschylus* (Oxford 1977) 78; B. Fowler, 'Aeschylus' imagery', *C&M* xxviii (1967) 3–10; Anderson (n. 4) 167–8; Winnington-Ingram (n. 2) 11.

[24] See J. Lembke and C. Herington, *Aeschylus' Persians* (Oxford 1981) on 343, who rightly note that Zeus, whose justice for many critics determines the narrative, is called εὔθυνος [assessor] at 828; *n.b.* also εὐθυντήριον [of government] 764, discussed below. G. E. M. de

out such checks (as Herodotus writes, iii 80 μουναρχίη τῇ ἔξεστι ἀπευθύνῳ ποιέειν τὰ βούλεται [monarchy in which it is possible for a man to do what he wants without being accountable] [*cf.* Soph. *Ant.* 506–7]). If Xerxes survives, the queen concludes, 'he will rule this land in the same way'. It is precisely the nature of Xerxes' rule that is brought to the fore.

Darius emphasizes a different aspect of this rule. On the one hand, he stresses how Persia is ruled (note σκῆπτρον εὐθυντήριον [the sceptre of government] 764, echoing 213) by a single man (762–4):

> ἐξ οὗτε τιμὴν Ζεὺς ἄναξ τήνδ' ὤπασεν,
> ἕν' ἄνδρ' ἀπάσης Ἀσίδος μηλοτρόφου
> ταγεῖν ἔχοντα σκῆπτρον εὐθυντήριον.

> [since our lord Zeus ordained this honour
> that one man should be ruler of all of sheep-rearing Asia
> and hold the sceptre of government.]

So, the catalogue that follows (756–86) is a named list of individual rulers (such as could never be constructed for the democratic *polis*). On the other hand, he distinguishes between the individual rulers in terms of their behaviour particularly with regard to the gods. So Cyrus is emphasized as a fortunate man whom the gods respect for his good sense (767–72), while Mardos and Artaphernes are distinguished for their disgraceful conduct (774–6). Here Aeschylus is concerned also to place the historical and genealogical narrative within a theological and moral framework. Darius, although a single ruler who too had attacked Greece, acts as a foil to his son. The young man (νέος 782; *cf. P.V.* 35, 309–10, on Zeus as νέος τύραννος [young tyrant]) and his recklessness are set in opposition to the now divine father, who is treated by the chorus and queen as a figure of great respect. The contrast between the entrance of the ghost and the entrance of Xerxes is marked.[25]

The opposition of Greek and Persian is strongly evident, of course, in the messenger's description of the battles themselves. The Greeks' well-omened song (388–9) is a holy paian [song of triumph] (393) which leads to their famous cry of freedom (402–6). The Persians raise in opposition a ῥόθος [rush] of noise (as befits *barbaroi* accord-

Ste-Croix, *The class struggle in the ancient Greek world* (London 1981) 285 writes 'It was a fundamental principle of democracy that everyone who exercised any power should be *hypeuthynos*, subject to *euthyna*, the examination of his conduct (and audit of his accounts) which every official had to undergo, at Athens and most if not all other democracies, at the end of his term of office, normally one year.' He adds in a footnote (601 n. 11) that critics of democracy were not fond of remarking on this aspect of democratic power.

[25] See Taplin (n. 23) 121–7, especially 126. On Darius and Xerxes, see S. Saïd, 'Darius et Xerxes dans les *Perses*', *KTEMA* vi (1981) 17–38.

ing to the usual derivation of the term). The Greeks advance εὐτάκτως ... κόσμῳ [in well-ordered arrangement] (399–400), the Persians flee ἀκόσμως [in disorder] (421). The Greeks encircle οὐκ ἀφρασμόνως [not injudiciously] (417), the Persians are unable to assist each other (414).[26] In the following action, the Persians flee ἀκόσμῳ ξὺν φυγῇ [in disordered flight] (470) and take οὐκ εὔκοσμον ... φυγήν [not well-ordered ... flight] (481). The order of the Greeks is stressed, then, whereas the troops under a monarch are in military disarray. But one of the most marked differences in the descriptions of Persian and Greek is in the use of names. At three points in the play, there are lengthy lists of Persian names, both of individuals and of races (see 12–58, 302–29, 950–1001);[27] no individual Greek is named, and only Athens of the Greek cities. This fact has often been remarked on and there have been numerous explanations suggested. Lattimore sees it as part of the emphasis on the enormity of the Persian losses.[28] Kitto regards it as focussing attention on the theological and moral structure of ideas in the play by understressing any Greek's personal involvement.[29] Broadhead, who regards Aeschylus as quite impartial, writes: 'This reticence was wholly fitting in a play that was to be primarily the presentation of the Persian tragedy as seen through Persian eyes'.[30] Both the exotic sound of the names and the heroic aspect of such name-filled battle narratives have been commented on. There is, however, a further element here. In talking of Athenian military ideology, I mentioned the values of collectivity, so important for the hoplite phalanx of the democratic *polis*. In particular, the anonymity of the soldiers in the Funeral Oration's eulogy was discussed with regard to Nicole Loraux's research.[31] I argued that it was important for the democratic *polis* in general and

---

[26] *Pace* J. Quincey in *CQ* xii (1962) 184, who calls this reading of ἀρωγή 'landlubberly'.

[27] On the relations between these three catalogues see U. Albini, 'Lettura dei *Persiani* di Eschilo', *PP* xxii (1967) 256; Holtsmark (n. 4) 20; Paduano (n. 2) 72. I have not the space here to discuss the relevant and complex issues of the relations between lists and epic narrative and the claims of κλέος [repute], or of the relations between lists, naming and mourning.

[28] (n. 2) 90.

[29] (n. 4) 33–45. A common view: see e.g. G. Murray, *Aeschylus, the creator of tragedy* (Oxford 1940) 126, who writes 'If one Greek general had been named the play would have become modern and been exposed to all the small, temporary emotions of the immediate present, the gratified vanity, the annoyance, the inevitable criticism.' I hope to be showing how the *Persae* is modern, though without the flaws Murray fears.

[30] (n. 2) xx. For further bibliography and discussion see Paduano (n. 2) 52 n. 3.

[31] *JHS* cvii (1987) 65–7. The connection between the anonymity of the ἐπιτάφιοι [funeral orations] and the *Persae* is briefly mentioned by M. Pohlenz, *Die griechische Tragödie* (Leipzig and Berlin 1930) 51. As Loraux remarks, there are exceptions to the general rule of anonymity. In Lysias ii 42, and ii 52, Themistocles and then Myronides are mentioned by name. Both, however, are not contemporary military figures being buried, but characters from the past history of Athens (and hence R. Seager [e.g.] *JHS* lxxxvii [1967] may be wrong to see con-

for the citizen army as a key element in the democratic *polis* that even in such a fiercely competitive society as fifth-century Athens the individual was seen in an essential way as being defined by his contribution to the *polis*. That is, the subsumption of the individual into the collectivity of the *polis* is a basic factor in fifth-century Athenian democratic ideology. This may provide an interesting light in which to view the anonymity of the Greek soldiers in the *Persae*. It is as if they are being portrayed as a unified, collective body (which can be contrasted with the lists of Persian contingents, Persian dead, and Persian kings). Although the Persian disaster is certainly seen as a disaster for the whole land (*cf.* e.g. 249–55, 531 ff., especially 548–9),[32] the queen can still talk of the 'great light' and 'day from night' that shines for her house because Xerxes is still alive (300–1); and the catalogue of fallen leaders, where, for example, Syennesis is singled out for praise (325–7), contrasts markedly with the κῦδος [glory] (455) that the Greek ships together win. The triumph of the Greek forces is a collective victory, as, indeed, the battle narrative was introduced by a dialogue which stressed such collective values over and against rule by one man. Perhaps, then, the contrast between the name-filled descriptions of the Persians and the anonymous collective view of the Greeks should be seen as part of the wider contrast between Greeks (or more specifically Athenians) and barbarians in terms of political and military systems. Aeschylus' *Persae* seems to suggest that the Greeks are victorious not only because of the gods, not only because of Persian *hubris*, but also because of the values of democratic *collectivity*, embodied in Athens, as opposed to barbarian tyranny.[33]

temporary party political significance in the failure to name Conon in this speech). The later example of Hyperides offers a more interesting case (discussed at length by Loraux, *L'invention d'Athènes* [Paris 1981] esp. 110–13 [translated as *The Invention of Athens*]). For Hyperides' speech contains an extensive ἔπαινος [eulogy] of Leosthenes, the general, quite out of keeping with earlier ἐπιτάφιοι [*epitaphioi*, funeral orations]. Loraux relates this to a move away from democratic norms towards the cult of the 'great man' (and presumably an early example of what becomes the norm in Hellenistic eulogy). Certainly it is easy to see some unease on Hyperides' part, especially when he writes vi 15: καὶ μηδεὶς ὑπολάβῃ με τῶν ἄλλων πολιτῶν μηδένα λόγον ποιεῖσθαι, [ἀλλὰ] Λεωσθένη μόνον ἐγκωμιάζειν συμβαίνει γὰρ τὸν Λεωσθένους ἔπαινον [ἐπὶ] ταῖς μάχαις ἐγκώμιον καὶ τῶν ἄλλων πολιτῶν εἶναι [Let no one suppose that I take no account of the other citizens and only praise Leosthenes. For the praise of Leosthenes in these battles is also a eulogy of the other citizens]. The difference between our examples of fifth- and early fourth-century democratic ἐπιτάφιοι [*epitaphioi*] and the epic or, say, Herodotean narratives with their concern for individual κλέος [repute] remains extremely important, despite these examples.

[32] *Cf.* Gagarin (n. 2) 44.

[33] It is interesting to note that the battle's success is preceded by a trick (δόλον 361) by a single Greek man, which is concerning, if not in, the night; *cf.* P. Vidal-Naquet, *Le chasseur noir* (Paris 1983) 125–74 [translated as *The Black Hunter*]. If the Persians and monarchy provide a contrast by which to understand the democratic, hoplitic collectivity, so perhaps the

If this is true, we see in the *Persae* the first written indications of what will become a major topic of fifth-century rhetoric, namely, the linked oppositions of tyranny and democracy, barbarian and Athenian. And typically enough, this is to be seen in the light of the developing *polis* ideology and the military values with which such ideology is necessarily linked. The narrative of the city's recent triumph may seem at first sight a surprising subject for a tragedy;[34] but in its interests in such a constellation of ideas the *Persae* may seem at least closer to other works written for the Great Dionysia.

To write a *kommos* for a defeated enemy (especially a *kommos* for the Persian invaders to be performed in a public Athenian festival) is in itself a remarkable event, and this is perhaps not sufficiently emphasized by critics.[35] (It is difficult to imagine anything similar in the years following the first or second world war, to take a perhaps tendentious example.) To insist that the fighting itself must be seen within a framework of a divine plan, a moral order and indeed a contrast of social and political systems is further evidence to suggest that the *Persae* is concerned to develop a complex understanding of the recent events of Athenian history, and to raise questions about a response to the victory. The *Persae* may not demonstrate the ironic questioning of a Euripides, but it is not hard to see it investigating attitudes within the *polis* to the recent victory, not least in the tension between the lauding of Athens and the values that led to triumph, and the extensive *mourning* for the enemy victims of that triumph. Nor is it hard to imagine a variety of reactions to its performance, as critics have reacted to it so variously since.[36] As such, the *Persae* may

δόλος [trick] of an individual (though still unnamed) Greek provides a different contrast by which the military values of the play are developed.

[34] It was Wilamowitz (*Hermes* xxxiii [1898] 382–98) who first suggested—and then recanted—that it was so surprising that we should consider the *Persae* to have been written first and foremost for production in Sicily.

[35] Though see the sensible comments of Gagarin (n. 2) 84–6. A complex model of weeping with (though not precisely for) an enemy is provided by the end of the *Iliad* in Achilles' tears for his father and Patroclus, shared with Priam's tears for Hector (*Il.* xxiv 471 ff., esp. 507–12). The *communitas*—and individualism—of mourning in Homer's scene in the tent and at night between two enemy warriors seems importantly different, however, from the public festival's representation of a *kommos* for a defeated invader and sacker of the (still ruined?) Athens. If sympathy for others is part of the 'tragic experience', it is none the less part of what I see as Aeschylus' boldness in this play to place an audience in the position of discovering tragic sympathy for such an 'other' as the Persian invaders. It is in the variety of possible reactions to such boldness—and what such variations imply for the self-definition of the Athenian audience—that a major part of the 'questioning' of the *Persae* lies.

[36] Winnington-Ingram (n. 2) 15 seems to me to show less than his usual awareness when he writes 'The interpretation of the East–West relations … does not seem to go much further than might be expected from an intelligent Greek of the time. Morally, it is a study in black and white, and so lacks subtlety.' For a somewhat simplistic view of a possible audience reaction to the play, see Gagarin (n. 2) 51–6.

be more easily appreciable as a tragedy for the Great Dionysia than had sometimes been suggested.[37]

[37] Thanks to Robin Osborne for all his help.

3 Greeks and Barbarians in Euripides' Tragedies: The End of Differences?†

SUZANNE SAÏD

The 'democratic' poet who dared to let women and slaves speak, if we are to believe Aristophanes,[1] also gave more space to Barbarians in his tragedies. If we take into account only the complete extant plays, as I do here, Euripides is the one of the three tragedians to use the word most frequently;[2] he is also the one who most often brought Greeks and Barbarians face to face:[3] half his plays show Barbarians installed in the heart of Greece (Medea in Corinth, Andromache in Phthia, a Phrygian slave in Argos, Phoenician women or 'Asian Bacchants' in Thebes) or Greeks temporarily settled in a Barbarian land (i.e. the Achaean leaders in Thrace or the Troad, Iphigenia, Orestes and Pylades in Tauris, Helen and Menelaus in Egypt). In the context of the Trojan war, the Barbarian world haunts even the tragedies that unfold on Greek soil and which put on stage only Greeks, such as *Electra* or *Iphigenia in Aulis*. Lastly, with the exception of *Alcestis* and the *Suppliants*, there is no tragedy that does not include an allusion to the Barbarians (memories of the Amazons in *Hippolytus*, *Heracles* and *Ion*)[4] or that does not use them as a point of comparison (like the *Heracleidae*).[5]

---

† Originally published as 'Grecs et Barbares dans les tragédies d'Euripide: le fin des différences', *Ktema* 9 (1984), 27–53.

[1] *Frogs*, l. 949ff.

[2] One hundred and one examples of βάρβαρος in the 18 extant tragedies of Aeschylus (to which must be added 7 examples in the fragments) as well as one example of βαρβαρόω and one of μειξοβάρβαρος, or a total of 110 attestations against 14 of βάρβαρος (plus 4 of κάρβανος) in the seven preserved tragedies of Aeschylus and 6 examples of βάρβαρος (and one of βαρβαρόω) in the seven preserved tragedies of Sophocles.

[3] However, what we know of the work of Phrynichus suggests that the Barbarians were very much present in the early stages of Greek tragedy: The *Egyptian Women* had a chorus composed of Barbarians, *Antaeus* a chorus of Libyan women; the *Phoenician Women* like the *Capture of Miletus* put Persians on stage. See W. Kranz, *Stasimon*, Berlin, 1933, p. 75.

[4] *Hippolytus*, ll. 10, 307, 351, 581; *Heracles*, ll. 414–16; *Ion*, ll. 1145–62.

[5] Cf. l. 130ff.

However, the Barbarians in Euripides have not caught the attention of the critics to a great extent. Euripides is largely eclipsed by Aeschylus in the chapter W. Kranz devoted to the 'Non-Greek in Greek tragedy'.[6] He appears only peripherally in a discussion in the volume of the *Entretiens sur l'Antiquité classique* devoted to *Greeks and Barbarians*.[7] The longest study that has been made of him is still that by H. Bacon in her book *Barbarians in Greek Tragedy*;[8] but she adopts a very reductive point of view, and is in fact concerned only with the Barbarians and the *facts* regarding them:[9] geographical details, linguistic features, physical characteristics, costume, objects or settings shown or evoked, religions and customs, in short, everything which, in the tragedy, reflects the common knowledge of fifth-century Greeks. But by isolating the elements in this way, we may perhaps miss the meaning they take on from an author who happily makes use of ironic quotation. The chapter devoted by K. Synodinou to Greeks and Barbarians in the framework of a much larger work on the concept of slavery in Euripides would suffice to demonstrate, were it necessary, the importance of the dramatic context and the need to put the passages commented upon in perspective.[10]

Euripides' ideas about Barbarians seem to give rise to a problem. Certainly, most critics agree in thinking that, for once, Euripides has made himself the spokesman for established values and the resolute advocate of Greek superiority.[11] But others, more careful and cautious, like W. Kranz[12] or H. Diller,[13] admit that the portrayal of the Barbarian in Euripides' drama is far from simple, and that the tragedian wavers between two opposite positions, regarding the barbarian now as a born slave, now as a fully fledged human being. Still others, like V. di Benedetto[14] or E. Lévy,[15] map out a process of evolution from the first tragedies, which give the Barbarian a positive image and bear witness to an effort to understand, up to the last (especially *Iphigenia in Aulis*) which exalt Panhellenic values. Yet

---

[6] *Op. cit.*, pp. 71–112. On Euripides, see pp. 108–12.

[7] *Entretiens sur l'Antiquité classique*, VIII, *Grecs et Barbares*, Vandoeuvres-Geneva, Fondation Hardt, 1962, p. 113ff.

[8] New Haven, 1961. On Euripides, see pp. 115–72.

[9] See the introduction, p. l: 'What follows is mainly an attempt to establish *facts* – to find out how much and in what ways Aeschylus, Sophocles and Euripides used the knowledge of their own days in representing foreigners.'

[10] K. Synodinou, *On the Concept of Slavery in Euripides*, Ioannina, 1977, pp. 32–60.

[11] See the references assembled by Synodinou, pp. 34–6.

[12] *Op. cit.*, p. 109.

[13] In his discussion of the paper by O. Reverdin, 'Crise spirituelle et évasion', *Grecs et Barbares*, p. 113.

[14] V. di Benedetto, *Euripide, teatro e società*, Turin, 1971, p. 217ff.

[15] E. Lévy, *Athènes devant la défaite de 404*, Paris, 1976, p. 157.

others, like K. Synodinou,[16] have striven (successfully, in my opinion) to prove that Euripides had never believed in the natural inferiority of Barbarians. One might go further and ask, as I shall here, whether Euripides does not call into question at almost all levels the validity of the Greek/Barbarian distinction and denounce, once more, 'the Manichean illusion of Greek order'.[17]

1 THE BARBARIAN: A REALITY ON STAGE?

In the *Suppliants* of Aeschylus, the Barbarians were defined by a very different physical type from that of the Greeks[18] and by a characteristic costume: the Danaids were of dark complexion[19] and wore 'veils of Sidon' (l. 121) and 'barbarian dress' (l. 235). In Euripides' plays, the Barbarian is recognisable only by his costume:[20] in the *Heracleidae*, Demophon is able to identify a Greek by his clothing and even his way of draping it (l. 130ff.), and the garment that enfolds the body of the Trojan Polydorus immediately indicates to Agamemnon in *Hecuba* that the dead man is not an Argive (l. 734ff.). There is nothing surprising about that. Was not Euripides famous for his talents as a costumier? Had he not created a beggar's outfit, the components of which Aristophanes gleefully enumerates in the *Acharnians*?[21] Had he not put on stage, in both *Helen* and *Orestes*, characters who looked as though they had been driven 'wild'?[22]

In *Orestes*, the 'Mycenaean boots' (l. 1470) of the hero are in contrast with the βαρβάροις εὐμάρισιν [barbarian slippers'] (l. 1370) of the Phrygian slave, that goatskin footwear that was, for the Greeks, characteristic of Barbarians,[23] whether Phrygian or Persian. But

---

[16] *Op. cit.*, pp. 32–60, *passim.*

[17] I borrow this expression from C. Nancy, who demonstrated the same questioning of commonplaces in Euripides' discourse on women in 'Euripide et le parti des femmes', *La femme dans les sociétés antiques* (ed. E. Lévy), Strasbourg, 1983, pp. 73–92, and 'ΦΑΡΜΑΚΟΝ ΣΩΤΗΡΙΑΣ: le mécanisme du sacrifice humain chez Euripide', *Théâtre et spectacles dans l'Antiquité, Colloque de Strasbourg*, 1981, Leiden, s.d. pp. 17–30.

[18] Ll. 496–8. See H. Bacon, *op. cit.*, pp. 24–6.

[19] Ll. 70, 154. See also regarding the Egyptians, ll. 719ff., 743, 888.

[20] Cf. H. Bacon, *op. cit.*, pp. 121–7.

[21] Ll. 414–79, with the 'rags' (ll. 415, 418) and tatters of a tunic (ll. 423, 427, 431, 432, 433, 438), 'the little Mysian cap' (l. 439), 'the beggar's staff' (l.448), the blackened 'little basket' (l. 453), the chipped bowl (l. 459), 'the little jug plugged by a sponge' (l.463), and 'the old peelings' (l. 469).

[22] In *Helen*, Menelaus, 'who has a savage aspect' (ἄγριος ... μορφὴν), (l. 544ff.) wears rags (ll. 416, 421–4, 1204, 1281); in *Orestes*, the hero, who is a man 'made savage' by illness (ll. 126, 387), is characterised by his filthy hair (ll. 224–6, 387) and his hideous appearance (ἀμορφία, l. 391).

[23] On this footwear, which appears on Greek vases as well as on certain Achaemenid documents, see A. Bovon, 'La représentation des guerriers perses et la notion de Barbare dans la première moitié du cinquième siècle', *BCH*, 87, 1963, pp. 579–602 (p. 594).

for plays that contain so many Barbarian characters, it is precious little.

Paradoxically, Euripides mainly draws the spectator's attention to items of Barbarian clothing when they are detached from their owner: for instance, the finely woven garment and gold headband that Medea gives her children so that they can pass them on to the Corinthian Creusa[24] or the 'splendour of Phrygian robes' (l. 1220) in which Hecuba will reclothe the body of Astyanax in the *Trojan Women.*

It is true that the dialogue sometimes supplements the spectacle: fleeting allusion to Thracian weapons, like the πέλτη (a kind of shield) of Diomedes (*Alc.*, l. 498) or the 'twin Thracian lances' of Polymestor (*Hec.*, l. 1155), the description of Tydeus' 'semi-Barbarian' Aetolian weapon (*Phoen.*, ll. 132–9), the evocation of the dazzling gold and splendour of the embroideries on Paris' costume when he carries off Helen, fairly vague in the *Trojan Woman* (l. 991) or *Iphigenia in Aulis* (ll. 74, 182–4), more detailed and more caricatural in the *Cyclops*, when Polyphemus jeers at breeches baggy enough to be likened to sacks and a gold necklace so heavy that it looks like a shackle (ll. 182–4).

Except for these few details, there is no trace of any local colour in the evocations of Barbarians. What predominates is rather a general impression of opulence resting on legendary memories and historical realities. For the Greeks, these barbarian lands were the first countries to which one went in search of riches.[25] The Egypt of *Helen* is the 'rich table' (l. 295) and the 'sumptuous palace' (l. 431) of its king Theoclymenus, to say nothing of the 'purple robes' (l. 181) drying in the sun. Lydia, the land of a ruler whose wealth had become proverbial, remains a land 'rich in gold' in the *Bacchae* (l. 13) as in *Iphigenia in Aulis* (l. 786).[26] The Trojan tragedies are full of references to the wealth of Troy: the Phrygian gold which accompanies Polydorus in his Thracian exile and is the cause of his downfall in *Hecuba*,[27] the adjective 'rich in gold' (πολύχρυσος) which qualifies the Trojans as well as their palaces,[28] the nostalgic reminders of Troy where the gold flowed freely (*Trojan Women*, l. 994ff.), of the pomp surrounding Andromache's marriage (*Andromache*, l. 2), of the

[24] *Medea*, ll. 786, 949, 977, 983, 1160, 1186, 1193.
[25] *Iphigenia in Tauris*, l. 417.
[26] *Heracles*, l. 645, also shows that the opulence of Asian rulers was proverbial.
[27] Ll. 10, 25, 27, 712, 772, 775, 994, 1002, 1148, 1206, 1219, 1245. See also, for Trojan gold, *Andromache*, l. 169; *Trojan Women*, l. 18.
[28] *Hecuba*, l. 492; *Helen*, l. 928.

'statues cast in gold' which adorn the temples (*Trojan Women* l. 1074) and of the gold mirrors in the women's hands on the eve of the capture of Troy.[29]

But this wealth is most often removed from its former possessors and has passed into Greek hands. This already applies to the spoils of the Amazons: the gold-brocaded materials and rich tapestries evoked in *Heracles* (ll. 414–16) and in *Ion* (ll. 1145–59) have been won by Heracles and henceforward adorn Apollo's temple at Delphi. This is even more true of the riches of Troy. In *Andromache*, Hermione wears a gold crown (l. 146), dresses in embroidered garments (l. 146) and can order her servants to collect water in gold urns (l. 165ff.). In *Electra*, the heroine recalls her mother amid the Phrygian spoils with captives who, as at Troy, wear robes fastened with gold brooches (l. 317ff.), and, on the arrival of Clytemnestra, does not fail to stress the brilliance of her chariot and garments (l. 966). In *Orestes*, Trojan luxury surrounds Menelaus and Helen with its brilliance: Menelaus, who makes a display of his splendour (l. 349) and prides himself on his beauty and fair curls (l. 1532), could almost be mistaken for Paris, his wife's Barbarian lover as described in the Trojan tragedies; Helen wears golden sandals (l. 1468) and is surrounded by Barbarian servants equipped with mirrors and perfumes (ll. 1110–12) or with the task of waving a feather fan 'in Barbarian fashion' around her head (ll. 1426–30), while she weaves purple fabrics taken from the booty of Troy. Thus Greece, which has become a haven of wealth, is no longer distinguishable from the Barbarian universe.

The *Bacchae* – which, with *Iphigenia in Aulis*, is Euripides' last work – marks the logical conclusion of this development, showing the gradual assimilation of the Greeks to the Barbarians and displaying it through costume. This tragedy opens, in fact, on a Dionysus who comes from Mt Tmolos in Lydia[30] and 'has adopted the costume of an eastern priest in his cult'.[31] It puts on stage a chorus of 'Asian Bacchants' (l. 1168) who also have left Mt Tmolos, the rampart of Lydia (l. 55). But it also shows '*Cadmean* Bacchants' (l. 1160) who become indistinguishable from their Asiatic sisters[32] as soon as they have donned the 'trappings (σκευήν) of his mysteries' (l. 34). It also

[29] *Hecuba*, l. 925; *Trojan Women*, l. 1107.

[30] Cf. ll. 12–14, 234, 462–4.

[31] Cf. D. Auger, '"Le jeu de Dionysos": déguisements et metamorphoses dans les *Bacchantes* d'Euripide', *Nouvelle Revue d'Ethnopsychiatrie*, 1, 1983, pp. 57–80 (p. 58).

[32] Well emphasised by C. Segal, *Dionysiac Poetics and Euripides' Bacchae*, Princeton, 1982, p. 121.

introduces two old men, the soothsayer Tiresias and Cadmus, the
founder of Thebes, with 'the trappings (σκευήν) of the god' (l. 180),
'rigged out in spotted fawn-skins' and with 'the narthex [wand] in
their hand' (ll. 249–51). Lastly,[33] Pentheus himself ends by becoming
the double of the effeminate priest he had pursued with his hatred;[34]
in his turn he dons 'the trappings' (σκευήν) of a woman, a Maenad,
a Bacchant (l. 915) and assumes 'the appearance' (μορφή, l. 917) of
a daughter of Cadmus. Paradoxically, then, Euripides' text includes
the most precise references to pieces of oriental costume, such as
the 'sash' (μίτρα)[35] and the ankle-length 'linen robes' characteristic
of the Barbarians.[36] This symbolic disguise marks the abolition of the
frontier that normally separates the Greek man from the effeminate
Barbarian:[37] once he is dressed up in 'apparel that counterfeits that
of a woman' (ἐν γυναικομίμῳ στολᾷ, l. 980), Pentheus becomes like
Dionysus in everything: the θηλύμορφος [female in form] which
qualified the one in line 353 is matched by the γυναικόμορφος
[womanly in form] which characterises the other in line 855. The
Greek has become the double of the Barbarian.

2 THE BARBARIAN: A CHANT?

Deprived of distinctive physical features, sometimes stripped by the
Greeks of the costume belonging to him, does the Barbarian in
Euripides at least retain the linguistic characteristic that had originally defined him? It has been known for a long time, as F. Skoda[38]
recently recalled, that 'in origin, βάρβαρος belongs to the vocabulary
of linguistics and refers particularly to pronunciation'. It is probably

---

[33] On this progression (first Greek women transformed into female Bacchants, then two
Greek men being transformed into male Bacchants, and lastly a Greek man transformed into
a Bacchant), see D. Auger, *loc. cit.*, pp. 66–9. This confusion between the three images
(Dionysus, the Bacchants and Pentheus) is marked especially by a detail, that of the long hair
waving on his shoulders (Dionysus: ll. 150, 235ff., 240ff., 455ff.; Bacchants: l. 695; Pentheus:
l. 831).

[34] The importance of this transformation has been underlined by several recent works. See
especially H. Foley, 'The Masque of Dionysos', *TAPA*, 110, 1980, pp. 107–33 (p. 129ff.);
C. Segal, *op. cit.*, pp. 118–24; and D. Auger, *loc. cit.*, p. 69.

[35] Ll. 833, 929, 1115. In Euripides' tragedies, the 'mitra' is worn by the Trojan women, who
are Barbarians (*Hecuba*, l. 924) and mentioned in *Electra*, l. 163, in reference to the sumptuous 'oriental' welcome that Clytemnestra was said to have given Agamemnon after his victory
over Troy.

[36] Ll. 821, 935–8. A byssus [linen] garment is also worn by Persian women in Aeschylus'
Persians, l. 125.

[37] One could also emphasise, though it is not my purpose to do so here, that, by donning
an animal skin (l. 835), Pentheus, like the Bacchants (l. 697), crosses the boundary separating
civilisation from savagery. See the remarks of C. Segal on this point, *op. cit.*, n. 32.

[38] F. Skoda, 'Histoire du mot βάρβαρος', *Actes du Colloque franco-polonais d'histoire*,
Nice-Antibes, 6–9 Novembre 1980, pp. 111–26 (p. 112).

not by chance that the oldest attested word of the βάρβαρος family is not the simple noun, but the compound adjective βαρβαρόφωνος, 'of Barbarian speech' (*Il.*, 2, 867). The difficulties – and arguments – begin when one tries to pinpoint what is meant by Barbarian speech. Is it a foreign language incomprehensible to a Greek ear, as is usually agreed and as F. Skoda[39] recently upheld, or, more subtly, 'a Greek distorted so much by Barbarian mouths that it became incomprehensible even to Greeks', as a quotation from Strabo[40] might lead one to think, and as F. Letoublon[41] suggested?

However it may be, in a tragedy in which all the characters conventionally speak a correct language and there is no question, as there is in Aristophanes,[42] of putting on stage the poor Greek of a Persian ambassador, a Triballian god or a Scythian archer, there cannot be Barbarian speech in the strict sense of the term. Euripides is even remarkably mean in his use of words of foreign origin to typify his Barbarian characters.[43] But he still has music. Euripides' liking for exotic rhythms was renowned in antiquity. In the *Frogs*, Aristophanes does not miss a chance of making fun of the 'Carian flutes' (l. 1302) of Euripides (we must not forget that the Carians were the first 'Barbarians' attested in Greek literature, since they appear in Homer)[44] and depicts him in the *Thesmophoriazusae* in the act of having a 'Persian air' played (l. 1175).

This exotic music may simply be evoked, as in *Iphigenia in Aulis*, when the chorus recalls the 'Barbaric sounds' modulated by the shepherd Paris, imitating the 'Phrygian flute of Olympus' (ll. 576–8). More frequently, it is presented on stage with choruses composed of Barbarian women or exotic characters.[45] Thus in the *Phoenician Women*, a chorus made up of women of that country bring Jocasta out of her palace with their 'Phoenician cries' (l. 301ff.). They then invoke Epaphus with clamour and 'Barbarian' prayers (l. 679ff.) and finally prepare to greet the death of Eteocles and Polynices with 'Barbarian cries' (l. 1301). Similarly, in the *Bacchae*, the chorus of Asian Maenads sing the *parodos* accompanied by exotic instruments (tambourines and lotus flutes),[46] uttering cries and 'Phrygian' calls

[39] *Loc. cit.*, pp. 112–14.
[40] Strabo, *Geography*, 14, 2, 28.
[41] In a lecture given at the University of Grenoble in 1982.
[42] Cf. *Acharnians*, ll. 100–4; *Birds*, ll. 1615, 1678ff.; *Thesm.*, ll. 1001–25.
[43] Cf. H. Bacon, *op. cit.*, p. 117: 'Of actual foreign words, Euripides uses only six (compare Aeschylus' 22 and Sophocles' 20).'
[44] Cf. *Il.*, 2, 867.
[45] On this point see W. Kranz, *op. cit.*, pp. 110–112.
[46] Ll. 58ff., 124, 156, 160.

(l. 159), and greet with 'Barbarian' songs (l. 1034) the news of the death of Pentheus. In *Orestes*, the monologue of the Phrygian slave is also distinguished by its 'Barbarian cries' (l. 1385) and by an exclamation, Αἴλινον, which is supposedly a 'Barbarian' word uttered 'in Asiatic voice' (ll. 1395–7).

But is not this supposed Barbarian exclamation in fact Greek? At all events, it can be found several times[47] on Greek lips, without a single indication of its exotic nature. The linguistic frontier is therefore far from being as clear cut as one might have thought at first. Of course, this is only a hint, and a tenuous one at that, but it finds its confirmation in *Iphigenia in Tauris*, a tragedy that is set among the Barbarians, but puts on stage a Greek chorus and heroes. For the chorus in this tragedy is just as exotic as the Barbarian choruses of the *Phoenician Women* or the *Bacchae*. Iphigenia's *Greek*[48] serving women in fact make the air resound with 'the *Barbarian* echo of Asiatic hymns' (ll. 179–81), and their mistress herself intones 'Barbarian' songs (l. 1337ff.) when she pretends to indulge in magic practices intended to cleanse the two Greeks of their stains, as if the stay on Barbarian soil had contaminated the Greeks and transformed them into Barbarians. So Barbarianism is infectious and it seems difficult, when one considers the complete extant plays of Euripides, to maintain the existence of a true linguistic frontier between Greeks and Barbarians.

3 THE IMAGE OF THE BARBARIAN: REALITY OR FANTASY?

Nevertheless, the image of a universe divided into two irreconcilable groups, free Greeks, on the one hand, and Barbarians who are by nature slaves or tyrants, on the other, is certainly present in Euripides' plays; but it is too much of a caricature to be taken seriously. Here again, 'The theatre of Euripides invites … the reader to look below the surface of the words he gives his characters … whose passion is often suspect and speech stereotyped.'[49]

This theme appears even in Euripides' earliest tragedies; but what had been a central motif in the *Persians* of Aeschylus or the *Histories* of Herodotus has become a rather hollow cliché in the *Heracleidae* or even a frankly suspect argument in *Medea*. In the *Heracleidae*,

---

[47] Cf. *Heracles*, l. 172; *Phoenician Women*, l. 1519.
[48] Cf. ll. 64, 132, 136.
[49] Cf. C. Nancy, 'Euripide et le parti des femmes' (see n. 17), p. 80.

the contrast between the 'tyranny of the Barbarians' (l. 422) and a
regime like that of Athens, where the ruler must act justly in order
to be justly treated in his turn, allows the Athenian Demophon to
conclude in grand fashion a tirade that was by no means heroic, since
he had just withdrawn from the Heracleidae the support which he
had at first promised them. In *Medea*, it is the heroine herself who
dares to say out loud what the Greek Jason is thinking: for a Greek,
union with a Barbarian woman is a degrading misalliance, which
'puts him on the road to an old age without glory' (l. 591ff.). But it
is clear that, by choosing to put this Greek viewpoint in the mouth
of a Barbarian woman, Euripides is thereby inviting us to look at it
with a critical eye.

We find this still more in the plays connected with the Trojan war,
from *Hecuba* to *Iphigenia in Aulis*. In *Hecuba*, it is the heroine who
clearly states that an unbridgeable gulf separates the two races and
that 'the Barbarian race (τὸ βάρβαρον ... γένος) will never become
the Greeks' friends, nor could they' (ll. 1199–1201). But that statement is only an argument appropriate to the circumstances, intended
to refute the declarations of the Thracian Polymestor, who claims to
have killed the Trojan Polydorus to serve the interests of the Greek
Agamemnon.[50] The argument is all the more suspect since it is put
into the mouth of a Barbarian woman who has herself, a little earlier,
begged for the help of that same Agamemnon, invoking the 'kinship'
that linked him to the brother of his paramour.[51] In *Andromache*, it
is Menelaus who becomes indignant at the idea that the Greek Peleus
could take the side of Andromache, a Barbarian woman who 'comes
from a continent where so many Greeks have fallen to the spear'
(l. 652ff.). He again, several lines later, denounces the scandal there
would be if 'Barbarians by birth' (βάρβαροι δ' ὄντες γένος) were
seen 'giving orders to Greeks' (l. 665ff.), which would happen if the
son of Andromache and Neoptolemus should succeed his father on
the throne of Phthia. But Menelaus is the villain of the tragedy, and
'the very manner in which he is presented prevents us from seeing
him as Euripides' spokesman'.[52] In fact, Euripides has denounced in
advance the sophism that lays responsibility for the Trojan war
on Andromache's shoulders. Through Peleus, he directly blames
Menelaus: 'You are the one', says Peleus, 'who has destroyed many
brave lives and left old women bereft of their children at home and

[50] Ll. 1175–7.
[51] Ll. 824–35.
[52] K. Synodinou, *op. cit.*, p. 43, n. 3.

robbed grey-haired fathers of their noble children. I am one of those unhappy men. I regard you like some polluted criminal, as the murderer of Achilles' (ll. 611–15).

The thesis of Barbarian inferiority sometimes takes a more clearly political turn, thus prefiguring what would become one of the major themes of the panhellenic discourse and political propaganda of the fourth century. For Isocrates in particular, from the *Encomium of Helen* to the *Panathenaicus*, the war with Troy would become a historical precedent to be called upon when preaching unity to the Greeks and summoning them to fight together against the Barbarians. In fact, to use Isocrates' words,[53] it was 'the most useful campaign (ὠφέλιμος) to the Greeks that was ever undertaken', for it changed the direction of history and marked a 'turning point' (μεταβολή) in the relations between Greeks and Barbarians: before that war, the Barbarians had played the colonisers and 'considered themselves fit to have control over Greek cities', but Agamemnon 'put and end to their insolence' and, since then, 'the [Greek] race had made such great progress that it had managed to win many towns and vast territory from the Barbarians'. Euripides had not read Isocrates. Nor could he have known the *Olympic Discourse* of Gorgias which foreshadowed him, when he composed *Andromache*, the *Trojan Women* or *Helen*.[54] However, these arguments can be found almost word for word in those three tragedies, but in a context of a kind that prevents us from taking them seriously.

In *Andromache*, it is in fact Menelaus (we saw earlier what must be thought of this character) who, to defend Helen, maintains that 'she rendered the greatest service to the Greeks' (πλεῖστον ὠφέλησεν Ἑλλάδα) by provoking the Trojan War, for by doing so she was the source of all the progress they had accomplished: until then 'inexperienced in arms and battle (or perhaps more exactly in hoplite warfare) they progressed to bravery' (ll. 681–3). In the *Trojan Women*, Helen says almost exactly the same thing when she tries to excuse herself against a Menelaus who assumes the stance of pitiless judge. Indeed, she presents 'her marriage' as 'Greece's good fortune' (ἃ δ' εὐτύχησεν Ἑλλάς, l. 935). 'My marriage,' she says, 'at least gave the Greeks this benefit (ὤνησαν), that you were not made subject to the Barbarians' (οὐ κρατεῖσθ' ἐκ βαρβάρων) (l. 932ff.).

[53] Cf. *Encomium of Helen*, 67–8, and *Panathenaicus*, 76–83 (eulogy of Agamemnon).
[54] The *Olympic Oration* of Gorgias was pronounced at the Olympic Games of 408. The *Trojan Women* dates from 415 and *Helen* from 412. As for *Andromache*, the date of which is disputed, it must be pointed out that the latest date proposed is 412–411 and that it is generally agreed that the tragedy falls between 423 and 420.

This would have been the case if Paris had accepted the suggestions of Pallas, who had 'offered him the chance of going to conquer Greece at the head of a Phrygian army' (l. 927ff.). Helen even goes so far as to claim that, like an Olympic victor, she deserves to 'receive a crown' (l. 937) for this exploit. The irony of the development is obvious, and one would have to be very naïve to claim that Euripides could have made such theories his own, all the more so since this speech of Helen's is followed by a rebuttal from Hecuba, and it is the queen of Troy who has the last word.[55] What must we think when we find in *Helen*, that tragedy which portrays an upside-down world and a perfectly innocent 'Egyptian' Helen, this well-turned sentence in the heroine's mouth: 'the Barbarians are all slaves, except one alone' (l. 277)? Should we, with R. Goossens,[56] see it as one of those passages in which 'the belief – deeply rooted in the Greek mind – in his own superiority over the Barbarians bursts forth'? Or should we, on the contrary, believe that Euripides is inviting us to distance ourselves from a cliché that is only a rhetorical development of the preceding line: 'I am a slave, I who was born of free parents' (l. 276). I would be more inclined to go in this latter direction.[57]

There remains the more thorny and more interesting case, in other words that of *Iphigenia in Aulis*, where this theme plays a role as ambiguous as it is central. In view of the foregoing, in order to be able to state that Euripides identified with his characters' statements about the inferiority of the Barbarians and the Greeks' right to command them, we should need to postulate a real conversion on Euripides' part: at the end of his life, from the distant Macedonia to which he had voluntarily exiled himself, he had finally adopted Greek values and rallied to the cause of panhellenism. But the notion of Euripides' conversion is perhaps rather too simple a solution to the problems posed by his last work (the example of the *Bacchae* should make us cautious, 'for it would take a close scrutiny of the play ... to discover in it the "conversion" of Euripides, finding his road to Damascus in Thessaly')[58] and we must take a closer look before choosing between the two opposite interpretations of the play proposed to us, for example, by R. Goossens[59] and P. Vellacott,[60] as

---

[55] On the *agon* of the *Trojan Women*, see S. Saïd, *La faute tragique*, Paris, 1978, pp. 525–6.
[56] R. Goossens, *Euripide et Athènes*, Brussels, 1962, p. 581.
[57] See also K. Synodinou, *op. cit.*, p. 46: 'It is tempting to suppose irony on the poet's part in view of the pretentious patriotism and uprightness of Helen in this play.'
[58] Cf. C. Nancy, *loc. cit.*, p. 91.
[59] *Op. cit.*, pp. 683–7. Among the supporters of Euripides' panhellenism in *Iphigenia in Aulis*, one may quote W. H. Friedrich, 'Zur Aulischen Iphigenie', *Hermes*, 70, 1935, p. 86ff.; A. Diller, *Race Mixture among the Greeks*, Urbana, 1937, p. 30; A. Bonnard, 'Iphigénie à Aulis:

a manifesto of panhellenism or a denunciation of Greek chauvinism.

The thesis of the Barbarians' natural inferiority as justification of the Greek expedition against Troy is explicitly affirmed on two occasions in the tragedy. It first appears in the mouth of Menelaus, when he protests at Agamemnon's change of mind and bewails Greece's misfortune, saying to his brother: 'She was planning a glorious action; and she is going to let the Barbarians, these nothings (βαρβάρους τοὺς οὐδένας) escape and laugh at us, because of you and your daughter' (ll. 370–2). Above all, it brings to a brilliant conclusion the speech in which Iphigenia agrees to die for Greece: 'That Greeks should command Barbarians,' she says, 'is normal (εἰκός) but not that Barbarians should command Greeks. *They* are the slaves, and we are free beings' (l. 1400ff.). This conclusion has been prepared by a development in which Iphigenia is shown as the potential liberator of Greece (Ἑλλάδ' ὡς ἠλευθέρωσα, l. 1384), for the departure of the fleet and the ruin of the Phrygians which will be the outcome of her sacrifice, if we are to believe the predictions of Calchas,[61] will henceforth protect Greece from the extortions of

tragique et poésie', *MH*, 2, 1945, p. 105; F. Wassermann, 'Agamemnon in Iphigeneia at Aulis: a man in an age of crisis', *TAPA*, 80, 1949, pp. 174–86; E. Delebecque, *Euripide et la guerre du Péloponnèse*, Paris, 1951, pp. 366–75; M. Pohlenz, *Die griechische Tragödie*, Göttingen, 1954, p. 466ff.; E. Valgiglio, 'L'Ifigenia in Aulide', *RSC*, 4, 1956, pp. 179–202, and 5, 1957, pp. 47–52; H. Vretska, 'Agamemnon in Euripides *Iphigenie in Aulis*', *WS*, 74, 1961, pp. 18–39; H. Diller, 'Die Hellenen-Barbaren-Antithese im Zeitalter der Perserkriege', *Grecs et Barbares, Entretiens sur l'Antiquité classique*, VIII, 1962, Geneva, pp. 39–68 (p. 55); B. M. W. Knox, 'Second thoughts in Greek tragedy', *GRBS*, 7, 1966, pp. 213–32 (p. 232); H. Steiger, *Iphigenies Opfertod*, Diss. Frankfurt-am-Main 1963, pp. 55–7; G. Mellert-Hoffman, *Untersuchungen zu Iphigenie in Aulis des Euripides*, Heidelberg, 1969, pp. 9–90; V. Di Benedetto, *Euripide, Teatro e Società*, p. 217; D. Goertz, *Iphigeneia at Aulis: A Critical Analysis*, Diss. Austin, 1972, pp. 17–35; E. Lévy, *Athènes devant la défaite de 404*, p. 157; H. Foley, *Ritual Irony: Poetry and Sacrifice in Euripides*, Ithaca, 1985, pp. 100–102. These studies, like those featured in the next note, will be henceforth recalled by the author's name only.

[60] P. Vellacott, *Ironic Drama: A Study of Euripides' Method and Meaning*, Cambridge, 1975, pp. 173–7 and 201–3. See also, for the same interpretation, E. M. Blaiklock, *The Male Characters of Euripides*, Wellington, 1952, p. 119; H. D. F. Kitto, *Greek Tragedy*, London³, 1961, p. 369; H. Funke, 'Aristoteles zu Euripides *Iphigeneia in Aulis*', *Hermes*, 92, 1964, pp. 284–99 (p. 287f.); K. Synodinou, *op. cit.*, pp. 33–42; G. E. Dimock, *Iphigeneia at Aulis*, tr. W. S. Merwin and G. R. Dimock, New York, 1978, pp. 4, 10; K. Matthiesen, 'Euripides: die Tragödien', *Das Griechische Drama*, ed. G. A. Seeck, Darmstadt, 1979, p. 148; H. Neitzel, 'Iphigeniens Opfertod', *Würzburger Anzeiger*, 6, 1980, pp. 61–70; H. Siegel, 'Self-delusion and the volte-face of Iphigeneia in Euripides' *Iphigenia at Aulis*', *Hermes*, 108, 1980 (cited as H. Siegel 1980), pp. 300–21 (pp. 315–17); 'Agamemnon in Euripides' *Iphigenia at Aulis*', *Hermes*, 109, 1981 (cited as H. Siegel 1981), pp. 257–65; C. Nancy, 'ΦΆΡΜΑΚΟΝ ΣΩΤΗΡΊΑΣ', p. 23; E. Masaracchia, 'Il sacrificio nell'Ifigenia in Aulide', *QUCC*, 14, 1983, pp. 43–77 (p. 71ff.). F. Jouan, in the introduction to his edition of *Iphigénie à Aulis*, Paris, 1983, refrains from deciding between the two arguments ('L'expédition panhellénique: précepte ou prétexte?', pp. 41–3).

[61] Cf. ll. 89–93. H. Neitzel, pp. 62–4, clearly shows that the oracle does not make sacrifice an absolute necessity. It simply makes it a condition for the annihilation of Troy. Thus the capture of Troy is necessarily bound up with an impious and unjust act (c.ll. 1089–97), which is a means of denouncing in advance the crimes that will accompany it.

the Phrygians: 'Even if the Barbarians try, they will no longer have licence to seize women from Greece's blessed land' (l. 1380ff.). The whole question is whether to infer from the profession of faith by Menelaus and, above all, by Iphigenia an expression of Euripides' conviction and his conversion to the panhellenic ideal and the racism it presupposes. It is made all the more problematic by the fact that elsewhere these two characters uphold exactly opposite arguments – by no means surprising in this 'tragedy of indecision and volte-faces',[62] entirely filled with characters who constantly change according to circumstance.

It seems difficult to allow, with R. Goossens,[63] that lines 370–2, which 'ring out like a panhellenic protest against Persia's insolent hegemony', reflect Euripides' thinking. For the patriotism of Menelaus which condemns a 'doom-laden message for the whole of Greece' (l. 308) and sees in its author a man 'who refuses to be associated with Greece's ordeals' (l. 410) is very suspect, and the general interest serves here as a convenient screen for a man who is only looking after his own interests. It is 'the spur of desire' (l. 77) and not love of Greece that has prompted Menelaus to raise an expedition which will allow him to hold a beautiful woman in his arms again and take his revenge on the worst of wives.[64] We must also remember that Menelaus' patriotic convictions are as ephemeral as they are loudly proclaimed. One hundred lines further on, Menelaus 'goes back on his earlier words' (l. 479) and stops urging Agamemnon to kill his daughter (l. 481), with the approval of the chorus and Agamemnon, who praise him equally for his noble words, worthy of him and his ancestors.[65] In fact, both the prologue and the whole of the exchange between the two brothers clearly reveal that the Barbarians' natural inferiority and the glory of Greece are here no more than convenient and hollow slogans, which Agamemnon does not even trouble to refute and which Menelaus seems to forget as soon as he has declaimed them, regardless of logic. Before comparing the Greeks with the Barbarians, 'those nothings', had he not precisely treated the leader of the panhellenic forces as a 'good-for-nothing' (οὐδὲν ἦσθ', l. 351)?

The true reasons for the expedition, as they have emerged up to this

---

[62] This is the title chosen by R. Goossens, p. 688, for a part of the chapter that he devotes to *Iphigenia in Aulis*. On the volte-faces in this tragedy, see also B. M. W. Knox, p. 229.

[63] *Op. cit.*, p. 682.

[64] Ll. 385–7, 397.

[65] Ll. 504–7.

point, are in fact quite different, as has often been stressed.[66] For the war stems first from the oath (ll. 57–65) which, to get him out of a tight spot (ll. 55–7), Tyndareus had 'astutely' (l. 67) demanded from his daughter's suitors and which they had sworn, 'led astray by the desire to wed' and possessed by hope (ll. 391–3). Now, this oath was not aimed at Barbarians as such, but concerned the possible kidnapper of Helen and 'his city, whether *Greek or Barbarian*' (l. 64ff.). We have seen the reasons that had prompted Menelaus to invoke the oaths already sworn.[67] When Calchas indicated that the sacrifice of Iphigenia was the necessary condition of the expedition's success, what carried the most weight, if we are to believe Agamemnon, were still the words of Menelaus in persuading his brother (l. 97ff.), or rather, if we are to believe Menelaus, the will of Agamemnon himself, who refused 'to be deprived of his command and lose a dazzling glory' (l. 317). To which must be added the 'ambition' of certain Greeks, such as Calchas (l. 520) or Odysseus (l. 527) and the 'madness' (l. 394) of all of them. In short, at the start of this tragedy, everything invites us to look for the causes of the war on the side of a Greece that 'is sick' (l. 411) and not on the side of the Barbarians and their alleged crimes.

But can one so easily set aside the conclusion of the tragedy and words which are worthy of a heroine, who agrees to die for the Greek cause, does not go back on her promise,[68] and deserves the eulogies of the chorus and Achilles?[69] In other words, is the death of Iphigenia enough to guarantee the value of the cause for which she is dying, or rather is claiming to die? For Iphigenia has no choice,[70] and the hundred lines separating the apparently decisive patriotic arguments of Agamemnon from his daughter's decision have no other purpose than to establish it. The news of the army brought by Achilles in fact confirms that Agamemnon is right at least on one point: Iphigenia's death is henceforth inevitable.[71] All the Greeks are demanding it, threatening to stone anyone who opposes it,[72] and making ready to come and seize the victim.[73] Now convinced that 'in the face of the

[66] Cf. H. Funke, pp. 287–9; K. Synodinou, p. 41; H. Neitzel, p. 65; H. Siegel, 1980, p. 308ff.

[67] Menelaus, who has only his personal interest in mind (cf. ll. 489, 493) and lets himself be dominated by his passions, is elsewhere taxed with depravity and madness (ll. 387, 407, 411) and himself recognises the fairness of this last reproach (l. 489).

[68] The possibility of a final change of mind by Iphigenia is envisaged by Achilles in line 1425, but given the lie by the messenger's account.

[69] Cf. ll. 1402, 1409, 1411, 1421.

[70] As H. Funke, p. 295, and H. Siegel, 1980, p. 311, have both emphasised.

[71] Ll. 1257–72.

[72] Ll. 1349–53.

[73] Ll. 1361–6.

impossible, it is not easy to stand firm' (l. 1370), Iphigenia no longer has any option but to find good reasons for making a virtue of a necessity. And this she does in her speech, as Achilles emphasises in line 1409: ἐξελογισω τὰ χρηστὰ τὰναγκαιά τε [you choose the thing that was good and fated].[74]

Are these reasons, and especially the last, all that good? Is there not a great deal of irony in having the liberty of the Greeks and the slavery of the Barbarians proclaimed by a Greek woman who has at no time had the possibility of deciding her own fate (she can choose only the manner of her death)?[75] Are not these slogans, inherited from the Persian Wars, here diverted from their proper meaning and wrongfully used to justify Greek imperialism and disguise a war of conquest as a war of liberation? Are they not placed at the conclusion of a development which is, to put it mildly, not notable for the rigour of its reasoning? Iphigenia's speech, which amasses arguments that are sometimes self-destructive[76] to justify her decision *a posteriori*,[77] has, in fact, been severely criticised.[78] But this jumble of absurdities is certainly put together on purpose. Indeed, by virtue of a clever piece of editing, it is a means of discrediting in advance the commonplaces of panhellenism.

But it is impossible to assess the real value of those commonplaces without going back to their true origin: in other words, Agamemnon. For Iphigenia merely takes up her father's words[79] and the one positive reason he had put forward to justify her death. When she presents herself as Greece's benefactress (l. 1446) and the 'light of salvation' (l. 1502) for a homeland she is 'defending' (l. 1383) and 'saving' (l. 1420, 1472–3) by destroying Troy (l. 1475ff.), she is echoing her father, who had proclaimed the army's desire to 'bring to an end the abduction of Greek wives' (l. 1266) and had also spoken of

[74] Cf. P. Vellacott, p. 176.

[75] Cf. H. Siegel, 1980, p. 314: 'What must have really struck the audience was that Iphigeneia distinguished the Greeks as being free. What greater irony could there be than to hear this from the mouth of an innocent girl, who has had, as a Greek, absolutely nothing to say about her own fate?'

[76] Thus, in lines 1392–4, Iphigenia claims to be dying to prevent Achilles entering battle with all the Argives and being killed: 'for it is better that one single man should see the light of day rather than ten thousand women'. But was not the entire expedition intended to cause the death of thousands of men in the defence of one woman alone?

[77] H. Neitzel, p. 69ff., clearly shows that Iphigenia, in her speech, is not describing a decision that is being made, but is justifying after the event (μοι δέδοκται, l. 1375) a decision that has been taken in spontaneous and thoughtless manner.

[78] Cf. H. D. F. Kitto, p. 369, 'all sorts of nonsense'; H. Funke, p. 292; P. Vellacott, p. 176, n. 14; and H. Siegel, 1980, p. 313.

[79] This point is stressed by most critics: see especially H. Funke, pp. 293–5; K. Synodinou, p. 37; H. Neitzel, pp. 68–70; H. Siegel, 1980, p. 315; and E. Masaracchia, p. 71.

a war of liberation: 'In conclusion, he had said to his daughter, Greece must be free, and it is up to you, my daughter, and to me, and the Barbarians must not be allowed to come and forcibly rob the Greeks of their wives' (ll. 1273–5). But what is this patriotic argument worth in the mouth of a man who has been accused of personal ambition?[80] Is it enough to transform him, as has been said, into 'an anticipation of Alexander'?[81] With C. Nancy,[82] I prefer to believe that 'it is difficult simply to give credit to the last argument of a man who has constantly vacillated and lied'. I would even go further and point out all the irony of this anti-Barbarian propaganda when it is put in the mouth of a man who matches, point for point, the image of the Barbarian he is creating.

For Agamemnon, far from personifying Greek liberty, constantly looks like a slave in *Iphigenia in Aulis*.[83] Certainly, when he himself speaks of it, he is sometimes able to impart a noble appearance to this servitude. In line 443, indeed, he presents himself as a victim of destiny and a man 'who has fallen under the yoke of necessity' (εἰς οἷά γ' ἀνάγκης ζεύγματ' ἐμπεπτώκαμεν). In the speech in which he proclaims the 'need' (δεῖ) for Greece to be 'free' (ἐλευθέραν) (l. 1273), he admits that he is himself 'the slave of Greece' (... με καταδεδούλωτο ... Ἑλλάς) and that it had placed him under the 'necessity' (δεῖ) of sacrificing his daughter, 'whether or not he wanted to' (l. 1271ff.). But the reality is more sordid. As he himself confesses, Agamemnon is 'the slave of the mob' (τῷ τ' ὄχλῳ δουλεύομεν, l. 450) and the 'necessity' (ἥκομεν γὰρ εἰς ἀναγκαίας τύχας) [we have come to these necessary destinies], l. 511) that weighs on him is to be identified with the will of the entire assembled Achaean army (– τίς δ' ἀναγκάσει σε τήν γε σὴν κτανεῖν; – Ἅπας Ἀχαιῶν σύλλογος στρατεύματος) [Men.: 'What do you mean? Who will force you to kill your own [daughter]?' Ag.: 'The whole assembly of the expedition of the Achaeans'], l. 512ff.). Moreover, he is reduced to this condition by none other than himself. If he is the slave of the mob and 'completely humbles himself' (ταπεινός, l. 339) before it, it is because he is 'ruled by vanity' (προστάτην γε τοῦ βίου τὸν ὄγκον ἔχομεν, l. 449ff.) and still more by fear.[84] For in spite of the advice of Menelaus ('You must not fear the mob too much', l. 517), 'he is a

---

[80] Cf. ll. 337–63.
[81] Cf. F. Wassermann, p. 185.
[82] 'ΦΑΡΜΑΚΟΝ ΣΩΤΕΡΙΑΣ', p. 23.
[83] Emphasised by P. Vellacott, pp. 219–22; K. Synodinou, p. 38; H. Siegel, 1980, p. 309, and 1981, pp. 262–4.
[84] The fundamental role of fear as motivation for Agamemnon's behaviour has been recently brought to the fore by H. Siegel, 1981, pp. 260–4.

coward and too afraid of the army' (l. 1012). This opinion of Clytemnestra is more than confirmed by Agamemnon's behaviour and the extravagant tirades in which he exaggerates the threat the army holds over him,[85] when, in lines 531-5, he pictures Odysseus persuading the Achaeans to massacre him, together with his brother and daughter: 'And even if I seek refuge in Argos,' he says, 'they will come and take us by storm, us and our Cyclopean walls, and ravage the land'; or when, in lines 1267-8, he states to his wife and daughter: 'they will come and massacre my daughters who have stayed in Argos, and yourselves with me if I infringe the oracle of the goddess'. It was probably the wish to broach this theme as early as the prologue[86] that justifies the curious dialogue between Agamemnon and the old servant which opens the tragedy. In fact, Euripides impresses upon us the image of an Agamemnon who dreams of slavery and envies the existence – without renown or glory, but also without any danger – of his slave (ll. 16-19). And it is the slave who, against his master, must become the defender of heroic values, affirming: 'However, that is where the beauty of life lies' (l. 20). This beginning seems to me to throw an ironic light on Agamemnon's final declaration about the liberty of Greece and the need to sacrifice everything for it.

One can give no more credence to Agamemnon when he denounces the kidnappings of the Barbarians. For this portrayal of the Barbarians who 'kidnap' (ἁρπαγή, ἁρπάζειν, ll. 1266, 1381) and 'plunder' (συλᾶν, l. 1275) Greek women has hardly any backing in the rest of the tragedy. It is only in Iphigenia's mouth, in line 1382, that Helen's departure is presented purely and simply as an 'abduction' (Ἑλένης ... ἣν ἀνήρπασεν Πάρις). Elsewhere, there is mention rather of Aphrodite's 'gift' to Paris (l. 181); emphasis is placed on the active role of Helen, who has 'fled her palace' (l. 270) and 'abandoned her husband' (l. 783), and the mutual attraction experienced by the two lovers.[87] In *Iphigenia in Aulis*, it is the Greeks who behave like abductors. For from the start the tragedy shows us a Menelaus who 'forcibly wrests' (ἐξαρπάσας ... βίᾳ, l. 315) from Agamemnon's slave the message he bears. It mentions Greeks who would come to 'abduct' Iphigenia even from Argos if Agamemnon took refuge there (ll. 531-5) and who are preparing, under the leadership of Odysseus, to 'abduct' Iphigenia and drag her off by her fair hair (l. 1365ff.).

---

[85] Cf. H. Funke, p. 289, n. 1, and H. Neitzel, p. 65.

[86] On the authenticity of the whole of the prologue, in the order in which it is given in the manuscripts, see B. M. W. Knox, 'Euripides' *Iphigenia in Aulide* 1-163 (in that order)', YCS, 22, 1972, pp. 239-61.

[87] Cf. ll. 75ff., 585ff.

It recalls (and this is important) the rape formerly perpetrated by Agamemnon himself. Clytemnestra in fact relates that Agamemnon married her against her wishes and took her by force, after killing her first husband, Tantalus, and crushing on the ground her living child, brutally torn from her breast (ll. 1149–52). As F. Jouan[88] reminds us, 'this legend appears here for the first time'. Should we not explain this invention of Euripides (or, if you prefer, this deliberate choice of a little-known version only rarely attested by later authors) in terms of an ironic intent[89] and a desire to demystify in advance the commonplaces about Barbarian abductions?

It remains to point out one last detail, which seems to me to be decisive, namely the Barbarian origin of Agamemnon himself. In fact, when Achilles is quite confident of preventing Agamemnon from laying a hand on Iphigenia, even with so much as a fingertip, he bases this confidence on the superiority of the Greeks over the Barbarians, and contrasts his Greek homeland, Phthia, with Sipylus, 'that Barbarian corner whence the leaders of the army (in other words, Agamemnon and his brother) have their origin' (l. 952ff.) Scholars have sometimes been surprised at this 'bizarre and forced' expression and have wondered 'what the Lydian origin of Agamemnon is doing here, since he is generally considered to be a very Hellenic character, the national hero of the first war waged against the Barbarians'. But rather than seeing it – as does R. Goossens[90] – as a (very veiled!) allusion to contemporary events and to an intervention by Cyrus the Younger (since Sardis lay at the foot of the Sipylus) to enforce the authority of Lysander at the head of the Peloponnesian forces, should we not infer from this little phrase the ultimate denunciation of panhellenism and the gulf it creates between Greeks and Barbarians? This would be not at all surprising in a tragedy that is completely dedicated to 'unmasking false claims of glory'.[91]

We have seen what to think of the clichés about the natural inferiority and servility of the Barbarians in Euripides' tragedies. Now we must compare these theoretical statements with what is shown on stage and first of all analyse the way in which prostration [*proskynesis*], which was for the Greeks a typically Barbarian custom, is presented by Euripides.[92] Certainly the Barbarians continued to pros-

---

[88] Edition of *Iphigénie à Aulis*, p. 105, n. 4.

[89] P. Vellacott, p. 176, n. 13, is the only one to connect the conclusion of Agamemnon's speech to Clytemnestra's account.

[90] *Op. cit.*, p. 683.

[91] Cf. H. Neitzel, p. 67: 'Demaskierung des falschen Ruhmes' so könnte man die Iphigenie in Aulis überschreiben.'

[92] Cf. Aristotle, *Rhet*, I, 1361 a, l. 36.

trate themselves in Euripides' plays, whether in the *Phoenician Women* (ll. 291–4) or *Orestes*. But they always manage to distance themselves from what they are doing by stressing that they are acting 'according to the custom among their own people' (*Phoen.*, l. 294) or 'in keeping with Barbarian custom' (*Or.*, l. 1507). Furthermore, unlike in the *Histories* of Herodotus, where the Greeks ignored or rejected such Barbarian conduct,[93] we also see Greek women delighting in others' prostration when they are transported to Barbarian lands, like Helen in the *Trojan Women* (l. 1020ff.), or even demanding it from their servants, while they are in Greece, like Hermione in *Andromache* (l. 165). And it is the Barbarian woman who then proudly refuses to fawn upon her Greek mistress (*And.*, l. 459).

If the Barbarians were proverbially servile, they were also known for their cowardice, which was explained sometimes by the soil, as in Book IX of Herodotus' *Histories*:

> For soft men are usually born in soft countries; and the same land is not capable of producing admirable fruit and men who are valiant in war (122),

sometimes by the climate, as in the Hippocratic treatise *Airs, Waters, Places*:

> As for the lack of courage in men, and their lack of virility, the fact that the Asians are less warlike than Europeans and of a gentler nature is chiefly because of the seasons, which undergo no great change in heat and cold (16),

and sometimes by the political regime: if the inhabitants of Europe are more warlike, 'it is also due to laws, because they are not ruled by kings like the Asians' (*Airs, Waters, Places*, 22).[94]

Relying upon the tragedies in which Euripides stages confrontations between Greeks and Barbarians, *Iphigenia in Tauris*, *Helen* and *Orestes*, one might think that he shares the common opinion, since these confrontations always turn out to the Greeks' advantage. But one needs only to take a closer look at the accounts of these combats to discover that this is by no means so, and that they are far from 'bringing to light the sporting and military superiority of the Greeks', as R. Goossens believes.[95]

In both *Iphigenia in Tauris* and *Helen*, the Greek victories over the Taurians or the Egyptians, with which these two tragedies end, have nothing very glorious about them. In both cases, it is a matter of attacks which are treacherous, resulting from perfidious deceptions

---

[93] Herodotus, II, 180. l. 6; VII, 136, l. 2.

[94] On these explanations for Barbarians' cowardice and their connection with the Persian Wars, see J. Jouanna, 'Les causes de la défaite des Barbares chez Eschyle, Hérodote et Hippocrate', *Ktema*, 6, 1981, pp. 3–15.

[95] *Op. cit.*, p. 581.

carried out by women. In *Iphigenia in Tauris* (ll. 1355–78), there is no more than a simple brawl in which stone-throwing and flights of arrows follow a fist fight. In *Helen*, the memory of the glory formerly won before Troy and the appeals to the victors of Ilium[96] cannot efface the unequal character of a battle which sets unarmed Barbarians against Greeks who carry their swords concealed beneath their garments.

But what of the combat that opens *Iphigenia in Tauris*, and contrasts Greek valour (Orestes and Pylades) with the Barbarian horde (people from round about, rushed up in a crowd)? Is it not tempting to interpret this as a repetition of Thermopylae and a glaring demonstration of Barbarian cowardice?[97] For, despite their numbers, the Barbarians at first remain 'silently clustered together, awaiting death' (l. 295), do not attack until they have seen Orestes fall (ll. 308–10) and 'fall back at the sight of the two naked swords' (l. 323ff.), whereas the Greeks exhort each other to die gloriously (l. 321ff.). But the account is too ironic and over-reminiscent of the madness of Ajax (with an Orestes who slaughters the flocks that he takes for enemies)[98] and even more of the fight which, at the end of *Andromache*, sets Neoptolemus against the Delphians assembled by Orestes (with the same reaction, on the part of the assailants, who flee before the naked sword of the hero)[99] to allow such an interpretation.

The case of *Orestes* is even more significant, because the superiority of the Greeks over the Barbarians is proclaimed in a much more insistent manner and because the context shows much more forcefully the derisory nature of this claim.

In this tragedy, the Greeks on several occasions emphasise the gulf that separates them from the Barbarians. Pylades proudly states that he could fear no Phrygian (in this instance the 'Barbarian servants' (ll. 1110–12) who wait on Helen), for 'the race of slaves is nothing by comparison with the free' (l. 1115) and 'the Phrygians are all cowards' (l. 1447). Electra too contrasts 'the cowardly Phrygians' with Orestes and Pylades, who are 'real men' (l. 1351). The appearance of the Phrygian slave[100] happens at just the right moment to confirm these statements.

---

[96] *Helen*, ll. 1393–5, 1603ff.
[97] Ll. 301–6.
[98] Ll. 293–300.
[99] *Andromache*, ll. 1140–6.
[100] On the entire scene, see the good analysis of C. Wolff, 'Orestes', in *Euripides: A Collection of Critical Essays*, ed. E. Segal, Englewood Cliffs, 1968, pp. 132–49 (pp. 137–42); K. Synodinou, pp. 46–50; and chiefly B. Seidensticker, '*Palintonos Harmonia*: Studien zu

His headlong flight and the terror by which the Phrygians have been struck by the arrival of Orestes and Pylades are indeed stressed.[101] But the contrast thus established between Greek valour and Phrygian cowardice is revealed as grotesque right from the start by the juxtaposition of the 'Argive sword' and the 'Barbarian babouches' (l. 1369ff.). And Euripides' irony bursts out in a gigantic monologue, with this portrait of a larger-than-life Barbarian – who himself draws the spectators' attention to the typically Barbarian nature of his flight (l. 1374: βαρβάροις δρασμοῖς) or his cries (l. 1385: βαρβάρῳ βοᾷ) – and a perfectly caricatured picture of Greek heroism. For, after all, it is only an attempted murder, in which two desperadoes, armed with a sword that they have concealed in their clothing, attack a woman surrounded by eunuchs (l. 1528) whose only weapons are their mirrors and fans (ll. 1112, 1426–30). And the 'prudent calm' (l. 1407) manifested by Orestes and Pylades here is merely another name for treacherous guile: they begin by feigning powerlessness and adopt the suppliant's traditional posture (ll. 1408–15) the better to deceive their victim. We must not allow ourselves to be deluded by the brilliance of an epic style which transforms this trick into a heroic exploit by comparing Orestes and Pylades to noble predatory animals or likening them to the heroes of the Trojan war. For Euripides is careful to couple the traditional references to 'twin lions' (l. 1401) or 'wild boar of the mountains' (l. 1459) with a comparison that throws into relief the madness of the aggressors and the impotence of the victim (the two young men are in fact likened to 'Bacchants (lacking only the thyrsus) falling upon a young mountain animal', l. 1492ff.). Although he compares Pylades to heroes renowned for their valour, such as 'Ajax with the triple-crested helmet' or the 'Phrygian Hector'[102] (the Achaeans do not have a monopoly of courage!), he also likens that 'perfidious' being (l. 1403) to Odysseus, the man who absolutely typifies the 'silent false-hearted rogue' (l. 1404). In this context, lines ll. 1483–5, 'Then indeed the Phrygians showed clearly how inferior we are to the Greek spear (ἥσσονες Ἑλλάδος ... αἰχμᾶς) when it comes to martial prowess (ἀλκάν)', ring out like a parody of the customary clichés of the Persian Wars. The 'Greek spear', which has no business here since the two heroes are both armed with a sword, reminds us of the contrast which Aeschylus' *Persians* made between Persian bow and

---

komischen Elementen in der griechischen Tragödie', *Hypomnemata*, 72, Göttingen, 1982, pp. 103–14.

[101] Ll. 1369–79, 1418, 1425, 1500.

[102] Ll. 1478–80.

Greek spear (ll. 146–9), and the Barbarians' inferiority from the point of view of courage, implicitly compared with their superiority in numbers and riches, constantly crops up in the descriptions of the combats that had set a handful of Greeks against the hordes of the Persian empire.[103]

Once in Orestes' presence, the Phrygian slave displays his spinelessness to the full; he throws himself at Orestes' feet, going along with him completely and affirming that Helen fully deserves to die, trembles at the sight of a sword and shows himself ready to do anything at all to save a life that in his eyes is the greatest possession (ll. 1506–27). But he is never anything but a grotesque caricature of Orestes,[104] which prevents one from interpreting this scene as a demonstration of Barbarian cowardice. If the Phrygian slave gains the hero's approval when he proclaims his love of life and its sweetness (ll. 1509, 1523), it is first of all because he is echoing him: did not Orestes state, before Menelaus, that his life was the dearest of his possessions (l. 644ff.) and that the search for one's own wellbeing was the aim of everyone (l. 679)?[105] If he tries to please Orestes by embellishing the remarks made by him,[106] has not Orestes resorted earlier to 'flattery' (θωπείᾳ, l. 670), even if he denies it? Did he not recall Menelaus' love for Helen, and implore him in Helen's name (ll. 669–71)? The Phrygian slave prostrates himself before Orestes, but had not that same Orestes crouched humbly in front of Helen and clasped imploring hands around her knees (ll. 1408–15)? And had he not beforehand entreated Menelaus (ll. 671–3)? From the point of view of cravenness, there is therefore nothing to choose between the Greek Orestes and the Phrygian slave.

If the Barbarians were renowned for their cowardice, their women were thought to be dangerous because of their magic practices. In *Andromache*, Hermione does not miss the chance to remind us that the women of the continent are clever in this field (l. 159ff.) and know how to make a woman barren or loathsome to her husband by means of 'secret potions' (l. 32).[107] But this accusation is purely gratuitous, and Andromache does not hesitate to refute it

---

[103] See for example on Marathon, Plato, *Menexenus*, 240d: 'They taught that neither numbers nor wealth fail to yield to valour.'

[104] Cf. C. Wolff, *loc. cit.*, p. 137; K. Synodinou, p. 49; F. Zeitlin, 'The closet of masks: role-playing and myth-making in the *Orestes* of Euripides', *Ramus*, 9, 1980, pp. 51–77 (p. 63); B. Seidensticker, *op. cit.*, p. 112.

[105] See also *Orestes*, ll. 1173–6.

[106] In line 1512, Orestes spoke of the 'just death' (ἐνδίκως) of Helen; the Phrygian slave, though, speaks of a 'very just' death (ἐνδικώτατ᾽, l. 1513).

[107] See also *Andromache*, ll. 157ff.

vigorously in lines 355–60. Hermione can blame only herself if she does not possess the potion to charm her husband (ll. 205–8). The only known appearance of love potions in Euripides' plays is in *Hippolytus*, and it is Phaedra's *Greek* nurse who resorts to them.[108] As for the potions (φάρμακον) used by Barbarians like Medea or Dionysus, they on the contrary are able to end the barrenness of Aegeus[109] or make men forget their troubles.[110] As for poisons, the Greeks have them just as much as the Barbarians, and the Athenian Creusa[111] has no cause to envy the Colchian Medea[112] in the matter of 'effective poisons' (*Ion*, l. 1185).

Lastly, what about the intelligence which, if we are to believe Herodotus,[113] had distinguished Greeks from Barbarians since time immemorial? In Euripides' plays, this opinion is expressed only by Pentheus, who, in the *Bacchae*, maintains, against Dionysus, that 'the Barbarians are much more stupid than the Greeks' (l. 483). But this judgement is immediately challenged by the god (l. 484), and discredited by the entirety of a tragedy which on several occasions emphasises the stupidity and ignorance of Pentheus,[114] and is careful not to favour any definition of wisdom, even less to admit that it is the exclusive possession of the Greeks.[115]

In general, the Greeks often contrasted a Barbarian universe, one that was still close to a state of animality, with a truly civilised Greek world. It would be easy to ascribe such ideas to Euripides, starting with a collage of quotations borrowed from his tragedies. One could then, with his Jason, make a distinction between a Greece that knows about justice (δίκη) and has recourse to the law (νόμοις χρῆσθαι) and a Barbarian land that obeys only force (*Med.*, ll. 536–8). With Odysseus, one could contrast the Greeks, who know how to be grateful for services rendered and honour their dead, with Barbarians, who behave without gratitude (*Hec.*, l. 328ff.). With Agamemnon,

---

[108] *Hippolytus*, ll. 479, 516, 699.

[109] *Medea*, ll. 717ff.

[110] *Bacchae*, l. 283.

[111] *Ion*, ll. 845, 1185, 1221, 1286.

[112] *Medea*, ll. 385, 709, 806, 1126, 1201. B. M. W. Knox, 'The *Medea* of Euripides', YCS, 25, 1977, pp. 193–225 (henceforth 1977), showed very well (p. 213ff.) how Euripides, far from emphasising Medea's Barbarian magic, on the contrary relegates this aspect to a secondary position; he says nothing of the marvellous rejuvenation of Aeson, nor does he make any mention of magic in the context of the death of Pelias, to whom he fleetingly alludes in lines 486–7.

[113] I, 60.

[114] Pentheus has been reproved for his ignorance and madness by Tiresias (ll. 312, 326, 359) and Cadmus (l. 332). He has just been treated as ignorant by Dionysus (l. 480). See the excellent remarks on this point by K. Synodinou, p. 53.

[115] *Bacchae*, ll. 395, 877.

one could point to Barbarians, who find it easy to kill their guests and Greeks for whom it is infamy (*Hec.*, l. 1247ff.). Above all, one would denounce the disregard of the Barbarians for the closest family bonds; recalling Jason's horrified cry at Medea's infanticide 'No Greek woman would have dared to do this' (*Med.*, l. 1339) and Hermione's scandalised words when faced with the customs current among Barbarians, 'Father couples with daughter, son with mother, sister with brother; the closest relatives kill one another and no law prevents it' (*And.*, ll. 173–6).

But this anti-Barbarian talk, whose spokesmen are very suspect, is always invalidated by the context.

This is obvious in *Andromache*; for it is hard to see how, logically, the immorality of the Barbarians can be inferred from the example of the heroine, who is a slave and has only against her will shared the bed of the son of her husband's murderer. And Hermione, who is a member of a house whose members have killed one another ceaselessly for several generations, seems ill-qualified to speak in this way.[116]

It is just as true in *Hecuba*.[117] For the Greek who waxes indignant about 'guest-killing' (ξενοκτονεῖν, l. 1247) is an army leader who has 'cut a human being's throat' (ἀνθρωποσφαγεῖν, l. 260)[118] and sacrificed Polyxena on Achilles' tomb. And in Odysseus' mouth, honours rendered to the dead are nothing but a sophistic argument to justify the unjustifiable.

Euripides' irony is equally plain in *Medea*.[119] Indeed, it would seem difficult to believe in a Greece that is the chosen land of law and justice when this eulogy is put in the mouth of Jason; in other words, a character who has himself 'violated the laws' (ἀνόμως, l. 1000) and treated Medea in a manner contrary to all justice.[120] And it is perfectly impossible to accept that infanticide is a Barbarian speciality in a tragedy that recalls the story of Ino[121] and puts on stage a Medea who, despite her Barbarian origin, conforms on all counts to the Greek heroic ideal.[122]

---

[116] K. Synodinou, p. 51.

[117] K. Synodinou, p. 52ff.

[118] The fact that these two verbs appear in Euripides only in *Hecuba* makes the comparison even more striking.

[119] Cf. P. E. Easterling, 'The infanticide in Euripides' *Medea*', YCS, 25, 1977, pp. 177–91 (p. 191); K. Synodinou, p. 45; C. Nancy, 'Euripide et le parti des femmes', p. 85.

[120] *Medea*, ll. 26ff., 314, 411, 578, 582, etc.

[121] Ll. 1282–9.

[122] On this point see the convincing demonstration by B. M. W. Knox, 1977, pp. 211–18, and P. E. Easterling, *loc. cit.*, pp. 180, 191.

But what are we to think of *Iphigenia in Tauris*? In this land where 'a Barbarian reigns over Barbarians' (l. 31), a cruel law exists which demands that the priestess of Artemis shall put to death all Greeks who land in these parts (l. 38ff.). Now, Euripides places this custom at the heart of his plot; he even embodies it physically, with an altar 'dripping with the blood of Greeks' and 'human trophies on the cornices' (ll. 72–5), and seems to cast responsibility for this on the natives rather than on the gods: 'I believe', says Iphigenia, 'that the people of this country, being themselves the killers of men, have ascribed to the goddess their own sin' (l. 389ff.). Everything therefore seems set to make the tragedy an illustration of Barbarian savagery.[123] But that would be to overlook Euripides' irony.[124] For the play's ending establishes unequivocally that the ritual had certainly been demanded by Artemis, since the memory of it would persist in the worship the Greeks would render to this deity.[125] And the whole tragedy continually invites us to parallel the crimes of the Taurians with those of the Greeks and to come down on the side of the former. For the Barbarians content themselves, if one can so express it, with sacrificing foreigners. The Greeks, however, go as far as to sacrifice members of their own families. Euripides never lets us forget this fact. On several occasions[126] he reminds us that in Aulis Agamemnon would have cut his daughter's throat, had the goddess not intervened. He also recalls the crimes that had preceded this sacrifice – the reminder of the feast of Tantalus, who offered the gods his son's flesh, counterbalances the denunciation of the Taurians' bloodthirsty instincts (ll. 386–90), and the series of killings brought about by the appearance of the golden lamb has a prominent place in the *parodos* [opening chorus] (ll. 195–201) – and those that had followed: Agamemnon himself has his throat cut by his wife (l. 552), and she, in her turn, dies at her son's hand (l. 556). This Greek matricide provokes an indignant exclamation even from the Barbarian Thoas: 'No one, even among the Barbarians, would have had such audacity' (l. 1174),[127] which makes an ironic counterpart to the Greek Jason's

---

[123] At all events, this is the interpretation proposed by R. Goossens, p. 581.

[124] This irony was also recognised by D. Sansone, 'The sacrifice motif in Euripides' *Iphigenia in Tauris*', *TAPA*, 105, 1975, pp. 283–95; K. Synodinou, p. 51; and H. Foley, *Ritual Irony…*, p. 58.

[125] Ll. 1458–61.

[126] Ll. 6–27, 177, 211ff., 339, 360, 770, etc.

[127] D. Sansone, *loc. cit.*, rightly compares these lines with a passage in the *Histories* in which the Persians 'maintain that no one as yet has killed either his father or mother, and that, in cases where there had apparently been such a crime, an inquiry would inevitably discover that the offspring were in fact not theirs or the product of adultery; for, they say, it is abnormal … that real parents should die at the hand of their son' (I. 137)

outburst at the infanticide committed by the Barbarian Medea. All
in all, the tragedy testifies less to Barbarian cruelty than to Greek
treachery, as the (Greek) heroine ironically recognises, at the very
moment when she is lying to the Barbarian Thoas: 'Greece knows
nothing of trustworthiness' (πιστὸν Ἑλλὰς οἶδεν οὐδέν, l. 1205).
We are a long way from the Persian Wars and the times when
Spartans could state as an unchallengeable truth that 'there is neither
trustworthiness nor truth among the Barbarians' (ὡς βαρβάροισί
ἐστι οὔτε πιστὸν οὔτε ἀληθὲς οὐδέν, Herodotus, VIII, 142).

So Euripides is no prisoner of the myth of Greek superiority. Far
from contrasting Greek νομός [law or custom] with Barbarian
ἀνομία [lawlessness], he merely notes the differences in customs in
matters of matrimonial practices,[128] sacrifice[129] and supplication.[130]
But he also stresses, especially in *Andromache*,[131] the universality of
certain rules, for 'over there [among the Barbarians] as here [among
the Greeks] shame dishonours' (l. 244) and the victims retaliate
(l. 438).

At the same time, he can completely disassociate the two aspects
of the notion of a Barbarian that most Greeks had a tendency
to confuse, that is, its use as an ethnic designation and its use as a
pejorative value term.[132]

4 THE BARBARISM OF THE GREEKS

'Barbarian' in fact acquires a purely moral connotation when it
describes the heart, as in *Hecuba* (l. 1129) or the mind, as in *Helen*
(l. 501). Certainly, it is applied then by Greeks to more or less
precisely designated Barbarians. In *Hecuba*, it is Agamemnon
exhorting Polymestor, who wants to get hold of those females who
have just blinded him and killed his children to 'feast on their flesh
and bones' (ll. 1071–2), 'to drive barbarism from his heart' (l. 1129).

---

[128] *Andromache*, ll. 215–18: Thracian polygamy is contrasted with Greek monogamy.
[129] *Helen*, ll. 1255–8; it is a Barbarian custom (ἐν βαρβάροις ... νόμος) to sacrifice a horse
or a bull to the dead.
[130] *Helen*, ll. 799–801: Menelaus asks Helen whether 'according to Barbarian custom'
(νόμοοσι βαρβάροις) a tomb can serve as a place of asylum for suppliants, in the same way as
an altar in Greece.
[131] On the central importance, in this tragedy, of the Greek/Barbarian antithesis, here
merged with the master/slave contrast, see K. Synodinou, pp. 55–8.
[132] On the semantic evolution of the term βάρβαρος, see F. Skoda, *loc. cit.*, *passim*, which
ends thus: 'Pure onomatopoeia originally, during the course of history it became a geographic
and ethnic denomination. Historical, political and economic circumstances helped to load it
with pejorative values. From then on, the word was used to express a very derogatory moral
or intellectual judgement' (p. 124).

In *Helen*, Menelaus condemns in advance a man with 'such a Barbarian mind' (l. 501) and so ignorant of the laws of hospitality that he can refuse food to a hero of the Trojan war.

But βάρβαρος can just as easily be used to denounce the behaviour of the Greeks. Thus in the *Heracleidae*, the Argive herald who, scorning the gods,[133] tries to snatch the Heracleidae away from the altars where they have taken refuge and 'do them violence'[134] finds himself reproached, despite his clearly 'Greek' costume (ll. 130–1), for his 'Barbarian deeds' (l. 131) by the king of Athens, Demophon.[135] To understand just how unheard-of such a reproach could be, here coming from a Greek, this scene must be compared with the one that has obviously been used as a model, namely, the episode in Aeschylus' *Suppliants* in which a herald who is as 'impious' as his masters[136] 'does violence'[137] to the Danaids and tries to drag them away from the altars where they too have taken refuge. For in the *Suppliants*, the herald is a Barbarian, characterised as such by the colour of his skin, as the text emphasises several times.[138] And the entire episode, which strongly foregrounds the Barbarian/Greek antithesis by contrasting κάρβανος 'Barbarian' with Ἕλλησι (Greek) (l. 914), 'the fruit of the papyrus' with 'the ear of corn' (l. 765), beer with wine (l. 952ff.), invites us to ascribe the *hybris* to the Barbarians, and to them alone.

Paradoxically, however, we find, in Euripides' plays, at least one Barbarian woman who denounces the barbarity of Greeks who have decided 'to put an innocent child to death' (*Tro.*, l. 765) and to invite them to 'feed on its flesh' (l. 775). (We thus find, for the purposes of denouncing Greek savagery, the very picture which, in *Hecuba*, emphasises the animal quality of the Barbarian Polymestor.) Andromache's indignant cry in the *Trojan Women*: 'O Greeks, inventors of barbarous tortures' (Ὦ βάρβαρ' ἐξευρόντες Ἕλληνες κακά) (l. 764) clearly shows the gap between Euripides' world and the time of the Persian Wars, when Pausanias, urged to have the head of the Persian Mardonius impaled and thus render 'like for like' (Τὴν ὁμοίην ἀποδιδούς, Herodotus, IX, 78) to those who had had the head of Leonidas at Thermopylae cut off and placed on a stake (*ibid.*), had

---

[133] Ll. 70–2, 78ff., 101–3, 112ff.
[134] Ll. 59–72, 79, 102, 106, 112, 127.
[135] On this passage, see K. Synodinou, p. 54.
[136] Ll. 750–9, 762ff., 872, 893ff., 908, 921–3, 927.
[137] Ll. 812, 821, 830ff., 943. See also ll. 835–41: 'Go then! Make for the ship, as fast as your legs can carry you! Or we shall see hair torn, yes, torn from sword–pierced bodies, decapitated heads, flowing with the blood of the massacre.'
[138] Ll. 719ff., 745, 888.

rejected in horror this 'proposal that is impious to the highest degree' (ἀνοσιώτατον λόγον), saying: 'Such conduct is more suitable to Barbarians than to Greeks' (IX, 79). It is understandable that, in reference to this passage from the *Trojan Women*, scholars could have spoken of a 'breaking down of the image the Greeks had of themselves',[139] since at that time they cease to identify themselves with law and right. It would seem that, in Euripides' view at least, the gulf separating Greek civilisation from Barbarian savagery at the time of the Persian Wars no longer had any *raison d'être* in a period when Greeks were competing in cruelty in the Peloponnesian War.

Was there still a real ethnic and geographical boundary between Greeks and Barbarians? Reading the last works of Euripides, the *Phoenician Women* and the *Bacchae*, one may well doubt it.

In the *Phoenician Women*, Euripides deliberately blurs the frontiers that Aeschylus had so firmly mapped out in the *Seven against Thebes*. This tragedy in fact contrasted the inside and the outside, the Greeks and the Barbarians. Within, there is a city that 'speaks the language of Greece' (Ἑλλάδος φθόγγον χέουσιν, l. 73)[140] and a chorus of Theban woman. Without, there are warriors characterised by their transgressiveness (*hybris*) and their boastfulness (κόμπος),[141] who, despite their incontestably Greek origins,[142] possess all the traits of a Barbarian: they 'speak another language' (ἑτεροφώνῳ στρατῷ, l. 170) and their mares 'whinny in Barbarian fashion' (l. 463), as if the invaders were Persian,[143] for the godless people[144] who want ignominiously to destroy a Greek city could be nothing other than Barbarians. On the other hand, in the *Phoenician Women*, there are Greeks and Barbarians in both camps. The second part of the prologue, which imitates the *teichoskopia* [lit. 'looking from the walls'] of Book III of the *Iliad*, in fact invites us to liken the Argive

---

[139] Cf. W. Beringer, *Studien zum Bild vom Unfreien Menschen in der Griechischen Literatur*, Diss. Tubingen, 1956, p. 203, quoted by K. Synodinou, p. 55.

[140] This insistence on a linguistic fact which seems self-evident appeared so strange that it was proposed to atheticise [set aside] this line; cf. R. D. Dawe, *The Collation and Investigation of Manuscripts of Aeschylus*, Cambridge, 1964, p. 180ff. He was followed by D. Page, *Aeschyli Septem quae supersunt Tragoediae*, Oxford, 1972, and L. Lupas–Z. Petre, *Commentaire aux Sept contre Thèbes d'Eschyle*, Paris, 1981, p. 38, despite the criticisms of H. Lloyd-Jones, *CR*, 16, 1966, p. 20ff.

[141] On the hybris and the κόμπος [boastfulness] which characterise the Argive aggressors (with the sole exception of Amphiaraus), see S. Saïd, *La Faute Tragique*, Paris, 1978, pp. 351–5.

[142] They are called 'Achaeans' (ll. 28, 324) or 'Argives' (ll. 59, 118, 679).

[143] As J. T. Sheppard clearly saw, 'The plot of the *Septem contra Thebas*', *CQ*, 7, 1913, pp. 73–82; W. Kranz, *op. cit.*, p. 79; F. Solmsen, 'The Erinys in Aischylos' *Septem*', *TAPA*, 68, 1937, pp. 197–211 (p. 208), etc.

[144] On the impiousness of the Argives in the *Seven*, see S. Saïd, *loc. cit.*, n. 141.

aggressors to the leaders of the Achaean army at Troy. But it also points out, in their midst, the presence of a semi-Barbarian Aetolian (μειξοβάρβαρος, l. 138) armed with mixed weapons,[145] who is however united with the Theban Polynices by the closest of family links.[146] Conversely, Euripides sets a chorus of Barbarians in the very heart of Thebes, in front of the royal palace, and in their first words they recall that they 'left the Tyrian sea ... and abandoned the Phoenician island' (ll. 202–4). And on several occasions he stresses their 'barbarian' character[147] and 'Phoenician'[148] origin. The meaning of this innovation by Euripides has been interpreted in various ways (the chorus of the *Seven against Thebes* consisted of Theban women). Was it motivated merely by a taste for exoticism?[149] By a concern to keep an equal balance between the two brothers by means of a chorus less dependent on Eteocles and less engaged in the action?[150] Probably. But also, and perhaps chiefly, by a desire to show the links connecting Thebes with Phoenicia,[151] to recall the oriental origin of its founder Cadmus and to give substance to a Barbarian past to which the lyric sections constantly refer.[152]

Certainly, Euripides was neither the first nor the only author to point out the link uniting Thebes with Cadmus: Homer, although mentioning Cadmus only once,[153] had already given the inhabitants of Thebes the name 'Cadmeans' (Καδμεῖοι[154] or Καδμείωνες),[155] and the tragedies of Aeschylus and Sophocles, to name only those two, constantly speak of 'the city of Cadmus' and 'Cadmeans'.[156]

[145] If his 'shield' (σακεσφόρος, l. 139) is like those of the other Argive leaders (cf. ll. 1107, 1114: σάκος) and makes him a Greek, his skill with the bow (ἀκοντιστῆρες, l. 140), by contrast marks him as a Barbarian.

[146] The text insists curiously on the fact that Tydeus made the same marriage as Polynices, for the two men married two sisters born of the same father: οὗτος ὁ τᾶς Πολυνείκεος ... αὐτοκασιγνήτας νύμφας ὁμόγαμος (ll. 135–7).

[147] Ll. 679ff., 819, 1301.

[148] Ll. 280, 301.

[149] J. de Romilly, 'Les *Phéniciennes* d'Euripide et l'actualité dans la tragédie grecque', *RPh*, 39, 1965, pp. 28–47 (p. 32).

[150] *Ibid*. It was already the opinion of the scholiast [ancient commentator] on line 202 of the *Phoenicians*.

[151] Cf. E. Rawson, 'Family and fatherland in Euripides' *Phoenissae*', *GRBS*, 11, 1970, pp. 109–27 (p. 112).

[152] Cf. M. Arthur, 'The curse of civilization: the choral odes of the *Phoenissae*', *HSCP*, 81, 1977, pp. 163–85.

[153] *Od.*, 5, 333.

[154] *Il.*, 4, 388, 391; 5, 807; 10, 288; *Od.*, 11, 276.

[155] *Il.*, 4, 385; 5, 804; 23, 680.

[156] In Aeschylus, the *Greek* city of Thebes and its inhabitants are always designated by expressions marking the link uniting them to Cadmus (see *Index Aeschyleus*, under Καδμεῖος, Καδμογενής, Κάδμος). By contrast, Sophocles speaks as much of 'Thebes' (Θήβη or Θῆβαι) as of the city of Cadmus and the Cadmeans (see *Lexicon Sophocleum*, under Καδμεῖος, Καδμογενής, Κάδμος).

But Euripides is the only tragedian and one of the earliest writers to mention 'Cadmus the Tyrian' (*Phoen.*, l. 638ff.). The question of Cadmus' eastern origin – the echo of a historical reality according to some, pure 'mirage'[157] according to others – has long been debated by the moderns, from K. O. Müller to R. B. Edwards.[158] What is certain is that, in the extant texts, the Phoenician Cadmus (unlike his sister Europa)[159] does not appear explicitly until the fifth century, with Herodotus.[160] Even in Euripides, with the exception of the *Phoenician Women* and the *Bacchae*, it is rare to find an allusion to his Barbarian ancestry.[161] The place occupied by this subject in the *Phoenician Women* is thus all the more significant.

For Euripides is not content just to mention in passing 'Cadmus the Tyrian' (l. 638ff.) and refer in the prologue to the day when he arrived in Thebes 'after leaving the maritime land of Phoenicia' (l. 6). He emphasises the bond that continues to unite the royal house of Thebes and the whole city to the Barbarian universe, by means of

---

[157] Cf. F. Vian, *Les origines de Thèbes: Cadmos et les Spartes*, Paris, 1963, p. 52.

[158] A good review of this debate, from the first query about the Phoenician origin of Cadmus by K. O. Müller, 'Orchomenos und die Minyer', *Geschichte hellenischer Stämme and Städte*, Breslau, 1820, right up to 1979, in R. B. Edwards, *Kadmos the Phoenician: A Study in Greek Legends and the Mycenaean Age*, Ch. III, 'The Phoenician origin of Cadmos in the ancient tradition and in modern scholarship', Amsterdam, 1979, pp. 50–64.

[159] From the time of Homer, Europa was the daughter of Phoenix (*Il.*, 14, 321), 'which proves nothing since the epic knew another Phoenix, purely Greek' – cf. F. Vian, *op. cit.*, p. 56, after A. Gomme, 'The legend of Cadmos and the *logographi*', *JHS*, 33, 1913, pp. 53–72, 223–45 (p. 54ff.). But the *Catalogue of Women*, which resumes this genealogy (frgt 140 M.W.), had a Phoenix indisputably linked to the East, since he was the father of Adonis (frgt 139 M.W.) and husband of a daughter of Arabus (frgt 137, 138 M.W); cf. F. Vian, *op. cit.*, p. 56ff., and R. B. Edwards, *op. cit.*, pp. 67–9. Certainly, these texts do not mention the kinship of Europa and Cadmus. But the presence in the *Europeia* of Stesichorus of an allusion to Cadmus (schol. to Euripides, *Phoenician Women*, l. 670) seems to establish the existence of a connection between these two characters in archaic lyric poetry; cf. F. Vian, *op. cit.*, p. 57.

[160] Herodotus, II, 49, speaks of Cadmus the Tyrian and mentions his Phoenician origins in IV, 147, and V, 57–61. The same applies to Europa (I, 2; II, 44; IV, 45). But as F. Vian rightly stresses, *op. cit.*, p. 56, 'Herodotus is certainly not the initiator of this transformation: his *Histories* testify that the legend was already widespread.' On the other hand, it must be noted that Bacchylides, XIX, 39–48 Snell, links Cadmus to Io and Egypt and seems to know the Phoenician genealogy of Io, whom he calls νύμφα φοίνισσα [Phoenician maiden] (XVII, 53 Snell). But one can also understand 'daughter of Phoinix'. Pherecydes of Athens, *FGrHist* I A 3, frgt 21, 86, 87, also established, in his genealogy, a connection between Cadmus and Egypt (his mother was the daughter of Neilos) and, more indirectly, Phoenicia (he is the half-brother of Phoinix). The case is more doubtful concerning Hellanicus, *FGrHist*, I A 4, frgt 1, 23, 41, 96, and still more Hecataeus (R. B. Edwards, *op. cit.*, p. 70: 'No fragment of Hecateus is preserved which mentions either Kadmos or Europe'). On the place occupied by Cadmus' eastern origins among the *logographi*, see A. Gomme, *loc. cit.*, and the discussion by F. Vian, *op. cit.*, pp. 21–5, and R. B. Edwards, *op. cit.*, pp. 69–73.

[161] One can only quote the prologue of the *Phrixos* (fr. 819 N₂) which mentions 'the day when Cadmus left the city of Sidon for Theban territory'. However, it must be added that, in the *Cretans* (fr. 472 N₂) the Phoenician origin of Europa is recalled and that a fragment of the *Hypsipyle* (I, III, 20 Bond) recounts the story of Europa, the young Tyrian girl who left the city and her paternal house of Phoenicia.

a chorus that hails Polynices as a 'relative' (l. 290), reminds us that the Thebans and Phoenicians belong to the same race (they are ὁμογενεῖς, l. 218) and stresses that Thebes' calamities are shared by the Phoenician land (ll. 243–6). This link goes back to Agenor,[162] the father of the eponymous heroes of the Cadmeans and Phoenicians, but also, further back still, to Io and her son Epaphus.[163] On this point, comparison with Aeschylus has much to teach us. For Io and Epaphus, who, like Agenor, are missing from the *Seven against Thebes*, occupy an important place in the *Suppliants*. But in this tragedy, Aeschylus' theme is the opposite of Euripides'. In fact, in the *Phoenician Women*, the evocation of the 'horned ancestor' (l. 828), whose Argive origin is never mentioned, enables the Cadmeans and Phoenicians to form a close bond, for they are equally the children of Io, and the same blood flows in their veins (κοινὸν αἷμα, κοινὰ τέκεα τᾶς κερασφόρου πέφυκεν Ἰοῦς, l. 247ff.). By contrast, in the *Suppliants*, the Danaids, who, like the Phoenicians, come from Asia (they have 'left the land of Zeus that borders on the Syrian country' (l. 5ff.) and have an appearance that is as un-Greek as possible),[164] hark back to the fertile heifer which was formerly the guardian of the temple of Hera in the Argolid (l. 291ff.) to establish their Argive breeding,[165] despite appearances, and lead Pelasgus to recognise, at the very least,[166] that they have ancient connections with this country (δοκεῖτέ (τοι) μοι τῆσδε κοινωνεῖν χθονὸς τἀρχαῖον, l. 325ff.).

Euripides, who thus gives an exceptional prominence to the link that binds Cadmus and the Cadmeans to Phoenicia, also weaves a very close relationship between Cadmus and his city. In the *Seven*, Cadmus was in fact merely the 'eponymous' hero (l. 135) of the Cadmeans. The *Phoenician Women* recalls explicitly that he had 'colonised' (κτίζειν, l. 135) the country and 'organised its population into a city' (κατοικίζειν, l. 643)[167] and makes the history and misfortunes of Thebes begin with Cadmus.[168] In this tragedy, a very close bond indeed unites the present to the most distant past, and it is doubtless the central purpose of the episode of Tiresias and, still more, the lyric passages (which are not as removed from the main

---

[162] Ll. 217, 281, 291.

[163] Ll. 246–9, 676–82, 828ff.

[164] They differ from the Greeks by their physical appearance (ll. 496–8) and the colour of their skin (ll. 154–6) as well as their costume (ll. 120ff. [= 131ff.], 134, 234–7, 279–91).

[165] Ll. 41–55, 274–323.

[166] On the restrictive value of Pelasgus' reply, see H. Friis Johansen–E. W. Whittle, *Aeschylus: The Suppliants*, Copenhagen, 1980, on l. 325ff., II, p. 261.

[167] On the sense of κτίζειν and κατοικίζειν in these two passages, see M. Casevitz, *Le vocabulaire de la colonisation en grec ancien*, Paris, 1985, pp. 35 and 171.

[168] Cf. ll. 1–6.

action as scholiasts,[169] and the majority of modern scholars[170] in their wake, have believed) to show this clearly.

For, according to Tiresias, the sacrifice of Menoeceus is a direct outcome of the 'ancient resentment conceived *against Cadmus* by Ares, who avenges the slaying of the dragon' (ll. 931–5).[171] The soothsayer's words even suggest the existence of a more complex connection between the fate of Menoeceus and the deeds of the founder of Thebes: the death of the 'child sprung from the dragon's jaws' (l. 941) – Menoeceus is in fact descended from the Spartoi ('Sown men'), those warriors born of the dragon's teeth that Cadmus threw into the ground[172] – also represents the compensation demanded by the earth for the harvest that had formerly been destroyed (ll. 937–40) and the blood spilled by the Spartoi when they killed one another.[173]

More indirectly, the second *stasimon* [choral song] suggests that the war which caused the death of Menoeceus was also the consequence of Ares' intervention (thus of his anger regarding Cadmus and his descendants). For it is Ares who has 'breathed' (ἐπιπνεύσας) the same homicidal madness into the Argive army (l. 789) and the race of the Spartoi (l. 794).

Going further back into the past, we discover that the arrival of the Sphinx, the episode that haunts the whole tragedy[174] and seems to rule the destiny of Oedipus and his house,[175] is closely connected with the slaying of the dragon, thus with Cadmus: first of all by the ὅθεν [whence] which in line 1065 establishes a relationship of cause and effect between the throwing of the stone that makes the dragon's blood flow and the divine calamity that befalls Thebes with the ravening monster; but also by details which show the continuity that exists between these twin menaces, both sited near to the fountain of Dirce.[176] Lastly, by echoes that invite us to parallel Ares and the

---

[169] Cf. schol. to the *Phoenician Women*, ll. 1019, 1053, and schol. to Aristophanes, *Acharnians*, l. 442.

[170] See for example W. Kranz, *op. cit.*, p. 251, and V. di Benedetto, *op. cit.*, pp. 254–6, 269ff.

[171] This murder has been mentioned in lines 657–665, and the text emphasises in lines 931–3, 1010ff., 1312, that the death of Menoeceus occurs at the place where the dragon had been killed by Cadmus.

[172] Cf. ll. 666–72.

[173] Ll. 672–5.

[174] It is mentioned already in the prologue (ll. 45–54), resumed in the second *stasimon* (ll. 801–11) and above all in the third (Str. 1: arrival of the Sphinx; Ant. 1: arrival of Oedipus, ll. 1018–54) and mentioned several times in the *exodos* [end, lit. 'going out'] (ll. 1352–5, 1505–7, 1728–31).

[175] It brought about Oedipus' incest (ll. 49, 1047–50) and appears as the true cause of the death of Jocasta and her children (ll. 1352ff., 1505–7).

[176] Cf. ll. 659ff. (the dragon), 1026ff. (the Sphinx). This parallelism has been pointed out by M. Arthur, *loc. cit.*, p. 179ff.

Sphinx, a god and a monster both equally 'bloody' (φόνιος, l. 1031)[177] and discordant: the 'most inharmonious revel' (l. 791) led by Ares is matched by the 'most discordant songs' (l. 808) accompanying the Sphinx.[178]

The direct cause of the main events affecting Thebes, the deed of Cadmus the Tyrian, is also the model that is endlessly reproduced by a repetitive history, one characterised entirely by 'disgrace' (ὄνειδος),[179] abduction (ἁρπαγή)[180] and 'discord' (ἔρις),[181] as if Thebes were for ever contaminated by the barbarian origin of its founder.

This presentation of Theban history in the *Phoenician Women* deserves our attention because of its unusual character. To effect it, Euripides had to distance himself from the more common versions of the legend of Cadmus and make a complete break with the Aeschylean model. In fact, as F. Vian[182] has shown, 'in versions earlier than that of Euripides, Ares finally made peace with Cadmus the moment he gave him his daughter in marriage'. In the *Seven*, Cadmus was even the eponymous hero of Thebes who earned Ares' protection of his city,[183] and the ills that befell the city and the members of the royal house were explained only by the 'ancient offence' of Laius, who had dared to disobey Apollo's oracle.[184] In the *Phoenician Women* Cadmus and Ares replace Laius and Apollo: the Barbarian seals the fate of the Cadmeans once and for all by leaving them the heritage of Ares' wrath, which is a way of saying that the Greek city,

---

[177] Cf. F. Vian, *op. cit.*, p. 209, n. 3.

[178] Cf. M. Arthur, *loc. cit.*, p. 177: 'The description of the Sphinx (Antistrophe) assimilates her to the Ares of the strophe.'

[179] The 'glorious disgrace' of the Spartans (l. 821) is followed by the 'disgrace' of the Sphinx (l. 1732), of the Mycenaean threat (l. 513), and of Oedipus' curse (l. 1555), which finally brought about the death of Jocasta and her children.

[180] It is doubtless not by chance that ἁρπαγή and ἁρπάζειν, which refer, in lines 46, 1021, 1066, to the abductions of the Sphinx, reappear in the description of the last phase of the two brothers' fight, in which they 'seize (ἁρπασάντε) the hilts of their swords' (l. 1404), and in the account of Jocasta's death when she 'snatches (ἥρπασ') a sword from the corpses' to stab herself (l. 1456).

[181] In the *Phoenician Women*, ἔρις not only refers to the 'discord' that sets the two brothers against each other (ll. 81, 798, 811, 1277, 1495) and then assails the Thebans and the Argives (ll. 1460, 1462). It also describes the 'discord' that formerly set Oedipus against his children (l. 351) and the one which, earlier, had been embodied in the Sphinx (l. 811).

[182] *Op. cit.*, p. 30. See also p. 209.

[183] L. 135: σύ τ' Ἄρης ... πόλιν ἐπώνυμον Κάδμου φύλαξον κήδεσαί τ' ἐναργῶς ['you too Ares ... guard and clearly care for the city that bears the name of Cadmus']. See also ll. 104–7.

[184] This offence is mentioned in the second *stasimon* (ll. 742–57), which connects the parricide and incest of Oedipus, as well as the bloodthirsty madness of his children, directly to Laius' disobedience. But l. 691 had already recalled that the 'entire race of Laius was hated by Phoebus'. The messenger who announces the death of the two brothers will similarly stress the decisive role of Apollo, who 'has reserved for himself the seventh gate in order to avenge the line of Oedipus for the punishment of Laius and his old errors' (ll. 800–2), while the chorus will acknowledge that the 'recalcitrance of Laius has prolonged its effects' (l. 842).

which continues to be the scene of fratricidal battles, is far from having finished with primitive barbarism.

Euripides' last tragedy is also the one that challenges most profoundly the conventional Greek/Barbarian distinction. Whereas the *Phoenician Women*, through the chorus and its songs, pointed out the kinship that united *one* Greek city, Thebes, with *one* Barbarian country, Phoenicia, the *Bacchae* did away with the idea of a boundary separating Greece and Asia, showing the gradual invasion of Thebes by a barbarism that no one could escape and establishing an incessant to-ing and fro-ing between the two continents so that in the end one no longer knows where the Greeks end and the Barbarians begin.

The beginning of the play presents the image of a Thebes peopled with emigrants. The prologue is spoken by a Dionysus who, to reach Theban territory, has had to 'leave the gold-rich fields of Lydia' (l. 13ff.). The chorus that follows him is composed of women who come from 'among the Barbarians' (l. 55)[185] and have also 'abandoned Mt Tmolos, rampart of Lydia' (l. 54). The first episode opens with Tiresias' call, which brings forth from the palace 'Cadmus, son of Agenor', who has formerly 'left the city of Sidon' (ll. 170-2).

This Barbarian east, so central to the scene, is therefore no longer confined to Phoenicia alone and Cadmus' homeland.[186] As well as Lydia, the land of Dionysus and the Bacchants,[187] it also includes Phrygia, which is the favourite setting for the rites[188] (in the *Bacchae*, Dionysiac music is completely under the sign of Phrygia, which has supplied the instruments),[189] 'the plateaux of Persia, all burnt by the sun, the walls of Bactria, the country of the Medes with its harsh winters, and fortunate Arabia' (ll. 14-16). In short, 'all Asia' (l. 17) is on parade, together with the countries crossed by Dionysus and his 'Asian Bacchants' (l. 1168),[190] and enters Greece with them. For, in the *Bacchae*, Thebes represents only the 'beginning'[191] for a god who 'will later turn his steps to another region' (l. 48ff.) and extend his cult to the whole of Greece,[192] finally making a name for himself at the very centre of Hellenism, namely Delphi.[193]

---

[185] See also ll. 604, 1034.
[186] In the *Bacchae*, Sidon (ll. 17, 1025) has replaced Tyre (*Phoenician Women*, l. 639) as Cadmus' homeland.
[187] Ll. 13, 234, 464: Dionysus; l. 55: the Bacchants.
[188] Ll. 86, 140.
[189] Ll. 58, 127, 159.
[190] See also l. 64.
[191] Ll. 20: πρῶτον; l. 23: πρώτας ... Θήβας.
[192] Ll. 86, 272-4, 309, 465.
[193] Ll. 306-9.

In the *Bacchae* the invasion of Greece by the 'Barbarian' cult of Dionysus[194] takes two forms.

It can take the form of an armed confrontation. Dionysus envisages this possibility, as early as the prologue, when he declares:

> If the city of the Thebans, yielding to anger, takes up arms to try to drive the Bacchants out of the mountains, I will fight it at the head of a band of Maenads (ξυνάψω μαινάσι στρατηλατῶν) (ll. 50–2).

In fact, in the first episode, Pentheus announces his intention of 'hunting down' the Bacchants and 'dislodging them from the mountains' to imprison them 'in nets of iron' (ll. 228–32). But in the 'hunt',[195] the quarry very quickly becomes the hunter: the Bacchants, armed only with their thyrsoi [wands] (l. 733),

> dash towards the plains that spread alongside the Asopos ... invade the villages of Hysiae and Erythrae situated at the foot of rocky Cithaeron; like enemies, they fall on the region, upset and carry off everything, snatch children from their homes (ll. 748–50).

Faced with this looting, the inhabitants 'run to take up arms' (l. 759), but are routed by the Bacchants, who make them turn tail (l. 763). Pentheus contemplates a new expedition which would mobilise against the followers of Dionysus all the military forces of Thebes, hoplites, cavalry, light infantry and archers (ll. 781–5). But Dionysus predicts another defeat and gives him a foretaste of a shocking picture, 'hoplites turning their bronze-circled shields and fleeing before the Bacchants' (ll. 798–9). This theme of Barbarian invasion, prefigured by the Bacchants' attack in the centre of the tragedy, is resumed in the conclusion. Dionysus in fact predicts a second invasion of Greece by the 'Barbarians'[196] in terms reminiscent of the Persian Wars. For in both cases it is a matter of a 'composite' horde[197] led by a monstrous chief (the Cadmus metamorphosed into a 'snake'[198] in the *Bacchae* irresistibly brings to mind the Xerxes who has 'the dark blue gaze of the bloody serpent' (l. 81ff.) of the *parodos* in Aeschylus' *Persians*), attacking all that is most sacred (the Persians had not hesitated to 'burn the temples' and 'destroy the altars' (*Persians*, l. 810ff.); Cadmus, 'at the head of a troop armed with spears', will attack 'the altars and tombs of the Greeks', l. 1359ff.).

---

[194] Ll. 482.

[195] Ll. 719, 732.

[196] Ll. 1333–8, 1354–60.

[197] Ll. 1336: μιγάδα βάρβαρον στράτον [mixed Barbarian army]. The beginning of the *Persians* (ll. 16–64) gives a lengthy list of the peoples who make up the Persian army.

[198] *Bacchae*, l. 1330: δράκων γενήσῃ μεταβαλών; l. 1358: δράκων.

And this expedition, like the other, will reach Delphi, which it will not be able to seize.[199]

But Thebes is not so much conquered by force as infected by a sort of contagion. When the tragedy opens, Semele's sisters have already been transformed into Bacchants 'forced to leave their homes' (l. 32). They are at once followed by all the women in Thebes whom Dionysus has driven from their houses and made mad (ll. 35–8).[200] The first episode shows two old Theban men 'changed into Bacchants'. The disease does not spare the head of the city. Pentheus, who had given the order 'to have brought to him his hoplite arms' (l. 809) in order to avenge his city for the 'outrage of the Bacchants' (l. 821), instead of the expected weapons in fact agrees to put on a 'linen robe' and ultimately appears, in the fourth episode, 'with a woman's costume, of a Maenad or Bacchant' (l. 915). So the staging gives the impression of a Thebes that has been entirely absorbed by the Barbarians who have penetrated it.

Even before Pentheus' transformation is complete, the first two *stasima* had mentioned a Dionysiac cult that ignores geographical boundaries and pays no attention to the difference between Greeks and Barbarians. Indeed, when the chorus 'from the land of Asia' (l. 64) dreams of better countries and places 'where Bacchants are allowed to celebrate their rites' (l. 415), it is not thinking only of Barbarian lands, like 'Cyprus,[201] the island of Aphrodite' (l. 402ff.) or the enigmatic city (should line 406 be Paphos or Pharos?)[202] 'made fruitful, in the absence of rain, by the hundred mouths of the *Barbarian* river' (l. 407); it is thinking also of Greece and 'the beautiful Pieria, home of the Muses, the sacred slope of Olympus' (l. 410ff.). The episode of the second *stasimon* similarly brings together Barbarian regions and Greek lands by means of a Dionysus who leads his maenads to 'Nysa, that nurtures wild animals' (l. 566ff.) (whether it is in the kingdom of Lycurgus, therefore

---

[199] *Bacchae*, ll. 1335–8; and Herodotus, VIII, 35–9.

[200] Cf. ll. 215–20.

[201] In Aeschylus' *Suppliants*, 'the Cypriot type' (l. 282) is put on the same level as the Libyan, Egyptian and nomadic Indian women, or the Amazons, so putting this island in the class of a Barbarian land. People have been astonished to the point of deleting this line on the pretext that in the fifth century the population of Cyprus comprised a strong Greek element (cf. H. Friis Johansen–E. W. Whittle, *Aeschylus' Suppliants*, II, pp. 223–6, on l. 282ff.). But in *Helen* also Cyprus appears as a Barbarian land destined to be colonised by Teucros (l. 148). In the *Bacchae*, Cyprus is again apparently regarded as a Barbarian land or, at least, as a frontier zone; cf. E. R. Dodds, *Euripides' Bacchae*, Oxford², 1960, on ll. 402–16: 'Cyprus represents the eastern limit of the Greek world.'

[202] E. R. Dodds, *op. cit.*, on ll. 406–8, convincingly defends the Πάφον of the manuscripts against the correction *Pharos* proposed by Reiske.

Thrace, as in the *Iliad*,[203] or 'near the river Aegyptus', as in the *Homeric Hymn*),[204] Mount Nysa belongs to the Barbarian world), and on 'the Corycian peaks' (l. 599) (doubtless those of Parnassus, but perhaps also of Cilicia)[205] and in 'blessed Pieria' (l. 565) (and he gets there only after crossing a river that evokes the name of Lydia,[206] even if it lies in Macedonia, the Lydias).

If Dionysus is equally 'at home' among Greeks and Barbarians, it is because he belongs to both worlds. If, for his appearance in Thebes, he has assumed the guise of an effeminate Barbarian,[207] he is nonetheless the offspring of Cadmus' daughter and is thereby part of the royal house of Thebes.[208] The *parodos* recalls that Thebes nurtured Semele (l. 195), and the beginning of the second *stasimon* evokes the day when Dirce received the son of Zeus in her fountain (ll. 519–21), and the journey which leads Dionysus 'from the mountains of Phrygia to the 'spacious streets' of Greece (εὐρυχόρους ἀγυιάς, l. 86ff.) is in fact a return, as the κατάγειν [to lead down] of line 85 emphasises.

The status of Cadmus is just as undecided. Both the *Bacchae* and the *Phoenician Women* recall the Barbarian origin of the man who formerly left the city of Sidon, but the tragedy also tightens the links that bind this Phoenician to Thebes. He is no longer merely the city's founder; he is also responsible for its defences (whether he has built them himself or simply 'had them built'),[209] whereas all tradition ascribes the construction of the ramparts to the Theban twins, Amphion and Zethos.[210] Lines 1024–5, which juxtapose Ἑλλάδα [Greece] and Σιδωνίου [Sidonian], underline the complex situation of a house that had known prosperity 'in *Greece*', but was descended from 'an old man from *Sidon*'. And the end of the tragedy takes the

---

[203] *Il.*, 6, 133.

[204] *To Dionysus*, III, 8–9. On the whole, commentators on the *Bacchae* (E. R. Dodds followed by G. Kirk and J. Roux) are in agreement in situating the *Nysa* of l. 556 in Thrace, and propose identifying it with Pangaeus. In fact, *Nysa* seems to be the name of Dionysus' mythical mountain, the siting of which varies according to the versions of his legend (cf. H. Jeanmaire, *Dionysos: Histoire du culte de Bacchus*, Paris, 1951, pp. 348–51), but it is almost always situated in Barbarian country.

[205] Cf. Pausanias, X, 32, 5. In the *Eumenides*, l. 22, as in *Antigone*, l. 1128, the Corycian Nymphs or rocks are similarly mentioned in a Delphic context.

[206] Cf. C. Segal, *op. cit.* (n. 32), p. 122.

[207] *Bacchae*, ll. 233–6, 454–9.

[208] *Bacchae*, l. 1250: οἰκεῖος γεγώς.

[209] *Bacchae*, l. 172. On the factitive sense, see J. Roux, *Euripide, les Bacchantes*, Paris, 1972, on l. 171ff.

[210] Cf. F. Vian, *op. cit.*, pp. 69–75. In the *Odyssey*, 11, 264ff., the twins are both the founders and the builders of the walls: 'they founded Thebes with the seven gates and built its ramparts …', usurping the role that is usually ascribed to Cadmus, just as here Cadmus is usurping theirs.

paradox to its height by presenting as an *exile* what is in fact a *return*. Indeed, when Cadmus learns from Dionysus' lips that a decree of the gods destines him to 'lead a mixed troop of Barbarians to Greece' (l. 1355ff.), he bewails a fate that condemns him to live 'as a metic'†† (l. 1355) among the Barbarians, which suggests that he considers himself to be a Greek.[211]

Seen in this perspective, lines 17–18 of the prologue, which depict an Asia 'of cities filled with a mixture of Greeks and Barbarians', are no longer only an allusion to the Greek colonisation of Asia Minor and a gratuitous anachronism.[212] They assume a programmatic value in a tragedy in which 'the boundaries between the Greek and Barbarian elements [have become] ethnically, socially and morally blurred'.[213]

It was the generation of the Persian Wars who really elaborated the Barbarian/Greek[214] antithesis. The Greeks, sure of their own identity, had at that time contrasted a Europe with a passion for liberty to Barbarians who knew no middle ground between tyranny and slavery. Aeschylus, who fought at Marathon, in the *Persians* (the first of his tragedies that have been preserved for us) gives us the most perfect defence and illustration of this bipolar vision of the world. Euripides belongs to another era. He is the contemporary of the sophist Hippias, who claims that 'from the point of view of nature, all men belong to the same family, the same house and the same city' (Pl. *Prot.*, 337 c). He could have heard Antiphon declare provocatively that 'from the point of view of nature, all men are alike in every way, whether they are Greeks or Barbarians' (DK 87 B 44 b 2). He doubtless knew the theories of the doctors who explained differences between Europeans and Asians by geographical situation or political regime, and was not unaware that, for supporters of the idea of progress, 'the Barbarians were distinct from the Greeks only because they were at an inferior stage of evolution'.[215] In its own way, his work testifies to this 'crisis of meaning',[216] which is also a crisis of

---

† A foreigner resident at Athens. See further Vidal-Naquet, 'The place and status of foreigners'.

[211] A. W. Gomme, *loc. cit.*, p. 69, has rightly emphasised this.

[212] See for example the commentary of E. R. Dodds on l. 17. C. Segal, *op. cit.*, p. 123, sees it more as an evocation of the mythical time of origins, when Greeks and Barbarians had not yet become clearly differentiated.

[213] Cf. O. Reverdin, *loc. cit.*, p. 92.

[214] See H. Diller, *loc. cit.* (n. 59), pp. 39–68, *passim*.

[215] Cf. J. de Romilly, 'Thucydide et l'idée de progrès', *ASNP*, 35, 1966, pp. 143–91 (p. 161), regarding the archaeology of Thucydides, I, 6, 1–6.

[216] Cf. K. Reinhardt, 'Die Sinneskrise bei Euripides', Fr. trans. 'La crise du sens chez Euripide', in *Eschyle Euripide*, Paris, 1972, pp. 293–328.

Greek identity. It tells us that the boundary dividing the Greek from the Barbarian and the civilised man from the savage can easily be crossed:[217] Greeks can always behave like barbarians and thus swing back to a Barbarism that is their past. And the better to express this, it seems to invent new words or give new meanings to those that already exist. Euripides is in fact the first of the tragedians to show us Greeks who, under the pressure of circumstances, have 'turned savage' (ἀγριόω).[218] He is also the only one to show us Greek men, like Menelaus in *Orestes*, whose stay among Barbarians has 'changed them into Barbarians' (βαρβαρόω).[219]

[217] The point has also been stressed as much in regard to *Medea* – P. Easterling, *loc. cit.* (n. 119), p. 191 – as to *Orestes* – F. Zeitlin, *loc. cit.* (n. 104), p. 56 – and the *Bacchae* – C. Segal, *op. cit., passim.*

[218] This verb is not attested in Aeschylus. It appears for the first time in Euripides' *Electra* (usually placed, for metrical reasons, between 420 and 417) regarding Clytemnestra: ἠγριώμην, l. 1031. To turn oneself into a savage (middle voice) is to cross the frontier that separates civilisation from a state of savagery by committing a horrible crime (killing her husband) under the pressure of circumstances: in this case the abuses inflicted by Agamemnon on Clytemnestra. It is found again in *Iphigenia in Tauris* (l. 348): the heroine has been 'turned savage' (ἠγριώμεθα) by misfortune, or more exactly through the dreams (ἐξ ὀνείρων) that have announced the death of Orestes to her, and she thereby loses all pity for those she sacrifices. Lastly it is used three times in *Orestes* (dated 408): twice it is used in the middle voice (ll. 226, 387) and refers to a physical appearance: the illness and lack of bathing have given the hero a savage air; once it is used in the active voice (l. 616) and indicates a violation of the most sacred laws: Electra has 'turned Orestes into a savage' (σ' ἠγρίως), has filled him with hatred for his mother and spurred him to matricide. The word is attested in Sophocles only in *Philoctetes* (dated 409), in line 1321, in relation to a hero 'reduced to a savage state' (ἠγρίωσαι) by illness and isolation, to the point where he no longer wishes to hear good advice.

[219] The only good use of βαρβαρόω attested in Sophocles, *Antigone*, l. 1002, is quite different. In fact it is applied to birds which 'under the effects of a fatal and barbarised dart emit sharp cries' (κακῷ κλάζοντας οἴστρῳ καὶ βεβαρωμένῳ). The meaning of this difficult passage becomes clear as soon as one recognises the inversion of a common comparison. The Greeks often likened the incomprehensible language of Barbarians to the twittering of birds; F. Skoda, *loc. cit.*, p. 112ff., quotes Herodotus, II, 57; Aeschylus, *Agamemnon*, ll. 1050–2; Aristophanes, *Frogs*, ll. 680–2, and *Birds*, l. 199ff.). Tiresias, for his part, compares the incomprehensible language of birds killing one another to Barbarian speech (cf. schol. *ad vers.*: ἐμηνευθῆναι μὴ δυναμένῳ).

4 The Athenian Image of the Foreigner[†]

FRANÇOIS LISSARRAGUE

translated by Antonia Nevill

To tackle the question of Greek identity in art, the use of the plural – identities – becomes necessary. Greek iconography in fact offers an entire series of plastic art forms and representations evoking various groups, peoples and races, mythical or real, which are just so many imaginary models to be compared with the Greek paradigm.

Otherness, often referred to by anthropologists as a dimension of self-consciousness, complementary to identity, is not a homogeneous category, but can assume many varied forms at the same time and within the same culture. It is not an immediate 'natural' fact, but the construction of such a culture, and the historian's interest lies in the way in which this category comes to be produced.[1] From this viewpoint, the Greeks are no different from others.

I shall concentrate in the following pages on a particular group of subjects, in a specific city: the Attic vases of the sixth and fifth centuries – not because of an Athenocentric complacency, but because there is available here an extraordinarily abundant, well-dated collection, whose many variants enable us to nuance the dualities and contrasts which are sometimes too mechanically applied to the ancient Greek world.

The vases, moreover, belong in the context of a particular use, well known in its time – that of the symposium – where the images they carry intermingle with the customs of wine-drinking and conviviality among men, among citizens. In this context the representations open onto an imaginary social world, a shared knowledge, some of whose

† Originally published as 'L'immagine dello straniero ad Atene', in S. Settis (ed.), *I Greci*, 2.II *Definizione* (Giulio Einaudi: Turin, 1997), 938–58.
    [1] Cf. W. Nippel, 'La construzione dell' "altro"', in *I Greci*, vol. 1, Turin 1996, pp. 165–96 [translated below, Ch. 12]; E. Hall, *Inventing the Barbarian*, Oxford 1989, also F. Hartog, *Mémoire d'Ulysse: récits sur la frontière en Grèce anciene*, Paris 1996 [translated as *Memories of Odysseus*, Edinburgh 2001].

aspects they manipulate and transform, offering to the viewer's gaze a variety of models on which to reflect.

In the course of this study, a selection of images will be examined which cover the essentials of those aspects. This is necessarily a selective path but, I hope, sufficiently broad to give some idea of the richness and variety of these Athenian points of view on the 'other', and on others in general. The analysis will move from the distant to the near: (1) we shall start from an imaginary ethnography, of fantastic peoples, at the farthest ends of the inhabited world; (2) from this 'faraway land' we shall go to the other end of the chain, the nearest to hand, when the Greeks themselves become others, in the context of the banquet, through the experience of wine; (3) from this experience we shall approach that of war where the hoplite-citizen turns himself, through images and poetry, into the epic hero and comes into contact with the 'other' as 'back-up' or enemy; (4) lastly we shall examine some mythical uses of the other that have the aim of defining the Greeks' own identity, and how, in the description of distant and barbarian societies, it is in fact Greek categories of culture that come into play.

1 THE DISTANT, THE PICTURESQUE, THE EXOTIC

One of the most notable items of archaic production, the François Vase, will be useful as a starting-point.[2] The vase offers an impressive number of figures, all (with the exception of the ornamental frieze) related to heroic subjects: Theseus and Ariadne, the Calydonian boar hunt, the battle between the Centaurs and Lapiths, the funeral games in honour of Patroclus, the marriage of Thetis and Peleus, Achilles' pursuit of Troilus, the return of Hephaestus to Olympus, and Ajax bearing the corpse of Achilles. There has been much argument about the coherence of the whole, the relationships between the various themes, the general composition and arrangement of the friezes. Here it is enough to emphasise one fundamental element: on the foot of the bowl there unfolds a continuous frieze picturing the battle of the Pygmies and the cranes (fig. 1).

The *Iliad* makes a fleeting allusion to this topic, at the beginning of the third book, after the long catalogue of ships in the second, where we find the inventory of the entire political geography of the

[2] The black-figure crater signed by the potter Ergotimus and the painter Clitias, known as the François Vase, preserved in the Archaeological Museum of Florence; *ABV* 76/1.

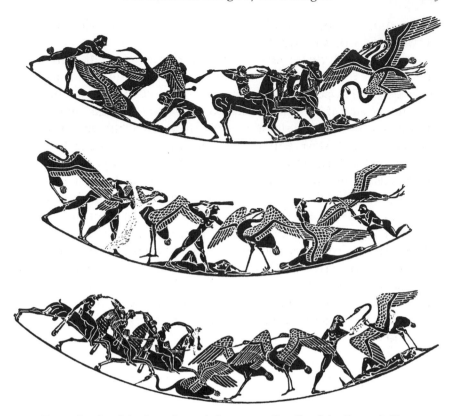

Fig. 1 Battle of the Pygmies and the cranes. Details of the François Vase
(*c*.570 BC), after Furtwängler-Reichhold

Greek world and the description of the Trojan leaders. The two
armies, Greek and Trojan, ready to confront one another, hurl themselves forward:

> Then, when all were in order, each with their leader, the Teucri [Trojans]
> went shouting and calling, like birds, as the cries of the cranes re-echo in the
> heavens when, fleeing the winter and the unending rain, they fly, screeching,
> on the currents of Ocean, bringing slaughter and death to the Pygmies.[3]

The brevity of the allusion implies that the fact was well known.
Homer's poem pays no heed to precise ethnographical information
because that is not its function, and no sign emerges of any particular interest in that distant and exotic universe which others such
as Ctesias, more enthusiastic about fables and fantastic accounts,
would later develop.[4]

---

[3] *Iliad*, 3. 1–6 (from the translation by R. Calzecchi Onesti).
[4] P. Janni, *Etnografia e mito*, Rome 1978.

The noteworthy element of the François Vase is the position reserved for the subject and the way in which it is treated. The episode is placed on the foot of the bowl, far from the other epic subjects; it is somehow marginalized, pushed out to the limits of the decorative space just as, in Homer, it is situated beyond the Ocean. Without wishing to force the interpretation, if we consider the volume of the vase as both a mythical and geographical space, we immediately grasp the gap which separates the heroic epics from those fabulous creatures, the Pygmies, whose function, in Homer as on the vase, is purely metaphorical.

Indeed, on the François Vase, the Pygmies are simultaneously put at a distance and treated on a different scale. Nothing in their physical characteristics – except for their size – differentiates them from the Greek or Trojan heroes. We see them riding goats instead of horses, and most have a youthful countenance (only two have a beard). They fight with cudgels and slings: it is a noisy battle, if we follow Homer, and parodic; it is not a hunt – for the birds retain their own size and are gigantic in relation to the Pygmies, who sometimes adopt a Herculean pose – but a battle against monsters.

There is nothing in ethnography to confirm the reality of such a struggle between Pygmies and cranes, but the motif persisted and developed in Greek tradition. It takes on the character of an actual fact and becomes part of common knowledge, to the point where the episode becomes popular at a later date in theatrical representations. Among the circus spectacles, Statius mentions the battle between Pygmies and cranes, and the hilarity which it arouses.[5]

In Attic iconography, the theme remains popular but undergoes a gradual transformation. For a long time artists keep to the formula of the François Vase: miniscule men confront giant birds. The fight is out of proportion, the positions assumed by the Pygmies recall those of Heracles, with the result that they look ridiculous. In the early fifth century significant changes can be noticed. The most obvious is found on a *rhyton* by the Brygos Painter (fig. 2),[6] where we see a double transformation. The first concerns the Pygmy, who has become deformed, afflicted with a caricatural dwarfism, a prominent belly, short thighs and a swollen face;[7] the representation of the Pygmies has passed from the distant to the grotesque. The second transformation involves the weaponry: the Pygmy uses a bow and wears

    [5] Statius, *Silvae*, I. 56–64.
    [6] St Petersburg, Hermitage, b. 1818; *ARV*²382/188
    [7] V. Dasen, *Dwarfs in Ancient Egypt and Greece*, Oxford 1993, especially pp. 175–88.

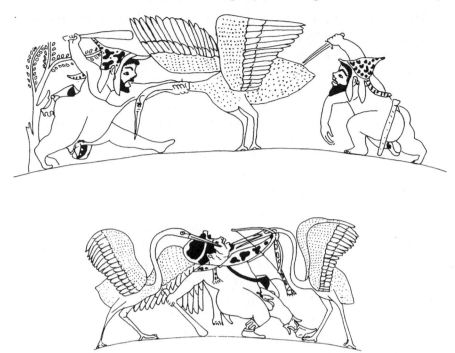

Fig. 2 Battle of the Pygmies and the cranes. Drawing by F. Lissarrague from a red-figure *rhyton* by the Brygos Painter (*c.*480 BC)

a leopard-skin Scythian cap; there is also a mixture of barbarian characteristics which further emphasise the gap between them and the little archaic Pygmies, who are simply human beings reduced in size.

Such imagery testifies to an elaboration that must not be generalised, but which reveals the fact that the painters are not handling a precise and documented ethnographic curiosity, to some extent descriptive, but are parodying established iconographic models: the epic hero and his double, the huntsman hero.

This elaboration is developed and accentuated in a particularly original and revealing group of vases. These are objects midway between small-scale sculpture and pottery: drinking vessels in the form of statuettes, sculpted vessels that seem to have been the speciality of the potter Sotades, who often signed his work.[8] They are about 30 cm high, mounted on a plinth, composed of a figure in the round and a turned neck, provided with a vertical handle; they therefore have a use other than purely ornamental. On a specimen from the

---

[8] On this potter and his workshop cf. *ARV*[2] 763–73 and the book by H. Hoffmann, *Sotades, Symbols of Immortality*, Oxford 1997.

Fig. 3 *Rhyton* in the manner of the Sotades Painter (*c.*460 BC)

museum of Erlangen (fig. 3)⁹ we see a person of small stature, ill-proportioned, with short legs and a long genital organ that reaches his knees, walking along carrying a dead crane on his shoulders. The black glaze accentuated the negroid characteristics attributed to him by the potter and the caricatural aspect of the statuette, in which the Pygmy has emerged as victor from the battle with the cranes. Other vases produced in the same studio offer a more cruel motif, as for example a specimen from Dresden (fig. 4).¹⁰ In this instance the Pygmy, in black, makes a horrible grimace; his right arm is imprisoned in the jaws of a crocodile which is devouring him, its left forefoot resting on the victim's chest. This second subject has no known iconographical or textual precedents or parallels; it seems to

⁹ Erlangen PI; *ARV*² 766/3.
¹⁰ Dresden 364; *ARV*² 764/11.

Fig. 4 Rhyton by the Sotades Painter (*c.*460 BC)

be an invention of Sotades, who thus develops in his own way the pictorial and anecdotal possibilities suggested by the stories of the Pygmies. Cranes and crocodiles, the Pygmies' mortal enemies, infest the air and water, making the world they live in uninhabitable.

Alongside these Pygmy-vessels, Sotades and some contemporary potters produced other sculpted vessels whose variety is revealing: vessels in the form of a Sphinx, an Amazon on horseback, a Persian leading a camel, accompanied by a small black slave.[11] Merely to list the subjects demonstrates the interest of these potters, and of their customers, in images that evoke distant and exotic lands, and mingle human beings and animals in a spirit of foreignness.

It has sometimes been suggested that the choice of such deliber-

---

[11] London E 788; *ARV²* 764/8 (sphinx). Boston 21.2286; *ARV²* 772/θ (Amazon). Paris, Louvre CA 3825; *Paralipomena* 461/i (Persian).

ately exotic motifs was dictated by the clients.[12] Many of these vessels have been found outside Greece: the Persian with the camel in Egypt, the Amazon at Meroe. But, besides the fact that there is no correspondence between the type portrayed and the place where it was found, many of the receptacles come from Greece or Italy: Pygmy–crocodile groups have been found at Thasos, Paphos, Capua, Locris and Ruvo; a Pygmy–crane group at Nola and Locris. For want of complete and consistent datings, the logic of their distribution almost totally eludes us; it does not seem possible, however, to interpret these 'exotic' vessels as the direct reflection of a 'barbarian' clientele.[13] In reality, they reveal a liking for these forms of alterity among the participants in the banquet; they are wine vessels which invite the drinkers to open up to a different and distant world. Through this kind of product, variations develop on these portrayals of the 'other' represented by the Pygmies, Persians or Amazons, which were first and foremost intended for Athenian drinkers in the context of the symposium.

2 EXPERIENCING THE OTHER

We may find confirmation of a similar interest in the depiction of the 'other' by analysing the range of sculpted vessels produced by the potters who came before Sotades.[14] The oldest are little perfume jars, but the most numerous are wine cups, with one head only. These usually take the form of a woman's head and are jugs (*oinochoai*). In this way the serving-maid gives her own appearance to the jug itself, since mixing the wine for men is effectively her role in the symposium.

There are sometimes vessels in the shape of a goblet with two vertical handles, canthari. The wall of the cup is modelled in the shape of a face, and the faces are in pairs, thus assuming a Janus-like appearance. Amongst the Janus cups, the potters seem systematically to choose to exclude the representations of men. The combinations of heads are as follows: woman/satyr (23 examples); woman/woman (21); woman/Heracles (13); woman/negro (11) (fig. 5);[15] and then

---

[12] F. Brommer, 'Themenwahl aus örtlichen Grunden', in H. Brijder (ed.), *Ancient Greek and Related Pottery*, Amsterdam 1984, pp. 178–84.

[13] F Lissarrague, 'Voyage d'images: iconographie et aires culturelles', in *Revue des Études Anciennes*, LXXXIX, 3–4 (1987), pp. 261–9.

[14] Beazley has classified them, labelling them 'Head-vases': *ARV²* 1529–52. Cf. F. Lissarrague, 'Identity and otherness', in *Source*, XV, I (1995), pp. 4–9.

[15] Boston, Museum of Fine Arts, 98.926; *ARV²* 1534/9, class G; the two heads on this specimen are female.

Fig. 5 Janiform cantharus (*c.*510 BC)
Henry Lillie Pierce Fund, courtesy Museum of Fine Arts, Boston

there are rarer variants: Heracles/satyr (2); Heracles/negro (2); Dionysus/satyr (1); Dionysus/woman (1).

The importance of the women is clear, and matches the predominant model followed in jugs for pouring wine. The other subjects are unsurprising: black slaves; Dionysus and satyrs in connection with wine and the symposium; Heracles, himself no mean drinker and the companion of Dionysus. In this way the figures put before the drinkers' eyes do not refer to their masculine image, but suggest the presence of divine or exotic companions.

The playful dimension of these portrayals seems to be confirmed by the inscriptions on an example in the Thessalonika Museum,[16] a cantharus pairing a female face with that of a negro. On the woman's side it says: 'I am Eronassa, most beautiful', which may be interpreted, like many inscriptions on vessels, as a compliment; on the side

[16] Thessalonika, Archaeological Museum, tomb 27 of the necropolis of Acanthus. Cf. the catalogue of the exhibition *I Macedoni*, Marseilles 1995, n. 196.

of the negro, whose features the potter has caricatured, giving him prominent teeth, there is an ironic inscription: 'I am Timyllos, as handsome as this face.' It would appear that the drinkers were making explicit with this graffiti the jokes of comparison made possible by the contrast of the goblet and the one using it.

This anthropomorphic collection must be considered together with all the drinking-cups in the shape of animal heads, the *rhyta* which in their turn introduce a picturesque element to the banquet.[17] Noteworthy among these is a dog's head, on which the decoration of the neck, attributed to the Brygos Painter, is adorned with the grotesque, deformed and barbarian Pygmies mentioned above (fig. 2).[18]

By using these vessels, double-headed cantharus or animal *rhyton*, the Greek drinker came face to face with forms of the animal world or otherness that took him outside his masculine universe. During the banquet these two ranges of vessels combined the human and animal world, but never referred to the central model of the city of drinkers, the Greek man in his civic identity. The choice, which seems deliberate, finds its logical equivalent in words ascribed sometimes to Thales, sometimes to Socrates:[19] 'He said ... that he was grateful to fate for three reasons: first, for being a man and not an animal; second, a man and not a woman, and third, a Greek and not a barbarian.'[20] This highly significant sentence is often quoted, and quite rightly.[21] In its layout, it makes clear the hierarchy underlying Greek anthropology: animal, woman, Barbarian, in that order, were the three degrees defining the male, allowing him to identify himself negatively, somehow by a process of elimination. At the banquet, it is the male, the Greek man, who lingers in company with his peers. Through their products, potters and painters put before the Greek drinker a series of objects that, by evoking various categories, favouring the image of the 'other' – barbarian, woman or animal – enable him to reaffirm his own identity.

In the same light, but on a different level, we must examine another series of images which, in the symposium, must be placed in relation to this same imaginary experience of the 'other'.

This time, it is a matter of trying out the forms of alterity which, in other contexts than the symposium, are kept at a distance, but

[17] The dossier is assembled by H. Hoffmann, *Attic Red-figured Rhyta*, Mainz 1962.
[18] Cf. above, n. 7.
[19] Diogenes Laertius 1/33 = Thales, DK 11 A I.
[20] From the translation by R. Laurenti.
[21] Most recently Hartog, *Memoire*, p. 31.

which in this instance are taken for the various customs of wine-drinking. Ways of imbibing wine were rigidly codified and defined by the Greeks, who were very careful about how wine and water were mixed. They did not drink unadulterated wine; it was mixed with water and the proportions to be observed were the subject of numerous rules and regulations. To drink pure wine would be both dangerous, because drunkenness could kill or send one mad, and barbarian, in that the violence which could result might enter the domain of barbarity. The Centaurs at Pirithous' wedding were the proof: having drunk too much, they tried to carry off the bride and transformed the banquet into a battlefield. But it was chiefly to the Scythians that the Greeks ascribed ways of drinking that were radically opposed to their own. To drink Scythian-style meant to drink wine neat, and the Greeks coined a word for this practice: *skythizein*.[22]

The iconography of the symposium takes up this motif, making some drinkers wear a Scythian cap, thus differentiating them from their table companions (fig. 6).[23] We can suppose in all probability that these played the part of masters of the feast – symposiarchs – organising the mixing and distribution of wine.[24] Marked out as 'Scythians', they were the symbol of unadulterated wine and of alterity, and supervised for the community of drinkers the use of the wine. Regarded as poisonous when it was consumed neat, wine had to be adapted to man, tamed, so to speak, made drinkable. In the same way, the Scythian presence at the banquet underlined that distance of the others from oneself, which had to be diminished by allowing the proper use of drinking.

It is possible to compare this Scythian presence at the banquet with other forms of alterity that the iconography of the vessels brings into play. There is a group of representations of the *kômos* (revel) or the symposium which introduces adult bearded drinkers, wearing long chitons, a *sakkos* [cloth] on their head, carrying a parasol and wearing earrings (fig. 7).[25] This type of apparel was often associated with eastern, Ionian practices, and especially with the arrival in Athens of the poet Anacreon, but its feminine nature must be emphasised,

---

[22] To drink like a Scythian: Anacreon: '*skythizein*'; Athenaeus, II.499ff (with a play on words between Σκύθης and σκύφος); cf. F. Lissarrague, *L'immaginario del simposio Greco*, Rome–Bari 1990, p. 133 and n. 12 [translated as *The Aesthetics of the Greek Banquet*].

[23] Rhodes 13 286; *ARV²* 139.23, Pithos Painter.

[24] See most recently M. C. Miller, 'Foreigners at the symposium?', in W. J. Slater (ed.), *Dining in a Classical Context*, Ann Arbor 1991, pp. 59–81, which emphasises the importance of the Achaemenid influence on the Greek world.

[25] London E 308; *ARV²* 673/7, Zannoni Painter. On the parasol as a sign of distinction cf. M. C. Miller, 'The parasol: an oriental status-symbol in late archaic and classical Athens', in *Journal of Hellenic Studies*, CXII (1992), pp. 91–105.

Fig. 6 Drinker with Scythian headdress. Red-figure goblet by the
Pithos Painter (*c.*500 BC)

when compared with the usual characters in contemporary Attic
iconography. Between oriental and feminine, this series, traditionally
termed 'the Anacreontics',[26] shows how forms of otherness were
elaborated in the area of the symposium, which therefore seems, at
least in some aspects, to be a place for experimentations with the
'other'.†

But these forms of alterity were neither mechanical nor homogeneous, since they went from the furthest possible distance – the
Pygmies fighting cranes and crocodiles – to a kind of interiorisation
of the other – the figure of the oriental or effeminate drinker.

[26] Cf. D. C. Kurtz and J. Boardman, 'Booners', in *Greek Vases in the J. Paul Getty Museum*,
III (1986), pp. 35–70, and F. Frontisi-Ducroux and F. Lissarrague, 'De l'ambiguité à l'ambivalence: un parcours dionysiaque', in *Annali dell'Istituto universitario orientale di Napoli.
Seminario di studi del mondo classico. Sezione di archeologia e storia antica*, V (1983), pp.
11–32.
    † For the symposium, see Murray, *Sympotica*.

Fig. 7 'Anacreontic' drinker. Red-figure neck-handled amphora
by the Zannoni Painter (*c.*460 BC)
© The British Museum

3 THE HOPLITE AND HIS DOUBLES

The same play, the same combination of the proximity and, at the same time, the distancing of the other – of the others in various forms – can be seen in another fundamental area of Greek culture: war.[27]

The picture of the Pygmies on the François Vase echoed, on a lesser scale, the heroic adventures displayed on the belly of the vessel. It is known that the heroic model was widely dominant in the ideology of war in archaic Greece, especially in Athens, and in the iconography of the goblets the drinkers are also often represented as warriors. The artists' work confers upon the hero the appearance of the solitary hoplite, who is marked out by particularly elaborate weapons, above all the shield hollowed out on both sides, known as Boeotian.[28]

[27] On the whole of this dossier cf. F. Lissarrague, *L'autre guerrier: archers, peltastes, cavaliers dans l'imagerie attique*, Paris–Rome 1991.
[28] So called by archaeologists because it appears on coins from Boeotia; cf. A. Snodgrass, *Early Greek Armour and Weapons*, Edinburgh 1964, pp. 58–60, together with the reservations of J. Boardman, 'Symbol and story in Geometric art', in W. Moon (ed.), *Ancient Greek Art and Iconography*, Madison 1983, pp. 29–32.

Fig. 8 Memnon and the Ethiopians. Black-figure neck-handled
amphora (*c.*520 BC)

What about 'barbarian' heroes, non-Achaean warriors? One of
the most noteworthy examples is presented to us by the picture of
Memnon, the leader of the Ethiopians, the men with the burnt faces,
leading an army of Africans before Troy (fig. 8).[29] While his companions and subjects are clearly portrayed as non-Greeks, as much
by their physical appearance (snub-nosed, curly hair) as by their
weapons (bow, club), Memnon has all the characteristics of a Trojan
or Achaean hero. When he is on his own, he is indistinguishable from
Hector or Aeneas, Trojan heroes, or from Achilles or Diomedes,
Achaean heroes. The figure of the heroic warrior corresponds to a
single model, individualised only through the situations in which he
is involved or the inscriptions that mention him and make him a
precise personality, a particular individual.

In the case of Memnon, for example, it is the presence of Aurora,
Eos with the divine wings, which enables us to identify him. And

---

[29] Munich 1507; *ABV* 375/207, group of Leagros.

when he appears together with his men, it is the difference between his heroic figure and his African companions that marks him out. Memnon and the Ethiopians constitute a sort of system, and the otherness of the African archers a part of the identity of Memnon.

At the end of the sixth century, we have a number of pictures which show various moments in the activities of warriors, more or less clearly heroicised: departures, libations, scenes of divination, the return of the dead. In a good many of these scenes, the warrior is seen in isolation rather than placed in the hoplite context of the phalanx and collective combat. At the same time, he is accompanied by archers in Scythian costume, characterised by a stitched tunic with sleeves and trousers and a tall cap, which contrast with the drapery of Greek garments. Through these representations a dual contrast between Greek and non-Greek, hoplite and archer, takes shape – that is to say, between a cuirassed warrior, protected for fighting face to face, body to body, and the archer who fights at a distance and hits the target without getting near it. For the Greeks the contrast between these two fighting techniques was strong; they took a dim view of the use of the bow in war; Paris, in the *Iliad*, both hero and archer, is neither a complete man nor a complete warrior. Euripides echoes this disdain for the bow in the argument which, in his *Heracles*, sets Amphitryon against Lycus. The latter, denigrating Heracles' deeds, exclaims:

> In himself he was worthless, but he has gained a name for bravery by coming down into the fields against wild beasts, though in other things he is not brave at all. He never held a shield on his left arm, never faced a spear or came near one, but with the basest of weapons, his bow in his hand, was ready to take flight. It is not with the bow that a man proves his courage, but by standing his ground, his eyes wide open and his gaze straight ahead at the spear swiftly cleaving the air, and remaining motionless at his post.[30]

The presence of archers in the ranks of the Athenian army in the fifth century is attested by casualty lists,[31] and we can be sure that no combat technique was unknown to the Greeks. The picture that was given in the iconography of the sixth century, however, emphasises the gulf dividing these two levels, and confers on the less noble weapon a strange appearance that enables the importance of the hoplite warrior, the citizen soldier seen as an epic hero, to be thrust into prominence. Here, too, as in the example of Memnon, the

---

[30] Euripides, *Heracles*, 157–64.
[31] *IG*, I², 950 (barbarian archers); *IG*, I², 929, 949, 950 (Greek archers). Lissarrague, *L'Autre guerrier*, p. 126.

Fig. 9 Peltast. Red-figure *oinochoe* by the Painter of Berlin 2268 (*c.*510 BC)

one and the other form a system and the identity of the hoplite is constructed upon the distance that differentiates him from the archer.

Early in the fifth century a series of images represents young
warriors armed with light shields in the shape of a half-moon (*peltê*).
They are not represented, like the archers, beside the hoplites, but in
isolation, and they seem to have a marginal role in the war (fig. 9).[32]

Between the warrior and his equipment there is a notable kind of
play on identity. His panoply is a sort of double of the hoplite's body,
and the tales connected with weapons – those of Achilles in particular – reveal their importance. To become a citizen means assuming all
the panoply, as is confirmed by the Cretan rite of passage from the
statues of ephebe to adulthood: the young man simultaneously
received 'military equipment, an ox, a goblet',[33] the sign of his status
as a full warrior, participant in sacrifices and the symposium.

In comparison with this picture of the hoplite warrior, Attic
iconography develops two models of alterity: that of the archer, who

[32] Paris, Louvre G 102: *ARV*² 156/52, Painter of Berlin 2268.
[33] Strabo, 10.4.21.

cannot be confused with the hoplite citizen, and that of the peltast, who has not yet attained hoplite status.[34] The identity of the warrior is thus constructed by contrast with these other models of combatants, archers and peltasts.

In the history of imagery, as in many other fields of Athenian history, the Persian Wars mark a pronounced break. The iconographic repertoire is opened up to the image of the barbarian, especially the Persian, and a number of very revealing transformations can be observed.[35] In the work of the Brygos Painter, we saw the Pygmies become both grotesque and barbarian; this transformation is matched by that of the image of the Persians, which begins to develop, causing the disappearance of the figure of the Scythian who accompanies the Greek hoplite. In place of the archers flanking the hoplites, we see the development of the representation of Persian archers confronting the Greek hoplites. The two are no longer parallel, but in opposition. Suddenly, this type of warrior, who had become an enemy, is belittled, reduced to a caricature.

A recently published document, from the excavations of the Ceramicus, is a good reflection of this change. It is an *ostrakon*, one of those pottery fragments on which citizens wrote the name of the person they wished to banish from the city. This is a well-known occurrence, and there are numerous preserved *ostraka*.[36] A small group of *ostraka*, recently studied by S. Brenne, is accompanied by graffiti qualifying the written name, and which Brenne has termed 'portraits'.[37] Quite rightly, he puts the term in inverted commas, because at this date the notion of portrait cannot be taken for granted. The hypothesis that such portraits are imitative is improbable; these graffiti serve rather as indications, marks of identity. We see, for example, a horseman accompany the name of Megacles, son of Hippocrates.[38]

A noteworthy *ostrakon* (fig. 10)[39] bears the inscription: 'ΚΑΛΛΙΑΣ ΚΡΑΤΙΟ ΜΕΔΟΣ' ('Kallias Kratiou, the Persian'). On the back of the potsherd a small outline figure of an archer is carved,

---

[34] Lissarrague, *L'Autre guerrier*, Ch. 7.

[35] T. Hölscher, *Griechische Historienbilder des 5. und 4. Jahrhunderts v. Chr.*, Würzburg 1973; W. Raeck, *Zum Barbarenbild in der Kunst Athens im 6. und. 5 Jahrhundert v. Chr.*, Bonn 1981.

[36] See most recently A. Martin, 'L'ostracisme athénien: un demi-siècle de découvertes et de recherches', in *Revue des Études Grecques*, 1989, pp. 124–45, and F. Willemsen and S. Brenne, 'Verzeichnis des Kerameikos Ostraka', in *Mitteilungen des Deutschen Archäologischen Instituts (Athenische Abteilung)*, CVI (1991), pp. 147–56.

[37] S. Brenne, '"Portaits" auf Ostraka', ibid., CVII (1992), pp. 161–85.

[38] Athens, Kerameikos O 2359; *ibid.*, fig. 1.

[39] Athens, Kerameikos O 849; *ibid.*, fig. 8 and tab. 39.4–5.

Fig. 10 Ostrakon, front and back (*c.*485 BC)

similar in all respects to those found on the vases of the preceding
generation, with pointed beard, tall rounded cap, curved-toed shoes
and a longbow in his hand (rather than the double bow). Here the
picture of the archer which on the *ostrakon* accompanies the epithet
'Persian' specifies the reason for the condemnation and acts as an
insult. At this date, the image of the archer can no longer serve to
qualify positively, by contrast, the identity of the hoplite-citizen; in
the case of Callias, the image fits him like a glove and serves to
condemn him.

Scorn for the Persian enemy finds caricatured expression on a little
wine-jar from the sixties of the fifth century.[40] It shows a Greek wearing a chlamys [short cloak], with his erect member in his hand,
advancing with long strides upon a Persian archer, who turns his
back on him, leaning forwards with his hands framing his face,
turned towards the spectator, whom he seems to be addressing. An
inscription details his name together with his position: 'κυβάδε
ἕστεκα, I am stooping. Εὐρυμέδων εἰμί, I am Eurymedon.' This is
simultaneously an obscene and a political witticism: his position is
that of a man about to be buggered; the Persian's gesture implies
defeat and its sexual equivalent; militarily he is vanquished, sexually
possessed. This Persian's name, Eurymedon, confirms the interpretation: Eurymedon is the name of the river near which a Persian force

<hr />

[40] Hamburg 1981.173: cf. fig. 18 of the essay by T. Hölscher in S. Settis (ed.) *I Greci*, 2.II;
L. Schauenburg, 'Εὐρυμέδων εἰμί', in *Mitteilungen des Deutschen Archäologischen Instituts
(Athenische Abteilung)*, XC (1975), pp. 97–121; M.F. Kilmer, *Greek Erotica on Attic Red-
figure Vases*, London 1993, p. 264 R 1155.

was beaten by Cimon after the Persian wars, around 468 BC.[41] But the word contains two significant roots: Μέδων evokes the ethnic Μῆδος, the Mede; εὐρύς means wide open, and fits the Persian's position to a T. Witticisms are amusing only when caught in flight. This laborious explanation must be forgiven. But such a picture aptly reminds us how, at the banquet, on this wine-jar, political values were the subject of games and jokes whose verbal repercussions may easily be guessed.[42]

4 MYTHICAL USES OF THE 'OTHER'

From the distant to the near at hand, from Pygmies to Persians, the play of variations on the theme of alterity in Greek culture could be, as we can see, both rich and complex. The iconography of the barbarians developed, in fact, a range of points of view on the Greek world itself, whose classificatory categories were themselves brought into play. In addition to the practices of war and ways of drinking, other aspects appear in this mosaic of images.

A range of scent bottles (*alabastra*) has an exceptional typology. They are oblong receptacles, decorated with figures, the design often made by broad black strokes, without incisions, which contrast with the vessel's white background. The majority of the scenes in this group represent black archers, often next to a palm tree, which underlines the exotic nature of these small perfume-containers and without doubt also that of their contents.[43]

Out of a desire for *variatio*, the artists represented other types in this group, for example Amazons: so we find two categories of warriors, black archers or Amazons, to contrast with the hoplite model.[44] In the case of the Amazons, there is a dual contrast, in that the feminine dimension is added to the barbarian. In one, exceptional, instance the painter has gone even further in this direction, since he has deepened the gulf between male and female by associating two feminine models in the same picture (fig. 11):[45] an Amazon

[41] Plutarch, *Life of Cimon*, 12.8.

[42] K. Dover, *Greek Homosexuality*, London 1978, p. 105, and F. Frontisi-Ducroux, *Du masque au visage*, Paris 1995, fig. 83, p. 118.

[43] C. Sourvinou-Inwood, *'Reading' Greek Culture: Texts and Images, Rituals and Myths*, Oxford 1991, pp. 106–18, on the significance of the palm.

[44] Negro and Amazon are together on an *alabastron* of Berlin, 3288; ARV² 268, close to the Painter of New York 21.131; published by F. Snowden, *Blacks in Antiquity*, Cambridge MA. 1970, fig. 16. Cf. also C. Benson, cat. no. 122, in E. D. Reeder (ed.), *Pandora: Women in Classical Greece*, catalogue of the exhibition, Baltimore 1995, pp. 379–80.

[45] Athens, National Archaeological Museum 15002; ARV² 98/2, group of the *alabastra* of Paidikos.

Fig. 11 Amazon and Maenad. Drawing by F. Lissarrague from a
white-ground alabastron (*c*.510 BC)

in eastern costume, armed with a bow, and a Maenad, clad in
leopard-skin, brandishing a hare that seems to be both the outcome
of the hunt and a love-gift. Such a picture does not refer to any
known myth, but it forms a syntagma of the feminine in terms of
marginality, the total overturning of the masculine – here we are
presented with the non-hoplite, the non-citizen.

Other series represent the male/female, man/animal, Greek/
barbarian categories, in a more explicit narrative context. This is
especially the case in the iconography of Orpheus, in the early fifth
century, for which the artists make revealing choices.[46] In preference
to the classic image that would make its name in Roman mosaics, for
example, of a musician Orpheus charming animals, the vase painters
chose to depict an Orpheus charming Thracian warriors. Orpheus
was then clothed in Greek style and contrasted with his clearly
barbarian audience. Sometimes this initial Greek/barbarian comparison is complemented, as on a *hydria* [water jar] in the Petit Palais
(fig. 12),[47] by the presence of a satyr symmetrical with the Thracian
warrior, introducing a man/animal contrast, since Dionysus' habitual companion combines in himself this dual dimension, in his hybrid
anatomy. On this vessel, the two listeners are motionless, their hands
extended towards Orpheus, their gesture indicating the object of
their attention. The musician is seated on a rock, and the satyr, hand

[46] On Orpheus see *LIMC* (M.-X. Garezou).
[47] Paris, Petit Palais, *ARV*² 1112/4, the Tarquinia Painter 707.

Fig. 12 Orpheus among the Thracians. Drawing by F. Lissarrague from a
red-figure *hydria* by the Tarquinia Painter (*c.*440 BC)

on hip, his tail resting on another rock, seems turned to stone by
Orpheus' music. This power of the musician, which immobilises
everyone and distracts the Thracian warriors from their lively
activity, provokes the jealousy of the Thracian women, as is well
known, and they decide to kill him. On the Paris *hydria*, we see some
of them, on the right, armed with a spear, like the Thracian who
stands in front of her. On the left, one of her companions arrives at
a run, armed with a pestle, both an agricultural and a domestic
implement. The immobility of the listeners is in contrast with the
woman's hasty movement, and this opposition shows the tension
between feminine and masculine that structures the episode.

Numerous pictures, like the one that appears on a *stamnos* [a large
jar with short neck and handles] from Basel (fig. 13),[48] privilege the
moment of Orpheus' death. In these scenes, where the women's
violence is unleashed against the Greek musician, the Thracian
warriors disappear. Orpheus defends himself with his lyre; the
women are armed with a variety of weapons: a sword to cut his
throat, but also a boulder, pestles, a skewer, a hatchet, which refer to
domestic life, agricultural work, cooking and sacrifice. By immobil-
ising the men, Orpheus paralyses the functioning of the *oikos*
[household]; the women's violence is not arbitrary, but seems to be
carried out to defend the survival of the *oikos* connoted by the imple-
ments with which they are armed. In this series, the artists are not
trying to describe the Thracian world; the barbarian element is only
one component of a whole range of signifiers in which the mascu-
line/feminine contrast is predominant.[49]

When Attic artists turn their gaze on peripheral worlds, Greek

---

[48] Basel, Antikensammlung, ex Bolla. *Paralipomena* 373/34 ter, the Dokimasia Painter.
[49] F. Lissarrague, 'Orpheé mis à mort', in *Musica e storia*, II, Bologna 1994, pp. 269–307.

Fig. 13 Death of Orpheus. Red-figure *stamnos* by the
Dokimasia Painter (*c.*490 BC)

categories are always at work. The story of Heracles and the pharaoh
Busiris offers us an excellent example of this.[50] In the course of his
wanderings, the hero reaches Egypt during a drought. Busiris, who
sacrifices all passing foreigners to the gods, welcomes Heracles not
as a guest but as a victim to be slaughtered; Heracles, crowned,
believes he is being received as a guest. Only at the moment when he
arrives at the altar does he realise the fate in store for him and the
horror of the cannibalistic feast being prepared. At this point he goes
wild and puts the Egyptian sacrificers to flight.

    This is the moment captured by the Pan Painter, to whom the
pelike [a type of *amphora* or jar with a sagging bottom] of the Athens
National Museum is attributed (fig. 14).[51] The artist pays particular
attention to the exotic character of the Egyptians, whose barbarian
appearance he emphasises: they have snub-nosed faces and shaven

    [50] On this series cf. J.-L. Durand and F. Lissarrague, 'Héros cru ou hôte cuit: histoire quasi
cannibale d'Héraklès chez Busiris', in F. Lissarrague and F. Thélamon (eds), *Image et céramique
grecque*, Rouen 1983, pp. 153–67.
    [51] Athens, National Museum 9683; *ARV*[2] 554/82, Pan Painter.

Fig. 14 Heracles at the court of pharaoh Busiris. Red-figure *pelike* by the Pan Painter (*c*.480 BC)

heads, and, above all, their tunics are carefully folded back to give a better view of their circumcised and deformed organ – in contrast, for example, to the exemplary discretion of Heracles' genitalia.[52] But, besides these clearly exotic physical features, the entire scene has been thought out in Greek terms. All the sacrificial instruments are obviously Greek: the altar near which Heracles is fighting, the tables and the spits carried by one of the Egyptians, the *hydria* and the knife-holder held by his two companions, even the upturned basket under the handle, from which falls the throat-cutting knife that is usually kept in the basket, its contents revealed by the violence of Heracles. In Greek ritual everything is aimed at making sacrifice an ordered and peaceful act, denying its murderous nature.[53] With Busiris, the horror of human sacrifice and the cannibalistic meal this implies turns the Greek norm upside down. But this overturning is

[52] Cf. Aristophanes, *Clouds*, 1114. Cf. Dover, *Greek Homosexuality*, p. 129, and T. Nonven, 'The unheroic penis: otherness exposed', in *Source*, XV, I (1995), pp. 10–16.
[53] J.-L. Durand, *Sacrifice et labour en Grèce ancienne*, Paris–Rome 1990.

entirely one constructed by the artist, beginning from the Greek elements of sacrifice and in keeping with Greek ritual, whose logic this picture – out of place but not different – reveals.

Once again, by representing 'others' in pictures, their authors tell us about themselves.

PART II

Themes

Introduction to Part II

In one of the most famous passages of Herodotus' *Histories*, the Athenians deny that they will ever come to terms with the Persians (8.144). This grandiose stand is almost immediately belied by events: suspicious that the Spartans will not come to their aid, the Athenians use the threat of an alliance with the Persians to stiffen the Spartans' resolve. The grounds on which the Athenians make their claim are significant in their own right, however: they appeal first to the images and temples of the gods, burnt by the gods and demanding vengeance, and then to *to hellenikon* (their common Greek identity), their being 'of the same blood' and 'of the same language', their common shrines, sacrifices and way of life.

Of these three constituents of Greek 'national identity' – blood, language and religion – that of blood is perhaps the least prominent in our sources. There is certainly evidence that some of the differences between Greeks and barbarians were considered innate. The 'natural slavery' that Aristotle ascribed to the barbarian world in his *Politics* is foreshadowed by the natural slavishness of foreign peoples in such sources as Aeschylus' *Persians* or Herodotus.[1] (On two occasions in the *Histories*, for example, foreign peoples – the Medes and the Egyptians – find themselves in a political vacuum, in the case of the Egyptians under the rule of twelve regional chieftains, in that of the Medes with no political order whatsoever.[2] In both cases, they swiftly revert to monarchy.) The Hippocratic *Airs, Waters, Places* develops the thesis that the softness of the peoples of the Near East was the inevitable function of their different climate.[3] As we have seen in Chapter 3, the tragedies of Euripides reflect (and subvert) the view that to be a barbarian was a matter of birth (*genos*).

[1] See Dörrie, 'Die Wertung der Barbaren im Urteil der Griechen'.
[2] Hdt. 1.96–101, 2.151–2.
[3] For Hippocratic medical writings, see above, introduction to Part I.

In general, however (as Edith Hall has written in justification of her use of terms such as 'xenophobia' or 'chauvinism' in preference to 'racism'), there is little stress on the biological differences between Greeks and barbarians; we find, at least, no biological theorising on the differences between peoples,[4] and little emphasis on differences in colour between peoples.[5]

What we do find is myth. It was, in particular, through the means of heroic genealogies, which traced the Greeks' descent from imaginary common ancestors, that they expressed their sense of their particular ethnic identities. But, as Edith Hall emphasises in her 'When is a Myth Not a Myth? Bernal's "Ancient Model"' (below, Ch. 5), it is important to distinguish between what the Greeks *thought* about their origins (their 'subjective ethnicity') and the reality ('objective ethnicity'). It is also necessary, as she again emphasises, to remember that there is no unitary Greek Myth – that the identities asserted through heroic genealogies are as likely to be those of an aristocratic *genos* (or family), of a phratry (or 'brotherhood', a group within a city based on imagined descent from a common ancestor), a *polis* or an *ethnos* (i.e. the Dorians or the Ionians), as of the Greeks in general.[6]

Edith Hall's discussion is in the first instance a critique of Martin Bernal's now notorious work *Black Athena*.[7] Bernal argues, as Hall puts it, first that the Greeks believed that they were descended from the Egyptians and the Phoenicians, and secondly that they were right in thinking so. Hall shows, however, that the Greeks' beliefs are far more complex: figures such as Cadmus and Danaus, who in myth settled in Thebes and Argos respectively, themselves formed part of highly developed *Greek* mythical genealogies; such myths, moreover, arose or were modified in specific cultural contexts. Above all, these myths cannot be interpreted on the assumption that they possess a historical kernel of truth. Just as the Greeks ascribed foreign origins to the eminently Greek god Dionysus, so myths of the foundation of Greek cities may have been 'Egyptianised' or 'orientalised' in the

---

[4] Hall, *Inventing the Barbarian*, p. ix; cf. Dench, *From Barbarians to New Men*, p. 46. See below, Ch. 12 (Nippel), on the development of physical anthropology in the eighteenth century.

[5] Snowden, *Before Color Prejudice*.

[6] A stress on 'intrahellenic' identities – on the articulation of the identity of Aeolians, Dorians etc., or of smaller units through the invention of mythical genealogies – is a feature of Hall, *Ethnic Identity*. See also Ch. 10 (Walbank), below.

[7] Bernal, *Black Athena*. For responses to Bernal, see e.g. M. M. Levine and J. Peradotto, *The Challenge of Black Athena* (a special issue of the journal *Arethusa*); subsequent articles in *Arethusa* 25 (1992) and 26 (1993); Lefkowitz and Rogers, *Black Athena Revisited*; Lefkowitz, *Not Out of Africa*; Coleman and Walz, *Greeks and Barbarians*; Berlinerbau, *Heresy in the University*.

light, for example, of the Greeks' colonising movement (as charter myths to justify Greek colonies) or as a result of the development of Greek ethnography. The integration of foreign figures into Greek mythology, far from reflecting a historical era of migration into Greece, may suggest the Greek *appropriation* – through the medium of myth – of foreign lands.[8]

None of this is to deny the influence of Near Eastern and Egyptian culture on the Greek world, or (one of Bernal's main arguments) that such influences have been systematically excluded in much past scholarship. Hall indeed observes that 'modern racial prejudice' accounts for the fact that 'cultural contact between ancient Helleno-phone communities and ancient Semitic and black peoples ... is still being played down' (p. 135). In recent years, however, there has been a good deal of research, from well-established figures in classical scholarship likely to command (at very least) lip service, which has sought to address precisely this problem.[9] I would give weight to weaker ideological explanations for the blindness of modern scholars to such cultural contact: the increased compartmentalisation of fields of scholarship, and the continuing need to prove the relevance and potency of the classical past in order to justify its study.[10]

The importance of language as a feature of Greek identity is then discussed by the comparative philologist Anna Morpurgo Davies in her piece 'The Greek Notion of Dialect' (Ch. 6). The distinction of dialect and language, Morpurgo Davies argues, is not one that has a linguistic basis; rather, it usually depends on other, broadly political, factors. Moreover, there is an added difficulty in talking of Greek 'dialect'. A dialect is a dialect of a language. However, though Greek writers switched *between* dialects (Doric, Ionic, Attic, Aeolic), they did not switch between a dialect and *Greek* for the simple reason that, before the *koine* or 'common' language of the Hellenistic period, no such common language existed. Morpurgo Davies first reviews the evidence for dialect switching in the classical period, and then turns to Greek attitudes towards dialect and language. Though there may have been no common language, her survey discovers

---

[8] See also Hall, *Inventing the Barbarian*, pp. 47–50 (on colonisation and Homer); Bickermann, 'Origines Gentium'; Buxton, *Imaginary Greece*, pp. 191–3; Ulf, 'Griechische Ethnogenese'; see now also Jones, *Kinship Diplomacy*; Erskine, *Troy between Greece and Rome*; and, for an emphasis on myth as a tool in mediation between Greeks and native peoples, Malkin, *Returns of Odysseus*.

[9] I am thinking, in particular, of Burkert, *The Orientalizing Revolution*, and M. L. West, *The East Face of Helicon*.

[10] See my comments, *The Emptiness of Asia*, pp. 111–15, and below (introduction to Part IV).

that an abstract notion of a single Greek language pre-existed the Hellenistic *koine*.

Morpurgo Davies's article can be supplemented by a huge range of recent work: on dialect and the attitudes to dialect;[11] on local scripts[12] or on the Phoenician origins of the Greek alphabet;[13] on language contact between Greeks and non-Greeks;[14] on the language used to describe 'acculturation' (reflecting the assumption that barbarians can become Greeks through the acquisition of culture, but Greeks barbarians only through mixed blood);[15] on the linguistic caricature of non-Greeks (and of different Greeks) in tragedy and comedy;[16] on the ascription of moral values to foreign languages (for example, the idea that barbarian speech was somehow slavish), on the later linguistic purism of the hellenism of the Roman empire or of the independence era;[17] or on Greek ideas of the structure of foreign languages and of the relation of foreign languages with Greek.[18] As Saïd observes in Chapter 3, it is open to question whether the Greeks even thought that foreign languages were distinct from Greek – or whether they saw them as 'Greek gone wrong'.

We turn finally to the last of Herodotus' three constituents of Greek identity: religion. As Jean Rudhardt points out in Chapter 7, Herodotus and the Greeks had no conception of Greek 'religion' as distinct from the religions of foreign peoples. In his descriptions of foreign peoples, Herodotus concentrates on differences in ritual practice; he classes these ritual practices as a subset of *nomoi*, customs. Foreign gods are simply Greek gods with different names and different rites associated with them. The Athenians' denial that they will ever contemplate an alliance with the Persians noticeably lays stress on the common *shrines* and *sacrifices* of the gods, not on their common Greek gods.[19]

---

[11] Hall, *Ethnic Identity*, Ch. 6; Colvin, *Dialect in Aristophanes*.

[12] Hall, *Ethnic Identity*, with further refs.

[13] See e.g. Hall, *Ethnic Identity*, pp. 143–53; Powell, *Homer and the Origin of the Greek Alphabet*; Woodard, *Greek Writing*.

[14] See e.g. Sherwin-White, 'Seleucid Babylonia', pp. 3–8.

[15] Dubuisson, 'Remarques sur le vocabulaire grec'.

[16] See e.g. Hall, *Inventing the Barbarian*, pp. 17–21, 76–9, 117–21, 177–81; Halliwell, 'Sounds of the voice'; Brixhe, 'La langue d'étranger'; Jannsens, 'Les étrangers comme élement comique'. There is a huge bibliography on individual passages in Aristophanes: see e.g. Harrison, 'Herodotus' conception of foreign languages', n. 49. For interpreters in Greek (and Latin) texts, see Rochette, 'Grecs et Latins'.

[17] See e.g. Swain, *Hellenism and Empire*; Herzfeld, *Ours Once More*; Horrocks, *Greek*.

[18] On all these aspects (and further bibliography), see Harrison, 'Herodotus' conception of foreign languages'.

[19] See Parker, *Cleomenes on the Acropolis*.

Rudhardt connects this apparent openness in (what we must call for convenience) 'Greek religion' to the diversity of religious cult within the Greek world. Against the background in which different Greek cities worshipped the gods under different epithets (e.g. Athena *Polias*), with different rites and with different associated myths, foreign cultures – with their different names for gods, but with sufficient small similarities in iconography or myth to establish identifications of Greek and foreign gods – appeared significantly less foreign. Rudhardt also connects this openness to a central principle of Greek religion, that of the unknowability of the names and natures of the gods:[20] because it is impossible to have certain knowledge of the nature of the gods, or of the best means of approaching them through ritual, each people must follow their own traditional rites. It is for this reason that Greeks often show an initial unwillingness to integrate the rituals of new gods (that is, gods without established cults) into their cities.[21] It is also for the same reason that for the Greeks to proselytise – to seek to convert foreign peoples to their own religious customs or beliefs – was unthinkable.

A different emphasis is possible in a number of areas. I have argued elsewhere, in the context of Herodotus' religious beliefs, that the Greeks found a range of ways to differentiate their own 'religion' from those of foreign peoples.[22] Some foreign gods – often, it seems, because of the barbaric rites associated with them – proved untranslatable: Herodotus terms them, for example, 'local gods'. Though the Greeks may espouse the ideal that one should give the benefit of the doubt to the gods of foreign peoples, they generally refrain (as Rudhardt points out) from participating in, or importing, foreign rituals. Moreover, when foreign peoples – pre-eminently the Persians – show a consistent disregard for Greek religious cults, this serves ironically to justify the Greek disapproval of Persian 'religion'. The diffusion of the 'names of the gods' described by Herodotus is also open to more than one explanation. When, for example, Herodotus asserts that the names of the gods came from Egypt to Greece – though he knows that in many instances the Egyptian names for gods differed – Rudhardt and others have interpreted this to mean that the

---

[20] For unknowability, see esp. Gould, 'On understanding Greek religion', 'Herodotus and religion', p. 94; Rudhardt, *Notions fondamentales de la pensée religieuse*, pp. 90, 101, 105; Sourvinou-Inwood, 'Tragedy and religion', pp. 162–3; Harrison, *Divinity and History*, Chs 6–7.

[21] For the integration of new gods into Athens, see esp. Parker, *Athenian Religion*, Ch. 9.

[22] Harrison, *Divinity and History*, Ch. 8 ('Foreign gods and foreign religion'); contrast Hall, *Inventing the Barbarian*, pp. 5, 86–93, 143–54, minimising the degree to which 'religion' was a criterion of Greek self–definition.

Greeks learnt from the Egyptians the *habit* of distinguishing these gods.[23] Following Richmond Lattimore, I have argued that this reading makes a nonsense of a number of neighbouring passages of the *Histories*: instead, an explanation must be sought in Herodotus' ideas of language, for example in his assumption that names may *change*.[24]

There are inevitably a number of issues that Rudhardt's important discussion leaves uncovered. Walter Burkert and John Gould have both emphasised Herodotus' concentration on differences in *ritual* between different peoples (Gould going so far as to comment that Herodotus '[almost] identifies religion with ritual process').[25] Christiane Sourvinou-Inwood, in a discussion of the theology of Greek tragedy, has demonstrated beautifully how the Artemis of the Taurians in Euripides' *Iphigenia in Tauris* relates to the Artemis of Attic cult.[26] Finally, there is the issue of the veracity of Greek representations of foreign religion. Greek sources consistently portray the Persians as sacrilegious destroyers of shrines[27] – Greeks only ever burn temples by accident (Hdt. 5.102) – and (sometimes, it seems, wilfully) represent the Persians' gesture of deference to their kings (or *proskynesis*) as a form of worship.[28] Greek identifications of their own gods with those of foreign peoples often rest on (what seem to us to be) extraordinarily slim resemblances in myth or iconography.[29] Here again we see the Greeks fitting their partial knowledge of foreign peoples into the structure of their own assumptions.

[23] For further bibliography, see Harrison, *Divinity and History*, Appendix 2.

[24] Lattimore, 'Herodotus and the names of the Egyptian gods'; Harrison, *Divinity and History*, Appendix 2. See now, however, Thomas' restatement of the alternative line, *Herodotus in Context*, Ch. 8 (written in knowledge of, but without engagement with, my own counter–arguments).

[25] Burkert, 'Herodot als Historiker fremder Religionen'; Gould, 'Herodotus and religion' (the quotation from p. 104); see, however, my comments, *Divinity and History*, pp. 220–2.

[26] Sourvinou-Inwood, 'Tragedy and religion', pp. 170–5, arguing against the simplistic distinction of the religion of tragedy and 'real life' pursued by Mikalson, *Honor Thy Gods*.

[27] See e.g. Kuhrt and Sherwin-White, 'Xerxes' destruction of Babylonian temples'.

[28] See further Harrison, *Emptiness of Asia*, Ch. 8; Bickermann, 'À propos d'un passage'; Badian, 'The deification of Alexander the Great'; Bosworth, *Conquest and Empire*, II.D.

[29] See further (and for bibliography) Harrison, *Divinity and History*, Ch. 8.

5 *When is a Myth Not a Myth?*
Bernal's 'Ancient Model'†

EDITH HALL

THE ANCIENT MODEL

The argument of Bernal's *Black Athena* sets up two rival models of Greek prehistory. The one, which he terms "the Ancient Model," was, he claims, the conventional view held by most Greeks in the classical and Hellenistic eras; according to this model, Greek culture had arisen as a result of colonization, around 1500 B.C.E., by Egyptians and Phoenicians who civilized the native inhabitants of (what was later called) Hellas. This model therefore sees ancient Greece as essentially a Levantine culture, on the periphery of the Egyptian and Semitic spheres of influence. The rival model, on the other hand, which he chooses to term "the extreme Aryan Model," was invented, he argues, in the early nineteenth century. It saw the Greeks as Indo-European-speaking invaders from the north, who had overwhelmed the indigenous pre-Hellenic culture; sometimes the myth of the return of the Heraclidae was interpreted as holding a kernel of the historical "truth" of these invasions from the north. Ancient Hellas, according to this model, is thus viewed as European, the pure Aryan *Ursprung* [origin] of modern Europe. Bernal argues from a historically relativist standpoint that the original "Ancient Model," though surviving until fairly recently, was overthrown by the "Aryan Model" as a result of the contingent ideological requirements of the late eighteenth and nineteenth centuries. The theory of the biologically distinct races of humankind and their congenital inequalities in terms of intelligence and so on, which was to develop so disastrously into the practical policies of National Socialism, was

† Originally published in *Arethusa* 25 (1992), 181–201; this version from Mary Lefkowitz and G. M. Rogers (eds), *Black Athena Revisited* (Chapel Hill: University of North Carolina Press, 1996), 333–48.

Reprinted, with revisions, by permission of the author and The Johns Hopkins University Press from *Arethusa* 25 (1992): 181–201. I thank the editor of *Arethusa* and the anonymous readers for helpful comments on a previous draft.

first promulgated in print by Blumenbach in 1775; it was a product of the racist tendencies of European artists, intellectuals, and academics, and it was fed by their romanticism. They found it intolerable to admit any Semitic or African influence on the "pure childhood" of Europe. The "Ancient Model" was officially overthrown by Karl Otfried Müller in 1820.

Modern classicists may have *adapted* the "Aryan Model" to accommodate the discovery of Levantine objects on Late Bronze Age and Early Iron Age sites in the Aegean, and would now mostly admit to the possibility of Bronze Age western Semitic settlements on islands and even at Thebes, as well as to Phoenician influence on Iron Age Greece dating back as far as the tenth century B.C.E. But they are still working, Bernal argues, within what he calls the "Broad Aryan Model." He urges that we must now decide whether we are to retain any respect at all for the "Aryan Model," and continue to work within it, or whether we are to discard it altogether and get back to the "Ancient Model." That is, are we to believe the ancient Greeks themselves, or the northern European thinkers of the eighteenth and nineteenth centuries? Bernal admits that there is no possibility that either model can be proven (*BA* 1:8) but submits that each of the two models must be assessed according to its "competitive plausibility."

The challenge the book presents is an important one; academic discourse is as ideologically laden as political discourse, journalism, art, and literature, and we must constantly review the assumptions we are bringing to bear on the ancient world, constantly try to understand ourselves, academics, as part of our own ideology and culture, indeed as some of the most influential makers or reproducers of ideology *for* our culture. Every era of classical scholarship looks into the ancient world and finds in it reflected its own contingent sociopolitical preoccupations. The clearest example from recent years of the way in which academic attitudes have altered as a result of political shifts has been the development of feminist theory and women's studies in all disciplines: this can in no way be separated from the rise and success of the women's movement in the political arena. Increasing political sensitivity in certain quarters to the problematic legacy of European imperialism, racism, and chauvinism has also at long last begun to produce academic work which admits to a latent ethnocentrism in almost all European historiography ancient and modern; such works as Preiswerk and Perrot's *Ethnocentrism and History* (1978), Diamond's *In Search of the Primitive* (1974), Said's *Orientalism* (1978), Hay's *Europe: The Emergence of an Idea* (1968), Barker's edition of a collection of essays entitled *Europe and*

Its Others (1985), Kabbani's *Europe's Myths of Orient* (1986), and now some works by classicists are beginning to impinge on the comfortable ethnocentric and racist assumptions of many establishment academics (Snowden 1983; Hall 1989). We therefore cannot dismiss Bernal's book out of hand.

Bernal's argument rests on many different kinds of evidence, but the three kinds of testimony on which his thesis ultimately depends are literary, archaeological, and linguistic. Others have done much better than I can at sorting out the archaeological and linguistic evidence. My remarks here are confined to what is the first, and really the most vital, plank in Bernal's argument, which itself breaks down into two separate subtheses: first, he asks us to accept that the Greeks themselves genuinely believed that they were descended from Egyptians or Phoenicians; secondly, he asks us to believe that they were right. This basic thesis is set out in chapter 1 of the first volume of *Black Athena*, "The Ancient Model in Antiquity." In that chapter Bernal also adduces testimony to the influence which the arts, crafts, religions, and technologies of Africa and the Levant continued to exert on Hellenic culture long after his proposed colonial invasions; we are not concerned here with that aspect of his argument, although I myself take a sympathetic view of academic works arguing that the amount of interchange between Hellenophone and other communities, whether commercial or cultural, was considerably larger than has generally been assumed (see, e.g., Burkert 1984). There is, moreover, little doubt that Bernal is correct in arguing that modern racial prejudice has been one of the reasons why cultural contact between ancient Hellenophone communities and ancient Semitic and black peoples has been and is still being played down.[1]

Bernal himself unfortunately often conflates his "cultural borrowing" arguments and his arguments for the return to the "Ancient Model"; attention here is primarily addressed to the latter. Did the Greeks think that they had come from Egypt and Phoenicia? Did they *all* think this, *all* the time? And is there any reason why their theories about their original ethnic derivation and provenance should be any more accurate or valid than our own?

Bernal's entire thesis rests ultimately on his argument that the versions of certain myths preserved in some ancient literary sources contain kernels of that nebulous entity "historical truth" and ought therefore to be believed. Most of these sources involve the mythical

[1] See esp. S. P. Morris 1989, arguing that Greek contact with Levantine culture was even greater than Bernal supposes.

pattern by which someone from outside of Hellas proper—Cadmus, Danaus—came to the Greek mainland, to Thebes or Argos, and settled there.[2] Bernal believes these myths, rather than the myth invented by nineteenth-century classical scholarship, that the Greeks were all Aryans coming down from the north. He thinks that the Greeks' myths actually crystallize a kernel of fact. This is, of course, an old-fashioned view of the generation, function, and nature of the truth expressed by myth, and I shall have more to say about it later.

SUBJECTIVE AND OBJECTIVE ETHNICITY

Bernal's work fails to take adequately into account the important distinction, first proposed by Max Weber (1921) and since used by social anthropologists, between objective and subjective ethnicity. Objective ethnicity is a biological category which defines groups of human beings in terms of their shared physical characteristics resulting from a common gene pool. Subjective ethnicity, however, describes the *ideology* of an ethnic group by defining as shared its ancestors, history, language, mode of production, religion, customs, culture, etc., and is therefore a social construct, not a fact of nature (see esp. Isajiw 1974). Objective and subjective ethnicity may and often do overlap, and the subjective, ideological boundaries between ethnic groups may be commensurate with objective ethnic boundaries (Barth 1969), especially where an ethnic group has been isolated or has rigorously avoided intermarriage. But there is a world of difference between saying that the Greeks *were* the descendants of Egyptians and Phoenicians, and saying that the Greeks *thought* that they were descended from Egyptians and Phoenicians. The first statement tries to define the ancient Greeks' ethnicity objectively, the second subjectively. When Bernal discusses "colonization myths" such as those of Cadmus and Danaus, he uses myths defining ethnicity subjectively as proof of the objective ethnic origins of the Greeks, which is a logical non sequitur and a methodological flaw. This will be discussed further later. But first it is important to state some simple empirical objections to Bernal's uses of literary sources.

---

[2] The third familiar myth following this pattern, often mentioned by ancient writers in conjunction with those of Cadmus and Danaus, is that of Pelops the Lydian or Phrygian, who colonized the Peloponnese. Bernal singularly overlooks Pelops, perhaps because the idea that Greece was colonized from the northwest corner of the Asiatic seaboard does not fit the argument of his book.

CADMUS

The cornerstone of Bernal's argument is the tradition that Thebes was founded by Cadmus the Phoenician. In Homeric epic the only tradition mentioned is the original foundation of Thebes by Amphion and Zethus (*Odyssey* 11.262). Yet Bernal implies (*BA* 1:19) that the story of Cadmus arriving from the east to *re*found the Thebes of Amphion and Zethus is likewise to be found already there.

Bernal (1:85–86) attacks Gomme's theory, put forward in an article in 1913, that Cadmus had only been Orientalized in the fifth century. Gomme pointed out that the word *phoinix* had many meanings other than "Phoenician" and that references in *Archaic* poetry to Europa as the daughter of Phoinix need not be understood as meaning the daughter of an ethnic Phoenician. To my knowledge Gomme's argument has not yet been rendered untenable, though R. Edwards has tried hard to make the ethnic significance of Phoinix's name an Archaic, even Mycenaean, rather than Classical-period tradition (1979, 65–87). Bernal makes much of the papyrus fragment of the pseudo-Hesiodic *Ehoiai* or *Catalogue of Women* (ca. 600 B.C.E.) referring to Europa (Merkelbach and West fragment 141). This, however, can still be interpreted as calling her "daughter of the noble Phoinix" rather than "daughter of the noble Phoenician" (*kou]r[e]i Phoinikos agauou*, line 7).

Lest anyone think that by arguing that Gomme may have been right I am here working only within the "Aryan Model" and failing to take a simple, sensible view of the ancient evidence, it is necessary to point out that several proper names occurring in early literature do not necessarily bear the same specific ethnic significance that they come to bear later. Homer's *Aithiopes*, for example, are not even described as dark of skin. Now although certain dark-skinned peoples were by the fifth century being described as *Aithiopes*, and their name interpreted as meaning "of heavily tanned complexion," the name *Aithiops* really is of perfectly good Greek etymology (*aitho*, "blaze, burn," + *ops*, "face"). It is, furthermore, just as plausible to argue that a fabulous people of Archaic epic, who lived in the furthest East or West and whose name indicated a brilliance in the eyes or face of reflected light from the rising or setting sun, were identified during the period of the rise of ethnography in the sixth century B.C.E. with real, outlying dark-skinned peoples, and that the name was reinterpreted accordingly (Forsdyke 1956, 97; Dihle 1965, 67–69). Can we discount the possibility that similar things may have happened to the word *phoinix*? Given that an unquestionably Greek hero on the

Achaean side in the *Iliad* is called Phoinix, and that the word *phoinix* really can and often does mean "purple," "red," "pertaining to the date palm," or a kind of musical instrument as well as to a Phoenician, and that it is cognate with such words as *phoineeis* and *phoinios*, "bloody, blood-colored," is anyone justified in insisting on the antiquity of the tradition that Europa was a daughter not of a hero called Phoinix, but of a Phoenician?[3]

DANAUS

The argument is just as difficult for Bernal when it comes to Danaus and the Archaic sources. He somehow overlooks two Hesiodic fragments of relevance: Merkelbach and West fragment 296, from a poem entitled the *Aegimius*, connecting Io's impregnation by Zeus not with the mouth of the Nile but with Euboea; and Merkelbach and West fragment 124 = [Apollodorus] *Bibl*[*iotheke*] 2.1.3, which makes Io a daughter not of Inachus but of Pieren. These fragments are important because they show (1) that the mythical tradition about the ethnicity of a particular character or family which succeeded in becoming the most widespread may not be the most ancient and (2) that there may have existed a whole alternative tradition about Io's descendants through Epaphus to the Danaids, and of course also to Heracles, which had a local mainland Greek color and very little to do with Egypt. Neither Bernal nor anyone else has to my knowledge *dis*proved that there was a process by which the story of Io and her descendants became Egyptianized, perhaps in the seventh century B.C.E. under Psamthek, when identification of the cow-maiden with the Egyptian horned goddess Isis would have been one of the more natural religious syncretisms made by the Greeks abroad (A. B. Lloyd 1975–88, 1:125). The mostly lost epic poem called the *Danais* or *Danaides* of which Bernal is forced to make so much is usually dated to the sixth century B.C.E.; anyway, by that time the story of Io's descendants had certainly brought them into connection with Egypt, for there was an important process, of which Bernal seems unaware, by which many traditional mythical figures were brought into connection with foreign peoples and places. This process was associated with *Greek* colonization, as the poet-genealogists sought to provide their Hellenophone public, now spread over all corners of the Mediterranean, with mythical progenitors and founders who had prefigured their own activities in foreign parts.

[3] See also Vian 1963, 52–75.

It is possible to argue, for example, that it is the widening horizons of the *Greeks* which are reflected both by the appropriation of oriental gods to Hellenic family trees in the *Catalogue of Women* (Adonis does indeed become a son of Phoinix, Merkelbach and West fragment 139; but then there is evidence that the Adonis cult had been adopted by Hellenophone communities by the time of Sappho [fragment 140.1, 211b ii Lobel-Page 1955], ca. 600 B.C.E.) and by its genealogical explanations of numerous foreign ethnic groups.[4] The (*Catalogue of Women* traces most of its Greeks back to the founding father Deucalion, including their eponymous ancestor Hellen. In its second and third books, however, it focuses on the descendants of the Argive Inachus. It was from one of them, Io (the Argive princess who, I would argue, is only now being diverted in myth to Egypt), that the largest group of non-Greek peoples was thought to have sprung. Argos became the center of a vast international genealogy, and Io's family the ancestors and descendants of the Egyptians, Arabs, Phoenicians, and Libyans. Belus (probably a Hellenization of the oriental cult title Baʿal) heads the family of Aegyptus and Danaus; Agenor's descendants include Cadmus. These genealogies are, however, actually profoundly ethnocentric from a *Hellenic* point of view, for they seek to trace the origin of all peoples of the world back to Greek gods and heroes (Bickerman 1952)—thus, it could be argued, legitimizing and mythically prefiguring the existence of Greeks in far-flung Greek colonies. It is significant that Danaus and Cadmus, though in family trees leading to foreign peoples such as the Egyptians and Phoenicians, are ultimately traced back to Hellas and Inachus; Bernal consistently forgets this in his interpretation of the narratives which recount their stories, and sees them purely as aliens coming in from outside.

The reason for focusing on this sparse Archaic literary evidence is that it is of the greatest possible importance to Bernal's argument: he wants the Greek myths to contain historical truth, and he would be most likely to convince us of the plausibility of this thesis if he could prove that Cadmus and Danaus had been Phoenician and Egyptian in the earliest extant testimony to the mythopoeic tradition. I hope to have shown by this time that even this step in his argument is susceptible to doubt. By the fifth century B.C.E., of course, myth was being reinterpreted, ornamented, manipulated, and transformed for many different purposes; using it now in any way as a factual historical record is methodologically even more dubious. And when Bernal

---

[4] See Merkelbach 1968; Drews 1973, 7–9; West 1985, 149–50; E. Hall 1989, 35–37, 48.

resorts to such late sources as writers from the first century c.e. (Strabo) or the second (Pausanias) (*BA* 1:79), credulity is stretched to the limit. Whether Plutarch regarded Greek religion as a borrowing from Egypt or not is irrelevant to the "truth"; at the time he was writing (second century c.e.), he was plugging into a centuries-old stream of discourse, a debate with its own goalposts and primary texts (such as Herodotus). He was in little better position to judge than we are.

COMPETITIVE GENEALOGIES

Subjective definitions of ethnicity, by their very nature as social constructs, are open to challenge. Different people can define a particular ethnic group's genealogy in different ways according to their contingent purposes at the time. A good illustration from ancient history is the argument waged over the provenance of the Romans. Once the Julio-Claudian family (especially Julius Caesar and Augustus) had taken it upon themselves to prove that they were descended from the gods via Aeneas, the hero of Troy, the problem of the Trojans' own ethnic origins wagged its head.[5] Poets were suborned to the cause of defining the Romans' ethnicity; Propertius, defending his practice of writing love poetry, complains to Maecenas that he has not the heart to trace the line of Caesar to his Phrygian forefathers (II.41–2). Virgil, of course, made Dardanus, the ancestor of the Trojans, into an Italian, thus presenting Aeneas' colonization of Italy less as an external imperial invasion than as a *nostos*, or homecoming, a reclaiming of what was rightfully his: the Trojans' return to their own autochthonous origins. On the other hand, the whole of the first book of Dionysius of Halicarnassus, who was writing for a different readership and with different aims, is concerned to demonstrate that all the tribes from which Rome sprang— Aborigines, Pelasgians, Arcadians, the followers of Heracles and Aeneas' Trojans—were more ancient and more Greek than any others (*toutōn gar an ouden heuroi tōn ethnōn oute archaioteron oute Hellē- / nikōteron*, 1.89.1–2).[6] Until the eighteenth century, however, numerous European royal families insisted, like the Julio-Claudians, on their derivation from Trojan exiles: to question their Trojan ancestry was to contest the legitimacy of the *ancien régime*

---

[5] Tiberius was supposedly so concerned about the Trojans' genealogy that he wrote a dissertation entitled *Quae Mater Hecubae Fuerit*; see Leaf 1902, comment on *Iliad* 16.717.

[6] See further H. Hill 1961, 88–89 and nn. 7–8.

(Vickers 1987, 481). In modern times our myths of ethnic provenance may seem no less incredible (see A. D. Smith 1986); the Mormons, for example, claim descent from the lost tribes of Israel.

Did the Greeks *all* believe that they were descended from Egyptians and Phoenicians, *all* the time? The simple answer to this is no. Rival traditions were propounded, along with competitive subjective ethnicities. A striking example is the "Pelasgian" theory. This may have been invented by Hecataeus (*FGrHist* 1 F119), but it is Herodotus who gives it its fullest exegesis. Greece, says Herodotus, had been in early times populated by the Pelasgians, a prehistoric, indigenous Mediterranean people, speakers of a non-Greek language (1.57). The Pelasgians had been supplanted in some areas, especially Sparta, by incursive Dorians, who were the original Hellenes (1.56). (The theory can thus be viewed as an ancient "Aryan Model.") Thereafter the Hellenic tongue had spread even to the autochthonous Pelasgians in Hellas, but not to the "barbarian" Pelasgians that Herodotus maintains were still to be found elsewhere in the Mediterranean—in the Hellespont, Thrace, Samothrace, Lemnos, Imbros, and the Troad (2.51, 4.145, 5.26, 7.42). Characters in both Sophocles (ft. 270.4, Radt 1977) and Hellanicus (*FGrHist* 4 F4) identify the barbarian Pelasgians also with the "Tyrseni" or Etruscans.

But Thucydides has a different argument: indigenous Pelasgians had been "Hellenized" by the Hellenes, the "sons of Hellen," who had of course originated in Phthiotis (1.3.2)—Hellas in the *Iliad* (9.395) is just one district in Thessaly. The early Argive historian Acusilaus offered yet another explanation, for he ratified Pelasgus' place in his own city's mythology by making him a brother of Argos and a son of Zeus (*FGrHist* 2 F25a). Hence Argos in tragedy is frequently described as "Pelasgia," for those peoples who made a claim to autochthony, like the Arcadians or the Athenians, tried to trace themselves back to a Pelasgian origin (Herodotus 1.56–57, 8.44). Argos indeed, said by many authors to have been founded for the second time by the barbarian Egyptian Danaus, was in fact thought to have had a particular claim to autochthony because of its Homeric epithet "Pelasgian." The whole Pelasgian/Hellene theory is therefore in a terrible state of confusion in the ancient writers, from the fifth century onwards,[7] reflecting the attempts of a disparate people, spread around numerous autonomous city-states, with very

[7] The ancient testimony to the "Pelasgian" theory is assembled in Lochner von Hüttenbach 1960.

little "national" Hellenic ethnic identity, to create for themselves an intelligible mytho-historical tradition of their ethnic provenance.

ATHENIAN SOURCES

A central problem with Bernal's argument, indeed, is that he believes in a homogeneous entity called Greek Myth; he is constantly talking about What the Greeks Themselves Believed or the Greek Patriotic Tendency. What he fails to account for is that the ruling families in every polis defined their subjective ethnicity by tracing their fore-fathers' genealogies in different ways: one only has to look at the contradictory and confusing family trees that Pindar so ingeniously devised for his parvenu tyrants around the edges of the Greek-speak-ing world. And the fact is that nearly every one of Bernal's sources for the barbarian provenance of Danaus and Cadmus is either actually Athenian, or has an Athenocentric interest (Herodotus), or is plugging into a narrative tradition probably ultimately deriving from Athenian sources. And what was the distinguishing feature of the Athenians' own view of their provenance and ethnic identity? Of course, that they were autochthonous.[8]

Athenian propagandists constantly sought to contrast their own compatriots' allegedly autochthonous ancestors with Cadmus, Danaus, and Pelops, the barbarian progenitors of the Thebans and Peloponnesians; this was to become one of the standard clichéd topoi of the Athenian funeral orations and of patriotic purple passages in other forms of oratory (see, e.g., Isocrates 10.68; Plato *Menexenus* 245c–d). It is interesting that Thucydides does not use these myths, although I do not think that that was because of "motives of national prejudice," as Bernal alleges (*BA* 1:102): perhaps it was because he (as we should) saw through their polis-propagandist origins. Bernal, of course, does use such sources without pointing out the significance of their Athenian provenance. I am not altogether sure whether he is aware of the problem with which this presents him. On the one hand, he constantly talks about "Hellenic nationalism" and "national pride" in the fifth century, as if he did not know about the Pelopon-nesian War or the almost incessant enmity between Athens and Thebes. But, on the other, we do get a brief hint that he may after all be aware of the problem presented by the myth of Athenian

---

[8] Bernal tries without success (1989a, 22) to counter the argument from the Athenians' myth of autochthony, which was apparently raised by S. P. Morris during discussion at the American Philological Association panel in 1989.

autochthony, for he feels the need to place the rare, late, alternative, Egyptian foundation myth as early as the fifth century B.C.E.: he claims in an aside, without any textual references, that the tradition that Kekrops (founder of Athens) was Egyptian, was "probably current in Herodotus' day" (*BA* 1:79). I would like to hear of a text which can support this claim.

Bernal uses an Athenian text, Aeschylus' *Suppliants*, a play about the arrival of Danaus and his fifty daughters from Egypt to Argos, as one of the linchpins of his argument. In this play a decidedly Egyptianized and black Danaus and his fifty daughters arrive at Argos to claim asylum from the indigenous Pelasgians, ruled by King Pelasgus but also described repeatedly as "Hellenes." Danaus and the Danaids are in flight from Aegyptus and his fifty sons: their claim for asylum is based on the blood tie that binds them to the Argives through their joint ancestress Io, and here Aeschylus uses something similar to the genealogy presented in the *Catalogue of Women*. It is fairly certain that in the rest of the trilogy, now lost, Danaus acceded to the throne of Argos and that the tragic myth presented an explanation of the doubleness of the traditions surrounding the foundation of the city. But what Bernal forgets is that this is an *Athenian* interpretation of the Argive foundation myths, and that this casts doubt on his entire argument that Aeschylus would have wanted to diminish the Egyptian element in the Argive tradition because of current "national" chauvinism. He goes through the play looking for references to Egyptian religion, equating Zeus Chthonios with Osiris and so on (*BA* 1:91–97); and indeed Aeschylus is undoubtedly exploiting all the new literary potential which had been opened up by the invention of ethnography, the idea of the barbarian, and the *logoi* which had sprung up during and in response to the Persian Wars. But the Egyptianness of the Athenian Aeschylus' Danaus and Danaids, though indisputable, cannot be taken as historical evidence for a "real" Egyptian colonization: Aeschylus, writing from an Athenian perspective, is attempting to make sense of the Argive foundation myths, and, as we have seen, the Egyptian element in them may not be much more than a century and a half older than Aeschylus' text itself. Bernal is skating not on thin ice but on water when he claims (1:97) that Aeschylus' sources were from the seventh century; the most plausible candidate for the poet's information about Egypt is undoubtedly the early fifth-century Ionian historian Hecataeus (E. Hall 1989, 133). In this same context (*BA* 1:97), we may pass over Bernal's observation that the title *Suppliants* (*Hiketes* or *Hiketides* in Greek), or rather *hikesios* ("pertaining to suppli-

cation"), its parallel form, "strikingly resembles the Egyptian Ḥkꜣ
ḫꜣst)"—which, even if it were rendered in a later century into Greek
as *Hyksos* (Bernal neglects to cite his source) strikes me as one of
the most implausible etymological suggestions in the book. (Cf.
Vermeule, Tritle [in Lefkowitz and Rogers, *Black Athena Revisited*].)

When Bernal starts to use later tragedy, such as Euripides'
Phoenissae, in which the Phoenician connection of the Thebans is
elaborated poetically and exploited in the use of the popular female
barbarian chorus, he makes the same mistakes. Athenians liked to
emphasize the tradition of the Thebans' barbarian origins and, moreover, in tragedy displaced their own stasis and internal strife to other,
historically hostile, Greek cities: the tragic Thebes is a countercul-
ture, a mirror opposite of the tragic Athens (Zeitlin 1986). Thebes
houses tyrants, incest, stasis, and sexual deviationists, whereas
the Athens of tragedy is nearly always presented as an idealized
polis, free from internal conflict and led by democratically minded
kings almost indistinguishable from democratically elected *stratēgoi*
[generals].

As we have seen, Bernal similarly misuses the works of such
Athenian propagandists as Isocrates and the writers of *epitaphioi
logoi* [funeral orations] when they are cataloguing the barbarian
roots of non-Athenian Greek city-states. In later writers the tenacity
of the fifth- and fourth-century Athenian versions of the Cadmus and
Danaus myths is surely not to be explained, as Bernal would have it,
as evidence of the historical truth of those particular versions of the
myths—but rather as evidence of the greater amount of Athenian
literature produced in comparison with that from other cities, and
the Athenocentrism of those who used and transmitted the texts in
the ancient intellectual world.

FLUIDITY OF ETHNICITY IN MYTH

Another problem which needs to be isolated is that subjective ethnicity is an extremely fluid social construct which can change
remarkably quickly (Banton 1981, Keyes 1981a, 14–28). In myth the
ethnicity of heroic figures is remarkably mutable. Heroes can change
their ethnicity altogether according to the ideological requirements
of the imaginations interpreting their stories. We often have a dia-
chronic perspective on the volatility of particular heroes' and dynas-
ties' ethnicities, and so the subtleties and complexities of the ideas
proposed and the changes involved can actually be illustrated.

Ethnicity could be proved or challenged by inventing genealogies and mythical precedents.[9] Euripides wrote propagandist plays for such peoples as the Macedonians (*Archelaus*) and probably the Molossians (*Andromache*), trying to prove by claims of mythical origins and genealogical manipulation that these peoples had a claim to Hellenicity, when their detractors in the Greek world insisted that they were barbarians. In Athenian hands Tantalus, Niobe, and Pelops are sometimes Lydian, sometimes Phrygian, but from their earliest appearance in literature in Greek they may also be of indeterminate provenance.

A change in ethnicity may take the form of a renaming process. It was only in the fifth century B.C.E., for example, that the Trojans become identified with Phrygia and called *Phruges*, as the Trojan myth was rehandled to provide a mythical precursor of the Persian Wars, a previous defeat inflicted by Hellenic conquerors on an eastern empire (E. Hall 1988). Alteration in ethnicity, on the other hand, may be a matter of localizing a hero whose ethnicity is indeterminate: Lycurgus, for example, the mythical king who (like Pentheus) was punished for rejecting Dionysus, is of indeterminate ethnicity in Archaic poetry but in fifth-century works becomes stabilized in Thrace, as Dionysiac themes are attracted to that country (E. Hall 1989, 107). But many mythical figures can be seen changing their ethnicity altogether. It is not just that the family of Atreus is derived variously from Mycenae, Argos, or Sparta, according to the political purposes of different literary presentations of the myth, for at least all three of these locations are within the Peloponnese: heroes and heroines can actually be transformed from Greeks into barbarians and vice versa.

Medea, for example, almost certainly began as the northern Peloponnesian Agamede of the *Iliad*, a sorceress and granddaughter of the Sun (11.740–41). In Eumelus' epic, where myth was manipulated in order to justify Corinthian claims to territory in the Black Sea (Drews 1976, 24–29), she was presented as the Corinthian daughter of King Aeëtes, who emigrated to the Pontus (Pausanias 2.3.10). Her name, by being confused with the ethnic Medes, may have suggested her mother's name, Perse, in the *Odyssey* (10.138–39), but there is no other evidence for a truly barbarian, Colchian Medea until Euripides' play of 431 B.C.E. (D. Page 1938, lxii n. i). Tereus, again, began as a Megarian hero, but by the time of Sophocles' famous tragedy had been transformed into a Thracian, probably an Odrysian Thracian, simply because his name was simi-

---

[9] The following owes much to E. Hall 1989.

lar to that of the fifth-century Odrysian king Teres (E. Hall 1989, 104–5). Similarly in the *Odyssey* the Cimmerians may once have been the Cheimerians, inhabitants of Cheimerion on the River Acheron, near the Thesprotian *nekyomanteion* (oracle of the dead), and were only assimilated to the "Cimmerians" when the Greeks heard of the strange tribes who inhabited the "Crimea," the Tauric Chersonese (G. L. Huxley 1958; J. H. Finley 1978, 58 and n. 3). Ritual names also became confused with ethnic terms: Artemis' cultic title Tauropolos ("Bull-hunting") almost certainly became confused with the tribe known as the Taurians in the Tauric Chersonese (Lloyd-Jones 1983, 96), giving rise to the myth represented in Euripides' *Iphigeneia in Tauris*.

ETHNICITY AS AN ARTICULATOR OF ABSTRACTIONS

It is also necessary to point out that ethnicity can be used to express real truths in terms of the Greeks' conceptualizations of different abstractions, without being *literally* true. The Greeks' picture of their own past, in particular, overlapped with their picture of the else-where—a pattern seen in Thucydides' drawing of parallels between what the barbarians still practice and obsolete Greek customs (1.5). The Protagorean vision of the linear progression up through techno-logical inventions to the Greek democratic polis relied on a concept of a less civilized past, and this past was often identified with the else-where. But a contradiction lay at the heart of the Greeks' view of the non-Greek world, for the rise, paradoxically, could also be defined as a fall (witness the complexities of Hesiod's myth of the cycle of gener-ations). The retrospective vision expressed the ideas both of primi-tive chaos and of a more virtuous era when men were nearer to the gods. Because the past and the elsewhere often merged and over-lapped, the notion of the special spirituality of the golden age, before humanity was estranged by technological progress, could also be reproduced in narratives about known, contemporary barbarian communities.

This schizophrenic vision of the ethnically other expressed a contradictory conceptualization of non-Greek lands. Tyrants and savages lurked in the barbarian world, but it also supported ideal-ized peoples and harmonious relations with heaven. The countries believed to be older than Hellas, especially Egypt, thus became the sources in ethnography of numerous gods and rituals (witness Herodotus) and in Platonic philosophy of original wisdom. In this

conceptual system, therefore, anarchy and tyranny and cruelty all
belonged to the non-Greek world, but so did mystics like Orpheus,
sages like Anacharsis, and the kinds of religious practices and
intellectual skills that the Greeks believed were derived from the
Egyptians. And a grammar of associations was built up connecting
different abstractions with specific areas of the world. The West was
often the home of post-mortem havens and of utopias; the North,
of shamanistic practices, nomads, and primitivism both savage
and utopian; the East, of sex, decadence, and tyranny; the South,
especially Egypt, of cults, medicine, and primeval wisdom.

A telling example is the figure of Dionysus. Nearly everyone[10] used
to believe narratives (such as Euripides' *Bacchae*) which tell of the
bringing of Dionysiac religion from Asia or Thrace to Hellas, and so
placed the introduction of this new religion at some time in the eighth
century. But the almost certain appearance of the name Dionysus
in Linear B (Burkert 1985, 162) has shown that the idea of a late-
arriving eastern god appearing in Greece after the "Dark Ages" is an
academic fiction derived from an overly literal reading of myth;
indeed, Dionysus does not seem to have become Orientalized in the
Greek imagination until the sixth century (T. H. Carpenter 1986,
74–75, 124). This process was no doubt partly a result of syncretism
with genuine eastern divinities such as Sabazius, but what is important is that calling Dionysus Phrygian or Thracian expressed something other than historical ethnic derivation: these lands were from
the sixth century onward always associated with mystery cults, with
liberation from self-control and the constraints of civic existence, and
with dangerous release of the emotions and physical passions.
Dionysus is also the god of epiphany who arrives from the sea: this
finds mythical expression in the narratives of his introduction. The
same associations of Thrace led to Orpheus' being located there. The
definition of that perfectly good Greek religious figure, The Mother,
was the result of a similar process. Epic already expresses the association of specific concepts with the Egyptians and the Phoenicians, but
without any of Bernal's colonization narratives. Egypt in the *Odyssey*
is the land of wise doctors and great riches; from Phoenicia derive
wily merchants and slave dealers. The ancient wisdom of Egypt and
the cunning of the Phoenicians were to remain elements in the Greco-
Roman stereotypes of these countries throughout antiquity.

---

[10] Otto (1965, 52–64) was a conspicuous exception.

CONCLUSION: MYTH AND HISTORY

Ultimately the decision whether to accept or reject Bernal's advocacy of the "ancient model" depends on whether we can accept his handling of ancient Greek myth. This would mean that we must accept that certain myths do contain unmediated literal, historical truths. *Black Athena* seems to present an unsophisticated view of myth in general, and Greek myth in particular (T. Green 1989). Of course in the nineteenth and early twentieth centuries myth used regularly to be treated as history, as if its value existed in the information it bore about the past, rather than the present, the "here and now" of the culture producing the myth. It used to be argued that the myth of the Olympian victory over the Titans and Giants held a folk memory of *Homo sapiens'* victory over *Homo neanderthalensis*; many once saw the myths of the successions of the ages of gold, iron, and bronze as holding an orally transmitted memory of technological innovations.

A prime example is the myth of the Amazons, which clearly used to be taken as near-literal historical truth. This is the story of the matriarchal tribe subordinated by Greek male heroes, which itself underwent transmutations as the conquering hero changed from Heracles to Theseus in Athenian sources, and as the Amazons took on features borrowed from the *logos* of the Persian Wars. Bachofen (1861), in his work on matriarchy in prehistoric cultures, used the Amazon myth to show that matriarchy had preceded patriarchy. He pointed to Herodotus' discernment of a matrilineal system of inheritance in Lycia (1.173) and argued that this was a vestigial matriarchy. He saw the Amazon myth as recording man's usurpation of power from woman. But few would now see the truth of the Amazon myth as residing in its historicity: since the work of Pembroke (1967) and others,[11] it has been taken rather to express the Greek male's own self-definition of himself as patriarchal, by the construction of an "other," a matriarchal society embodying the exact opposite of his gender hierarchy. The myth of the conquest of the Amazons by Greek males defined by ahistorical aetiology the contemporary social structure.

Are we to abandon the sophisticated theories of the twentieth century which have helped us to understand how mythology works? Are we going to return to a simple nineteenth-century model which ignores all the post-Malinowskian, post-Freudian, and post-Lévi-

---

[11] See also Bamberger 1974, Tyrrell 1984, 23–25.

Straussian work on myths as ideological charters for social institutions, as expressions of subconscious desires, or as mediators or abstractions of concern to the contemporary world? Are we to ignore all the work done by social scientists in recent decades, since Weber's pioneering labors, on the way subjective ethnicity is constituted? Accepting Bernal's "Revised Ancient Model" requires us to do all this.

What he has done for us is to make us reject forever the "Aryan Model" and leave the question of who the Greeks actually were, biologically at least, buried with a proper degree of contempt. But in altogether abandoning the "Aryan Model," the nineteenth century's Myth of the Northern Origin of the Greeks, we ought not simply substitute another myth, the Myth of the Egyptian and Phoenician Takeover of Pre-Greece. What we must do is reject the historical validity of both myths and turn ourselves to the three really important questions which do need to be asked in greater detail, and with more sensitivity than hitherto, in regards to ethnicity as a social, subjective construct which signifies abstractions having little to do with ethnicity: who on earth did the Greeks *think* they were? Why did they think it? And what is it about the late twentieth century which renders the issue so important to *us*?

REFERENCES

Asterisks indicate reviews or critiques of *Black Athena*; daggers indicate recommended further reading.

BA 1 = Bernal 1987a.
BA 2 = Bernal 1991a.
Bachofen, J. J. 1981. *Das Mutterrecht: Eine Untersuchung über die Gynokratie der alten Welt nach ihrer religiösen und rechtlichen Natur.* Stuttgart: Krais & Hoffman.
Bamberger, J. 1974. "The Myth of Matriarchy: Why Men Rule in Primitive Societies." In W*oman, Culture, and Society*, edited by M. Z. Rosaldo and L. Lamphere, 263–80. Palo Alto: Stanford University Press.
Banton, M. 1981. "The Direction and Speech of Ethnic Change." In *Ethnic Change*, edited by C. F. Keyes, 32–52. London and Seattle: University of Washington Press.
Barker, F., ed. 1985. *Europe and Its Others.* Proceedings of the Essex Conference on the Sociology of Literature. Colchester: University of Essex.
Barth, F., ed. 1969. *Ethnic Groups and Boundaries.* Results of a Symposium held at the University of Bergen. Boston: Little, Brown.
Bernal, M. 1987a. *Black Athena: The Afroasiatic Roots of Classical Civilization.* Vol. 1, *The Fabrication of Ancient Greece 1785–1985.* London:

Free Association Books; New Brunswick: Rutgers University Press.

——. 1989a. "*Black Athena* and the APA." In Levine and Peradotto 1989 = *Arethusa* 22:17–38.

——. 1991a. *Black Athena: The Afro-Asiatic Roots of Classical Civilization*. Vol. 2, *The Archaeological and Documentary Evidence*. London: Free Association Books; New Brunswick, N.J.: Rutgers University Press.

Bickerman, E. J. 1952. "Origines Gentium." *Classical Philology* 47:65–81.

Blumenbach, J. F. 1795. *De Generis Humani Varietate Nativa*. Göttingen: Vandenhoeck & Ruprecht.

†Burkert, W. [1977] 1985. *Greek Religion: Archaic and Classical*. English translation of *Griechische Religion der archaischen und klassichen Epoche*. Oxford: Blackwell; Cambridge: Harvard University Press.

†——. [1984] 1992. *The Orientalizing Revolution: Near Eastern Influence on Greek Culture in the Early Archaic Age*. Translated by M. E. Pinder and W. Burkert. Cambridge: Harvard University Press.

Carpenter, T. H. 1986. *Dionysian Imagery in Archaic Greek Art*. Oxford: Clarendon Press.

Diamond, S. 1974. *In Search of the Primitive: A Critique of Civilization*. New Brunswick, N.J.: Transaction Books.

Dihle, A. 1965. "Zur Geschichte des Aithiopennamens." In *Umstrittene Daten: Untersuchungen zum Auftreten der Griechen am roten Meer*, 65–79. Cologne: Westdeutscher Verlag.

Drews, R. 1973. *The Greek Accounts of Eastern History*. Cambridge: Harvard University Press.

——. 1976. "The Earliest Greek Settlements on the Black Sea." *Journal of Hellenic Studies* 96:18–31.

†Edwards, R. 1979. *Kadmos the Phoenician: A Study in Greek Legend and the Mycenaen Age*. Amsterdam: Adolf M. Hakkert.

Finley, J. H. 1978. *Homer's Odyssey*. London and Cambridge: Harvard University Press.

Forsdyke, J. 1956. *Greece before Homer*. London: Max Parrish.

Gomme, A. W. 1913. "The Legend of Cadmus and the Logographoi." *Journal of Hellenic Studies* 33:53–72, 223–45.

*Green, T. 1989, "Black Athena and Classical Historiography: Other Approaches, Other Views." In Levine and Peradotto 1989 = *Arethusa* 22:55–65.

Hall, E. 1988. "When Did the Trojans Turn into Phrygians? Alcaeus 42.15." *Zeitschrift für Papyrologie und Epigraphik* 73:15–18.

——. 1989. *Inventing the Barbarian*. Oxford: Clarendon Press.

Hay, D. 1968. *Europe: The Emergence of an Idea*. 2d ed. Edinburgh: Edinburgh University Press.

Hill, H. 1961. "Dionysius of Halicarnassus and the Origins of Rome." *Journal of Roman Studies* 51:88–93.

Huxley, G. L. 1958. "Odysseus and the Thesprotian Oracle of the Dead." *La parola del passato* 13:145–58.

Isajiw, W. 1974. "Definitions of Ethnicity." *Ethnicity* 1:111–24.

Kabbani, R. 1986. *Europe's Myths of Orient: Devise and Rule.* Bloomington: Indiana University Press.

Keyes, C. F. 1981a. "The Dialectics of Ethnic Change." In *Ethnic Change* (Keyes 1981b), 3–30.

——, ed. 1981b. *Ethnic Change.* London and Seattle: University of Washington Press.

Leaf, W., ed. 1902. *The Iliad.* Vol. 2. 2d ed. London and New York: Macmillan.

†*Levine, M. M., and J. Peradotto, eds. 1989. *The Challenge of Black Athena.* Special issue, *Arethusa* 22 no. 1 (Fall).

Lloyd, A. B. 1975–88. *Herodotus Book II.* 3 vols. Leiden: E. J. Brill.

Lloyd-Jones, H. 1983. "Artemis and Iphigeneia." *Journal of Hellenic Studies* 103:87–102.

Lobel, E., and D. Page. 1955. *Poetarum Lesbiorum Fragmenta.* Oxford: Clarendon Press.

Lochner von Hüttenbach, F. 1960. *Die Pelasger.* Vienna: Gerold.

Merkelbach, R. 1968. "Les papyrus d'Hésiode et la géographie mythologique de la Grèce." *Chronique d'Egypte* 43:133–55.

Morris, S. P. 1989. "Daidalos and Kadmos: Classicism and 'Orientalism.'" In Levine and Peradotto 1989 = *Arethusa* 22:39–54.

Müller, K. O. [1820] 1844. *Orchomenos und die Minyer* (= *Geschichten hellenischer Stämme und Städte*, vol. 1). 2d ed. Breslau: Josef Max.

Otto, W. F. 1965. *Dionysos: Myth and Cult.* Translated by R. B. Palmer. Bloomington: Indiana University Press.

Page, D., ed. 1938. *Euripides' Medea.* Oxford: Clarendon Press.

Pembroke, S. 1967. "Women in Charge: The Function of Alternatives in Early Greek Tradition and the Ancient Idea of Matriarchy." *Journal of the Warburg and Courtauld Institutes* 30:1–35.

Preiswerk, R., and Perrot, D. 1978. *Ethnocentrism and History.* New York: NOK Publishers International.

Radt, S. 1977. *Tragicorum Graecorum Fragmenta.* Vol. 4, *Sophocles.* Göttingen: Vandenhoeck & Ruprecht.

†Said, E. W. 1978. *Orientalism.* London: Routledge & Kegan Paul.

Smith, A. D. 1986. *The Ethnic Origins of Nations.* Oxford: Blackwell.

†Snowden, F. M., Jr. 1983. *Before Color Prejudice: The Ancient View of Blacks.* Cambridge: Harvard University Press.

Tyrrell, W. B. 1984. *Amazons: A Study in Athenian Mythmaking.* Baltimore: The Johns Hopkins University Press.

Vian, F. 1963. *Les origines de Thèbes: Cadmos et les Spartes.* Paris: C. Klincksieck.

*Vickers, M. 1987. *Review of BA 1. Antiquity* 61:480–81.

Weber, M. 1921. 'Ethnische Gemeinschaften." *Wirtschaft und Gesellschaft: Grundriss der Sozialökonomik* Abteilung 3, Teil 2:215–26. Tübingen.

West, M. L. 1985. *The Hesiodic Catalogue of Women.* Oxford: Oxford

University Press.

Zeitlin, F. 1986. "Thebes: Theater of Self and Society in Athenian Drama."
In *Greek Tragedy and Political Theory*, edited by J. P. Euben, 101–41.
Berkeley and Los Angeles: University of California Press.

6 *The Greek Notion of Dialect*[†]

ANNA MORPURGO DAVIES

1. We frequently speak of Greek dialects but hardly ever try to explain what is the meaning of 'dialect' in this phrase. If we did, we would be reminded that dialects should not be discussed without making reference to their ethnolinguistic background. In general it seems impossible to call a dialect a dialect (rather than a language) and to study its development without considering the speakers of that dialect and the way in which they understood their linguistic situation or reacted to it. In the specific case of Greek the concept of dialect is so nebulous that a study of the ethnolinguistic data is especially relevant. What follows offers a few considerations which bear on the problem.[1]

2. We start with one of the best known passages of the late Byzantine grammarian, Gregory of Corinth, who lived in the twelfth century A.D. and wrote a manual Περὶ διαλέκτων [*On Dialects*] marked by little originality and much repetition.[2] It contains a definition of dialect which sounds singularly modern in its formulation: Διάλεκτός ἐστιν ἰδίωμα γλώσσης, ἢ διάλεκτός ἐστι λέξις ἴδιον χαρακτῆρα τόπου ἐμφαίνουσα "a dialect is a special form of a language or a dialect is a form of speech which indicates the special character of a place". It is noticeable that nineteenth or twentieth century dictionaries echo the sentiment and sometimes even the wording. It is also remarkable that the same dictionaries tend to use as exemplification of the use of the word 'dialect' (an obvious

† Originally published in *Verbum* 10 (1987), 7–27.
[1] Some of the points made here were first mentioned in the Semple Lectures on "Greek Attitudes to Language" which I delivered in 1983 at the invitation of the Department of Classics, University of Cincinnati. I greatly profited from the comments made then and from the discussion which followed the presentation of this paper at the Pont-à-Mousson Rencontre. For clarification, new ideas and new information I am especially indebted to Professors Albio Cassio of Naples and Jean Lallot of Paris.
[2] For a recent summary of the information available about Gregory of Corinth c.f. N.G. Wilson, *Scholars of Byzantium*, London 1983, 184–90.

Greek borrowing) phrases or sentences which refer to ancient Greek dialects.[3]

In current speech a dialect is now seen as a form of language which can be given a specific geographic or social definition. By contrast a language is seen as standardized and spoken over a wider area or by a larger group of people. In our modern literate world languages are likely to be both spoken and written, while dialects may simply exist in spoken form; we speak of dead languages, meaning presumably languages which are known only in written form, hardly ever of dead dialects. Until the recent wave of 'ethnicity' a language tended to have higher status than a dialect: the Sardinians were proud to speak a Romance language, not an Italian dialect.

The distinction between language and dialect which is so clear to the layman is less so to the linguist. We are now aware, as perhaps our nineteenth century predecessors were not, that it cannot be made in purely linguistic terms. It is simply not true, for instance, that the structural distinctions between two so-called dialects of a language are always smaller than those between two so-called languages. The criterion of mutual intelligibility which is often invoked in this

---

[3] It is a singularly instructive to read through some of the definitions; I quote a few at random. *Oxford English Dictionary* s.v. 'dialect' 2: "One of the subordinate forms or varieties of a language arising from local peculiarities of vocabulary, pronunciation and idiom. (In relation to modern languages usually *spec.* A variety of speech differing from the standard or 'literary' language; a provincial method of speech, as in 'speakers of dialect')". One of the examples quoted (ibid.) is "1614 RALEIGH Hist. World ii 496 The like changes are very familiar in the Aeolic Dialect." *Deutsches Wörterbuch* von Jacob und Wilhelm Grimm, Bd. 6 (1885), col. 2684 s.v. 'Mundart': "die wissenschaftliche bedeutung, die auf die in die einzelnen landschaften geltenden unterschiede der lebendigen volkssprache gegenüber einer allgemeinen, haupt- oder schriftsprache zielt, ist schon bei SCHOTTEL vorhanden, ist vielleicht die älteste des deutschen wortes". The *Neubearbeitung* of the Grimm Dictionary, Bd. 6 (1983) col. 852, s.v. 'Dialekt' has: "landschaftlich begrenzte Teilsprache, überwiegend mündlich. 1748 bey den Griechen schrieb ... jedes volk seinen dialekt wie es ihn zusprechen pflegte GOTTSCHED *Sprachkunst* 38". *Dictionnaire de l'Académie française*, vol. I (1932), p. 394 s.v. 'dialecte' gives a brief definition: "Variété régionale d'une langue" and exemplifies "La langue grecque ancienne a différents dialectes. Le dialecte attique. Le dialecte ionique. Le dialecte dorique ...". *Trésor de la langue française. Dictionnaire de la langue du XIXe et du XXe siècle*, vol. 7 (1979), p. 150 s.v. 'dialecte, A. linguistique': 1. Forme particulière d'une langue, intermédiare entre cette langue et le patois, parlée et écrite dans une région d'étendue variable et parfois instable ou confuse, sans le status culturel ou le plus souvent social de cette langue. ... 2. Forme régionale parlée et surtout écrite d'une langue ancienne. Comme ça m'est égal, que certaines des idylles de Théocrite soient en dialecte ionien (RENARD, Journal, 1895, p. 290). N. Tommaseo e B. Bellini, *Nuovo Dizionario della lingua italiana*, vol. 2 (1885), p. 133 s.v. 'dialetto': "Particolare linguaggio parlato da uomini d'una o più provincie, che per la differenza d'alcuni vocaboli o modi o costrutti o desinenze o pronunzie, si scosta dall'uso delle altre provincie che parlano la lingua stessa. Nel greco distinguonsi i dialetti Attico, Dorico, Jonico, Eolico, Comune = Infer. Sec. 254. S. Battaglia, *Grande Dizionario della lingua italiana*, vol. 4 (1966), p. 321 ff. s.v. 'dialetto': "Parlata propria di un ambiente geografico e culturale ristretto. ...'; contrapposta a un sistema linguistico affine per origine e sviluppo, ma che, per diverse ragioni ..., si è imposto come lingua letteraria e ufficiale. ... Varchi V-137 Ha (il greco), oltre la lingua comune, quattro dialetti, cioè quattro idiomi ...".

context cannot be used as a magic dividing line; first, it is part of our normal experience that we sometimes understand other so-called languages even without specific training in them while we may fail to understand the so-called dialects of our own language.[4] Secondly, there are instances where some form of intelligibility exists but is not mutual because social factors intervene. In an old article Hans Wolff[5] described the situation in the Eastern Niger Delta, where two structurally very close languages, Nembe and Kalabari, are spoken in adjacent areas. The Nembe claim that they understand Kalabari without difficulties. The Kalabari claim that to them Nembe is completely obscure except for a few words. It is noticeable that the Kalabari are a prosperous group while the Nembe have neither political nor economic power. In other words the labels 'language' and 'dialect' are applied on the strength of factors that need not be exclusively or even primarily linguistic.

We may now return to the similarities between the current lay understanding of a dialect and Gregory's definition. These are neither due to chance nor are they prompted by identical reactions to similar sets of observable facts. Though the current views fit admirably with the linguistic situation of the modern European nations (or of most of them) they have not been reached independently; they are clearly derived from the Greek views. It is the latter which call for an explanation rather than the former. How did Gregory or his predecessors reach their definition? Was this meant to reflect the linguistic situation of the ancient Greek world? If we answer in the affirmative, as is only natural, we encounter a curious paradox. Gregory and his predecessors are not interested in the theory of dialectology or linguistics, they are interested in describing Greek. But if so, and if Gregory thought that a dialect was a dialect of a language, as is implied by his statement, what was the language he had in mind? In Gregory's period, and indeed in the period of the earlier scholars from whom he may have borrowed his data and his thoughts, there was indeed a Greek language, the product of the Hellenistic koine [common Greek language], but in those periods it is also true that the koine had replaced the very dialects (Ionic, Attic, Doric and Aeolic) which Gregory lists and discusses.[6] On the other

---

[4] As a native speaker of Italian I can read Spanish, which I have never studied, but I cannot read Sicilian or Milanese, two Italian dialects, without the help of a translation.

[5] Hans Wolff, "Intelligibility and Inter-Ethnic Attitudes" in D. Hymes ed., *Language in Culture and Society*, New York 1964, 440–445.

[6] This is the current view; what exactly happened in spoken language and how far some of the earlier distinctions survived beyond the Hellenistic period is, needless to say, difficult to establish.

hand in the earlier period, when the dialects in question still flour-
ished, there does not seem to have been a standard language of which
those dialects could be dialects. Attic, Boeotian, etc. had equal status;
there may have been a certain amount of dialect switching for
the purpose of communication but there was no switching from
the dialect to a standard common language simply because such a
standard common language did not exist. If so, how did the grammarians reach their definition in the absence of suitable linguistic
conditions to which to anchor it?

3. The paradox could be solved in a number of ways. It could be
argued, for instance, that our interpretation of the data is wrong.
There may have been, even before the creation of the koine, some
form of standard language which could be called Greek and which
could have counted as the language of which the dialects were
dialects. An alternative possibility is that, even if such a standard
language did not exist before the koine, the grammarians reached
their concept of dialect *after* the creation of the koine; the fact that
they then applied it to the earlier period and spoke as if Attic, Ionic
etc. were simply dialects of Greek (i.e., on this interpretation, of the
koine) would simply be due to the normal absence of feeling for
historical development which characterized most of Greek gram-
matical work. This second hypothesis is not intrinsically contradictory; it is indeed plausible but, as I hope to show, is unnecessary.
On the other hand the first hypothesis conflicts with all the data we
have, as a brief review will show. In what follows I propose to argue
that, even though there was no standard language in Greece before
the koine, an abstract notion of Greek as a common language which
subsumed the dialects was present among Greek speakers at a relatively early stage, i.e. from the fifth century B.C. onwards; it is this
notion which the grammarians inherited and developed in the direction which opened the way to Gregory's definition of dialect, and,
in the last resort, to the concept of dialect currently used by the
European layman.

4. The case first depends on the demonstration that before the
development of the koine, i.e. before the Hellenistic period, there was
no standard language in Greece – this calls for a linguistic inquiry.
Secondly, we shall have to move from linguistic to 'metalinguistic'
data and try to find out how the ancient Greeks at various periods of
their history understood their linguistic situation. Here rather than

with linguistic phenomena we shall be dealing with ethnolinguistic or folk-linguistic data.

4.1. What do we know about the linguistic position of Greece in the prehellenistic period? We may rehearse here some well known facts about the written language (for which we have various types of data) and about the spoken language (about which we can only extrapolate from the written data).

The contemporary data we have for prehellenistic Greece show in the case of inscriptions a great deal of linguistic variety. Texts from different regions are written in different linguistic forms and the odds are that the writing conceals a greater amount of differentiation in the spoken language. It is sufficient to remember Herodotus' reference (I.142) to four different varieties of speech in Ionia which is not supported by epigraphical or literary data.[7] It also seems likely that in progress of time both Boeotia and Thessalia adopted a standardized regional spelling which ignored the phonological differences which must have existed in the various areas of the these two regions.

The literary evidence is less reliable because of the uncertainties about the manuscript tradition but can still lead us to some broad conclusions. The texts are written in a number of different linguistic forms; there is no standard literary language. There is on the other hand an interesting pattern of dialect or language switching tied to the view that some linguistic forms are more suitable than others for certain linguistic genres. Epic verse is written in some form of Ionic. Attic tragedy is written in Attic except for the choruses which are in a modified form of Doric. Lyric poetry can be in Aeolic; literary prose cannot. In a number of instances the choice of dialect is independent of the origin of the author; Pindar was from Thebes but did not write in Boeotian. Hesiod was also from Boeotia but composed in epic language, i.e. in a composite form of Ionic. We have Ionic prose, Doric prose and Attic prose, but, for instance, the Hippocratic corpus is written in Ionic, though Hippocrates himself was from Cos, a Doric place. The literary dialects are no perfect match for the epigraphical dialects: the Doric of Attic choruses is far less Doric than that of, e.g., the Peloponnesian inscriptions. These facts are far from new but a further point needs stressing. The dialect switching practised by poets and writers must have contributed to the contem-

---

[7] For a detailed discussion cf. O. Hoffmann, *Griech. Dialekte*, III, Göttingen 1898, 218–225 and more recently K. Stüber, *Zur dialektalen Einheit des Ostionischen*, Innsbruck 1996.

porary feeling that the various Greek dialects were joined by a special relationship which separated them from other non-Greek speech varieties. A different form of dialect switching also occurred in comedy for comic purposes but we may have to discuss that later in connection with spoken language.

Finally we must turn to epigraphical verse. The language of Greek verse inscriptions has been studied by K. Mickey in an Oxford dissertation and in a 1981 article;[8] her conclusion is that before ca. 400 these relatively humble verses were neither in the local dialect nor in any other dialect. The authors, in her view, aimed at a purified forms of the local dialect from which the most specifically local forms were excluded. That this is so is perhaps most clearly shown by Thessalian; the local genitives in -οιο or patronymic adjectives in -ιος are omnipresent in all prose inscriptions but are obstinately absent from verse inscriptions, though they could have been supported by the epic model.[9] If this avoidance of local forms is not due to chance, one may well wonder what is the language that the local poets were really aiming at. Could they think of it as a form of Greek which was not too Thessalian, not too Boeotian etc.? Do the verse inscriptions, in other words, confirm the impression we received from the literary dialects that the writers or speakers recognize a special link between the various 'Greek' dialects?

4.2. Any information about spoken language must be extrapolated from written texts. Parodies of various forms of speech in comedy confirm what we guess from the inscriptions, viz. that different regions used different linguistic forms. What our written evidence irritatingly does not reveal is how much dialect switching existed for the purposes of spoken communication. Did the sophists for instance always speak in Attic when in Athens? Did Socrates' interlocutors always switch to Attic in the course of their discussions (as Plato would have us believe) even if they were, for instance, Boeotian? We do not know how to interpret the odd examples of dialect exclamations in the context of normal Attic speech which we find e.g. in Plato or Xenophon.[10] They may be there as reminders of the

---

[8] K. Mickey, "Dialect Consciousness and Literary Language: an example from Ancient Greek", *TPS* 1981, 35–66; *Studies in the Greek Dialects and the Language of Greek Verse Inscriptions*, unpublished D. Phil. dissertation, Oxford 1981.

[9] Morpurgo Davies, *Glotta* 46 (1968), 96 with note 2; Mickey, *TPS* 1981, 50 ff.

[10] Cf. e.g. Plato *Phaedo* 62a, where Cebes, a Boeotian, starts his (Attic) talk with a dialect expression: Ἴττω Ζεύς, ἔφη, τῇ αὑτοῦ φωνῇ εἰπών κτλ ['"Indeed, by Zeus", he said, speaking in his own dialect'] (see also the same exclamation attributed to the Thebans in the Seventh Epistle, 345a3). In Xen. *Anabasis* VI.6.34 the Laconian Cleandrus replies to Xenophon

nationality of the speaker and of the way in which he in fact spoke. Yet it is also possible, at least in the case of the Plato example, that they are there for emphasis; the speaker had switched to Attic but to express strong emotion reverted to his own dialect. In general we cannot assume that speech reported in Attic or Ionic was in fact pronounced in Attic or Ionic; literary conventions do not normally allow reported speech in a different dialect from that of the main text (the same principle also applies to the speech of foreigners). On the other hand it is again Plato from whom we gain the impression that speech in one's own dialect was respectable even in Athens: at the beginning of the Apology (17d) Socrates pleads ignorance of the correct expressions to be used in a tribunal, explains it with his inexperience and concludes ἀτεχνῶς οὖν ξένως ἔχω τῆς ἐνθάδε λέξεως ['I am therefore, like a foreigner, without skill in this form of speech']. He then argues that if he had really been a ξένος [foreigner] he would have certainly been forgiven if he had spoken in the accent and manner in which he had been brought up ('Ώσπερ οὖν ἄν, εἰ τῷ ὄντι ξένος ἐτύγχανον ὤν, συνεγιγνώσκετε δήπου ἄν μοι, εἰ ἐν ἐκείνη τῇ φωνῇ τε καὶ τῷ τρόπῳ ἔλεγον ἐν οἵσπερ ἐτεθράμμην κτλ). Terminology (the use of ξένος) and context guarantee that here the reference is to a Greek dialect and not to a foreign language;[11] we can infer that it was feasible to speak in an Athenian tribunal in one's own dialect.

That dialect switching was possible for specific purposes is, however, known. We may remember Orestes stating in the Choephoroe (563–4) that he will address the porter of his palace in Phocian in order not to be recognized; that he then proceeds to speak in beautiful Attic trimeters does not alter the import of the statement.[12]

in Attic but starts with a Laconian exclamation: Ἀλλὰ ναὶ τὼ σιώ, ἔφη, ταχύ τοι ὑμῖν ἀποκρινοῦμαι κτλ [Well, by the twin gods, I will answer you quickly ...']. We have no reason to think that a Spartan would have switched to Attic for the sake of Xenophon and in this instance it seems likely that he spoke in Laconian all through. In the *Hellenica* (IV.4.10) Pasimachus begins with the same exclamation a sentence which is wholly in Laconian.

[11] Obviously we remain in doubt about the exact reference of φωνή and τρόπος in this context; Maurice Croiset (Platon, *Oeuvres complètes* vol. 1 Paris 1953[6], p. 141) translates with 'accent' and 'dialecte' respectively.

[12] For the purposes of this paper it is of course irrelevant whether on the stage Orestes spoke or did not speak with a Phocian accent; a minority of commentators has argued for the first hypothesis (cf. e.g. T.G. Tucker, *The Choephoroi of Aeschylus*, Cambridge 1901, p. 131 ff. on Choe. 561) but this seems to stretch credibility. The scholia [ancient commentaries] to Eur. *Phoen.* 301 (ed. Schwarz 1 p. 287) state that in the passage of the Phoenissae under discussion the chorus of Phoenician women spoke in Greek but with an accent which revealed its foreign origin; as a parallel they quote a fragment of the Sophoclean Ἑλένης ἀπαίτησις [*The Demand for Helen's Return*] (fr. 178 Nauck, 176 Pearson) which is taken to presuppose the use of a similar dramatic device to indicate Laconian origin (the text is not beyond suspicion: καὶ γὰρ χαρακτὴρ αὐτός· ἐν γλώσσῃ τί με / παρηγορεῖ Λάκωνος ὀσμᾶσθαι λόγου ['Yes, the accent is

Finally we ought to consider the extent of exposure to dialect forms other than their natives ones undergone by the various speakers. We must assume that in normal intercourse between people of different regions only a minimum of dialect switching occurred. So much at least seems to be implied by comedy; it should follow that some or most of the dialects were mutually intelligible. We also know – again from comedy – that Doric doctors were more popular than others. Various passages imply that doctors spoke Doric and were understood.[13] A last point is that long periods spent in cities other than one's own must have had linguistic consequences. One of the speeches in the Demosthenic corpus (57: mid fourth century) concerns the citizen status of an Athenian whose father was accused of being a non-Athenian because he used to ξενίζειν, i.e. to speak with a strange accent. This is explained by the defendant as due to the fact that his father had spent a long time away from Athens as a war prisoner and consequently had acquired that accent.[14] We have here some evidence for dialect mixture to use together with the evidence offered for instance by the disgruntled complaints of the Old Oligarch (*Ath. Pol.* 2.7) about the adulterated dialect spoken by the Athenians as a result of the outside influences to which they were exposed because of their commercial activities.[15]

Literary dialects in their recited and their written form offered a different type of exposure. All through Greece Homeric poetry was known and appreciated, the Spartan soldiers listened to Tyrtaeus' poems in the epic language, in Athens no one objected to the mild Doric of tragedy choruses; the language of Greek verse inscriptions also shows that at a local level dialect forms other than one's own

the same! Something about his speech coaxes me into scenting a Laconian way of talking', tr. Lloyd-Jones]). H.H. Bacon (*Barbarians in Greek Tragedy*, New Haven 1961, 65 ff.) is certainly right in her interpretation of the scholia but I have great difficulties in assuming that in the classical period a dialect accent was used in the performance of tragedy more or less in the same way it was in that of comedy; if that did in fact happen it is not clear why the playwriter would not have modified his text accordingly as the comoediographers did. Sophocles' fragment cannot reveal whether there were other indications of Laconian origin in the speech.

[13] The motif starts in the Old Comedy and is continued through the Middle and New Comedy; cf. for the references A.W. Gomme and F.H. Sandbach, *Menander, A Commentary*, Oxford 1973, in the commentary to *Aspis* 374 (at p. 92 ff.) and 439–64 (p. 99); Colin Austin, *Menandri Aspis et Samia*, Berlin 1970, vol. 2, 35 ff. on Aspis 374 ff.

[14] From the context it seems more likely that the accent was influenced by another Greek dialect than by a foreign language and this view is supported by the use of ξενίζειν; in Plato (*Crat.* 401c) ξενικὰ ὀνόματα [foreign words] refers to words of dialects other than Attic.

[15] Cf. the recent discussion by A. Cassio, "Attico 'volgare' e Ioni in Atene alla fine del 5. secolo a.C.", AION Sez. ling., 3 (1981) 79 ff. It is unfortunate that the famous verses by Solon (36, 11–12 West) about Athenians γλῶσσαν οὐκέτ' Ἀττικὴν ἱέντας, ὡς δὴ πολλαχῆι πλανωμένους ['no longer speaking the Attic language, so far and wide have they wandered'] are ambiguous; they may refer to the influence of foreign languages or to that of other dialects.

were appreciated. Finally, and perhaps most importantly, it has not been realized how crucial from a linguistic point of view were the decisions taken by the various oracles about the language they used in their responses. Delphi's choice of the epic language in preference to the local dialect was meant to guarantee to the oracle panhellenic importance.[16] Yet it also guaranteed panhellenic diffusion to the language chosen; it led to memorization and close scrutiny of the message – almost a linguistic *explication de textes* – by a vast number of people to whom the responses mattered: a misunderstanding could have been fatal.

5. What do we learn from this quick survey? There is no evidence before the Hellenistic period for a standard language used in Greece for either the purposes of literature or those of communication. There is on the other hand some evidence for a complicated pattern of dialect switching (if nothing else for literary purposes) and for an extensive passive knowledge of different dialects. The linguistic forms used differ extensively from region to region but the patterns of use and understanding create links between the different dialects and contribute to mark them off as a unit which can be contrasted with non-Greek languages.

I turn now to the second question: what do we know about the Greek attitudes to dialect or language?

We start from scholarship and technical terminology. Dialects in the early period are referred to with the generic terms γλῶττα/ γλῶσσα [*glōtta/glōssa*] and φωνή [*phōnē*] which can also be used for foreign languages; after Aristotle we have the impression that διάλεκτος 'speech, conversation, language' etc. begins to have its later specialized use but we remain in doubt about the exact date. There is no evidence that the Περὶ διαλέκτου [*On Dialect*] of Antisthenes, a pupil of Socrates, did indeed talk about dialects; the first conventional studies about dialects must have belonged to the first century. The word διάλεκτος (in the plural) is used with refer-

---

[16] L.E. Rossi (in *I poemi epici rapsodici non omerici e la tradizione orale*, Padova 1981, 223) reiterates that "da tutto il *corpus* delfico si vede un palese *sforzo* di essere omerici ... Delfi fa una *scelta* linguistica precisa: Omero. Evidentemente per ragioni di universalità panellenica". It is difficult to know what has priority; could it be that the choice of the Homeric language was determined by a choice of the hexameter as the obvious form? If so, we would still have to argue that the choice of the hexameter was determined by the prestige of Homeric poetry, which would of course have led to the choice of the language as well as of the metrical form. It is of course otiose to speculate, but if the choice had already been made by the seventh century this might imply that as early as that period there was in existence some notion of panhellenic language.

ence to Attic in a fragment of the third century B.C. (FGH II p. 263)[17] but 'dialect' may not be the right rendering.[18] Δωρίς refers to the Doric dialects in Thucydides (iii.112, vi.5), but the classification of the Greek dialects into Ionic, Attic, Doric and Aeolic which is frequently found in the first century may be first attested in the third century text just mentioned. Even then it seems clear that this classi-

[17] Ἕλληνες μὲν γάρ εἰσιν οἱ τῷ γένει καὶ ταῖς φωναῖς Ἑλληνίζουσιν ἀφ' Ἕλληνος. Ἀθηναῖοι δὲ οἱ τὴν Ἀττικὴν κατοικοῦντες Ἀττικοὶ μέν εἰσι τῷ γένει, ταῖς δὲ διαλέκτοις ἀττικίζουσιν, ὥσπερ Δωριεῖς μὲν οἱ ἀπὸ Δώρου τῇ φωνῇ δωρίζουσι‹ν›, αἰολίζουσι δὲ οἱ ἀπὸ Αἰόλου, ἰάζουσι δὲ οἱ ἀπὸ Ἴωνος τοῦ Ξούθου φύντες ['For Hellenes [i.e. Greeks] are those who descend from Hellen and "hellenize" in their language [i.e. speak Greek]. The Athenians who inhabit Attica are Attic by descent and "atticize" in their way of speaking [i.e. speak Attic], just like the Dorians who descend from Doros "doricize" in their language [i.e. speak Doric], and those who descend from Aeolos "aeolize" [speak Aeolic], while those who originate from Ion son of Xouthos "ionize" [speak Ionic]']. I quote from the new edition by F. Pfister, "Die Reisebilder des Heracleides", *Sitzungsberichte der Akademie der Wissenschaften (in Wien), Philosophisch-historisch Klasse*, 227 2 (1951), p. 90 l. 27 ff. The text used to be attributed to Dicearchus and is now attributed to Herakleides Creticus (or Kritikos) who according to Pfister (op. cit. p. 44 ff.) must have written between 275 and 200 B.C.

[18] It is normal to refer in this context to R. Münz, 'Uber γλῶττα und διάλεκτος und über ein posidonianisches Fragment bei Strabo', *Glotta* 11 (1921), 85–94, and some data can also be found in R. Calabrese, "I grammatici antichi e i dialetti greci", *Atene e Roma* 12 (1967), 159–165, but now we also have some precious references in an article and a book by W. Ax: "Ψόφος, φωνή und διάλεκτος als Grundbegriffe aristotelischer Sprachretlexion", *Glotta* 56 (1978), 245, and *Laut, Stimme und Sprache*, Göttingen 1986, esp. pp. 100, 113, 120, 201 ff. What emerges is that from its first attestations (e.g. Aristophanes fr. 706 Kassel-Austin, Hermipp. fr. 3 (Koch) διάλεκτος has a generic meaning such as 'talk, manner of speech', which is also that found in Plato. In Aristotle we also find a better defined meaning 'articulated language', and perhaps the beginning of the connection with local distinctions (Arist. *Hist. an.* 536 10). According to Ax the first instance of διάλεκτος in a sense which approaches that of the modern 'dialect' is in a passage by the Hellenistic doxographer Diocles, quoted in Diog. Laertius VII 56, who reports a statement by the Stoic Diogenes of Babylonia (*fl.* between the second and the first centuries B.C.). The passage reads διάλεκτος δέ ἐστι λέξις κεχαραγμένη ἐθνικῶς τε καὶ Ἑλληνικῶς, ἢ λέξις ποταπή, τουτέστι ποιὰ κατὰ διάλεκτον, οἷον κατὰ μὲν τὴν Ἀτθίδα θάλαττα, κατὰ δὲ τὴν Ἰάδα ἡμέρη ['A dialect is a form of speech marked ethnically and hellenically, or also a form from a certain place, that is to say such according to a dialect, as for instance *thalatta* "sea" according to [the] Attic [dialect] or *hemere* "day" according to [the] Ionic [dialect]']. The interpretation is not obvious (contrast the translation by Steinthal, *Gesch. der Sprachwiss.*, I 293 and that by Hicks in his edition of Diogenes Laertius; cf. also Wackernagel, *De path.* quoted below, p. 51 ff.); for Ax (op. cit. 201) it implies that διάλεκτος indicates linguistic variants of λέξις [*lexis*, speech] which are nationally or regionally defined and may therefore refer to Greek in contrast with foreign languages or within Greek to Attic or Ionic in contrast with other dialects. The doubt remains whether Diogenes really believed that διάλεκτος could (or should) be used to indicate the contrast between a foreign language and Greek; we could also interpret the text in such a way as to exclude this possibility – and this in spite of the use of διάλεκτος with *barbaros* in Diod. v. 6. However, if so, the difference between the first and second definition would be non-existent. After Diogenes the 'modern' meaning clearly appears in Strabo viii.333 and in Trypho: see J. Wackernagel, *De pathologiae veterum initiis*, Diss. Basel 1876, 57 ff. (= Kleine Schriften, iii, 1483 ff.) where, however, some of the information is outdated. Finally, Jean Lallot points out to me that in order to understand the history of διάλεκτος it would be important to understand why the word is feminine; is it because it belongs to a semantic field which includes a number of feminine nouns such as φωνή, γλῶττα, λέξις (which may have appeared later on the scene) or because it was originally an adjective in agreement with one of these nouns?

fication is largely done on ethnic rather than on linguistic bases.[19] Admittedly there was from an earlier period a lively interest in dialect words and Latte has argued that Plato may have had at his disposal earlier collections of lexical correspondences between dialects.[20] Yet so far nothing obliges us to think that the Greeks had before the period of the koine a concept of dialect similar to our own or to that which is presupposed by Gregory's definition.

Should we then think that the 'modern' concept of dialect, that found in Gregory, arose after the diffusion of the koine, so that a Greek dialect was seen as a dialect of the koine? Unexpectedly it is just the work of the late grammarians that gives us pause. Gregory, as we have seen, is not original. His definition is obviously based on earlier material. We may compare the not too dissimilar definition by Clemens Alexandrinus (*Stromateis* I.142; second/third centuries A.D.), who must also have made use of earlier sources: Διάλεκτος δέ ἐστι λέξις ἴδιον χαρακτῆρα τόπου ἐμφαίνουσα ἢ λέξις ἴδιον ἢ κοινὸν ἔθνους ἐμφαίνουσα χαρακτῆρα. Φασὶ δὲ οἱ Ἕλληνες εἶναι τὰς παρὰ σφίσι πέντε, Ἀτθίδα, Ἰάδα, Δωρίδα, Αἰολίδα, καὶ πέμπτην τὴν κοινήν· ἀπεριλήπτους δὲ οὔσας τὰς βαρβάρων φωνὰς μηδὲ διαλέκτους, ἀλλὰ γλώσσας λέγεσθαι, "A dialect is a form of speech which shows the individual character of a place or a form of speech which shows the specific or common character of an *ethnos*. The Greeks say that they have five (dialects), Attic, Ionic, Doric, Aeolic and fifth the koine. The *phonai* of the barbarians since they are incomprehensible are not called 'dialects' but *glossai*." The striking point here is the listing of the koine as a fifth dialect. A careful reading of Gregory of Corinth shows that he too treats the koine as a dialect, and in general the scholia are unanimous in including the koine among the five dialects.[21] There are earlier examples: in the second century the koine is treated as one of the dialects or as the fifth dialect by Apollonius Dyscolus and by Galen.[22] It is also poss-

---

[19] See J.B. Hainsworth, "Greek views of Greek Dialectology", *TPS* 1967, 62–76.

[20] K. Latte, 'Glossographica', *Philologus* 80 (1925), 136–175 (= *Kleine Scriften*, 631–666).

[21] Gregory, after his initial definition lists the four dialects, Ionic, Attic, Doric and Aeolic, and for each mentions a main exponent (Homer, Aristophanes, Theocritus, Alcaeus). He then continues Κοινὴ δέ, ᾗ πάντες χρώμεθα, καὶ ᾗ ἐχρήσατο Πίνδαρος, ἤγουν ἡ ἐκ τῶν δ συνεστῶσα ['The common language is that which we all use and which Pindar used, that is to say, that which is formed from all four']. The scholia to Dion[ysius] Thrax repeat the same statements with monotonous regularity (cf. the references in the index to *Gramm. Gr.* I 3 [Hilgard] 607 s.v. διάλεκτοι ε΄).

[22] Ap[ollonius] Dysc[olus] *de coniunctionibus* p. 223, 24 Schneider: Ἆρα. Οὗτος κατὰ πᾶσαν διάλεκτον. ὑπεσταλμένης᾽ τῆς κοινῆς καὶ Ἀττικῆς, ἦρα λέγεται ['*Ara*. This in all dialects, except for the koine and Attic, is said *era*']. I owe to Albio Cassio an important reference to an Arabic translation of a lost text by Galen *de vocibus in arte medica usitatis*. In the context of an anti-Atticistic debate Galen reproaches his adversaries for teaching a language

ible that in the first century A.D. the same analysis is reflected in Quintilian's anecdote about Crassus (P. Licinius Crassus Dives Mucianus consul 131 B.C.) who mastered *quinque Graeci sermonis differentias* [the five different forms of the Greek language] so that he could give judgement in all of them (*inst.* 11.2.50). Quintilian obviously borrows from the same source as the somewhat earlier Valerius Maximus (viii.7.6) who reports that when Crassus went to Asia as consul *tanta cura Graecae linguae notitiam animo comprehendit ut eam in quinque divisam genera per omnes partes ac numeros penitus cognosceret* ['He was so careful to master the Greek language that, divided as it was into five branches, he learned each of them thoroughly in all its parts and aspects (tr. Shackleton Bailey)'].[23] We have the impression that the much later Grammaticus Meermennianus (Schaefer ii p. 642) who maintains that koine was the beginning of all other dialects and a model for the rest (Διάλεκτοι δέ εἰσι πέντε, Ἰάς· Ἀτθίς· Δωρίς· Αἰολίς· καὶ Κοινή· ἡ γὰρ πέμπτη, ἴδιον οὐκ ἔχουσα χαρακτῆρα, κοινὴ ὠνομάσθη, διότι ἐκ ταύτης ἄρχονται πᾶσαι. ληπτέον δὲ ταύτην μὲν ὡς (πρὸς) κάνονα, τὰς δὲ λοιπὰς πρὸς ἰδιότητα ['There are five dialects, Ionic, Attic, Doric, Aeolic and the Common dialect [Koine]. The fifth [dialect], which has no specific characters of its own, was called "common", because all [dialects] originate from it. This one must be taken as the canonical form, while the others are specific cases']) represents a still later tradition and remained relatively isolated.[24]

which is incomprehensible to the representatives of the four groups of Greek dialects and even to those of the fifth which is known as the koine (M. Meyerhof, J. Schacht, "Galen über die medizinischen Namen Arabisch und Deutsch herausgegeben", *Abhandlungen der preussischen Akademie der Wissenschaften, Philosophisch-historische Klasse* 1932. Nr. 3, p. 30: "... wenn sie uns eine ihnen eigentümliche Sprache lehren, welche die Vertreter keiner einzigen der vier Gruppen von griechischen Mundarten verstehen und auch nicht die der fünften, welche als die allgemeine bekannt ist"). Conceivably a reference to the five 'dialects' may also be found in Porphyry *de abst*[*inentia*] 3.4.6 where in the course of a controversy about the language of animals it is pointed out that no man is so εὐμαθὴς ἢ μιμητικός ['good at learning or able to imitate'] that he can learn πέντε που διαλέκτων τῶν παρ' ἀνθρώποις ['the five languages of men'], let alone the language of animals.

[23] A. Thumb, *Die griechische Sprache im Zeitalter des Hellenismus*, Strassburg 1901, 167 ff., rejects the suggestion that the passage refers to the four Greek dialects and the koine on the ground that in Crassus' time Aeolic and Ionic were no longer spoken and that Quintilian (he does not mention Valerius Maximus) would not have used *sermonis differentias* for dialects. Both points do not seem decisive and even if Thumb was right in assuming that the koine split into five linguistic areas it is unlikely that the source of Quintilian and Valerius Maximus would have referred to this division. That the two authors depend on a common source is shown by the reference in both of them (Quint. loc. cit., Val. Max. loc. cit. and viii.7 ext. 15.16) to Themistocles, Cyrus and Mithridates (see PWRE XIII.336).

[24] We wish we knew more about the sources of this statement, but its very formulation seems to imply that it is late. There is a basic inconsistency between the first and the second part. On the one hand we are told that the koine is a dialect like the others, on the other hand we are told that it does not have a specific (ethnic?) character of its own, that it is the origin of

These statements are bizarre: why should the koine count as a fifth dialect instead of counting as the language of which the other dialects are dialects? If the koine, at a later stage at least, is seen as just one of the dialects, can we still think that the concept of dialect which we find in Gregory is based on an interpretation of the Greek data which was only possible after the creation of the koine? At this stage it is perhaps necessary to reconsider the earlier evidence for the concept of dialect.

5.1. Before the fifth century there is little to say; the ancients already discussed whether Homer had the concept of 'barbaric' or 'barbarian'.[25] It is possible that the epic poems made a distinction between barbaric languages and Greek forms of speech but this is far from certain.[26] In the fifth century, on the other hand, though the texts do not give us any technical terminology for dialects, we find first an awareness of the existence of linguistic variety which seems more pronounced than in e.g. Homer; secondly, an awareness of the contrast between foreign languages and Greek dialects; thirdly, an awareness of the 'Greekness' that all dialects have in common, joined to a feeling that in some sense 'Greek' can serve as an umbrella for all dialects. We may illustrate these three points, however sketchily.

The examples of deliberate dialect switching for specific purposes which I mentioned earlier (Orestes in the Choephoroe etc.) imply that the Greeks (or at least those who left us some evidence) not only made use of dialect variety but were also conscious that they could do so and, *a fortiori*, were conscious of the existence of dialect variety. The use of dialects to create laughter in comedy leads to the same conclusions.

Starting with the fifth century, and obviously as the results of political events, the contrast between Greeks and *barbaroi* is frequently mentioned. From a linguistic point of view it is clear that a conscious distinction is now made between all dialects on the one hand and all barbarian languages on the other. Linguistic facts are perhaps not prominent, though they are certainly not absent in the famous passage of Plato (*Politicus* 262d) where he attacks the type of

---

all dialects and that it is a *kanon*. Either the grammarian (or his source) used different and contradictory sources or he repeated parrot fashion what he had learned but could not resist adding some thoughts of his own. [Cf. now C. Consani, ΔΙΑΛΕΚΤΟΣ, *Contributo alla storia del concetto di 'dialetto'*, Pisa 1991, 62 ff.]

[25] Thuc. i.2.3; Strabo xiv.2.28.

[26] Mentions of different languages are very rare in the epic poems but the odd descriptions of linguistic confusion (*Il.* 2.204; 4.437) tend to refer to non-Greek languages. On the other hand in the famous description of linguistic mixture in Crete (*Od.* 19, 172 ff.) non-Greek languages and Greek dialects are mentioned together.

classification which divides mankind into two, separating on the one hand τὸ Ἑλληνικόν, the Greeks, and on the other hand all other races "though they are endless and unmixed and do not speak the same language" (ἀπείροις οὖσι καὶ ἀμείκτοις καὶ ἀσυμφώνοις πρὸς ἄλληλα). It is perhaps more important that even the parodies of barbarians and Greeks are different; in Aristophanic comedy the Persian Pseudartabas and the barbarian Triballos produce incomprehensible gibberish as contrasted with the funny utterances of those who speak dialects other than Attic. Barbaric languages, at a popular level, are compared to the twittering of birds; Greek dialects are not similarly treated. In the Trachiniae (1060) Heracles contrasts Ἑλλάς [Greece] and ἄγλωσσος [and without language]. The implication is that the Greeks have a (real) language in contrast with the barbarians who do not. We may ask what language.

Even more striking are the frequent references which show that different forms of local speech are all labelled Greek and that Greek (Ἑλλάς) can represent them all. A few examples are necessary even if the enumeration may be tedious.

The statement by Herodotus (viii.144) about τὸ Ἑλληνικόν which is defined as including among other things community of blood and of language (ἐὸν ὅμαιμόν τε καὶ ὁμόγλωσσον) is too well known to be striking but cannot be forgotten. It implies that the Greeks have a common language and again we ask which one. Herodotus also provides a multitude of passages where various dialects are all labelled "Greek". In iv.78 we are told that a Scythian learnt the Greek language and letters (γλῶσσάν τε Ἑλλάδα καὶ γράμματα) from his mother who came from Istra. Presumably the mother was Ionian and consequently Greek subsumes Ionian. In viii.135 Herodotus relates the long story of the Carian Mys sent by Mardonios during the Persian wars to consult all oracles. When he came to the Ptoion sanctuary, which belonged to the Thebans, he was accompanied by three selected citizens who were going to write down the oracle's statement. Yet the promantis [prophet] started to prophesize in a barbaric language; the three Thebans were astonished hearing a barbaric language instead of Greek (ἀντὶ Ἑλλάδος), but Mys took the tablet from their hands and started writing because he said that the language was Carian. If the oracle normally prophesized in Boeotian here it is Boeotian which is called Greek.[27] The list could continue but Herodotus also gives us evidence of how Greece, the

---

[27] Herodotus' story was discussed at length by Louis Robert, "Le carien Mys et l'oracle du Ptoion", *Hellenica* 8 (1950), 23–28; cf. also G. Daux, "Mys au Ptoion", *Hommages*

whole of Greece irrespective of dialect, could be treated as a linguistic unit. In describing the cruel acts perpetrated by the Lemnians against the Athenians (vi.138 ff.) he adds that as a result through the whole of Greek or Greece (ἀνὰ τὴν Ἑλλάδα) all cruel acts are called Λήμνια [Lemnian deeds]. The general impression is that Ἑλλάς has become a cover term for a number of linguistic forms which if necessary can be further defined. This point may be hammered home by a story told somewhat later by Xenophon.

In the *Anabasis* we find a certain amount about foreign languages, interpreters, etc.; we find an immense amount about ethnic differences within Greece (Athenians vs. Spartans etc.); we find very little indeed about dialect differences. There is an exception. In a difficult moment for the expedition Xenophon himself gives a firm speech (iii.1.15 ff.) exorting the Greeks to show courage and initiative. There is no opposition, but a certain Apollonides, who spoke in Boeotian (βοιωτάζων τῇ φωνῇ), objects that it is dangerous and unwise to oppose the Great King (iii.1.26). Xenophon replies in indignation: the man dishonours his country and the whole of Greece because being a Greek he behaves in this manner (iii.1.30): Ἕλλην ὢν τοιοῦτός ἐστιν). At this stage a third person intervenes who shouts: "But this man has nothing in common with Boeotia or Greece in general; I have seen that he has ears pierced like a Lydian" (iii.1.31: Ἀλλὰ τούτῳ γε οὔτε τῆς Βοιωτίας προσήκει οὐδὲν οὔτε τῆς Ἑλλάδος παντάπασιν ἐπεὶ ἐγὼ αὐτὸν εἶδον ὥσπερ Λυδὸν ἀμφότερα τὰ ὦτα τετρυπημένον). It is true and the man is sent away in ignominy. The dialect, Boeotian, is mentioned at the beginning to show that the man is a Greek; other facts, cultural facts, prove that he is not.

Clearly in the fifth and fourth century those which we now call dialects could be subsumed under 'Greek'. The use of the verb ἑλληνίζειν 'to speak Greek' confirms this point. Thucydides (ii.68) uses it for people who started to speak Greek under the influence of the Amprakiotai; these, we know, must have spoken a form of Doric. Later the meaning of the verb shifts to include a criterion of correctness: it means to speak or write correct Greek (Ar. *Rhet.* 1407 a 19). It is likely that in Athens this was taken to refer to correct Attic; at the beginning of the third century a New Comedy poet, Poseidippus (fr. 28 Koch), reminds the Athenians through one of his characters that in speaking they can only ἀτθικίζειν [speak Attic] while he and

W. *Déonna*, Bruxelles 1957, 157–62. I have not been able to establish for certain whether the Ptoion prophecies were normally uttered in Boeotian or not.

his compatriots can ἑλληνίζειν [speak Greek]; the reference may
be to the Thessalians who boasted that they were descendants of
Hellen.[28] By contrast in the fourth century and possibly earlier the
derivatives of ξένος [foreigner] (ξενικός [foreign], ξενίζειν [to speak
a foreign language], ξένως [in foreign fashion]) may be used to refer
to dialects other than that of the speaker.[29]

To sum up: at some stage, conceivably well before the fifth
century, the inhabitants of Greece (or at least some of them) started
to feel that they spoke and wrote Greek. Yet Greek as such did not
exist; there were instead a number of linguistic varieties distinguished
by important structural differences of which the speakers were well
aware. Some of these varieties must have acquired higher prestige
than the others, but in the classical period at least none of them came
to be identified with Greek. Aristotle in the *Rhetoric* is still able
to exemplify his stylistic points about correct Greek by quoting
Herodotus (who wrote in Ionic) and Homer (whose language is
dialectically mixed). The Greeks presumably did not worry about
this situation because they could not envisage a different one.
"Greek" was and remained an abstract concept which subsumed
all different varieties, much as a federal government subsumes the
component states or an *ethnos* subsumes a number of individuals and
a *polis* a number of citizens. A still closer comparison is that with
denominations such as Doric, Aeolic etc. The obvious distinctions
are those between the dialects of specific cities and regions and yet as
early as the fifth century Thucydides speaks e.g. of the Messenians as
Δωρίδα ... γλῶσσαν ἰέντας ['speaking the Doric language'] (iii.112).
He also says (vi.5), however, that at Himera, a joint Chalcidic and
Syracusan foundation, the language was mixed between Chalcidian
and Doric – where Doric obviously refers to the Syracusan dialect.

---

[28] The verses are quoted by Herakleides Creticos (op. cit., see note 17) in an interesting
passage where the author rejects the normal meaning of ἑλληνίζειν, 'to speak correct Greek'
in favour of a meaning 'to speak an inherited Greek language': Ἡ δὲ καλουμένη νῦν Ἑλλὰς
λέγεται μέν, οὐ μέντοι ἐστί. τὸ γὰρ ἑλληνίζειν ἐγὼ εἶναί φημι οὐκ ἐν τῷ διαλέγεσθαι ὀρθῶς
ἀλλ᾽ ἐν τῷ γένει τῆς φωνῆς· αὕτη ‹δ᾽› ἐστὶν ἀφ᾽ Ἕλληνος· ἡ δὲ Ἑλλὰς ἐν Θετταλίᾳ κεῖται·
ἐκείνους οὖν ἐροῦμεν τὴν Ἑλλάδα κατοικεῖν καὶ ταῖς φωναῖς ἑλληνίζειν, ['What is now
called Hellas is something which we speak of, but does not exist. For I say that to "hellenize"
[speak Greek] does not depend on speaking correctly but on the origin of the language. This
derives from Hellen, and Hellas is in Thessaly; we shall say then that only those [who live in
that region] inhabit Hellas and "hellenize" in their language'].
[29] Cf. R. Pfeiffer, *History of Classical Scholarship*, vol. I. Oxford 1968, 41 note 2, and see
above note 14 and the passage of the Apology quoted at p. 159. Plato's use of ξενικὰ ὀνόματα
[foreign names] is discussed by P.M. Gentinetta, *Zur Sprachbetrachtung bei den Sophisten
und in der stoisch-hellenistischen Zeit*, Diss. Zürich, Winterthur 1961, 54–6. For ξενικόν
Aristotle offers a definition (*Poe[tics]* 1458a 220) which presupposes a related but more general
meaning.

And yet there was no such thing as Doric; Doric was as abstract a concept as Greek.

6. Against the general background of these assumptions we may now explain why the grammarians when confronted with the koine could treat it as an another variety of Greek. That 'Greek' existed had been known at least since the fifth century, and since then (if not earlier) the different forms of speech of the Greek towns and regions were treated as forms of Greek. By the third century B.C. at the latest all Greek dialects were also classified into Attic, Ionic, Doric or Aeolic. Consequently when the existence of the koine was acknowledged it was possible to accept this new linguistic form as yet another variety of Greek. To give it a respectable pedigree the grammarians concluded, somewhat anachronistically, that it was the language used by Pindar so that all main varieties of Greek had their own writer. Some argued, on the basis of a concept of language mixture which is at least as old as Thucydides, that it had arisen from a mixture of the four other varieties of Greek.

The conclusion must be that the concept of dialect (even if not necessarily the word) precedes the formation of the koine.[30] In prehellenistic times the dialects are seen as different linguistic forms subsumed by an abstraction, Greek; in the later period the koine is added to the list but Greek, for some grammarians at least, remains an abstract concept which can subsume the koine as well as the dialects.[31] From this point of view when our modern or not so modern dictionaries speak of a dialect as "a variety of speech differing from the standard or literary language" (OED s.v.) they do indeed innovate with respect to the Greeks who at first did not have a standard or literary language and later failed for a while to identify the newly created koine with the standard language. Yet the existence of Greek as an abstract entity should not really surprise us. First, we are

---

[30] W. Ax. *Laut, Stimme und Sprache*, op. cit., p. 201 note 267, correctly observes that the definition of 'διάλεκτος' by Diogenes of Babylonia offers the first evidence for the term in its modern meaning, but this is "ein Primat, der allerdings nur für den Terminus gilt. Das Faktum regionalsprachlichen Varianten selbst war natürlich schon vorher, z. B. Platon bekannt".

[31] Jean Lallot (per litt.) obliges me to clarify my thoughts on this subject. As he points out, on one interpretation of the passage quoted above (cf. *supra* [in n. 18]) Diogenes of Babylonia may have wanted to contrast his examples of Attic and Ionic (θάλαττα, ἡμέρη) with the relevant koine forms (θάλασσα, ἡμέρα). If so, we *could* think that the koine was first identified with the abstract concept of Greek and only later came to be treated as one of the varieties of Greek (though this is not a necessary conclusion). An alternative view is that in the Diogenes passage the various dialects are contrasted with each other and not with the koine. If so, it would be possible to argue that as soon as the koine was recognized as a linguistic form with its own individuality it was treated as the fifth dialect. Obviously we cannot exclude the existence of different schools with different views on the position of koine.

now more aware than we used to be of the great speech variety which exists even in the most closely knit linguistic community; yet we are not amazed when the layman speaks of such communities as if they had one and not many linguistic forms. For whatever reason the speaker's assessment of the speech of his own community abstracts from the variety of performance. Secondly, in the history of Greek scholarship we have, at a more sophisticated level, innumerable examples of how the grammarians operated with an abstract concept of language and language forms. One example may be sufficient. Some one hundred and ten years ago Jacob Wackernagel published his doctoral dissertation where he discussed the various works dedicated from the first century B.C. onwards to the study of language πάθη (accidents).[32] Here we are concerned with one point only which is best illustrated with the quotation of a fragment by Herodian (649 Lentz): ὁ δελφὶς ὁ Τελχὶς οὐ καταλήγουσι φύσει εἰς ς ἀλλ᾽ εἰς ν, τροπὴ δὲ ἐγένετο τοῦ ν εἰς ς κατὰ Δορικὴν διάλεκτον ὥσπερ ἦν ἦς, εἴρπομεν εἴρπομες … καὶ οὕτω λοιπὸν ἀπετελέσθη ἡ εἰς ς κατάληξις οἷον δελφὶν δελφὶς, Τελχὶν Τελχίς ['*delphis* "dolphin" and *Telkhis* do not end by nature in -*s* but in -*n*; there was a change from -*n* to -*s* in the Doric manner, as *en* [becomes] *es* or *eirpomen* [becomes] *eirpomes* … Thus eventually the ending -*s* came about as in *delphis* from *delphin* and *Telkhis* from *Telkhin*'].

The problem here is that a regular declension would call for a nominative such as δελφίν (Gen. δελφῖνος) but the normal nominative is δελφίς. The solution suggested is that the 'real' nominative is indeed δελφίν but a change has taken place and the final -ν has been replaced by an -ς. Similar alternations, it is pointed out, occur between dialects: thus a final -ν in, for instance, the ending of the first person plural -μεν is 'replaced' by -ς in the Doric first person plural -μες. These statements are not historical statements, i.e. it is not implied that δελφίν was effectively pronounced as such at an early stage; nevertheless δελφίν is taken to be the 'real' Greek form (we feel tempted to say the underlying form), though this form has undergone a change just as the -μεν ending has undergone a change in Doric. In other words those concerned with 'pathology' operate with an underlying form of Greek which through the operation of various rules can be made to yield the attested form. In an even more outdated terminology we could say that the abstract δελφίν is 'real-

---

[32] Cf. Wackernagel, op. cit. (in note 18), and more recently D.L. Blank, *Ancient Philosophy and Grammar*, Chico California 1982, 41–49.

ized' in the concrete δελφίς.[33] Is this attitude at all connected with that which, at a much lower level of sophistication, led to the notion of dialect which we have been exploring and to the abstract concept of Greek which we have found in existence in the fifth century B.C.? If so, perhaps we do not need to ask why it was possible in Greece to have 'dialects' of a non-existing language and why the koine was not instantly identified with the language of which Doric, Ionic etc. were the dialects.

[33] Blank, op. cit., 45, points out that in Apollonius Dyscolus the same methodology is applied to syntax: a construction like τρέμω σε [I tremble in front of you] is treated as irregular because the verb behaves as if it was transitive but does not have a passive. Hence Apollonius concludes that the phrase is an elliptical form of ῍τρέμω διά σε [I tremble on account of you] (which is not attested). Pathology then not only explains the divergent forms of the dialects but also explains the anomalous forms of current language (i.e. of the koine) which are treated as realizations of underlying regular forms. It is tempting, but probably farfetched, to assume that at this stage the abstract concept of Greek which we discussed earlier was identified with the (abstract) set of regular forms from which both the forms of the dialects and those of the koine are derived. This would explain the equal 'dialect' status of the koine and the four dialect qroups. On the other hand it is possible that the studies of pathology started with the specific purpose of explaining the differences between the dialects and the koine, and if so the hypothesis would probably not work.

7 The Greek Attitude to Foreign Religions†

JEAN RUDHARDT

translated by Antonia Nevill

How did the Greeks view foreign religions? What did they think of them? I am not sure that such questions are pertinent; in fact, I doubt whether the Greeks would have understood them in the way that I have just put them.

They have no equivalent word for our noun *religion*. Of course, certain phrases such as *ta hiera* [the holy or sacred], *ta nomima* [customs], *thrêskeia* [worship or cult], *eusebeia* [reverence or piety], for example, can be translated as *religion* in certain texts, but only approximately. They have different uses in other places, where each takes on a particular meaning. Actually, the ideas to which they correspond have neither the same range nor the same comprehensiveness as our concept of religion. So the Greeks had no means of referring to religions in a general way, as we do. It was difficult for them to place all foreign religions in a clearly defined category or to ponder over them systematically.

Nevertheless, to try to answer the questions I have posed, in studying Greek thinking and behaviour I shall have to apply alternately our own conceptual framework and that of the ancients.

I

It is evident that, in speaking of non-Greek peoples, the Greeks deal with what seem to us to constitute a religion. Sometimes they do so incidentally, in the course of an account or description whose immediate subject is not, in our view, religious. Recalling an Egyptian town, for instance, Hellanicus informs us that there is a temple there

† Originally published as 'Les attitudes des Grecs a l'égard des religions étrangères', *Revue de l'Histoire des Religions* 209 (1992), 219–38.

adorned with plants and flowers; he then tells us the beliefs that give a meaning to this decoration.[1] Similarly, introducing the town of Babylon, Herodotus mentions its most striking monuments: the defence walls and an immense temple in the form of a tower. Describing this ziggurat, he informs us that a hierogamy [sacred marriage] is celebrated there, and devotes a few words to this.[2] The same historian elsewhere mentions a Syrian goddess whom he identifies with Aphrodite Urania, and says that her cult has spread from Ascalon to Cyprus and Cythera. This information, so valuable to a historian of religions, he supplies almost casually, as if in passing, in the course of an account of the events whereby the temple of the goddess was destroyed.[3] However interesting they may be, such passages are not very significant, but the systematic nature of certain others gives them a greater scope. There we find, indeed, a collection of numerous pieces of information concerning institutions, beliefs or behaviour that we consider to be religious.

In the first place, let us note that these passages are most frequently introduced by phrases that define their subject, of the type: νόμοισι τοιοισίδε χρέωνται ..., νόμοισι δὲ χρέωνται τοιοισίδε ..., ['they use these customs'], νόμοι δὲ οἵδε καθεστᾶσι ..., τὰ νόμαια διακεῖται ... ['these customs are established'].[4]

For the Greeks, the beliefs, institutions and customs that in our eyes constitute a religion are *nomoi* or *nomaia* – in other words, customary rules, traditional ways of acting and thinking.

Secondly, we will observe that chapters defined as expositions of *nomoi* or *nomaia* contain what seem to us heterogeneous material. Dealing with the customs of the Scythians, Herodotus provides us with a list of their gods, mentions some of their rituals of sacrifice, divination, oath-swearing and funerals, but also speaks of their military practices and their use of flax and hemp.[5] Writing of those of Persia, he tells us that the Persians never represent their gods with anthropomorphic features and that they make no statues of them; he lists these gods and describes the sacrifices that the Persians make in their honour, but also speaks of their communal meals, their gestures of greeting and the way in which they bring up their children.[6] As for the Babylonians, the historian writes of their funerary or purificatory

[1] Hellanicus, *Athenaeus*, XV, 679f–680a.
[2] Hdt., I, 180–3.
[3] Hdt., I, 105.
[4] Cf. Hdt., I, 94, 196, 199, 216; II, 35ff.; III, 20, 99; IV, 26, 59, 168, 169, 170–2, etc.
[5] Hdt., IV, 59–80
[6] Hdt., I, 131–8.

rituals, their marriage customs and the prenuptial prostitution to which their women are compelled and which doubtless fulfils a ritual function, but he also describes the way in which they behave towards the sick.[7]

In short, in Greek minds, material that we think of as religious is bracketed with beliefs and customs of all kinds. Within the overall category of *nomoi*, they do not distinguish a subset equivalent to what, in our view, could form one of the 'religious'. Was there then no religion in Greek antiquity, or indeed was *everything* religious?

At all events, one thing is fundamental: *nomoi* vary from one people to another. Herodotus notes this, and sometimes emphasises the differences that distinguish foreign customs from Greek ones. 'They (the Egyptians) differ from any of the Greeks on another point: instead of exchanging words of greeting when they meet in the street, they bow, lowering their hand to their knee.'[8] 'The Medes and the Lydians swear an oath by carrying out rites similar to those of the Greeks, but those making the oath also make incisions in their arms and lick each other's blood.'[9] In noting differences of this kind, Herodotus does not condemn the foreign *nomos*, though without doubt he sometimes criticises it. He finds the prenuptial prostitution practised among the Babylonians the most shameful of all their customs, αἴσχιστος τῶν νόμων.[10] He reveals a certain scepticism when speaking of the hierogamy practised in the temple of Zeus-Belos: contrary to what the priests affirm, he does not believe that the god comes in person to share the bed of the Babylonian woman chosen to celebrate the rite.[11] He rejects then some of the foreign *nomoi* for reasons of morality or probability; he never does so solely on the grounds of the differences that distinguish them from Greek customs. Moreover, Herodotus adopts towards Greek *nomoi* an attitude similar to the one he takes with regard to African or Asiatic customs. He rejects, for example, the Greek myth of Heracles and Busiris; bearing in mind all he knows of Egypt and Egyptian customs, he finds this myth implausible.[12] Besides, he sometimes feels a sympathy towards the foreigner. He enjoys emphasising the worth of the Arabians, who accord special respect to sworn oaths.[13] He is able to approve of the *nomos* of a distant country precisely for its difference.

---

[7] Hdt., I, 196–200.
[8] Hdt., II, 80.
[9] Hdt., I, 74.
[10] Hdt., I, 199.
[11] Hdt., I, 182. [See further Harrison, *Divinity and History*, pp. 88–90.]
[12] Hdt., II, 45.
[13] Hdt., III, 8.

In Persia, he writes, 'before the age of five, a child is kept out of its father's sight and lives among the women; this is done so that, if the child should die while still an infant, its death will not grieve the father. I approve of this custom. And I also approve of this one: the king himself puts no one to death in punishment of a single offence, and for a single offence no other Persian makes anyone in his household suffer irreparable punishment.'[14] I will not go on. Whether in approval or disapproval, in the many texts where the historian deals with foreign *nomoi*, value judgements are exceptional. Most frequently he describes them in a neutral tone of objectivity, no matter how good his information is. *Nomoi* vary; this is a fact; he takes note of it without showing himself shocked by these variations.

II

Beyond these variations, Herodotus is witness to a remarkable universality.

Whatever the customs may be that are peculiar to each people, all peoples seem to him to address the same gods. For him, these are the gods named and honoured by the Greeks in their own fashion. He recognises a Zeus in the person of the Egyptian Ammon,[15] in that of the Babylonian Baal-Marduk,[16] and in that of the great god worshipped by the Persians;[17] he sees a Demeter in Isis,[18] an Aphrodite in the Alilat of the Arabians, the Mylitta of the Assyrians and the Hator of the Egyptians;[19] a Heracles in the Melqart of Tyre;[20] and so on.

To explain such identifications, reference is made to a theory expounded by Herodotus on several occasions. When this or that cult spread from Egypt or Libya, it ultimately reached the Greeks, who adopted it.[21] It would therefore be natural for the Greeks to recognise the imported god when they came across him in his country of origin. I have little belief in the value of an explanation of this kind. Herodotus identifies foreign and Greek gods in too universal a manner for it to be possible to justify all the comparisons he makes by resorting to diffusionist theories, each one valid only in a particular instance. Actually, Herodotus himself in most instances

---

[14] Hdt., I, 136–7.
[15] Hdt., II, 42; cf. I, 182; II, 54, 56; IV, 181.
[16] Hdt., I, 181; III, 158.
[17] Hdt., I, 131.
[18] Hdt., II, 59, 123, 156.
[19] Hdt., I, 131; IV, 59; I, 105; II, 41.
[20] Hdt., II, 44.
[21] E.g. Hdt., II, 5off.

identifies the foreign deity with a Greek one without suggesting a single historical circumstance which could justify the identification. The equivalence of the two deities impresses him straightaway, to the extent that he gives a Greek name to the foreign god before mentioning – or even without mentioning at all – its native name.

Let us consider, for example, what he says about the gods of the Scythians: 'These are the only gods whose favour they try to win: first of all, Hestia, then Zeus and Earth ... then Apollo, Aphrodite Urania, Heracles and Ares. All Scythians worship these, but those who are known as Royal Scythians sacrifice also to Poseidon. In the Scythian tongue, Hestia is called "Tabiti"; Zeus "Papaios"...; Earth "Api"; Apollo "Goitosyros"; Aphrodite Urania "Argimpasa"; Poseidon "Thagimasadas".'[22] Let me underline that Herodotus makes no mention of any contact, either direct or indirect, between the Scythian and Greek worlds that might explain his identifications. In a more significant passage, the historian distinguishes explicitly between foreign and indigenous deities. Speaking of the Persians, he writes: 'It is their custom to carry out sacrifices in honour of Zeus by going up the highest mountains – they call the entire vault of heaven Zeus. They sacrifice to the Sun, the Moon, Earth, Fire, Water and the Winds. To these gods alone they sacrificed originally, but they learned from the Assyrians and the Arabs to sacrifice also to Aphrodite Urania. The Assyrians call Aphrodite "Mylitta", the Arabians "Alilat" and the Persians "Mitra".'[23] For Herodotus, therefore, the Persians had always honoured certain gods; they had received them from no other source. The historian does not say that they introduced the Greeks to them; but he has no hesitation in identifying them. Of course, it is an easy matter where some are concerned, whatever their Persian name. There is an objectivity to stars, elements and meteorological phenomena, and all men are capable of recognising them. It will be observed, however, that not all peoples hold them to be gods; in Persia Herodotus casts no doubt on their divine nature, although they are not all equally the object of worship in Greece. It will be noted, besides, that the case of Zeus is different; however closely associated with the sky he may be in Greek thinking, he is not confused with it. Now, although the historian immediately sees Zeus in Ahura-Mazda – whose Persian name he does not mention – he classes him among the gods whom the Persians have worshipped for all time. We cannot suppose that he takes him to be a god imported

[22] Hdt., IV, 59. Thamigasadas: conj. Stein.
[23] Hdt., I, 131.

from Anatolia to Greece, since elsewhere he assigns him an Egyptian origin.[24] The identification he uses in this case can rest on no diffusionist theory. In fact, the inclination to recognise the same deities under the different names they receive according to the various peoples is not peculiar to the historian of Halicarnassus; it is common to all Greeks. We see it, for example, in Diodorus, the rest of whose theories differ from those of his predecessor.[25]

Let us try to measure the true scope of diffusionism in Herodotus' thinking, and to this end examine the chief examples he has left to us. The Syrian temple at Ascalon, he writes, is the oldest temple erected in honour of Aphrodite Urania; the one in Cyprus was constructed on its model, as was that of Cythera, founded by Phoenicians from Syria.[26] It is not, therefore, knowledge of the goddess that has spread throughout regions, but the custom of erecting a temple to her and, perhaps, some of the details of its construction. The historian does not think that the cult of Dionysus, which had little in keeping with Greek customs, originated in Greece. As he perceives similarities between certain Egyptian sacrifices and Greek sacrifices dedicated to Dionysus, between the Egyptian use of statuettes with an erect member and the phallophoria [procession of the phallus], he supposes that such rites had been imported from Egypt into Greece. In his view, they would have reached Phoenicia first, then Cadmus and his companions, arriving in Boeotia, would have taught the prophet Melampus about them, and he then made them known throughout the country.[27] It was therefore not acquaintance with the god which the Greeks received from Egypt but several of the rituals that were part of his cult. Similarly, we have noted that the Persians did not receive the goddess Aphrodite from the Assyrians, but the custom of offering her sacrifices.[28]

Herodotus distinguishes between two Heracles: one the son of Alcmene, honoured according to heroic rites, and an older figure of the same name, honoured according to divine rites. Herodotus is convinced that the son of Alcmene is of Egyptian origin, since he refers to the mythical geneaologies that make him the son of Aegyptus, but in this instance he is a hero. As regards the more ancient Heracles, Herodotus does not claim that the god came from Egypt to Greece; he simply says that the Greeks received his appel-

[24] Hdt., II, 42, 50, 54ff.
[25] Diod., I, 25, 1–2; cf. II, 38, 3–39, 4, 3ff., etc.
[26] Hdt., I, 105.
[27] Hdt., I, 49.
[28] Hdt., I, 131.

lation, *ounoma*, from Egypt.[29] This transfer of the *ounoma* is the most usual form of diffusion in Herodotus. Apart from the particular cases I have quoted, where he mentions the spread of a ritual, he teaches that divine names were passed on from one people to another; when he speaks in general terms of the origin of Greek beliefs, he does not query the provenance of the gods but that of their *ounomata*. What does this expression signify exactly? In its most common sense, the word *onoma* means 'the name'. Now, it is precisely the names of the deities that change, when passing from one people to another. Herodotus takes care to translate them into Greek, without ever intimating that the Greek name is derived from the foreign one. As Burkert has suggested,[30] for the historian the word *ounoma* does not mean the name of the god but the simple fact of giving him a name. This is an important point. To name a god is not to meet him for the first time; it is to recognise in him, when he has already been encountered, enough characteristic features to be able to identify him. So what is passed from one people to another is not the god himself, or what has been experienced of him at close quarters, but a means of picking him out amid the overall divinity whose presence is felt. On contact with the foreigner who names a god, in whatever fashion he does so, one may thus learn to identify a divine reality which is already familiar. In other words, although the *ounoma* belongs to the ensemble of *nomoi* and, like all of them, varies from place to place, the divine being whose appellation enables him to be distinguished from the other gods may already be omnipresent.

Since the *nomoi* vary from one place to another, the resemblances that one perceives between those of certain peoples require an explanation. Herodotus resorts to diffusionist theories to account for them; conversely, he never advances such theories to explain the universality of the same deities in all the regions of the world. It is for him self-evident; wherever he encounters it, the identity of a deity compels recognition because he holds it to be universal. In this regard, I find one phrase significant: 'Among the gods, the Arabians think that only Dionysus and Aphrodite exist, Διόνυσον δὲ θεῶν μοῦνον καὶ τὴν Οὐρανίην ἡγέονται εἶναι';[31] 'among the gods, the Sun is the only one honoured by the Massagetai, θεῶν δὲ μοῦνον

    [29] Hdt., II, 43ff.
    [30] W. Burkert, 'Herodot über die Namen der Götter', *Museum Helveticum*, 1945, pp. 121–32.
    [31] Hdt., III, 8.

῞Ηλιον σέβονται'.[32] The use of such a formula implies a conviction: the gods are everywhere, alike one another and thus identifiable, but certain peoples name and revere only some of them.

The conclusions I have reached find confirmation in the famous theory by which Herodotus explains the origin and gradual formation of Greek religion. 'First of all, the Pelasgians used to sacrifice by addressing prayers to the gods ... but without giving any name or designation to pick out especially any one of them. They had called them gods (*theous*) in view of the fact that they were masters of all things and their governance, having established them (*thentes*) in the universe. Later, after a long time had elapsed, they learned the names of the gods from Egypt, with the exception of Dionysus, whose name they learned later still ...'[33] Despite the insistence with which Herodotus stresses the influence exerted by Egypt on Greek religion, it is noticeable that in no way does he say that the Greek gods were imported from the Nile Valley. The first inhabitants of Greece, the Pelasgians, he says, revered the gods immediately without being subject to any foreign influence, seeing them quite naturally as the initiators of cosmic order. In his view, the gods are well and truly universal; men spontaneously recognise their existence and honour them everywhere. The Pelasgians did so at first by addressing them all collectively, before learning from foreign masters the art of naming them individually. That was the preparation for a new stage. Among the Greeks who succeeded the Pelasgians and continued their traditions on this matter, the first poets, Homer and Hesiod, would be able to teach people to distinguish more clearly each one of the gods, whom their names would henceforth make identifiable. The poets conferred upon them a face and a history, and ordered them by situating them in a genealogy.

The gods are thus omnipresent, but men, who do not identify them all equally, name, imagine and talk of them in ways that vary from place to place. The images and names they use are not empty; they serve to distinguish from one another the forms of an encounter with the divine which Greeks seem convinced that all men alike experience. Everyone can then relate the images and names of the gods he meets abroad to those of his own tradition, even if those images and names differ from place to place, like the category of *nomoi* to which they belong.

Here we are brought back again to the remark I made at the

[32] Hdt., I, 216.
[33] Hdt., II, 52ff.

beginning of this account. If, on the one hand, what we think of as religious is mixed up in the overall collection of traditional practices in each place, if, on the other hand, the Greeks show themselves to be convinced that men everywhere address the same deities, do we not find ourselves (from their point of view) in the presence of a single religion, even though hard to define, which inspires all human behaviour, but in different ways depending on the region? Given that, it seems that for the Greeks the idea of foreign religion would have been difficult to conceive.

Several features peculiar to Greek cults prepared the Greeks for the understanding of foreign religions, as we will come to see. Although they are all related, their forms of worship assume differing forms according to the cities; the myths they recount about the same gods vary, and the same myths have numerous different versions depending on local traditions. The plurality and diversity that the Greeks encounter in observing foreign peoples are then easily incorporated for them through an extension of those which are familiar to them within their own country. Another feature produces a similar result. In Greek cult practice, the Greeks rarely call Zeus, Athena or Artemis by their name alone; depending on circumstances or the place, they address Zeus Ktesios, Zeus Agoraios, Zeus Polieus, for example; in the same way, they call upon Athena Chalkeia, Athena Ergane or Athena Lemnia; Artemis Propylaia, Artemis Okylocheia, Artemis Mounichia, and so on. In fact, a god manifests himself to man in several different ways: man addresses him in each instance with an appropriate epithet. However, despite this diversity of aspects and names, the Greek has no doubt that Zeus, Artemis or Athena remain themselves, inaccessible to man in the totality of their power. Thus each god is situated beyond the phenomena by which he reveals his presence, beyond the names that man gives him and the images he makes of him. If that is how things are within Hellas, a Greek will naturally accept that they must happen in a similar manner abroad, even though the observable differences between divine images and nomenclature grow larger when peoples who are farther away from one another are considered.

Several authors have already made similar observations.[34] I believe these to be pertinent; in the final analysis, however, it seems to me that the Greeks' attitude towards foreign religions rests on still more fundamental characteristics of Greek religion.

[34] See for example F. Graf, 'Religion in gegenseitiger Wahrnehmung: Die griechisch-römische Antike', *Bulletin de la Société Suisse pour la Science des Religions*, 13, August 1991, pp. 5–16.

We have noted that, in the Greek view, since all men perceive the presence of gods in the world, they are naturally inclined to pay them honour. Their consciousness of these relations between mortals and the divine deepens with time and is expressed in an increasingly elaborate manner, in the development of the *nomoi* peculiar to each people. Texts tell us that two types of person played a decisive role in this evolution: prophets and poets. According to Herodotus' theory, for instance, the Pelasgians consulted the oracle of Dodona before adopting the Egyptian custom of naming the gods; the poets Homer and Hesiod later gave them their forms.[35] Numerous testimonies teach us that poets and prophets are inspired; a god lives within them and speaks through their lips.[36] Greek religion thus rests on a tradition which preserves the memory of inspired lessons, chiefly those of prophets in matters of ritual, and chiefly those of poets in matters of belief. Inspiration, on the other hand, differs in some essential characteristics from the revelation with which we are more familiar.

Whatever the duration of the events during which it operates, revelation is unique; it is whole; it is complete. It brings to man the sum total of what he can, and what he must, know about the divine. The result is that a revelation is exclusive. It cannot abide any other revelation beside itself, unless it is presented as the definitive fulfilment of previous revelations, which at the same stroke it relegates to non-fulfilment.

Inspiration is different. The oracle replies to the one question it is asked. The poet makes use of a given myth and reworks it to deal with a particular problem that preoccupies him, as it may also preoccupy his contemporaries. Inspiration is thus always partial, incomplete, valid in a particular circumstance, a particular place. It can always prove a useful complement to other inspirations. Inspired religion, as a consequence, is not exclusive. Anyone who belongs to a tradition that conveys the memory of inspirations – the scope of which, despite their importance, is limited and the pertinence relative – will easily admit that elsewhere also traditions can carry the memory of similar inspirations, equally limited but entirely legitimate, in the circumstances in which they are produced.

Such relativism may surprise us. To understand it, we must bring our attention to bear on another feature of Greek religious psychology. Although, in each place, it enables man to give better expression to, and deepen his experience of, an encounter with the divine, inspir-

---

[35] Hdt., II, 53.
[36] E.g. Hes., *Th.*, 22–34, 103–15; Pl., *Ion*, 533 d–535 a; *Phdr.*, 244 a–245 a.

ation does not give him an exact knowledge of it. When they feel the presence of the divine, the Greeks perceive both its nearness and its distance. They use names, appropriate for establishing a relationship between man and a deity, but they know that these names have a relative value; they realise that the divine eludes their intelligence. Each in their own way, authors of all tendencies tell us so. Here are some of their words. Aeschylus writes: 'Zeus' purposes are not easy to grasp ... Hidden and covered in profound shadows, the paths of divine thought go their way in such a manner that they cannot be known.'[37] Among the prose-writers, we find many cautious expressions, like that of Isocrates: 'If it is really necessary, since we are mortals, to make conjectures about the thinking of the gods';[38] or of Andocides: 'If at least we may make conjectures regarding the gods'.[39] In a later period, Plutarch advises us to proceed with regard to the divine 'with the pious reserve of the philosophers of the Academy and purging ourselves of every claim to speak on the subject as if we had any knowledge about it'.[40]

Even more significant, one of Plato's texts emphasises the uncertainty of the names by which men designate the gods. 'By Zeus, Hermogenes, if we had any good sense, to put it in the best way we should say that we know nothing of the gods, either of their proper nature or the names they give themselves – for it is obvious that they call themselves by their true name. There would be a second way of speaking correctly, doing as is done in prayers, where it is the rule that we should invoke them *by the names they like*, whatever they may be and whatever their origin, and that we should speak as people who know nothing more.'[41] This distinction between the ritual name of the god and the god himself, as his true name would reveal his nature, is not the product of an exceptional philosophical reflection. In a tragedy addressed to the entire Athenian public, Aeschylus had already said 'O Zeus! whoever Zeus is, if he likes to be addressed by this name, thus do I invoke him.'[42] Euripides would develop the same idea: 'You who bear the earth and have your dwelling on the earth, whoever you may be, so difficult to know, Zeus, whether you are the necessity immanent in all things or the intelligence of (the same nature as that of) mortals, it is you that I invoke.'[43] Put briefly, the

[37] Aesch., *Suppl.*, 86–7, 92–4.
[38] Isoc. 1, *Demonicus*, 50.
[39] And. 1, *Mysteries*, 139.
[40] Plut., *De sera numinis vindicta*, *Mor.*, 549 e.
[41] Pl., *Crat.*, 400 d–e.
[42] Aesch., *Ag.*, 160–1.
[43] Eur., *Tro.*, 884–8.

traditional divine names do not correspond to an exact knowledge. Used in prayers and evocations, they none the less possess a ritual efficacy. This is what Aeschylus and Plato teach when they say: such names are pleasing to the gods.

Since the name used by men is not the god's true name but simply an instrument they employ according to their traditions, their *nomoi*, there is nothing disturbing in the fact that peoples use different names to designate the same gods. And since the god himself eludes our knowledge, there is nothing disturbing in the fact that they create different images, from one instance to another. For the Greek, such images do not form an adequate representation of the gods, who hide from view just as they elude human understanding. Traditional tools, they serve to express the feelings man experiences when he encounters the divine. If he gives these images the material reality of a statue, they are also useful to him to commemorate that encounter and, at the same time, encourage a beneficial repetition of it. On this point, past events of which tradition retains the memory have shown the effectiveness of images – even when it is known that images do not give an adequate representation of the deity.†

Names and divine images are in effect part and parcel of mythical language. Paradoxically, for all that they are aware of their inability to know the divine reality, the Greeks say a lot about it, but the language that they use has particular characteristics. It is suggestive rather than straightforward; the truth of mythical accounts lies in what they evoke rather than in the historicity of the events they relate. In this symbolic fashion, myths express not only what a man has sensed when experiencing a remarkable encounter with the deity, but also the consistency he perceives between all the similar experiences he has had.[44]

If we submit wisely to the evocative power of myths, paying attention to the links that connect them, we shall be able to penetrate a little way into Greek religious thinking. I believe that we shall then discover the most profound reason for the tolerance which Greeks evince in matters of religion regarding foreign *nomoi*. Through the image of an apportionment of *timai* [honours], the cosmogonic myths and the great divine myths simultaneously recall the way in which the universe received its shape and the gods were allocated their special functions and privileges; they thus throw light on the

---

† For the ancient conception of divine images, see Gordon, 'The real and the imaginary'.

[44] Cf. J. Rudhardt, 'Du mythe, de la religion grecque et de la comprehension d'autrui', *Cahiers Vilfredo-Pareto. Revue européenne des Sciences sociales*, IX, 58, 1981, pp. 105–205; 'Comprendre la religion grecque', *Kernos*, 4, 1991, pp. 47–59.

sacred governance of the world. Similar myths, several of which also refer to a distribution of *timai*, tell of the origin and history of the first men, recounting how they were gradually distanced from the gods and endowed with a civilisation. This is how they clarify man's situation in the world and in the sight of the gods. Other myths complement these by telling of the origin of the great human races, of families and cities and of their chief institutions. They throw light on a sacred ordinance in which man's condition is defined by more than the general framework of a relationship between mortals and immortals; the condition of each and every individual is defined also by his belonging to such and such a family, such and such a city. The sacred ordinance in which both gods and mortals participate simultaneously involves the world and human communities, in all their diversity. This is why, within this ordinance, the relationship of men to the gods assumes different forms in different places. The plurality of the *nomoi* and their variations can be seen then to have a religious basis.

The Greek, as he travels, does not only recognise his own gods in those of the countries through which he journeys; he accepts the legitimacy of the names or images which his hosts attribute to them, of the forms of worship devoted to them. Thus in Armenia, Xenophon, fearing the death of a horse which has been seized by mercenaries and which he learns had been pledged to the Sun-God, restores the horse to the headman of the village, so that the animal can be well fed and correctly sacrificed.[45]

A few facts seem to contradict all the propositions I have just set out, so I will conclude by examining them briefly.

Dinarchus,[46] Demosthenes and one of his scholiasts [ancient commentators][47] inform us that the Athenians put the priestess Ninos to death because she had introduced the worship of foreign gods. Flavius Josephus gives us the reason: 'Among them, this was prohibited by law, and the punishment for those who introduced a foreign deity was death.'[48] It was by virtue of this law that Theoris was condemned[49] and Phryne accused.[50] Socrates' writ of indictment refers to it, even though improperly.[51]

---

[45] Xen., *Anab.*, IV, 5, 35.
[46] Din., *Catalogue de ses discours*, XXVIII; *Oratores Attici*, II, p. 450, C. Muller.
[47] Dem., XIX, 181 and scholia; XXXIX, 2; XL, 9.
[48] Flav. Jos., *Contra Apionem* II, 267
[49] Dem., XXV, 79–80 and scholia.
[50] *Hyperides Oratores Attici*, II, p. 408, fr. 116; pp. 425–7, introd. and fr. 211–19. M. Müller; Aristogiton, *ibid.*, II, p. 436, fr. 7; Euthias., *ibid.*, II, pp. 447–8; *Athenaeus*, XIII, 590d–e.
[51] Cf. E. Derenne, *Les procès d'impiété intentés à des philosophes à Athènes*, Bibliothèque

However, the Athenians allowed several foreign forms of worship to be celebrated in the city, for instance that of Bendis.[52] How was that possible? The cult celebrated by Ninos and for which she was condemned to death was that of Sabazius. We later see the mother of Aeschines take part in this cult, and introducing new initiates to it, without being disturbed. Scholiasts teach us that it had been authorised in the meantime, as the result of a process about which they give us little precise detail; they do say, however, that it had included consultation of an oracle.[53]

These items of information are coherent and perfectly intelligible. A Greek recognises the existence and divinity of a foreign god, under whatever name he is described, as well as the legitimacy of his cult, in places where it is practised in conformity with an old tradition; conversely, he hesitates to introduce that cult into his own city. The *nomoi* are appropriate to each people. We have noted, when considering the system in which all Greek mythical accounts tend to become integrated, that the forms of the relationship that unites man with the gods vary according to the position that man occupies in the religious order of things. It is therefore not certain that transferring a cult from one area to another is beneficial. On the contrary, it might upset relations between mortals and immortals in the country to which it is imported. However, the approval of an oracle can placate that anxiety. The inspired oracle, in fact, legitimises an innovation in ritual matters. Reassured by the oracle of Dodona, says Herodotus, the Pelasgians accepted the Egyptian custom of naming the gods.

Apparently contradictory, the attitude adopted by the Greeks towards foreign cults practised outside Hellas, and that adopted when it is a matter of those foreign cults being practised in their own city, are clearly the outcome of one and the same logic. This logic has other consequences. In the same way that the Greeks find it difficult to accept imported foreign cults, they make little effort to export their own. However pious a Greek may be, it never crosses his mind to proselytise. He would not dream of altering either the beliefs or forms of worship of others, even less of destroying them.

de la Faculté de Philosophie et Lettres de l'Université de Liège, XLV, 1930.
[52] Pl., *Resp.*, I, 327 *a–b*, 354 *a*; Xen., *Hell.*, II, 4, 11; *IG*, II, 1361, 1283, etc.
[53] Dem. XVIII, *On the Crown*, 259–60, and scholia.

PART III

Peoples

Introduction to Part III

Perhaps the most exciting event in Greek history since the early 1980s has been the transformation in the writing of the history of Achaemenid Persia, the foreign land which, more than any other, cast its shadow over the classical Greek world. Through a series of volumes of the *Achaemenid History Workshop*, and in Pierre Briant's monumental *Histoire de l'Empire Perse*, the history of Persia has been rewritten both by a re-examination of Persian evidence and through a bypassing of the pejorative attitudes to Persia of Greek sources. It is difficult to imagine what event could bring about a change in the history of classical Greece or Rome comparable to that which these scholars have effected in the case of Persia. However, there are grounds for some caution over the use of Greek sources by recent historians of Persia. Lurid stories, for example, of the excessive influence and cruelty of Persian royal women are dismissed as motivated by the misogyny of Greek authors, yet the same stories are used as the basis for painting a sometimes implausibly apple-pie portrait of the role of women in the Persian court: such women are 'active, enterprising and resolute';[1] their cruelty is, they argue, the 'duty of a mother', a duty circumscribed by quasi-constitutional rules limiting the influence of royal wives over the king.[2] Is it legitimate to use sources so selectively? At any rate, the use of Greek sources for Persian history depends upon the prior examination of those sources in their Greek context.

It is exactly that which Pierre Briant's 'History and Ideology: The Greeks and "Persian Decadence"' (Ch. 8) achieves. Briant looks at the representation of the Persians by Plato, Xenophon, Isocrates and

---

[1] Wiesehöfer, *Ancient Persia*, p. 185. Similar language is used of the queen (possibly identifiable as Atossa) of Aeschylus' *Persians*: see Sancisi-Weerdenburg, 'Exit Atossa'; Harrison, *Emptiness of Asia*, pp. 44–7, Ch. 8.

[2] See esp. Brosius, *Women in Ancient Persia*, pp. 105–22.

other Greek authors.[3] Their characterisation of Persia – as militarily weak, steeped in luxury, dominated politically by women and eunuchs – is, he argues, motivated by ideological rather than historical aims, and must be interpreted in the context of Greek political ideas rather than as evidence of the reality of the Persian court.

Briant's account, concentrating on fourth-century sources, can be read as a companion-piece to James Redfield's account in Chapter 1 of the Persians' degeneration from 'hard' to 'soft' in Herodotus' *Histories*. It can also be read against a number of works which (from different perspectives) argue that the Greek–barbarian antithesis was 'gendered': discussions of the Athenian or Greek ideal of masculine austerity of dress and eschewal of luxury;[4] the Greek portrayal of, often strikingly masculine, barbarian women from the fringes of the earth;[5] or the Greek projection of matriarchy on foreign peoples.[6] This theme can be over-simplified. Edith Hall has argued that 'the oppositions man–woman and rapist–raped are transferred to the Greek-non-Greek relationship'.[7] Her evidence for this is the Eurymedon vase, on which a Greek is pictured on the verge of anal penetration of a barbarian 'Eurymedon' (see Ch. 4 and introduction to Part I, p. 22).[8] In general, however, the Greeks associated sexual violence with *effeminacy*, an attribute of the Persians rather than the Greeks: in Herodotus' narrative of the Persian Wars, it is the Persians who, like Greek tyrants, display a sexual insatiability.[9]

We move then to 'The Greeks as Egyptologists' by François Hartog (Ch. 9), well known for his *The Mirror of Herodotus*.[10] Hartog

---

[3] For Isocrates, see below, introduction to Part IV. There have been a number of recent studies of Xenophon's treatment of the Persians: Due, *The Cyropaedia* (for philosophical content and literary background); Tatum, *Xenophon's Imperial Fiction* (on the combination of politics and fiction, and on reception); Dillery, *Xenophon* (esp. on panhellenism and idealism); Georges, *Barbarian Asia*, Ch. 7; Hirsch, *The Friendship of the Barbarians* (with an excessive stress on Persian influence on the *Cyropaedia*); superior is Deborah Levine Gera, *Xenophon's Cyropaedia*. See also (from a Persian historian's viewpoint) Sancisi-Weerdenburg, 'The fifth oriental monarchy and hellenocentrism', 'The death of Cyrus'.

[4] Geddes, 'Rags and riches'; Kurke, 'The politics of *habrosyne*'; Lombardo, '*Habrosyne e habra*'; see also my comments, *Emptiness of Asia*, pp. 105–8.

[5] See especially Rosellini and Saïd, 'Usages de femmes'; also below, Ch. 12 (Nippel).

[6] See Pembroke, 'Women in charge'; for the gendering of foreign peoples, see also now Dougherty, *The Poetics of Colonisation*; Cartledge, 'Machismo'; Gray, 'Rhetoric of otherness'. For comparison, see Gittings, *Imperialism and Gender*; Hall, *Civilizing Subjects*.

[7] Hall, 'Asia unmanned', p. 113.

[8] See above, introduction to Part I. Better evidence of an association of sexual 'conquest' and military victory would be Hdt. 2.102 and 7.57; see further Harrison, 'Persian dress and Greek freedom'.

[9] See Harrison, 'Herodotus and the ancient Greek idea of rape'; Davidson, *Courtesans and Fishcakes*, e.g. p. 180 (of the Eurymedon vase).

[10] See also now his *Memories of Odysseus*.

distinguishes clearly between the reality of the contacts between Greece and Egypt and (the object of his study) the Greek *representation* of Egypt.[11] He highlights a series of defining moments in the history of that representation and shows how the most persistent images of Egypt – its religious aspect, for example – underwent significant shifts in the course of time from Hecataeus and Herodotus through to late antiquity. From being a source of wonder to Herodotus, Egypt became the source exclusively of religion.

The Persians and Egyptians in many ways represent two poles in the representation of foreign peoples. Egypt, as James Redfield shows in Chapter 1, presents in its climate and many of its customs a reversal of Greek norms. Yet, perhaps more than any other, it is the land from which the Greeks believed that they derived features of their culture.[12] With the exception of Xenophon's idealisation of Cyrus in the *Cyropaedia*, Persia remained – at least until Alexander's conquest of Asia – for the most part a negative model for the Greeks. Other peoples present a combination of these features: they are variously (and often simultaneously) idealised, distanced, and appropriated to provide analogies for Greek history and society. Several barbarian peoples have been the subject of specialised studies of Greek representations;[13] in those areas where archaeological material is plentiful, there have also been studies attempting to correct or balance the Greek perspective.[14]

We should never forget, finally, that the Greeks were far from being a united group, either in their imagination or in reality. Differences in religion, language and myth have already been discussed in Part II. Ethnographers such as the early fifth-century Hecataeus detailed the customs of Greek cities and peoples as well as foreigners. Herodotus devotes an 'ethnographic digression' to the Spartans.[15] Likewise, the fourth-century Theopompus of Chios ascribes dicing, drinking and debauchery seemingly to everybody,

[11] For the Greek representation of Egypt, see also (at greater length) Froidefrond, *Le mirage égyptien*; Lloyd, 'Herodotus on Egyptians and Libyans'; Preus, 'Greek philosophy in Egypt'.

[12] See further Harrison, *Divinity and History*, Chs 7–8.

[13] See Burkert et al., *Hérodote et les peuples non-Grecs*; Lévy, 'Les origines du mirage scythe' (and a number of other articles in the same volume); see also e.g. Archibald, *Odrysian Kingdom*, pp. 94–102; Hartog, *Mirror of Herodotus*; Snowden, 'Greeks and Ethiopians'.

[14] See e.g. now Archibald, *Odrysian Kingdom*. Often, in the case of northern peoples, we may suspect that historians and archaeologists subscribe too easily to the static ethnic labels of ancient writers, labels which sometimes coincide uncannily with the boundaries of modern nation states. See e.g. Fol et al., *The New Thracian Treasure from Rogozen, Bulgaria*; Fol and Mazarow, *Thrace and the Thracians*. For an exemplary treatment of a comparable situation in late antiquity, see Heather, *Goths and Romans*.

[15] See here Cartledge, *The Greeks*, pp. 80–2; Hartog, *Mirror of Herodotus*, esp. pp. 152–6; Munson, 'Three aspects'.

Greek and barbarian.[16] The political disunity of the Greek world is the subject, in Part IV, of F. W. Walbank's 'The Problem of Greek Nationality' (Ch. 10).

---

[16] See Flower, *Theopompus of Chios*. Flower finds a marked lack of emphasis, by contrast, on *Persian* decadence, and on Panhellenic idealism (pp. 83–90).

8 History and Ideology: The Greeks and 'Persian Decadence'†

PIERRE BRIANT

translated by Antonia Nevill

I

In Book III of the *Laws*, which is dedicated to the development of political societies, Plato reserves a relatively long exposition (III, 693 c–698 a) for Persian society. As Athens is the prototype of democracy, so Persia is that of autocracy. Unlike Sparta and Crete, which knew how to maintain the balance of their traditional institutions, Persia rapidly lost its equilibrium between the principles of monarchism and liberty. The exposition dedicated to the decadence of the Persians is intended to illustrate this theme. As a basis for his argument, Plato calls upon history, and in cavalier fashion recreates the development of Persian government and society between Cyrus the Elder and the period in which he himself is writing. In Plato's opinion, the Persians had never regained the balance between 'servitude and freedom' achieved under Cyrus; it had been an era when 'complete freedom of speech' reigned, and when 'there was progress in everything among them at that time, thanks to liberty, friendship and co-operation' (694 a–b). But things soured very quickly under Cambyses and, in spite of a kind of renaissance in the time of Darius I, there was a continuous deterioration from the time of Xerxes. 'The Persians failed to halt on the downward slope of decadence' (697 c), remarks the Athenian, adding 'that governmental regime of the Persians is currently tainted by an excess of servitude among the populace and an excess of despotism among their masters' (698 a). Thus the equilibrium of Cyrus' era had been broken. 'The cause, I say, is that by taking too much liberty away from their people and pushing the despotism of the master to limits beyond what is appro-

---

† Originally published as 'Histoire et idéologie: les Grecs et la "décadence perse"', in M.-M. Mactoux and E. Geny (eds), *Mélanges P. Lévêque II* (Bésancon, 1989), 33–47.

priate, they have ruined the feelings of mutual friendship and community of interest within the state' (697 e).

The credibility of Greek writings on Achaemenid history has often been the subject of argument among historians. In this case, it is known that the open battles between the sons of Cambyses and the subsequent accession to the throne of Darius did not fail to catch the attention of Greek authors (Herodotus, Ctesias, Xenophon, Aeschylus and many others). It is also known that Cyrus the Elder always enjoyed great prestige in Greek literature. From this point of view, the passage from Plato fits very neatly with Greek political discourse. Obviously, the historical value of Plato's explanations on the fragile balance between freedom and monarchy at the heart of Persian political society is open to doubt. The passages devoted to Cyrus, Cambyses and Darius seem to indicate that the Greeks thought the struggles in the time of Cambyses and the Magus (the Smerdis of Herodotus, in other words, Bardiya, alias Gaumata)† are written within the framework of relations between the dynasty and the aristocracy, the conditions of Darius' accession having paradoxically marked a fleeting restoration of the position of the aristocracy vis-à-vis the monarchy.[1]

However, for the historian of representations, the most interesting aspect lies less in the stages of evolution as Plato reconstructs them than in the causes to which he ascribes them. Now, from this point of view, Plato is very clear: the entire history of Persian society is determined by the relations that the royal family has maintained with the educational institutions of the Persian people. Plato recalls what was relatively well known, thanks chiefly to Herodotus, Xenophon and Strabo, about the harshness of the training imposed on young aristocratic Persians. 'A hard method, one capable of producing shepherds who are absolutely robust and capable of sleeping out in the open, even passing the night without sleep, and of fighting a campaign' (695 a). This is obviously the explanation for all Cyrus' virtues, especially his military ones. But contradictions quickly appear; by very reason of the fact that Cyrus 'was, so it would seem, always on campaign', his children's upbringing was left to the women of the palace. Instead of giving his sons the rough education he had himself received, 'he viewed with indifference his sons receiving an upbringing in the Median fashion, an education corrupted by so-called happiness, in the hands of teachers who were women and

† For the truth of this complex episode, see Briant, *Histoire de l'empire Perse*, pp. 109–18.
[1] Cf. my remarks in *Iranica Antiqua* XIX, 1984, pp. 111–14.

eunuchs' (695 a): an education wholly imprinted with 'softness'. If the accession of Darius marked a restoration, it was because *he* 'was not a king's son; he had therefore received an education free from softness' (695 c). 'Then, after Darius, came Xerxes, whose upbringing, once again, had been that of the Palace, all softness ... and it may be said that since that era there has been no king among the Persians who has truly deserved, except only in name, to be called Great King' (695 e). Thus Plato thinks he has brought to light the internal contradiction of the system: when he conquered the empire, Cyrus brought wealth and happiness to his children, who received no education suitable to teach them to use their power properly (694 d). The reason for the decadence is therefore to be sought 'in the kind of life most often lived by children of men who possess exceptionally great wealth or else absolute power' (696 a).

The most visible symptom and consequence of this moral decline are revealed in military discipline. The strengthening of the sovereign's autocracy 'has ruined the feelings of mutual friendship and community of interests within the state' (689 c). In these conditions, peoples do not respond to the demand for troops that kings seek to impose; the latter 'find no echo of their appeal among their peoples or any eagerness to run the risks of combat; quite the opposite; they may well have innumerable thousands of men at their disposal; all those thousands are no use at all, and just as if they were lacking soldiers, they engage more for pay, judging that they will one day owe their safety to mercenaries and foreign troops. An abundance of gold and silver has completely perverted their way of looking at things' (697 e–698 a).

II

An analysis that is no less schematic, yet at the same time more detailed, is to be found in the last chapter of Book VIII of Xenophon's *Cyropaedia* (VIII, 8). For the biographer of Cyrus and extoller of a benign model of monarchy, the decline set in 'immediately after the death of Cyrus', when his children (Cambyses and Tanyoxarkes [Smerdis/Bardiya]) struggled for power and the subject peoples rebelled (8, 2). This disintegration first showed itself on the moral plane. The Persian kings violated their commitments (8, 2–3) and rewarded people who had performed morally reprehensible acts (8, 4): 'Witnessing these things, all the inhabitants of Asia chose the paths of impiety and iniquity; for, with a few exceptions, subjects follow their leaders.' The other symptom of this decline was the inability of the Persians to defend their territories, for 'they avoided contact with those who were stronger than themselves, and no longer dared to join the royal army' (8, 7). In those conditions, 'whoever makes war on the Persians can, without a fight, stroll at his ease in the country' (8, 7), and 'enemies walk around everywhere in Persian lands more freely than friends' (8, 21), all the more so because 'they arrest not only serious delinquents but henceforth perfectly innocent people' (8, 6). From now on 'the cavalry does not hunt people down any more than it fights hand-to-hand' (8, 22); the footsoldiers themselves 'no longer seek hand-to-hand combat' (8, 22); as for chariot-drivers, they refuse to engage with the enemy (8, 24–6). All in all, 'those men make a crowd, very possibly, but they are no use at all for war'. This military incapacity is in any case obvious because of their call for mercenaries, whereas 'in bygone times' landowners supplied levies of horsemen (8, 20): 'No longer did they ever enter a campaign without Greeks, either when making war among the Persians or when they were the object of a Greek campaign; and even against these Greeks they chose to make war using Greeks' (8, 26). When all is said and done, 'in matters of war, the Persians and their people are more cowardly today than they once were' (8, 27).

As for the reasons and origins of this decline, Xenophon, like Plato, stresses the abandonment of traditional educational practices, not only among royalty but among all the Persians. 'The custom still survives that children are brought up at court; but the learning and practice of horsemanship have fallen into disuse, for want of the kind of events that would bring it into renown' (8, 13). Generally speaking, they no longer practise 'as they used to, physical workouts' (8, 8), or seek 'to toughen their bodies by exercise and sweat' (8, 8). In particular, they have given up hunting, which formerly 'had been sufficient exercise for themselves and their horses' (8, 12). From then on, they have fallen into the luxuriousness and softness of the Medes (8, 15). They eat and drink continually until they are inebriated (8, 8–11); they stuff themselves with sweetmeats (8, 16). They reject the constraints of a soldier's hard life, preferring to lounge on thick carpets (8, 16), and they fearfully protect themselves against cold and heat rather than courageously confront sudden changes in temperature (8, 17). These are exactly the same themes as those developed by Xenophon in Chapter IX of the *Agesilaus*, where he strongly contrasts the frugal life-style of *Agesilaus* and 'the boastfulness of the Persian' (9, 1).

III

Persia's weakness in the fourth century is a theme tirelessly taken up by the Athenian orator Isocrates, the eulogist of Panhellenism and the war against the Great King. It is to be found again, developed with a notable complacency, in the *Panegyric* (IV) and *Philip* (V). Isocrates intends to combat 'certain people who admire the king's greatness and resources' (IV, 134), as well as 'the many Greeks who believe the Great King's power to be invincible' (V, 139). It is inappropriate 'to make the sovereign of Asia appear too energetic or too important' (V, 76). Although the Barbarians actually 'have many possessions, they are quite unable to defend them' (IV, 184), as is attested in particular by the large number of countries that have seceded (IV, 161–2; V, 102–4). If the king has managed to win certain victories, he owes them not to his own might but to the folly of the Greeks in their divided state (IV, 137); in any case, the Great King has never had a victory over the Greeks, since the time when Athenians and Spartans were united (IV, 139) and 'when they (the Persians) passed into Europe, they were punished, some perishing wretchedly, and the others shamefully fleeing' (IV, 149). So difficult is it for them to assemble contingents, and so grudgingly do the subjected peoples give their support to the Persians (IV, 165), that the immense hordes of the Great Kings' armies are no more than an illusion. They therefore have to call upon Greek mercenaries (V, 126).

Among the reasons for Persian military inferiority, Isocrates makes reference to the logistical difficulties encountered by the king in assembling an army, because it is so hard to act rapidly in such an immense empire (IV, 141, 162, 165): this is a characteristic frequently emphasised by Greek authors, especially Xenophon himself (*Anab.* I, 5, 9) and Diodorus (XV, 9, 2; XVI, 44–6). However, in Isocrates' view, that is no more than a circumstantial factor. The 'softening' of the Persians is much more the result of the socio-political regime under which they live:

> Anyway, none of that is illogical and it all seems most likely: it is impossible for people brought up and governed as they are to have any virtue and, in battle, to raise a trophy over their enemies. How could either an able general or a courageous soldier exist, given the habits of those people, the majority of whom form an undisciplined mob with no experience of dangers, grown soft when confronted with war, but better instructed in slavery than our own servants; and among whom those with the highest reputation, without exception, have never experienced concern for the interests of others or of the state, and spend all their time gravely offending some, being the slaves of others, in the most corrupt way that men can? They immerse their bodies

in luxury because of their wealth, their souls are humiliated and terrified by the monarchy, they let themselves be inspected at the palace gate, grovel on the ground, indulge in every kind of humility when worshipping a mortal whom they call god and caring less for divinity than for men. (IV, 150–1)

Rather than considering, as Xenophon and Plato do, that this softening is the result of a decline in education, Isocrates on the contrary thinks that the education given to young Persians leads them inevitably into paths which he denounces:

Consequently, those who go down to the coast and whom they call satraps [provincial governors] do not show themselves unworthy of the education of their country and keep the same customs, acting treacherously towards their friends and like cowards towards their enemies, living now in humility, now in arrogance, despising their allies and flattering their adversaries. (IV, 152)

These explanations were taken up again, in their entirety or in part, by numerous authors of the Hellenistic period. In Arrian,† Darius III is shown as the archetype of a power that has lost all substance:

More than anyone, he was spineless and not very knowledgeable in matters of war, but, for the rest, he never showed cruelty, or else he had never had occasion to do so, because his accession to power coincided with the opening of hostilities by the Macedonians and Greeks against him; so, even if he had wanted to, it would not have been possible for him to behave arrogantly towards his subjects, seeing that he was going through greater dangers than they. His life was an uninterrupted succession of misfortunes from which he knew no respite from the time he came to power. (III, 22, 2–3)

Contempt towards the Barbarians erupts still more in the speech that this same Arrian (II, 7) puts in Alexander's mouth before the battle of Issus. Here we find all the traditional Greek arguments: the Macedonians, 'having long been inured to danger', are much superior, both physically and morally, for the Persians 'had lived in luxury for a long time. It will be above all the struggle of slaves against free men.' And Alexander also quotes the precedent of Xenophon (of whom Arrian was an ardent admirer) and the Ten Thousand who 'had routed the Great King and his whole army, near Babylon itself, then in their descent towards the Black Sea had vigorously attacked all the tribes which had tried to block their route'. In many other passages, Arrian – to cite him alone – contrasted the bravery of Alexander with the cowardice of the Persians, apparently unaware

† Writing in the second century AD, but relying on Ptolemy and Aristobulus, both contemporaries of Alexander.

that by doing so he was devaluing the Macedonian's victories (e.g. VII, 8, 6–7).[2]

In his treatment, intended to distinguish the beginning, causes and pretext of the wars, Polybius too does not hesitate to make the expedition of the Ten Thousand and that of Agesilaus the 'causes' of Philip II's expedition. In fact, Xenophon and the Greek mercenaries 'returned from the satrapies of the interior by crossing the whole of Asia without any Barbarian force daring to stand up to them'. As for Agesilaus, 'he met no adversary strong enough to oppose his undertakings ... All that gave Philip food for thought. Bearing in mind the cowardice and nonchalance of the Persians on the one hand, and the fact that he himself and the Macedonians excelled in warfare, he pictured the great and brilliant advantages he could reap from this enterprise ...' (III, 1). Polybius makes use of the memory of the Persian Wars to recall that sheer numbers of soldiers do not always make armies strong if the people attacked can stand up to the aggressors. Again the Persian Wars, and probably Darius' expedition to Scythia, are the basis for this other remark about the Persians, whom he contrasts with the Romans of his own time: 'The Persians who, in a certain era, ruled over a vast empire but who, each time they ventured outside the boundaries of Asia, put their domination and their very existence at risk' (I, 2).

I V

There is no need to multiply such references *ad infinitum* to show that the military incapacity of the Persians was clearly one of the favourite topics of Greek authors in the classical and Hellenistic periods. What is surprising is that the Greek thesis has sometimes been accepted by historians of today, a good many of whom, until quite recently, suggested that Darius III's kingdom was the picture of an empire in the throes of internal disintegration and a very advanced state of military enfeeblement. It is not my intention here to set out the state of the Achaemenid kingdom in the time of Darius III: let me say simply that, on the majority of points in dispute, the thesis of the Greek authors is contradicted by the facts. On the other hand, it is not a matter of denying the weaknesses of the Achaemenid empire, but merely of remarking that the Greek writings in no way allow an analysis of what they present as decadence. It is an odd sort of decadence at all events, since according to Plato it began with the

[2] See my study in *Mélanges Labrousse* (=*Pallas, n° hors-série*), Toulouse 1986, pp. 11–22.

disappearance of the founder, Cyrus the Great, and continued to worsen despite a short respite under Darius I. If one adds that, according to Isocrates, Persian weakness was linked to its political regime,[3] one ought even to dismiss the term 'decadence'; it is difficult to see, in these conditions, when and how such a state could have experienced the slightest apogee!

True, Isocrates and Xenophon lay particular emphasis on the catastrophic development supposedly undergone by the empire in the fourth century: the former dwelling on the seccessions of the countries that had been conquered, the latter describing the abandonment of educational practices among the Persians. Is that any reason for inferring a clear-cut contrast between a fifth century of Achaemenid might and a fourth century of decadence, with the expedition of the Ten Thousand, based on this hypothesis, forming both a symptom and a landmark? Not at all. It is in the fifth century that we see the theme of Persian military weakness develop, correlative to the Greek victories in the Persian Wars. The latter, as we know, rapidly became the favourite theme of Athenian history, a theme situated poles apart from any historical truth whatsoever.[4] In the 'Persian Wars' as imagined, the fifth-century Persians were obviously worth no more than those of the fourth century. This same theme is to be found, for example, in the speech which Herodotus (V, 49–50) ascribes to Aristagoras of Miletus, who has come to Sparta to try to persuade Cleomenes to send an expeditionary force to Asia Minor: 'It will be easy for you to succeed. Indeed, the Barbarians are without military strength, whereas *you* have reached your peak for warfare.' Moreover, the Persians are not only weak but also wealthy: 'The inhabitants of that continent possess more riches than all the other peoples put together.' We find the same argument in Isocrates (IV, 184) and Xenophon (*Anab.* III, 2, 25–6), both eager to urge their fellow citizens to colonise in Asia Minor. In the fourth century, in Athens, the use of the 'Persian Wars' theme continued to increase, and Isocrates himself handles it with evident delight in the *Panegyricus.*[5] In any case, the expedition of the Ten Thousand soon formed an

---

[3] Cf. also Hippocrates, *Airs, Waters, Places* (§ 16): 'Where men, far from being their own masters and autonomous, are under the authority of a despot, they do not have the reputation of taking much part in warlike activities, but are regarded as not very bellicose ... (§ 23). Where there are kings, there we find the most cowardly people.' Hippocrates adds climatic reasons: in Asia, 'the seasons do not bring change ... Now, change stimulates people's character and prevents their remaining passive ... For uniformity produces softness, whereas from change is born strenuous effort of body and soul.'

[4] See N. Loraux, *L'invention d'Athènes: histoire de l'oraison funèbre dans la cité classique*, Paris-The Hague-New York 1981, pp. 133ff. [translated as *The Invention of Athens*].

[5] Cf. Loraux, in *REA* 75, 1973, pp. 13–42.

ideal precedent for proving Persian military decline to the Greeks, since, for the first time Greek mercenaries – on the orders of an Achaemenid, it is true – had reached as far as Babylonia. This was soon followed by the expedition of Agesilaus, who had been the first to dare to wage war against the Persians by going a little farther from the coast of Asia Minor, before being overcome by the division among the Greeks and the money of the Great King. Their position strengthened by these heroic examples, Xenophon and Isocrates were able to hammer home the military decadence of the Persians.

Without undertaking a word-for-word commentary on the assertions of the Greek authors, it is very clear to everyone that neither Xenophon nor Isocrates nor Plato had much concern for historical analysis. Their primary aim was ideological. The realities of the Persian empire in their time were not their intellectual priority. The true subject of the speeches of Plato and Xenophon was not so much Persia as Sparta and Athens.[6] The Greek authors used the example of Persia only in as much as it allowed them to develop a discourse which was internal to the city. By way of a last example, let us take the speech delivered by Demosthenes in 354, *On the Symmories* (Dem. 14). The author wishes to challenge those who want to declare war on the Great King, the size of whose naval preparations had just become known. Adopting a form of reasoning that was exactly the opposite of Isocrates' (IV, 138ff.), Demosthenes does not hesitate to denounce those who are urging war by glorifying the Athenian past (§ 1). Of course, the Persian King 'is the common enemy of all Greece', but the Athenians are not ready to confront him; let them not, therefore, be lulled by illusions about their military abilities or the union of the Greeks (§ 2–10). Even if superior in courage, Athens is inferior in triremes, fortresses and money. To overcome this handicap, the tax reforms proposed by Demosthenes must be put into effect. At this point in his exposition, the orator's tone changes. Once the city is assured of these new resources – he underlines – it can face the future with confidence. After all, the king's wealth is not inexhaustible (§ 29–30); furthermore, the Greeks – whose lack of unity he has just demonstrated – would never agree to enlist under the orders of the Great King, for 'is not war against the Barbarian a war for one's native country, for the national way of life and customs, for liberty and all that we hold dear?' In the course of a few sentences, the king's strength has turned into weakness, and the disunity of the

---

[6] Cf. my paper to the Achaemenid Workshop of Groningen in 1984: 'Institutions perses et histoire comparatiste dans l'historiographie grecque'.

Greeks into community spirit! Which of today's historians could use such texts as a basis for evaluating the military capacities of the Achaemenid empire?

V

But, if such speeches could have been delivered, the cultural conceptions underlying them, or which they openly express, were also very widespread and common in Greek public opinion. Among the most frequently advanced explanations for Persian decadence is their luxurious manner of living (*tryphè*). It was precisely this lesson which, according to Plutarch (*Art.* 20, 1), the Greeks learned from the expedition of the Ten Thousand. 'By their action, they proved that the greatness of the Persians and the king was no more than gold in large quantities, luxury and women; beyond that, all was play acting and boastfulness'! Belief in the degenerative power of wealth can be found in many Greek authors confronted with the opulence of oriental courts. These were often portrayed as hotbeds of corruption, a corruption itself associated with luxury and the women of the palace. This is certainly the picture presented in the work of Ctesias (*Persika*), for instance, in which the Persian court, dominated by eunuchs and women, is riddled with rumours of conspiracies and assassinations, which are often conducted at the instigation of eunuchs and women.[7]

It seems, indeed, that in the view of classical authors the feminisation of the palace is a characteristic feature of oriental societies. We have the example of Ninyas, who lived solely with his women and eunuchs (Athenaeus XII, 538ff.): 'He had no ambition other than pleasures, idleness and a life free of troubles and cares; for him, the joy of reigning consisted in the ceaseless enjoyment of sensual delights' (Diodorus II, 21, 1). For his part, Sardanapalus lived like a woman, among women, dressed and made up like a woman (Athenaeus XII, 528–9 a–d). According to Ctesias (quoted by Athenaeus XII, 530 d), the same could be said for Annaros, the Great King's representative in Babylonia, who wore the garments and jewels of a woman. And Mnaseas, in his book *Europe*, gave a fairly

---

[7] In a suggestive work (*Structure du Sérail: la fiction du despotisme asiatique dans l'Occident classique*, Paris 1979), A. Grosrichard dwells chiefly on Aristotle's texts. It is a pity that the author did not subject Ctesias, Plato, Xenophon and many others to the same pattern of reading (cf. P. Briant, *Rois, tributes, et paysans* [henceforth *RTP*], Paris 1982, p. 296, nn. 17–18). [The fragments of Ctesias are collected as *FGrHist* 688; a French translation exists by Janick Auberger, *Ctésias*.]

similar description of Andrakottos the Phrygian (Athenaeus XII, 530 c). It was the same for the Lydians who – effeminate in spirit – swiftly adopted the lifestyle of women (Athenaeus XII, 515 f). According to Plato, the same development was experienced by the representatives of the Achaemenid dynasty entrusted to the care of women, 'away from all masculine guidance'. Now, such an upbringing necessarily softened up the body and spirit and lessened military prowess. This is what Agesilaus had wanted to make his soldiers understand when he ordered them to strip Persians who had recently been taken prisoner and take them to the slave market. 'The soldiers, seeing their white skin because they never removed their clothes, their soft, flabby bodies, because they went everywhere in chariots, thought that in this war it would be as if they were having to fight women' (Xenophon, *Hell.* III, 4, 15; cf. *Agesilaus* 1, 28; cf. Plutarch *Cimon* 9, 5: 'Bodies that were flabby and not used to work').

But, as Xenophon puts it very clearly in the last chapter of the *Cyropaedia*, that physical enfeeblement was equally caused by the excesses of eating and drinking and the rejection of physical exercise. He returns to it in *Agesilaus* (9, 3): 'For the Persian (the Great King), men scour the whole land in search of what he may enjoy drinking, and thousands of others are busy finding something to excite his appetite ... He must have people searching to the ends of the earth for something he can enjoy' (also quoted by Athenaeus IV, 144 b). The theme was taken up by Theophrastus in his *Peri Basileias*, writing that, to satisfy their taste for luxury (*tryphè*), Persian kings offered huge sums of money as a reward for those who invented a new pleasure (Athenaeus IV, 144, c). Other authors (such as Clearchus) cited this trait as characteristic of Persian royalty (cf. XII, 528 d; 539 b; 545 d and f). The abundance and variety of dishes at the king's table were well known to classical and Hellenistic authors; aside from Xenophon, Herodotus and Aristophanes, Athenaeus quotes Theophrastus on this subject (IV, 144 c), Theopompus (144 f and 145 a), Heraclides (145 b–146 a), Ctesias and Dinon (146 c–d).[8] For the supporters of the decadence thesis – such as Xenophon – there was no doubt that the misuse of heavy meals, sweetmeats and drink was the source of the Persians' military weakness. That was the opinion of Clearchus, writing about Darius III in his work *Peri Biôn*: 'The Persian king gave prizes to those who furnished his pleasures,

---

[8] See my study: 'Table du roi, tribut et redistribution chez les Achémenides' (*Table Ronde de Paris*, March 1986), to be published [subsequently published in P. Briant and C. Herrenschmidt (eds), *Le tribut dans l'empire perse: actes de las table ronde de Paris* (Paris 1989), pp. 25–44].

but he led his kingdom to defeat, and did not realise that he was destroying himself until the moment when others seized his sceptre and were proclaimed [kings]' (Athenaeus XII, 539 b). We find the same judgement in Strabo (XV, 3, 22), when he writes: 'In the end, excess of wealth plunged the kings of Persia into all the refinements of luxury (*tryphè*): for example, they would eat no other wheat than that from Assos in Aeolis, drink no other wine than the best Chalybonian from Syria, or no other water than that from the Eulaeus, on the pretext that the water from this river is lighter than any other.' Did not the story go that Darius I had the following inscription carved on his tomb: 'I was able to drink a lot of wine and still feel fine' (Athenaeus X, 34 d)? As for the tomb of Sardanapalus, it bore an inscription which, according to Athenaeus (XII, 530 c), ended with these words: 'Eat, drink and be merry!' – by which he meant that one should make the best of a short life!

We see then the contours of a general theory of the birth and death of great empires taking shape. According to this logic, their decline is inscribed in a development that brings great riches to the conquerors, riches that themselves create a taste for luxury and luxuriousness, leading inevitably in their turn to the weakening of native qualities. This is how Plato explains it, taking as an example the transition, among the Persians, from a 'rough shepherd's' upbringing to an education left in the hands of women: 'Now the latter brought them up as if, in their childhood, they had already reached the heights of happiness and as if, from this point of view, they wanted for nothing' (*Laws* III, 694 d).

The best soldiers, on the other hand, and therefore the most valiant conquerors came from societies which cultivated poverty and simplicity of habits. This was obviously the case with the Spartans, as Xenophon emphasises in his comparative portrayal of Agesilaus and the Great King, or in the contrast he finds between the simplicity of Agesilaus and the luxury of Pharnabazus (*Hell.* IV, 1, 30). It had also been the case with the Persians, whose original virtues and customs were often compared, implicitly or explicitly, with those of the Spartans (cf. e.g. Arrian V, 4, 5). In the era of Cyrus' conquest, they had indeed been a people who were young, vigorous and poor. According to Aelian (*VH* X, 14) moreover, Socrates contrasted the Persians with the Lydians and Phrygians: 'He said that Idleness is the sister of Freedom. As proof he maintained that the Indians and Persians are the most courageous and most free, for both are the most hostile to doing business for the sake of getting rich (*pros chrematismon*); on the contrary, the Phrygians and Lydians, who are the most industrious, are in a state of slavery.' Socrates' remark was certainly alluding to a trait reported by Herodotus (I, 153) in a speech ascribed to Cyrus: 'The Persians, in their own country, know nothing of the use of markets, and have no place for this practice.' For his part, Strabo writes: 'Throughout this time (from [age] 20 to 50 years), the Persians do not set foot in a market, seeing that they have nothing to sell or buy' (XV, 3, 19). Xenophon (*Cyr.* I, 2, 3) also speaks of the poor reputation of merchants among the Persians. Whatever the foundations of such assertions, it is clear that the use which Socrates makes of them refers to conceptions of social ethics comparable to what was current in Sparta at the time of 'Lycurgus': the true Spartans, the Peers, had no thought of getting rich by trading (which was prohibited), they were soldiers. The same applied to the original Persians – completely oriented towards war – and the Indians (cf. Arrian V, 4, 4).[9]

It was entirely due to these virtues (cf. Herodotus I, 89) that the Persians were successful in gaining the upper hand over kingdoms corrupted by luxury and wealth, the Medes, Lydians and Babylonians. When they were poor, the Persians were all the more tempted to launch themselves into the conquest of existing kingdoms and their riches (cf. Herodotus I, 126).[10] In a conversation reported by Aristoxenus in his *Life of Archytas* [a Pythagorean philosopher and mathematician] (ap. Athenaeus XII, 545 a–546 c), Polyarchus, the ambassador of Dionysius the Younger and himself a disciple of Archytas, stated that the aim of every conquest was in effect to seize wealth accumulated by previous kings: when they were rich, the new victors thought of nothing but satisfying their physical pleasures. Hence the risks run by the Medes to conquer the Assyrians. The same occurrence was to be observed at the time of the Persian conquest of the Medes. The ultimate goal (*télos*) of the conqueror was indeed to satisfy his physical desires to the utmost (545 c): the Assyrian, Lydian, Median and Persian kingdoms illustrated this law of history. The unprecedented luxury of the Great Kings provided the proof, whether in the variety of foodstuffs, the various sorts of perfumes and incense that they used, the beauty of their carpets, their clothing, their goblets (545 d–f), or their great sexual licence. The Persians therefore joined a long series of sovereigns of Asia who, from Ninyas on, had given themselves up to *tryphè* – as Ctesias stated (Athenaeus

---

[9] Cf. also Herodotus V, 6 on the Thracians, who hold 'the state of idleness to be the most honourable, that of the man who tills the soil to be the basest'.

[10] Cf. my remarks in *État et Pasteurs au Moyen-Orient ancien*, Paris-Cambridge 1982, pp. 32–4.

XII, 528 c). As for the Great King's habit of moving from capital to capital, it caused Athenaeus to say (XII, 513 a) that 'the first men in history to become famous for their *tryphè* were the Persians'. But, by taking possession of the kingdom of the Medes, they gained access to their luxury (Plato, *Laws* 695 a; Xenophon, *Cyr.* VIII, 8, 15) and were led into the same excesses and the same decadence. Hence their defeat at the hands of the vigorous Macedonians (cf. Arrian II, 7), before Alexander himself, in his turn, copied Persian courtly customs! The causes of Sparta's decline are in any case no different, in the eyes of a Xenophon or Plutarch: 'the love of gold and silver' (*Agis and Cleomenes* 3, 1); a man like Leonidas, in complete contrast to Agis, the 'new Agesilaus', is an emblematic figure of these new customs, learnt through contact with oriental courts: 'As he had stayed for a long time in the palaces of the satraps and paid court to Seleucus, he transferred, unharmoniously, the haughtiness of those distant countries to the practices of Greek law and a constitutional government' (*ibid.*). It is striking to note to what extent the processes of evolution of Persia and Sparta are envisaged in parallel by Xenophon: to be persuaded, it is enough to compare the last chapter of the *Cyropaedia* and the last chapter of the *Lakedaimoniôn Politeia*.[11]

The decadence of the Persians was therefore ineluctable, so true is it that wealth and luxury corrupt even the strongest bodies and souls. This is certainly what is implied in the advice given by Croesus to Cyrus to avoid a rebellion by the Lydians: 'Impose upon them a ban on possessing weapons of war, order them to wear tunics under their cloaks and slippers on their feet, urge them to teach their children to play the cithara and pluck stringed instruments, to engage in trade; and you will soon see, O king, men become women, so that you will never have to fear that they will rebel' (Herodotus I, 156). Thus, from renowned warriors (cf. I, 79), the Lydians became 'the least warlike of men' (Polyaenus VII, 6, 4). In fact, 'they were reduced to being publicans, wandering entertainers and procurers. These people, formerly so powerful because of their activeness, and intrepid in war, henceforth rendered effeminate by soft living and debauchery, thus lost their ancient virtue, and those whom the habit of battle had made invincible before Cyrus, letting themselves slide into debauchery, were vanquished by idleness and sloth' (Justin I, 7, 11–13). According to Plutarch (*Apoptht. Reg. C3*), these measures were imposed by Xerxes on the Babylonians after their revolt: 'He forbade

---

[11] See F. Ollier, *Le mirage spartiate: étude sur l'idéalisation de Sparte dans l'antiquité grecque de l'origine jusqu'aux Cyniques*, Paris 1933, pp. 434–9; also my study quoted above, n. 6 (3, 2). On the last chapter of the *Lakedaimoniôn Politeia*, see *ibid.*, 386–9.

them to carry weapons, and forced them to play musical instruments, drink, amuse themselves and wear long robes.' Judging by the last chapter of the *Cyropaedia* the Persians underwent a comparable evolution, one which allows us to understand why, 'having lived a long time in the lap of luxury', they found themselves in an inferior position vis-à-vis the Macedonians, 'who had long been accustomed to danger' (Arrian II, 7, 4). Then, in their turn, the Macedonians succumbed to the pernicious pleasures of the East (cf. Athenaeus XII, 539 c–540), imitating Persian habits and thereby drawing down upon themselves the thunderbolts of Cicero (*Verr.* III, 33).[12]

Such a theory obviously offered the advantage of simplicity. It none the less gave rise to contradictions, for it was unable to take account of the complexity of historical reality. Here, for instance, is how Plutarch (*Art.* 24.10–11) describes and comments on the conduct of Artaxerxes II on his return from a difficult expedition against the Cadusians:

> Neither gold, nor the royal garment, nor the ornaments with which the king was always covered, and which were worth 12,000 talents, hindered him from striving and enduring as much as the next man: his quiver on his back, his shield in his hand, he himself marched at the head up steep mountain paths, without using his horse, so that the sight of his drive and energy gave nimbleness and wings to his troops, for every day he opened up a distance of 200 stades.

Here we find – this time in positive form – the contrast that was frequently remarked on by Greek authors between the sumptuousness of the Persians' clothing and the difficulty they have in moving around under awkward conditions (see especially Xenophon, *Anab.* I, 5, 8). The royal portrayal given here in any case differs from the one Plutarch draws in the first chapter of the same Artaxerxes, where he is contrasted with his young brother Cyrus the Younger: 'Whereas at the earliest age Cyrus exhibited vigour and energy, Artaxerxes seemed gentler in every respect, and of a less passionate disposition.' Quite simply, Plutarch is here repeating a version that made Cyrus the paragon of all the traditional royal virtues, compared with an older brother described as a less good soldier (cf. Xenophon, *Anab.* I, 9). The episode of the Cadusian campaign led Plutarch, conversely, to emphasise the exemplary vitality and courage of the king, which he links to a general reflection in the following manner: 'The king in this instance demonstrated that cowardice and softness do not

---

[12] Speaking of the custom of giving lands and towns to queens, Cicero – as part of his prosecution of Verres – writes: 'Thus they (the barbarian kings of the Persians and Syrians) have entire peoples not only as witnesses but also as agents of their pleasures' (*Verr*, III, 33).

always, as is commonly believed, stem from pleasures and luxury' (24, 9).

Similarly, ancient authors were not in agreement over the military virtues of Sardanapalus. Some (Duris and others) turned him into the archetype of the weak and cowardly king, simply because of his effeminate way of life (Athenaeus XII, 529 a). Ctesias, on the other hand, underlined his dignified and courageous death (529 a–b). Others stressed the importance of the works of construction he had achieved (529 c). The divergences in the judgements of Plutarch on Artaxerxes II give an account of the imperatives of the ideological struggle between the two brothers.[13] As for his commentary on the *tryphè*, he refers to a continuing debate on this subject that was going on in the classical and Hellenistic eras. The whole of Book XII of Athenaeus' *Deipnosophistae* is devoted to quoting the best known examples of *tryphè*, among peoples and cities (510–28 e) and also private individuals (528 f ff.), and setting out the points of view of philosophers and political thinkers on this problem. The Persians' role in this lengthy development was naturally not forgotten. Indeed they are even pointed out as being the first in history to have acquired a reputation in this field (513 f): Dinon cited the head-dress and foot-stool of the Great King (514 a–b), Heraclides of Cyme his 300 concubines and courtesans (514 b–c), Chares of Mytilene and Amyntas the unheard-of sumptuousness of the royal bed (514 e–f). On this subject, Athenaeus (515 a–d) does not fail to pass on the judgement given by Xenophon in the VIIIth book of the *Cyropaedia*. But Athenaeus' work clearly shows that not all ancient authors shared Xenophon's point of view. In the Hellenistic period especially, the word *tryphè* was not systematically taken in a pejorative sense. Quite the reverse. In the context of Hellenistic courts, the word referred rather to the wealth of the king, and therefore also to the favour of the gods.[14] *Tryphè* was a symbol of power and a matter of prestige, as is shown for instance in the bitter rivalry between Straton of Sidon and Nicocles of Paphos on the subject of their respective wealth and luxury (XII, 531 a–c), or again, the desire of Tachos to prove to Artaxerxes that the pharaonic banquets were still more sumptuous

[13] There were similarly two opposite versions of the courage of Darius III: cf. my remarks in *RTP*, pp. 373–5.
[14] See A. Passerini, 'La *tryphè* nella storiographia ellenistica', *SIFC* 11, 1934, pp. 35ff.; J. Tondriau, 'La *tryphè*, philosophie royale ptolémaïque', *REA* 50, 1948, pp. 49–54; C. Preaux, *Le monde hellénistique* (Coll. Nouvelle Clio 6), I, Paris 1978, p. 228. See also C. Nenci, '*Tryphè* e colonizzazione', in *Modes de contact et processus de transformation dans les sociétés anciennes*, Pisa-Rome 1983, pp. 1019–29. [See also in English Kurke, 'The politics of *habrosyne*'; Davidson, *Courtesans and Fishcakes*.]

than those of the Great King (Athenaeus IV, 150 b–c; Aelian, *VH* 5, 1). In these conditions – as Plutarch's opinion of Artaxerxes II shows – 'luxury' was not regarded by all the authors of antiquity as the antithesis of physical courage. Heraclides of Pontus actually supported the opposite theory in his work *On Pleasure (Peri Hèdonès)*, in which he wrote (Athenaeus XII, 512 a–b):

> Tyrants and kings, masters of all the good things in life, and well versed in them, grant the first place to pleasures, for pleasure ennobles human nature (*megalopsychotera*). In any case, all who give themselves up to pleasure and choose a life of luxury are noble and generous: for example, the Persians and Medes. For, more than any people in the world, they devote themselves to pleasure and luxury, and yet at the same time they are the noblest (*megalopsychotatoi*) and the bravest (*andreiotatoi*) of the Barbarians. In fact, enjoyment of pleasure and luxury is the mark of free men; it liberates and elevates the spirit. Conversely, to live a life of work (*ponein*) is the mark of slaves and men of low birth.

The contradictions are obviously informed by the various authors' convictions about the best political regime: they passed judgement on the Achaemenid empire less in the light of a documentary inquiry than according to their own philosophical standpoints.[15] The contradictions also reflect the ambiguity of the feelings nurtured by Greek public opinion towards the Persian empire. Let us not be confused by the polemical portrayals of the last chapter of the *Cyropaedia* and the speeches of Isocrates. From polemical motives (specific ones, moreover) both authors systematically devalued the Persian society and kingdom of their time. Not that they were systematically lying; it was rather that they often interpreted in a systematically biased manner Achaemenid institutions whose very existence could not be placed in doubt.[16] We must not infer that they are the sole representatives of fourth-century Greek opinion. In reality, in Greece, what ruler would regard the venture of the Ten Thousand and Agesilaus'

---

[15] The same goes for Polybius' condemnation of *tryphè* (VI, 7–9) in the course of a reflection on the 'mixed constitution' which leads him to compare the Roman constitution with that which Lycurgus had instituted in Sparta (VI, 10, 48–50).

[16] This is the case, for instance, with the denunciations uttered by Xenophon in particular against the Persians' immoderate love of food and drink. So Xenophon does not hesitate to take advantage in the *Agesilaus* (9, 3) of the king's desire to vary the pleasures of the table to see it as a proof of his weakening. He refers to the Royal Table, which the Greeks know imitated the tables of the Persian nobility (Herodotus I, 133; Strabo XV, 3, 20), being set out with stupefying abundance (cf. Polyaenus IV, 3, 32). Starting from an existing institution, Xenophon presented and used it for purely polemical ends. Rather than the weakness of the king, the variety of dishes at his table bears witness to his power to attract tribute. And, as Heracleides of Cyme (Athenaeus IV, 145 d–f) remarked, far from being a proof of waste and prodigality, the abundance of fare was evidence of economic management, so many people did the king feed every day: 15,000 according to Dinon and Ctesias (Athenaeus VI, 146 c). (On all these problems, see my study quoted above, n. 8.)

expedition as promises of victory over the Achaemenid armies? What ruler would take at face value Isocrates' arguments on the many repeated revolts in the empire? In actual fact, what dominated in Greece was rather an intense fascination with the immense riches, and therefore the *tryphè*, of the Great King,[17] together with deep-rooted fear of his armies and fleets.[18] Certainly, the idea of the decline of the oriental courts, ruined by luxuriousness and women, formed a convenient 'philosophy of history' for the Greeks, who knew that they were incapable of conquering that vast empire on their own; but it cannot deceive the historian who has learnt to read between the lines of Greek observers, and to decode their writings – with the help (in the best instances) of genuinely Achaemenid sources.[19] Today all evidence shows that in 334 the Achaemenid empire was not the moribund entity complacently described by Plato, Xenophon, Isocrates and others.[20]

[17] See the example of Pausanias, all the more enlightening because it is about a Spartan: Thucydides I, 130 (cf. Athenaeus XII, 535 e–f).

[18] Cf. Demosthenes, *On the Symmories*, Summary of Libanius.

[19] Cf. *RTP*, pp. 491–506 ('Sources grecques et histoire achéménide'), and the whole of the *Achaemenid Workshop* of 1984 (Groningen): 'New Approaches to Greek Historiography and their Relevance for Persian History' (to be published in 1987) [subsequently published as H. Sancisi-Weerdenburg and A. Kuhrt (eds), *Achaemenid History II: The Greek Sources* (Leiden 1987)]. See also the *Achaemenid Workshop 1983*, whose theme was 'The Last Century of the Achaemenid Empire: Decadence?', with the article of H. Sancisi-Weerdenburg in particular: 'Decadence in the empire on decadence in the sources?', to appear under the title *Achaemenid History I* (Nederlands Instituut voor het Nabije Oosten) [subsequently published as H. Sancisi-Weerdenburg (ed.), *Achaemenid History I: Sources, Structures and Synthesis* (Leiden 1987); Sancisi-Weerdenburg's article at pp. 33–45].

[20] We are immediately faced with the fundamental problem of the reasons for the Achaemenid defeat by Alexander. There is obviously no question of treating such a vast problem in a footnote (cf. a few words in my paper to the *Achaemenid Workshop* of 1985 in London: § 9, 4) [subsequently published in A. Kuhrt and H. Sancisi-Weerdenburg (eds), *Achaemenid History Workshop III: Method and Theory* (Leiden 1988), pp. 137–73]. I simply observe that the downfall of the Assyrian empire in 612 has often been regarded as a 'historical scandal': by using that expression, the authors wished to express their astonishment that a state as apparently powerful as the Assyrian kingdom could have disappeared so rapidly. From this aspect, the fall of the Achaemenid empire raises equally difficult questions. In any case, there is no reason to suggest that the disappearance of an empire is proof of earlier decadence: the problem lies elsewhere and must be put in other terms.

9 *The Greeks as Egyptologists*[†]

FRANÇOIS HARTOG

translated by Antonia Nevill

For Jean-Pierre Vernant

Egypt had been known to the Greeks as early as the Mycenaean era, and over the centuries they had enjoyed very positive relations with it, before installing themselves as its masters with the Ptolemies; they never viewed it with indifference. What I propose to do here is not to give a history of those relations, but solely to outline the ways in which the Greeks viewed Egypt, how, from Homer to the Neoplatonists, from the eighth century BC to the third AD, these views were developed and modified. I will pick out certain moments when the views on that strange country were formed and transformed, not from the standpoint of the degree of their reality or truth, but from that of the logic which, within Greek culture itself, organised them and gave them meaning. I will also show how the same theme, passed on and taken up again – the importance of the religious dimension, for example, heavily stressed from Herodotus to Porphyry – in fact witnessed a change in its scope in a Greek culture which itself was undergoing profound transformation.

The Greek *logoi* on Egypt are numerous – there was a Greek Egyptology, if not an Egyptomania – but unlike their modern manifestations, they were not centred on the mystery of the hieroglyphs and the passions, even hysteria, these aroused, or on the paradigm of their decipherment. Although Greek science – that is to say, at first, Ionian science – in its reports on that distant land always took account of its writing, this was not something mysterious, but simply a very ancient technical invention and a tool for the accumulation of knowledge.[1]

[†] Originally published as 'Les Grecs égyptologues', *Annales* 41 (1986), 953–67.

[1] Nevertheless, Plutarch (though seven centuries later), comparing Pythagorean precepts, enigmatic at first sight, with hieroglyphic texts (*De Iside* 354 E), supports the idea that it was a matter of a symbolic language, which Pythagoras had tried hard to imitate and transpose, with the aid of aphorisms, to a Greek world where orality was predominant. On the other

WHAT IS EGYPT?

The Egypt of Homer, a far-off land of medicinal plants and doctors, and magicians too, where Proteus and his seals frolicked, and whence Helen brought back the drug which makes mortals forget their cares,[2] was succeeded by an Egypt that was the object of inquiry, that of Ionian science, but also by another quite different and wholly conventional Egypt, that of Busiris, for instance, an unpleasant host who indulged in the lamentable practice of sacrificing passing foreigners, to say nothing of a fashionable Egypt, if one refers to several allusions in the plays of Aristophanes.

During the sixth century, erudite Ionians applied their method of inquiry (*historiê*) to devise a representation of the world in which Egypt enjoyed an especially important position because the Nile had caught their attention and stimulated their intelligence. That every investigator should feel bound to advance an original theory about this exceptional river was a matter of his scientific credibility. In his *Histories*, Herodotus recapitulates and makes fun of them before then, of course, propounding his own theory.†

Evidence of its importance is that Herodotus devotes an entire book to Egypt.[3] Since it is the country that offers the most marvels to the traveller's eyes, it is also the one that gives rise to the longest account. But no sooner is it stated – even if one repeats that the *thôma* (marvel) always outdoes its report – than the otherness of places and people is apprehended, 'domesticated', by a series of processes which the narrator unfolds, like a hunter casting his net: first, inversion, a very convenient ploy that changes the reality of the other into the simple opposite of the same thing or of our own; and, then, the constant concern to survey, measure, enumerate and quantify.

More broadly, the space of Egypt finds its place in Herodotus' representation of the world, and thus obeys the schemes that produce it: symmetry and inversion between the north and the south, on either side of an 'equator' crossing the Mediterranean, the farthest

hand, Plotinus (originally from Lycopolis in Egypt), putting 'the thing before one's eyes in a synthetic manner, without discursive conception or analysis', would see each hieroglyph as the expression of 'a kind of science and wisdom' (*Enneads*, V, VIII, 6).

[2] For the whole of this first part, see C. Froidefond, *Le mirage égyptien dans la littérature grecque d'Homère à Aristote*, Paris, Thesis, 1971.

[3] F. Hartog, *Le miroir d'Hérodote: essai sur la représentation de l'autre*, Paris, Gallimard, 1980 [translated as *The Mirror of Herodotus*], and *id.*, *Hérodote: Histoires*, Paris, Découverte, 1980, pp. 5–21.

† For the investigations into the Nile, and their context in Ionian scientific inquiry, see now Thomas, *Herodotus in Context*, Ch. 6.

reaches of the sun or 'tropics' being formed by the upper courses of the Danube (Istros) in the north and the Nile in the south. On this canvas, the geographer brings into play the figure of analogy, which allows him, for example, to discover the sources of the Nile by pure reasoning (2, 33). Egypt is put in its place and on the map.

A strange space at once completely artificial – created by the river, modelled by men – and very ancient, Egypt is even more remarkable for its relationship with time: it is a very old country, an unchanged land (2, 142), uninterrupted, where 'the time of men' – purely human time separate from the gods – goes back much further than the Greeks, who create many illusions for themselves in matters of both divine and human chronology, may think. One such Greek, Hecataeus of Miletus, though a learned man, when spelling out his genealogy before the priests of Thebes, imagined himself meeting a god in the sixteenth generation (1, 143)!

Through the regular practice of writing, this antiquity makes of the Egyptians men of memory and therefore of knowledge. It also explains why, in the religious domain, they had been inventors; the first to determine relations between men and gods, to fix the rules of piety and organise forms of worship. So Herodotus has no doubt that the religion of the Greeks is, in its essentials, of Egyptian origin. A diffusionist, he locates the route and marks off the staging posts. Not only do Dionysus, the Orphic cults, belief in metempsomatosis [transmigration of the soul], divination and even the Thesmophoria come from Egypt, but still further back in time, the *ounomata*, the 'names' of the gods. Until then there had certainly been gods (*theoi*), but these were undifferentiated, the gods whom the Pelasgians (the first inhabitants of Greece) had revered as 'organisers of the universe' (*Kosmôi thentes*). Herodotus resorts to etymology to explain this primitive religion in which the deity, a faceless power, is apprehended only as the principle of order (*theos* being related to *tithêmi*, I place upright).[4] But after hearing (*akouein*) the 'names' that had come from the Barbarians, and receiving the consent of the oracle of Dodona to use them, a new era began for the Pelasgians, and in turn for the Greeks who would receive the names from them; henceforth people knew how to pronounce the names and how it was appropriate to divide up the divine.[5]† In short, polytheism was born

---

[4] According to P. Chantraine, *Dictionnaire étymologique de la langue grecque*, under *theos*, the etymology is unknown.

[5] It may be noted that not for a moment does Herodotus envisage the question of translation (or even the translation as a question). Nor does the distinction appear, made by Plutarch, for example, in *De Iside*, between the 'name' (*onoma*) and the power (*dunamis*) of a deity.

† For the names of the gods, see my comments, introduction to Part II.

and became organised. With the arrival of Homer and Hesiod, very much later, there was a new stage: the arrangement of the pantheon, through the fixing of genealogies, areas of competence and honours (2, 53). But that was almost yesterday – barely 400 years earlier.

Thus Egypt appeared, across long stretches of time and, through various interventions, a land from which the Greeks borrowed. But borrowing did not, for Herodotus, mean mere imitation, or dependence upon the Egyptians; still less the latter's superiority. On the contrary, a clear cultural gap existed, something revealed by several indications, notably through the treatment of information. At a single stroke, Herodotus can demonstrate the Egyptian origin of Greek religion and note the difference of certain Egyptian practices by a comparison, often implicit, with what is done in the Greek world. Thus the division of men and animals, as set out by Hesiod in the myth of Prometheus and reactivated, in the city, with each sacrifice,[6] works differently: the divergences of Egyptian sacrificial ritual (2, 39), the existence of sacred animals – even extraordinary and sacred ones, like the crocodile – bear witness to this. The same framework of reference prevents Herodotus from interpreting and condemning, as in later times, the rapport the Egyptians had with certain animals as zoolatry, to see the Egyptians as prostrating themselves before idols in the form of animals. Moreover, the panoply of the Greek sacrificer (knife, spit and cauldron) served to circumscribe a Greek identity, and therefore also an Egyptian identity (2, 41): the Egyptian refusing outright to use these instruments, which were considered impure the moment they came into a Greek's possession.

But if sacrificial practices revealed a distance between Greeks and Egyptians, Herodotus also used them to reject a story suggestive of an excessive distance – the story of Busiris.[7] As a consequence of a long drought that had afflicted his country, Busiris had come to sacrifice one foreign passer-by every year. Then Heracles arrived. At first he was welcomed by his host, but subsequently he was on the point of being treated like a sacrificial 'animal'. Heracles, however, performed true to type: he broke his bonds and spread carnage, killing the impious king and his son. Herodotus sweeps aside this story (which has more to do with the adventures and character of Heracles

    [6] M. Detienne and J.-P. Vernant, *La cuisine du sacrifice*, Paris, Gallimard, 1979 [translated as *The Cuisine of Sacrifice*], pp. 37–132.

    [7] Apollodorus II, 5, 11. A satirical drama by Euripides had this title. Above all, an entire iconographic dossier is extant. See J.-L. Durand and F. Lissarrague, 'Héros cru ou hôte cuit', *Actes du colloque de Rouen*, Rouen, 1983, pp. 153–67.

than with Egypt) as *muthos*,† on the grounds of its improbability: a man on his own cannot slaughter whole battalions (Heracles then was a mere man); it also contradicts the very regulated sacrificial practices of the Egyptians, who sacrifice a few carefully selected animals only at certain precise times. Their practice could have no place for these excesses.

The same gap is also apparent in the description of funeral rituals. In order to contain the ever-possible outbursts of grief and mourning, the Greek city carefully regulated everything connected with the treatment of the deceased.[8] From this point of view, Egypt (like the funerals of the Scythian kings, or of those special Greeks, the Spartan kings) tended towards excess (2, 85). And the practice of embalming, even if his meticulous description of it constitutes rather a bravura passage in Herodotus' account, is – no less for this fact (indeed possibly more) – one that is very alien to Greek cultural logic: a corpse is for burying.

It was the same with Dionysus. Many Greeks are mistaken concerning his origins. Dionysus, that is to say Osiris, was Egyptian, introduced into Greece by Melampus, a Greek well versed in Egyptian religion (2, 49). For Herodotus, two pieces of evidence corroborated that statement: he had only recently made his appearance in Greece, and his cult 'was not identical to Greek customs' (*homotropos*). If he were Greek, his cult would have to be in harmony with Greek *nomoi*. But it was not, and therefore he came from elsewhere, from Egypt. Even with the passing of time this borrowing did not blunt the perception of the god's strangeness.[9]

The Egyptians had been writing for ages. They had archives and they read books. But this undeniable knowledge implies for Herodotus neither the appreciation of the value of writing as such, a mark of the superiority of Egyptian civilisation, nor the devaluation of orality. Of course, he himself wrote, but in the fifth-century Greek world, oral expression was preponderant.[10] In his relations with priests, there is no hint of his being given a 'writing lesson'; he is neither the uncivilised nor even the semi-civilised among these learned men, because they themselves are Barbarians.

---

† But for an alternative view of Herodutus' conception of *mythos*, see Harrison, *Divinity and History*, pp. 196–207.

[8] G. Gnoli and J.-P. Vernant, *La mort, les morts dans les sociétés anciennes*, Cambridge, Cambridge University Press, and Paris, Maison des Sciences de l'Homme, 1982.

[9] On Dionysus, as embodiment of the figure of the Other, see J.-P. Vernant, 'Le Dionysos masqué des Bacchantes d'Euripide', *L'Homme*, 93, 1985, XXV (1), p. 38.

[10] E. Havelock, *Preface to Plato*, Cambridge MA, Harvard University Press, 1963. [For a more complex investigation of this simplistic assertion, see Thomas, *Literacy and Orality*.]

From the point of view of the narrator, revealing the borrowings made by the Greeks also has a meaning as part of his strategy of persuasion; he displays his investigative ability and succeeds in disturbing, or at all events questioning, several certainties of Greek culture. Without really acknowledging it, on occasion, even presenting borrowings from Egypt as their own discovery, Greek religious reformers had acquired considerable fame. So, for example, in the case of the immortality of the soul and metempsomatosis: 'There are Greeks who have professed this doctrine as if it belonged to them exclusively. I know their names, but I do not set them down' (2, 123). But everyone had recognised Pythagoras or Orpheus. With such little touches, it was not so much a matter of aggrandising the Egyptians as of humbling certain Greeks.

If we consider the Egyptian *logos*, not in itself but in relation to the founding division which runs throughout the *Histories* – the Greek/Barbarian division – the Egyptians, very ancient, pious and learned 'others', are none the less inevitably included on the side of the Barbarians; on several occasions they are explicitly placed on that side (2, 50; 52). But 'Barbarian' did not carry with it the sense of barbarity (the accusation of sacrificing foreigners was rejected). Even more than a distinction of language – the fact, in other words, of their not speaking Greek – the term 'barbarian' designated someone who was ignorant of the *polis* and who lived in subjection to a king. To be a 'Barbarian' was first and foremost political. Now, the Egyptians had for centuries been unable to live without kings, of whom their history was merely a succession (2, 147). The object of inquiry and site of a thousand wonders, Egypt was a reservoir of knowledge – one which the Greeks tapped widely – but it was not, and had never been, a school for Greece.

WHAT IS TRUE CIVILISATION? WHERE IS THE REAL CITY?

At the end of the fifth century a veritable Egyptian archive had been established, with a whole repertoire of characteristics, amenable to rehearsal, critique and variation, but which clearly designated Egypt. Book 2 of Herodotus forms a fundamental part of it, and one that was clearly well known, since, without naming him, Aristophanes allows himself to parody certain of his descriptions in the *Birds*.

Plato, too, on several occasions indulges in 'Egyptian discourse'. Clearly very knowledgeable about this dossier, notably Herodotus' contribution, he is able to take up, imitate and even parody the *aiguptiaka*. But to what end, and why precisely Egypt? 'What a facility you have for composing Egyptian stories (*logoi*)!' exclaims the admiring Phaedrus; to which Socrates retorts sharply that what counts is the truth of what is said, not who says it or about where it is said.

More broadly, these Egyptian stories are an important part of the never-closed file on Plato and the Orient. Did he travel in Egypt, as an entire later tradition claims? Did he 'see' Egypt?[11] Or what, then, is the meaning of this presence, the purpose of that reference? Without directly addressing this point or the subject of the philo- sophical journey to Egypt, one may remark that, for Plato, the question is complicated – or simplified – if one picks out the link that exists between Egypt and Atlantis. Because, as the beginning of the *Timaeus* records, it was in Egypt that Solon learned from the lips of the priests of Sais the story of that distant hubristic power conquered by ancient Athens. Just as, despite the mountains of books and gener- ations of discoverers, Atlantis is a fiction of Platonic discourse, we may suppose that Egypt also served as a largely fictitious land, avail- able and plausible, that could be inhabited by Platonic discourse, setting up its own stage and enacting its own drama. Just as Atlantis is a *logos* which is primarily about Athens,[12] so the Egyptian *logos*, which also deals with Athens, would set out an authentically Platonic discourse: Plato speaks Greek there, in other words the language of Plato.

Let us take two moments from these stories: the inventions of Theuth and the opening of the *Timaeus*.[13] Pondering on writing, Socrates makes a detour by way of Egypt and recounts to Phaedrus an earlier tradition that he had received by *akoê* (by word of mouth). In a few words the Egyptian setting is established: near Naucratis. Doubtless Theuth, the inventor, is a copy of the Egyptian Thoth, but the latter's configuration goes beyond the mere features of the civil- ising hero recalled by Plato. And as soon as Theuth, with his new *technai* [skills], comes to find the king Thamus (with the strange name),[14] we are without a doubt in the Greek world and with Plato. The contrast between the king and inventor, the *krinein* [judging] and

[11] With Cicero and Diodorus, see A. S. Riginos, *Platonica*, Leiden, Brill, 1976, pp. 64–5.

[12] P. Vidal-Naquet, *Le chasseur noir*, Paris, Maspero, 1981 [translated as *The Black Hunter*], 'Athènes et l'Atlantide', pp. 335–60.

[13] *Phaedrus*, 274c–275d. *Timaeus*, 21c–24c. On this point, see the article by H. Joly (which I follow), 'Platon égyptologue', *Revue philosphique*, 2, 1982, pp. 255–66. J. Gwyn Griffiths, in a recent article, 'Atlantis and Egypt', *Historia*, XXIV, 1985, pp. 3–28, tries to demonstrate that Platonic Egypt has a basis in Egyptian etymologies and an Egyptian background.

[14] However, encyclopaedias find the name Ammon in it (*RE* Pauly, Wissowa, under Ammon and *Lexikon* Roscher, under Thamus).

tekein [engendering], are Greek: the user, the consumer, wins the day over the inventor, the producer.[15]

Above all, the king depreciates writing, invented by Theuth, in the name of the Platonic theory of knowledge and education. For Theuth, writing is a *pharmakon* (remedy) that must be of advantage to human memory and increase knowledge. For the king, on the contrary, it is clear that by making souls forgetful, it would encourage oblivion: he contrasts *anamnesis*, remembrance of the essence, something positive, with *hypomnesis*, the simple recollection of what is written. Exterior, hypomnesis forestalls the interior anamnesis. Theuth's *pharmakon* thus proves to be more a poison-remedy.[16] Lastly, Theuth's *grammata*, as described in the *Philebus* (18 b), are much more like the characters of the Greek alphabet: a writing which is '*phonographic*' much more than *hieroglyphic*.

Playing on the association between Egypt, antiquity and writing, the story of Theuth in any case helps to fix the idea (by giving it learned support) that writing was born on the banks of the Nile, in that land of origins.

At the beginning of the *Timaeus*, Egypt returns, with a similar montage of an Egyptian setting. Nothing is missing – neither the names, nor the parodic touch (à la Herodotus) on the name of the goddess, nor the in-depth account passed on by a succession of *akoai* [reports].[17] Then a scene opens, also fairly Herodotean in construction: Solon, already a very old man, is in Egypt and evokes for his hosts the farthest point the Greeks can reach in their past (the story of Phoroneus and Deucalion). These few lines recall those in which Hecataeus, before the priests of Thebes, is so proud to recite his 'long' genealogy. The same comic device is at work in both instances: the difference is in the chronological scale. The priests answer Hecataeus by silently pointing out to him the 331 statues of the high priests, men and nothing but men, who succeeded one another; to Solon, entangled in his calculations, the very old priest tosses the famous remark 'Solon, you Greeks are always children: a Greek is never old.'

From this point, and in the name of the theory of periodic cata-

---

[15] J.-P. Vernant, *Mythe et pensée chez les Grecs*, Paris, Maspero, 1971, 'Le travail et la pensée technique', pp. 16–43.

[16] On all this text, and especially on the inherent ambiguity of the word which the translation by 'remedy' or by 'poison' suppresses, see J. Derrida, *La dissémination*, Paris, Édition du Seuil, 1972 [translated as *Dissemination*], pp. 108–20. [See further Pickstock, *After Writing*, Part 1, Ch. 1.]

[17] 'In Egyptian (*Aiguptisti*) her name is Neith, but in Greek (*Hellênisti*), so they say, it is Athena.' The story was passed from the priests of Sais to Critias the Younger, by way of Solon and Critias the Elder.

clysms, he goes on to develop a picture which, recapitulating the elements already present in the *aiguptiaka*, contrasts Greece and Egypt. Thanks to the 'saviour Nile', Egypt in fact escapes catastrophes. In comparison with a Greece that is constantly changing and does not last, Egypt, as it was already for Herodotus, is the land of continuity and immutability. Each time that things get a little organised, and writing starts to take over from memory, a cataclysm arrives and forgetfulness spreads with the waves. Egypt, on the other hand, from the vantage point of its continuous archives, surveys these youngsters who are perpetually starting afresh. So those very 'ancient' accounts, which the venerable Solon was struggling to date, in reality are little more than children's stories. Greece is the land, not of history as it might think, but really of *mythology*; and Egypt is the land of *archaeology*, or rather of *archaeography*.[18] From this point of view, which is not that of anamnesis, but of memory of the past and its recollection (hypomnesis rather), writing prevails over the word, *grammata* [letters] over *logoi* [oral tales] which can be forgotten and lost.

At this point then in a well-constructed and near-orthodox Egyptian account, Plato executes a *coup de théâtre*: the city that is in fact the most ancient is Athens, by exactly a thousand years, the city with the best constitution, *philosophos* [wisdom-loving] and *philopolemos* [war-loving], the city of heroic deeds (*erga megala*) – again, a Herodotean nod† – that is to say, the city that battled against Atlantis. The chronology is turned upside down: from now on, the first inventors are no longer the Egyptians, but the Athenians, and Egypt is no more than an ancient Athens, remembering.

To be anything more than a simple game with and on Egyptian tradition, this reversal, however, must have a meaning within Platonic discourse itself. Egyptian archaeography takes the place of Greek memory, but 'by a stroke of genius and a mirror effect, this very ancient memory exactly intersects with the memory of the (Platonic) Forms: the prehistoric Athens of the *Timaeus* and the *Kallipolis* [fair city] of the *Republic* are one and the same city'.[19] The

---

[18] Thus what the Greeks recount about Phaethon, the son of the Sun, is a *myth*, 'but the truth is that an alternation of the things that go round the earth in the sky takes place at long intervals and the consequence for the things on the earth is destruction by fire' (from L. Brisson, *Platon, les mots et les mythes*, Paris, Maspero, 1982, p. 138). See also M. Detienne, *L'invention de la mythologie*, Paris, Gallimard, 1981 [translated – poorly – as *The Creation of Mythology*], pp. 163–6. [See now Murray, 'What is a *muthos* for Plato?'.]

† To the Proem, or opening paragraph, of his *Histories*.

[19] Joly, *op. cit.*, p. 261. [See here also Planinc, *Plato's Political Philosophy*, e.g. pp. 157, 262, 297.]

present-day construction of the philosopher is incarnate in a city of a bygone age. Whether in the philosophical city, the forgotten Athens, or Egypt, we find the same tripartite division of society (into priests, warriors and producers). Egypt is not there for its own sake, or in a Greece/Egypt dialogue, but to bear witness through its archives and by the 'actual' tripartite division of its society[20] that the city of the *Republic* had once been in existence; as fiction, therefore, intended to give proof, within a purely Greek discourse. This Platonic Egypt would have a lasting effect on the way that the Greeks would look at it.

With the fourth and third centuries, although the Greek/Barbarian polarity is still present, and still serves as the starting point for classifying and thinking of the Greeks on the one side, the Barbarians on the other, its definition changes; less and less political, the distinction becomes more and more cultural (Greekness becomes first and foremost a matter of *paideusis*, upbringing or education).[21] To hold the Egyptians as both ancestors and Barbarians, as Herodotus had no problem in doing, becomes more difficult, therefore. Those who had been at the origins of culture, masters of *paideia*, can no longer be called Barbarians, for fear of inconsistency.

This change goes hand in hand with another, initiated in the fourth century by Xenophon or Isocrates: a modification of the status of monarchy. The king, in the fifth century synonymous with the Barbarian, no longer appears as the negation of the values of the *polis*, but as the condition perhaps of its survival, the one who by his very exteriority is capable of putting an end to the excessive *stasis* [faction or civic strife] that is breaking it up. In this sense, also, the definition of the Barbarian is no longer political, and the gap between Greeks and Barbarians is abolished, or at any rate diminished. Thus Isocrates, in a rhetorical treatise (which explicitly claims to be a fiction), makes Busiris, the almost anthropophagous [cannibalistic] pharaoh, a first civilising king, the organiser of society and of its division into castes: the model of just monarchy.

Resuming earlier texts, Diodorus of Sicily would devote a section of his own *aiguptiaka* to the pharaoh, who is presented as a king of justice. Several commentators reckoned that these chapters plagiarised lost treatises of the fourth and third centuries *On Kingship* and,

---

[20] The subject recurs often in the fourth century (cf. Isocrates, *Busiris*, 15 for example). Herodotus had already mentioned a division into classes, but made them seven in number (2, 174).

[21] Isocrates, *Panegyric*, 50.

notably, passages from Hecataeus of Abdera.[22] Without opening up discussion over Diodorus' sources or the nature of Hecataeus' work, let us remember that in symmetry with these men of the South (philosophers, and thus religious) Hecataeus was interested in the distant men of the North, who also had a simple and pious way of life, the Hyperboreans.

An 'ethnography' such as this, drawn to the margins, is part of a broader intellectual movement, one which elaborates a theory on the types of life (and their debasement) of humankind since its origins. With the association antiquity–knowledge–South, Herodotus contrasted, with the Scythians, that of youth, ignorance and the North. Anacharsis, Scythian and sage, he who had gone to study in Greece, was the exception that proved the rule.[23]

With the fourth century, this system of contrasts, which no longer seemed to function, tended to be replaced by another in which primitivism came to the fore (by simple reversal, notably among the Cynics) and what had until then been considered as civilisation was devalued: the good savage at the expense of the faux-civilised, who was transformed into a real savage. And the Scythian way of life could be offered as a model.

According to this logic, the blood sacrifice, situated at the very heart of the ideology of civilised life, was denounced as savagery (murder), whereas true civilisation consisted of 'abstaining from all living things', that is to say offering the gods only bloodless (vegetable) sacrifices. Thus Ephorus finds good Scythians, abstaining from all living things, whose primitivism in fact denotes a pure life, close to the gods, a primitivism which makes them truly civilised people.[24] Dicearchus, similarly, develops similar considerations on these men of the North and on sacrifice;[25] while Theophrastus praises the same attitude in the South, precisely among the Egyptians, 'the most learned people in the world, inhabiting the most holy land', who also abstain from all living things and have 'for an incalculable time' practised vegetable sacrifices.[26] Whether it is in the North or the

---

[22] *FGrHist*, 264 F1–14 Jacoby. For Jacoby, Hecataeus' *Aigyptiaka* (written between Alexander and Ptolemy son of Lagus) must have been presented as a philosophical novel or an ethnographical utopia – see A. Burton, *Diodorus Siculus*, I, *A Commentary*, Leiden, Brill, 1971. In fact, there is no proof. In the few quotations extant, he is associated with Manetho, his contemporary, in writing on the meaning of the name of the god Ammon, the way kings have of drinking wine and the principles of Egyptian philosophy (in the prologue by Diogenes Laertius).

[23] F. Hartog, 'Le passé revisité: trois regards grecs sur la civilisation', in *Le temps de la réflexion*, IV, 1983, pp. 168–73.

[24] *FGrHist* 70 F 42 Jacoby.

[25] F. 49, F. Wehrli (Porphyry, *On abstinence*, IV, 228–31 Nauck).

[26] Porphyry, *On abstinence*, II, 5, 1.

South, among the young and good savages or the old wise men, one can find true wisdom – if not uniquely, in any case more – in that middle region which, still quite recently, had been constructed by its thinkers as the site of excellence.

Anacharsis, the Scythian philosopher, is transformed into a master of the art of life, at least for Diogenes or the Cynics, while Egypt firmly becomes a school, where everyone that mattered in Greece must have spent some time – no longer only hastily, for just enough time to borrow something, but to learn and be converted to the philosophical life. Pythagoras takes the first step: a disciple of the Egyptians, for Isocrates he is the first to bring philosophy back to Greece (*Busiris*, 28). According to Eudoxus of Cnidus (a student of Plato, who spent some time in Egypt), Pythagoras not only made the journey, but wanted to share in the priests' training; faced with his stubbornness and the privations he imposed upon himself, they finally admitted him into their company.[27] Diodorus (in the first century) would recapitulate the canonical list of the great minds who had made the pilgrimage: Orpheus, Musaeus, Melampus, Daedalus, Homer, Lycurgus, Solon, Plato, Pythagoras, Eudoxus, Democritus and Oinopides of Chios (I, 96). Lastly, in this chorus of eulogies, Aristotle says of the famous division into castes and its advantages that 'Egypt was the cradle of mathematics, because the priestly caste was allowed much leisure time': it offers the first example of an organisation favouring the contemplative life, a land that 'has always possessed laws and a political organisation' (*Metaphysics*, I, 1, 981b).

With discussion of these matters we move perceptibly further away from the Herodotean perspective. Inversion, a convenient figure which allows one precisely to locate and distil the alterity of the other,[28] tends to be replaced by a more global attitude, characterised by a dual devaluation in space and time: the devaluation of the centre to the advantage of the margins, and, in the name of a mythical time (bygone or yet to come), which the good savages or the old sages have more or less been able to preserve or rediscover, the devaluation of the present. In this new space the figure of Pythagoras is imposed, or rather, taken up again – a student of the Egyptians, needless to say.[29] And Plato too, a follower of Pythagoras, could do

---

[27] Porphyry, *Life of Pythagoras*, 7–8.
[28] It is of course understood that Herodotus' ethnography cannot only be reduced to this figure.
[29] As well as Isocrates, the biographies of Aristoxenus and Timaeus devote space to the Egyptian episode.

no other than make the journey to that Egypt, civilised since time immemorial, and initiator, then model (thanks to its good *politeia* [constitution]), of the contemplative life.

At this point of the story, and now that the Ptolemies are ruling the country, it would be pleasant to be able to call on a chosen witness, contemporary of Ptolemy II, who offers the rare advantage of being on both the Egyptian and Greek side at once: Manetho. In fact an Egyptian, he is also a priest of Heliopolis, and wrote several books in Greek. Tradition ascribes eight to him, one of which is against Herodotus. He is also credited with an important role in the introduction into Alexandria of the new cult of Serapis, that mixed Greco-Egyptian deity. Was he acting for a cultural policy of the Ptolemaic rulers? A translator or mediator of the two cultures? At all events, as with Berossus in Babylon and Fabius Pictor in Rome, with him there appear the first indigenous people writing books on their own history, but in Greek.

Unfortunately, our witness hides from view, for only a very little of his work is preserved (perhaps it was not simply chance, but also the sign of the limited interest of Greek readers in his works?). These fragments, in addition, are recorded either within the framework, with Flavius Josephus, of a violent polemic against his assertions (or what purport to be his assertions) on the origins of the Jews, or as part of another undertaking with apologetic ends: that of the Christian chronographers, Africanus and Eusebius, challenging the traditions of the other nations on the basis of the Bible.[30] Thus, from the viewpoint of a cultural history, when Manetho is called upon for his contribution he is ultimately a witness for neither the defence nor the prosecution, nor does he even provide a counterweight.

THE LAND OF RELIGION

Although Strabo, who stayed for a long time in Alexandria and even went up the Nile, dedicates a book of his *Geography* to Egypt, he views it in a rather matter-of-fact way. He found without doubt that from the outset the Egyptians had lived a 'disciplined and civilised' life (*politikôs* and *hêmerôs*), but he scarcely lingered over cultural, philosophical or religious considerations. The course of the Nile was well known and its flood easily explained, now that eye-witnesses could be relied on (XVII, 1, 5); exit the *thauma* [marvel]. For the rest, we have a somewhat dry description of places. The traveller's eye is

[30] *FGrHist* 609 Jacoby.

more that of an official, noting the setting up of good Roman order, and finding that overall the country could be easily held with a few soldiers (XVII, 1, 13).

Very different is the presentation of Egypt of Diodorus, who had visited the country half a century earlier when it was not yet subject to Rome. As Egypt was held to be the country where the gods made their appearance, where the first astronomical observations had taken place and where great men had performed great exploits, he would begin his book with it, he writes (I, 9, 5–6) – even though he does not adopt as his own the statement of Ephorus concerning the anteriority of the Barbarians in relation to the Greeks.

From the long exposition – more interesting than has often been observed – in which he records, notably on divine matters, what the Egyptians 'say' (I, 29, 6), one will recall only that Osiris is presented as the civiliser of the *oikoumene* [inhabited world] through which he travels to spread communal life and agriculture (I, 20). Before him, men had practised cannibalism. Thanks to the Nile and the fortunate balance of its climate, Egypt, the land of origin of the first men, was also the source of religion: being the first to use articulate speech, the Egyptians had been the first to distinguish and name the two primordial deities, Isis and Osiris (I, 10–12, 2). It was therefore not surprising that they had sent numerous colonies throughout the whole world, and especially to Greece: the Athenians were descended from the original settlers from Sais (I, 27, 4).[31] An image of Egypt finally takes shape, both traditional and composite (not only because Diodorus cobbled together scraps from a variety of sources), divided between *thauma* [marvel] and *paideia* [education], the origin of civilised life and birthplace of religion.

Such a portrayal, although not organised around the affirmed conviction of the superiority of Barbarian over Greek wisdom, nevertheless does not contradict it. And Greek intellectuals as a whole increasingly made it the postulate, hypothesis or conclusion of their reflections: Barbarian wisdom was older and profounder.[32] At the beginning of his *Lives of the Illustrious Philosophers*, Diogenes Laertius (in the third century AD) would echo this long tradition: 'Some would have it that philosophy began with the Barbarians: in fact there were the Magi among the Persians, Chaldaeans among the Babylonians or Assyrians, Gymnosophists in India, Druids among

---

[31] The vague kinship noted by Plato (*Timaeus*, 21e) has become a relationship of direct descent (I, 28, 6).

[32] A. Momigliano, *Sagesses barbares*, Paris, Maspero, 1979 [original version: *Alien Wisdom*].

the Celts and Galatians.' Each of these philosophies is then briefly described.[33] Of course, the moment that 'Barbarian wisdom' was mentioned, arguments began about who were the first initiators, or who was the most genuine sage among the Barbarians. The Egyptians were good traditional candidates, but the Persians, with the Magi and the great Zoroaster, seemed to be serious contenders ...[34] Still in the third century, Philostratus made his hero, the wise Apollonius of Tyana, a great disciple of Pythagoras, utter a definitive opinion on the matter: when it came to wisdom and purity of lifestyle, the Gymnosphists of India were way ahead of the Egyptian priests, who, forgetful of their origins, were in fact descended from settlers from India. A sure sign of inferiority was to be seen in 'the strange and ridiculous forms' they gave to their gods (VI, 19).

Going beyond these sophistic discussions, what had Egypt become? It was certainly no longer an object of inquiry in the sense of Herodotus: neither its *nomoi* nor its *politeia* nor its history were of interest any more, and the *thauma* was much diminished. It was no longer anything more than a simple province, even worse, a possession of the emperor. Almost all that remained were the Nile, the pyramids and chiefly 'its' religion, in other words, above all what Greek tradition had elaborated over the centuries under this title.[35] For although the number of those who wrote about Egypt and 'its' religion is large, in total there were only two priests of Egyptian origin, Manetho, already mentioned, and Cheremon, later under Nero, a Stoic priest and philosopher; all the rest were Greek.[36] As for evaluating the genuinely Egyptian content of, for instance, all the Hermetic literature, I am incapable of doing so, even though

[33] According to the Egyptians, Hephaestus was the son of the Nile and philosophy had begun with him. The summary of Egyptian philosophy (I, 10–12) is ascribed to Manetho and Hecataeus.

[34] Zoroaster, whose dates were calculated (6000 years before Xerxes), would see his fame grow, with the number of works attributed to him, starting from the fourth century. [For Zoroastrianism, see esp. Boyce, *A History of Zoroastrianism*.]

[35] On the perception of Egypt, other documents could be referred to that I shall just list: Greek and Latin inscriptions left by travellers, either official or private, tourists or pilgrims, on various monuments: those of the tombs of kings or syrinxes [*sic*] (J. Baillet) and chiefly those of the colossus of Memnon (A. and E. Bernand) – to which real worship was paid – most often have a religious dimension. Thus on the kings' tombs, visitors inscribe their admiration, adoration and the wishes they make for themselves and their families. One might also recall the episode of the 'miraculous rain' recorded by Cassius Dio: a certain Harnouphis, an Egyptian magus in the entourage of Marcus Aurelius, summoned the deities by magic art, notably Hermes Aerius, and through their agency brought on rainfall that saved the army, during the course of the Danubian campaign; J. Guey, 'Encore la pluie miraculeuse', *Revue de Philologie*, 1948, pp. 16–62.

[36] See the list given by Festugière, *La révélation d'Hermès Trismégiste*, Paris, Lecoffre, 1944, I, p. 86.

that content exists and proves larger than was originally thought.[37]

Simply – and this is all I want to emphasise – it seems clear that the process of reducing the signifier Egypt to religion alone (given, of course, that this dimension had been present at the formation of the tradition, and had been necessary so that the reduction could one day be possible) also makes sense in that long-lasting movement of Greek culture, self-doubting and reworking itself in complex fashion, notably by the movement of reversal mentioned earlier, but also by the growing place given to 'care of the self', as Foucault called it,[38] in which the relationship with the divine represents one of the fundamental methods of approach.

Porphyry is a good example, not so much of doubt as of a very learned reworking. Of Syrian origin, named Malco, he came to Athens to study with Longinus, before winning over Rome and the school of Plotinus, leadership of which he assumed in 268, after the death of the master.

Egypt in fact appears at various moments of his work and reflection. Let me swiftly recall two examples taken from his *Letter to Anebo* and the treatise *On abstinence*. In the letter, he is addressing an Egyptian priest (real or fictitious?) 'on the gods, good demons and the philosophical doctrines relating to them'. But, in view of the reputation of that religion, choosing to question a hierogrammateus [sacred scribe] (such as Cheremon, whom Porphyry quotes several times) was a decision to address the highest authority on the subject. And when those questions were also critical, they were criticisms of the most developed form of paganism. Christian apologists did not fail to take them up for their own use, seeing them as 'the admissions of a pagan disgusted with paganism'.[39] Asking, for instance, about the manner of invoking the gods, 'What do all these unintelligible words mean, and why pretend to resort to the barbarity of foreign names? If the Being who is listening cares only for the meaning of the prayer, the thought alone is important, and not the choice of words! For the god invoked is not, I imagine, Egyptian by birth? And even if he were, he would speak Egyptian no more than any other language of men ...'[40]

---

[37] P. Derchain, 'L'authenticité de l'inspiration égyptienne dans le *Corpus Hermeticum*, *RHR*, 161, 1962, pp. 175–98.

[38] M. Foucault, *Le souci de soi*, Paris, Gallimard, 1984 [translated as *A History of Sexuality*, vol. 3], pp. 53–85.

[39] J. Bidez, *Vie de Porphyre*, Gand, Université de Gand, 1913, p. 87.

[40] *Porfirio Lettera ad Anebo*, A. R. Sodano ed., 2 10 (Bidez for the translation of this passage).

To which Iamblichus would reply, in his *Mysteries of Egypt*, in the very name of the antiquity and immutability of the land. 'Since the Egyptians were the first to receive the privilege of communication with the gods, the latter like to be invoked according to the rules of that people.' Then he continues, taking up (but inverting) the Greek–Barbarian comparison, 'contrary to the Greeks, who are lovers of novelties, the Barbarians, constant in their customs, are equally faithful in maintaining the old ways of speaking: thus they are well regarded by the gods and offer them speeches that please them; no one is permitted to change them in any way' (VII, 4).

Egypt is still cited, this time positively, in the treatise *On abstinence*, in which Porphyry defends vegetarianism at length, and by various means. It first appears, through a long quotation from Theophrastus,[41] as a region which, unaware of blood sacrifice, was at the origin of vegetal sacrifices: 'They are so far from killing a single animal, that they use their forms for the images of gods, so true is it that they regard them as fitting (*oikeia*) and related (*suggenê*) to gods and men' (II, 26, 4).[42] Further on in the same book (II, 47, 1), to justify abstinence, the authority of 'the Egyptian' is invoked, an appellation that applies precisely to Hermes Trismegistus and his revelations.[43] We are then in the area of demonology: the souls of animals that have died a violent death can in fact be a danger, especially for the philosopher, and impede him in his 'one-to-one' progress towards god.

Further on, Egypt returns once more, with a resumption of reflections on the kinship of animal, human and divine souls, and through the intermediary of a long quotation from Cheremon (IV, 6–10). Presenting the temple as the site of philosophy and the priest as philosopher, he puts his emphasis on a particular lifestyle, marked by separation from the profane, purity, abstinence (total or partial), sober bearing, a solitary life, mathematical research and the hymns that are sung in honour of the gods. This was the very model of the contemplative life: the path to god.

---

[41] Theophrastus, Aristotle's successor at the head of the School, author of a treatise *On piety*, among many others, in which he calls into question traditional religion, and which we know from the long quotations given by Porphyry. On Book II *On abstinence*, see J. Bouffartigue, *Porphyre*, note to Book II, Paris, CUF, 1979, pp. 3–71.

[42] However, in II, 55, 2, with Manetho, a time is recalled when human sacrifice existed, to which the pharaoh Amosis put an end; he substituted wax statuettes. See J. Yoyotte, 'Héra d'Héliopolis et le sacrifice humain', *Annuare E.H.P.E.*, 5th section, LXXXIX, 1980–1, pp. 31–102.

[43] A. J. Festugière, *Études d'histoire et de philologie*, Paris, Bibliothèque d'histoire de la philosophie, 1975, pp. 141–50.

The philosopher-priest, living in his temple's cloister, in the company of others and yet solitary, fairly well represents an intermediary or pivotal character between one era, ruled (to use the terms of Peter Brown)[44] by a model of parity (including the management of its relations with the divine), and another characterised by ambition (with the rise of the figure of 'the friend of god'). In this area, better than elsewhere, the holy man can, then, approach 'the supreme principle privately and by his own doing' (II, 52, 3).

The same phenomenon is targeted by Lucian, in satirical mode, in order to denounce it, through his ambitious characters (therefore charlatans) such as Alexander, Peregrinus or Pancrates, hierogrammateus of Memphis. The last of these, completely erudite in Egyptian sciences, had been in retreat for twenty-three years (one year more than Pythagoras) in a subterranean temple, where Isis in person had taught him the art of the Magi. All the prodigies he had performed, especially riding astride crocodiles, make him unquestionably recognisable as a holy man.[45]

Originally the far-off land of doctors and a thousand wonders, Egypt became, within the framework of understanding of a self-confident culture, the land from which Greek religion borrowed (the matter of the divine '*onomata*' [names]). Then, as if inserted between the two figures of Pythagoras and Plato, themselves linked, it dwindled until it was no more than a space that was both abstract – a sort of pure signifier, inhabited by philosophers – and at the same time one which teemed with that profuse anonymous literature, ascribed (among others) to the 'thrice-great' Hermes.

Although for the Greeks the Egyptians always represented special 'others', in general things had moved on from a time when, with Herodotus and his 'political' picture of the world, one thought about others in relation to oneself, to an era when, with politics having given way to a cultural frame of reference, using a new strategy and a new logic, one would think about oneself in relation to others. Except that one could not 'go outside' oneself: for that other person, whether Egyptian, Indian or Persian ... was largely a fictitious creature, by means of whom Greek intellectuals created and dismantled their own culture, re-examining or reconstructing it, according to a world they had lost and for a world they had changed.

[44] P. Brown, *Genèse de l'antiquité tardive*, Fr. trs., Paris, Gallimard, 1983 [original English version: *The Making of Late Antiquity*], pp. 121–2.
[45] *Philopseudès*, 34, edition and commentary J. Schwartz, Strasbourg, Editions Ophrys, 1951.

PART IV

Overviews

Introduction to Part IV

Finally, we turn to a series of overviews of the history of Greek identity and of the Greek–barbarian antithesis. We begin with the classic article of Frank Walbank, 'The Problem of Greek Nationality' (Ch. 10), which examines the different responses in nineteenth- and early twentieth-century literature to the relative lack of political unity of the Greek world.

Walbank steers a course between two extreme models of Greek history. The first is a story of the failure of the Greeks to achieve political unification. Not only is this model one-sidedly negative, but it also tends to focus on only a fraction of the Greek world (the mainland of Greece);[1] the unification of 'Hellas' as a whole – that is, of the Greeks of the Black Sea, Sicily and Italy, North Africa and Asia Minor as well as the 'mainland' – was, by contrast, unthinkable. The alternative model, also rejected by Walbank, is that of a fragmented group of autonomous *poleis* struggling to maintain their autonomy or to assert a hegemony over others. This model, one which envisages 'Hellas' as no more than a cultural unit, underplays the positive values and achievements of the Greek cities, and ignores what was developed: the Greeks' sense of 'nation' and of a common ancestry. Though the Greeks may not have formulated any idea of unification, with hindsight, Walbank suggests, we may be able to glimpse movements towards integration in larger units that form some kind of pattern.

Walbank's article has a grand sweep and flourish that are rarely seen now in such scholarly articles. 'Fifty years hence,' he writes, 'it will be quite obvious that the themes chosen by historians today, and the treatment accorded to them, were directly related to contemporary problems.' Many of those contemporary concerns, however –

[1] See, however, Weiler's demonstration, 'The Greek and non-Greek world', pp. 27–8, of an implicit *territorial* definition of 'Hellas' as the Greek mainland in Herodotus (see also Walbank, n. 29).

notably the preoccupation with nations and nationalism[2] – are still with us. The model of the history of Greece as a failure of unification has recently been revived.[3] Walbank does not only look backwards to the historical imagination of the nineteenth century. He also foreshadows many of the concerns more marked today, for example the emphasis on *imagined* community, on kinship 'real or pretended'.[4] If 'The Problem of Greek Nationality' still appears fresh, it is in part, however, because historians now shrink away from the big picture, preferring to isolate individual 'ethnicities' or to distinguish the reality of political institutions and structures of power from questions of imagined community.[5]

Robert Browning then provides (Ch. 11) an introductory overview of the history of the Greek–barbarian antithesis in Greek thought from the classical world to the end of the Byzantine empire. Browning looks, for example, at how the Greeks responded to the Romans – by classifying them as barbarians, as Greeks, or as a third group[6] – or how the later Byzantine Greeks kept alive a 'Roman' identity in opposition to the Latins or Franks of the west. Browning's broad survey demands to be supplemented. His brief discussion of the Hellenistic period needs to be read, in particular, against the work of Amélie Kuhrt, Susan Sherwin-White and others on 'Hellenism'.[7] His brief nod forward to the importance of the historical past in the forging of Greek nationhood in the nineteenth century may be supplemented with the excellent *Concise History* of Greece by Richard Clogg or by Michael Herzfeld's study *Ours Once More*.

Finally, Wilfried Nippel (Ch. 12) first provides a survey of the Greek–barbarian antithesis in classical antiquity and then follows this with a history of its continued exploitation in later European

[2] See pre-eminently Hobsbawm, *Nations and Nationalism*; Anderson, *Imagined Communities*.

[3] By the historical sociologist Runciman, 'Doomed to extinction'. See also below, n. 5.

[4] See esp. (in a Greek context) Hall, *Ethnic Identity* (with emphasis on the Argolid). See also the regional studies of McInerney, *Folds of Parnassos*; Luraghi, 'Der Erdbebenaufstand'; or (in a Roman context) the excellent Dench, *From Barbarians to New Men*, Ch. 5.

[5] For more recent work in similar areas, see Finley, 'The Ancient Greeks and their nation'; Saïd, *Hellenismos*; for Panhellenism (emphasising the narrow interests underlying Panhellenic idealism), see Perlman, 'Isocrates' *Philippus*', 'Panhellenism'; Dillery, *Xenophon*, Part II. Another focus for research is the conception of Europe: see Momigliano, 'L'Europa come concetto politico'; de Romilly, 'Isocrates and Europe'; Hartog, 'Fondements grecs de l'idée d'Europe'; Sordi, *L'Europa nel mondo antico*.

[6] See also now Erskine, 'Money-loving Romans', *Troy between Greece and Rome*.

[7] Sherwin-White and Kuhrt, *Hellenism in the East, From Samarkand to Sardis*; for the cultural Hellenism of the Second Sophistic, see Swain, *Hellenism and Empire*.

history.[8] Nippel shows how, for example, in the colonial age, Europe's new 'barbarians' were seen in the light (and sometimes under the name) of ancient barbarian peoples, how colonialism was justified by the adoption of an Aristotelian idea of natural slavery, or how modern scholarship on the ancient world has been informed by the idea of the superiority of classical Greek culture and of an unbroken line of descent from the ancient past to the European present. The influence of the classical past on western Europe cannot be denied. But, as the anthropologist Jack Goody recently demonstrated in his *The East in the West*, many of the characteristics deemed unique to the 'western' tradition – the rationality of the logical syllogism, for example – developed independently in other cultures of the Far East. The influence of Greek philosophy and science, moreover, was never restricted to Western Europe.

Claims of the essential cultural superiority of the Greeks are sometimes said to be a thing of the past.[9] Yet, though the forms in which claims of Greek superiority are made out have mutated, the Greeks remain a privileged 'source' of our ideals. The beliefs, for example, in their lack of triumphalism after the Persian Wars,[10] or in the mirage of an ancient world free from sexual taboos,[11] have more to do with modern aspirations than ancient reality. As David Lewis commented in the context of the continuing tension between Greeks and others along the western seaboard of Asia Minor, so in this area also 'we should not think that our story is yet at an end'.[12]

---

[8] Nippel's essay draws in large part on his earlier, longer study, *Griechen, Barbaren und 'Wilde'*.

[9] See e.g. Ober, *Political Dissent*, p. 2.

[10] See here Harrison, *Emptiness of Asia*, pp. 111–15.

[11] See the review by W. V. Harris, *Times Literary Supplement*, 28 April 2000, p. 6.

[12] Lewis, *Sparta and Persia*, p. 158.

10 *The Problem of Greek Nationality*†

F. W. WALBANK

I

The problem which I propose to discuss in this paper is one which must strike anyone who ponders at all about the history of Greece. Can we speak of a Greek nation? Greece, as we all know, was never united until the Roman conquest within a single state; consequently there can be no history of Greece in the sense that there is a history of Rome. But the concept of a Greek nation trying to realise itself (and failing) has been adopted by many historians as the most fruitful criterion for interpreting the kaleidoscopic relations of the Greek cities. A few quotations will make this clear. 'The story of the Greeks possesses coordination and the true dignity of history only where it strives continuously, and with ever broader results, towards effective political unity, namely in Greece proper.' These words of De Sanctis[1] can be paralleled from Volume 6 of the *Cambridge ancient history*,[2] where Cary writes, '[The Athenian Empire] represented the first resolute attempt to solve the key problem of Greek politics, the assembling of the scattered Greek communities into a United States of Greece', or from a recent work by Pohlenz,[3] 'The League of Corinth brought to fruition that unity of the Hellenes for which the best elements in the people had for so long yearned.'

The authors I have just quoted differ in many ways in their interpretation of Greek history; but all share what may fairly be called the orthodox view of Greek history as the struggle for the unification of the Greek nation. It is perhaps worth observing, even at the risk of covering well-trodden ground, that this interpretation has not always been current. It does not, for instance, occur in the work of the banker and liberal politician who, in the years between 1846 and

---

† Originally published in *Phoenix* 5 (1951), 41–60.
[1] G. De Sanctis, *Storia dei Greci* (Florence, 1939) 3.
[2] *CAH* 6 (Cambridge, 1933) 26.
[3] M. Pohlenz, *Der hellenische Mensch* (Leipzig, 1947) 137.

1856, was publishing what is still perhaps the most noteworthy English history of classical Greece. For its origins we must turn not to George Grote,† but to the nineteenth-century Germans,[4] and in particular to the *History of hellenism* of Johann Gustav Droysen.[5] In his first edition of 1833 Droysen set out to bridge the gap between classical Greece and the coming of Christianity, and he found his link in what he called the Hellenistic Age. Droysen had a passion for progress and the wide horizon. His object was to study Greek history as part of universal history, and his sympathies were always with the *victrix causa*. 'My enthusiasm', he wrote,[6] 'is for Caesar, not Cato, for Alexander, not Demosthenes.' Small wonder that such a man living in the Germany of Bismarck should conceive a devotion to the rising state of Prussia, with its manifest destiny to unite the Fatherland; and Droysen's second edition, published its 1877, under the spell of Prussian success, laid special stress on the forces making for panhellenism and the unity of Greece – above all Isocrates and the kings of Macedon.

It was Droysen who really raised the national issue in Greek history. But it reached its apogee in the twentieth century with Eduard Meyer and Julius Beloch.[7] For many years yet Beloch's *Greek history* will be indispensable. But for all its factual learning it is marred by a curious schematism and tendency towards abstraction. To Beloch the Greeks are one race which at an early stage in its history lost the consciousness of unity, and spent the rest of its span on earth gradually, and never quite successfully, recovering it. 'Particularism', we read,[8] 'was the hereditary curse of the Greek people.' Athens, Sparta, Macedon, and the third-century Confederations, with their 'republican movement', were the successive incarnations of this spirit of national unity striving to be born. Each in turn proved abortive, and finally in the early second century the Symmachy of

---

† For whom see the classic article of Momigliano, 'George Grote and the study of Greek history'.

[4] See J. R. Knipfing, *AHR* 26 (1920–1) 658ff. As P. Treves, *LEC* 9 (1940) 285 n. 3, points out, it is inexact to attribute the 'unitary' view of Greek history (and particularly of the issue as between Isocrates and Demosthenes) exclusively to the German historians; but historically this view was nurtured mainly on German soil, and against the background of German nineteenth-century political developments.

[5] On this see A. Momigliano, *Filippo il Macedone* (Florence, 1934) Introd. xvi (with bibliography); H. E. Stier, *Grundlagen und Sinn der griechischen Geschichte* (Stuttgart, 1945) 25ff.

[6] J. G. Droysen, *Briefwechsel* 1 (Berlin–Leipzig, 1929) 66ff.; quoted by Stier, *op. cit.* (n. 5) 28. The remark was made in a letter to Friedrich Gottlieb Welcker.

[7] See for example E. Meyer, *Kleine Schriften* (Halle, 1910) 1–78, 'Zur Theorie und Methodik der Geschichte'; K. J. Beloch, *Griechische Geschichte* 1–4 (Strasbourg–Berlin–Leipzig, 1912–27) *passim*.

[8] *Op. cit.* (n. 7) 3.1.515.

Antigonus Doson was trampled down beneath the feet of the Roman legions. On this interpretation Greek history shows one highlight – the Persian Wars – when for a short space the cities forgot their quarrels and won deathless glory at Thermopylae, Salamis, and Plataea.

To De Sanctis, a pupil of Beloch, the unity of 481 has become a touchstone for the definition of Greek history. The solidarity then shown in Greece was based, he rightly observes, upon the liberty of the *polis*, and designed for its defence;[9] but this liberty was in reality 'the germ of the greatness of the nation'. Those Greek cities in Crete and western Greece which failed to respond at this historic moment forfeited their place in Greek history, and were henceforth fated to pursue a different path right down to the last days of Greek independence.

The Persian Wars thus occupied an unchallenged place in these histories of Greek unity similar to that which they had long ago enjoyed in the more expansive prose of the Attic orators. But the other supposedly great moment of Greek unification – the setting up of the League of Corinth by Philip II after Chaeronea – very soon because the centre of polemic. For in proportion as the stock of Philip and Isocrates rose, the reputation of Demosthenes fell, until he began to look like a petty and narrow patriot, blind to the swelling tide of history. Recently, therefore, several historians have brought considerable emotion to the task of rehabilitating Demosthenes, and illuminating the causes for which he fought – the freedom and autonomy of Athens, and (they would argue) ultimately of the other Greek states as well.

The opposing sides in this dispute have tended to mass round the symbolic figures of Demosthenes and Isocrates; but the issue has not been allowed to remain one of Greek unity versus Greek particularism. A careful examination[10] of what Isocrates really advocated led to a toning down of the exaggerations which had made him 'a man of 1848', the ideological forerunner of Philip and Alexander; in the last resort Isocrates, no less than Demosthenes, was shown to have based his aims on the *polis*, and to have fostered unification as the means to a new Athenian hegemony. Simultaneously it was being argued[11] that Demosthenes' whole policy after the Peace of Philo-

---

[9] *Problemi di storia antica* (Bari, 1932) 11ff.

[10] Especially by G. Mathieu, *Les idées politiques d'Isocrate* (Paris, 1925), and U. Wilcken, *SBBerlin* (1929) 313, and *Alexander der Grosse* (Leipzig, 1931).

[11] See W. Jaeger, *Demosthenes* (Berkeley, 1938) 170ff.; P. Treves, *Demostene e la libertà greca* (Bari, 1933) *passim*; LEC 9 (1940) 270ff.

crates in 346, down to Chaeronea, and even down to the Lamian War after Alexander's death, was designed to secure Greek unity in the fullest sense, that is, unity which maintained the liberty and autonomy of the city-state. But in fact this formulation concealed an irreconcilable contrast. For the urge towards the autonomy of the *polis* was a force working against, and not in the direction of, Hellenic unity; and in an acute and pessimistic study Ferrabino demonstrated that this liberty, admitting no restraint, and developing whenever circumstances allowed into domination over others, was the one really potent factor in Greek history. In such domination, taking the form of hegemony, the denial of someone else's liberty was implicit; and not only did this lust for power constantly nullify the quest for liberty, but because any hegemony based on power could only reflect a temporary balance of forces, to be overthrown as soon as that balance changed, there could be no question of national unity.

The impasse seemed complete; Demosthenes and Isocrates were both, it appeared, the spokesmen of the *polis*. Panhellenism and the crusade against Persia, which the latter so sedulously preached, had no more to do with a united Greek nation than had the anti-Macedonian coalition which the former built up in 340 and 339. The conclusion seemed to be that the Greeks had a weak or ineffective national sense; and that conclusion was quickly drawn. 'The concept of the Greek nation', wrote Berve,[12] 'is best left out of the picture.' But if this was so, what I have called the orthodox account of Greek history was due for revision. What was to take its place?

There have been roughly three answers to this problem. The first is that of Berve, just mentioned; leave nationality out of the picture and concentrate on what really mattered to the Greeks – or those of them who were vocal – the liberty and autonomy of the city, the attempt to establish a real peace, the urge towards hegemony. A second answer draws a distinction, along the lines suggested by several German sociologists, and in particular by Friedrich Meinecke,[13] between the *Kulturnation* and the *Staatsnation*. These expressions are not wholly happy,[14] but they sum up the thesis that a nation need not necessarily be united under a single state to enjoy a consciousness of its own identity; nationhood, on this argument, is something which depends on the possession of several – but not

[12] *NJbb* (1938) 15.

[13] See F. Meinecke, *Weltbürgertum und Nationalstaat*[7] (Munich–Berlin, 1928) 3 (and works by A. Kirchhoff and F. J. Neumann there quoted); H. E. Stier, *op. cit.* (n. 5) 108, connects the idea with a remark of Jacob Burckhardt to Arnold von Salis in December 1870 that it is impossible to be at once a culturally important and a politically important people.

[14] But E. Meyer's use of *Volk* and *Nation* (*op. cit.* (n. 7) 1.38ff.) is even less apt.

necessarily all – of the following factors: a common habitation, a common language, a common spiritual and intellectual life, and a common state or share in a federation of states.[15] The Greeks possessed sufficient of these in common to rank as, and feel themselves, a nation; but without political unity, they must be regarded as a *Kulturnation* only.

This view has won many adherents; but in the course of the last decade a third answer to the problem has been propounded in two important and very diverse works, Martin's study of the international relations of the Greek city-states, published in Geneva in 1940, and Stier's *Foundations and meaning of Greek history*, published at Stuttgart in 1945.[16] Quite independently, the former implicitly, the latter explicitly, these two scholars have restated the problem of Greek history in national terms; only the nation is now identified, not with Hellas, but with the individual *polis*. The novelty of this procedure may be obscured by the fact that in practice we have always treated the Greek cities for what they were and claimed to be – independent, autonomous states. Grote,[17] realising this and feeling some difficulty in reconciling it with the idea of a Greek nation, coined the term 'interpolitical' to describe relations between *poleis*, so that 'international' might be reserved for relations with non-Greek states; but the distinction was not made by the Greeks themselves, and it has never been adopted.

However, if we are to understand the foundations of Greek political thought and action, Stier's thesis will require some consideration, for (as Meinecke rightly insists) the identification of State and Nation is by no means an automatic occurrence. A state like Switzerland (or Great Britain) can contain several distinct cultural units, and conversely a single cultural unit like the German people may, as in the centuries before Bismarck and again at the present time, be divided amongst several states.

---

[15] Meinecke, *op. cit.* (n. 13) 1, who adds 'a common origin'; but this is manifestly lacking in the population of most nations throughout history and seems therefore somewhat irrelevant. Cf. F. Schulz, *Principles of Roman law* (Oxford, 1936) 109–39, but one may question his view that there was ever a single 'Roman' nation covering the whole Empire. J. Stalin, *Marxism and the national and colonial question* (New York, 1936) 8 (reprinting an essay of 1913), defines a nation as 'a historically evolved, stable community of language, territory, economic life, and psychological make-up, manifested in a community of culture', and treats each factor as essential. But this somewhat rigid definition would exclude Switzerland with its three (or four) tongues, and contemporary Germany with its economic division along the frontier between the eastern and western zones of occupation.
[16] V. Martin, *La vie internationale dans la Grèce des cités (VI–IVe siècle av. J.-C.)* (Geneva, 1940); Stier, *op. cit.* (n. 5).
[17] Grote, *History of Greece* 2 (1846) 340ff.

II

A full examination of the thesis that the Greeks regarded the *polis* and not the whole Greek people as the nation would require a comprehensive survey of the whole of Greek history, and this is clearly beyond the scope of a paper. We must therefore content ourselves with considering the general case, and the more convincing of the evidence with which Stier supports his thesis, accompanying it with such qualifications as seem necessary. First, then, the arguments for identifying the *polis* with the nation.

It has been widely assumed in the past that the word *Hellene* began by having a 'national' sense and later, especially in Hellenistic times, came to mean 'possessing Greek culture'. For instance, in Ptolemaic and Roman Egypt the Hellenes were also known as οἱ ἀπὸ τοῦ γυμνασίου, 'those from the gymnasium', and frequently had non-Greek names. From Tebtunis we have a list of five Ἑλλήνων γεωργ[ῶν], 'Greek farmers', of whom only one has a Greek name.[18] And it has been thought that the beginning of this extension in the meaning of the word can be traced to the fourth century, when Isocrates wrote,[19] 'Athens has become the teacher of the other cities, and has made the name of Greek (τὸ τῶν Ἑλλήνων ὄνομα) no longer a mark of race (γένος) but of intellect (διάνοια), so that it is those who share our upbringing (τῆς παιδεύσεως) rather than our common nature (τῆς κοινῆς φύσεως) who are called Hellenes.' This passage has attracted great attention, Jaeger going so far as to claim it as[20] 'a higher justification for the new national imperialism, in that it identifies what is specifically Greek with what is universally human'. 'Without the idea which [Isocrates] here expresses for the first time', he continues, '… there would have been no Macedonian Greek world-empire, and the universal culture which we call Hellenistic would never have existed.' Unfortunately for this claim, it has been shown[21] that in this passage Isocrates is not extending the term Hellene to non-Greeks, but restricting its application; he is in effect saying, 'Hellenes are no longer all who share in the γένος and common φύσις of the Greek people, as hitherto, but only those who have gone to school to Athens; henceforth "Greece" is equivalent

---

[18] See F. Zucker, *Das neue Bild der Antike* 1 (Leipzig, 1942) 380; W. Otto, *Kulturgeschichte des Altertums* (Munich, 1925) 117. *P. Tebt.* 1.247 = 4.1107.

[19] *Paneg.* 50.

[20] *Paideia* 3 (Oxford, 1945) 79–80.

[21] By Wilcken, *SBBerlin* (1922) 114 n. 3; *cf.* J. Jüthner, *Hellenen und Barbaren* (Leipzig, 1923) 34ff.; *WS* 47 (1929) 26ff.

to Athens and her cultural following.' Thus Isocrates gives the term a cultural value; but he cannot be regarded as initiating a wider concept of Hellas.

So far Stier's argument seems well based; what follows is more controversial. There is, he claims, evidence for the view that from the earliest times (and not merely from the fourth or third century) the word 'Hellene' was a cultural, not a national term.[22] It is now generally agreed that the original *Hellēnes* were a small tribe in south Thessaly, and that this name was extended in a way which can easily be paralleled – consider for example the names *Graeci* or *Allemands* – to cover the Greeks in a wider sense. Both Hesiod and Archilochus know the form *Panellēnes*;[23] and Hesiod was evidently acquainted with the shorter form *Hellēnes* since it is to him we owe our first reference to Hellen, the eponymous hero of the Hellenes. The extension of the name first in the longer, and then in the abbreviated form can, therefore, perhaps be attributed to the eighth century. Stier, however, now argues that since the Macedonians were excluded from the *Hellēnes*, yet appear to have been a Greek-speaking people, the criterion for inclusion was evidently not race or tongue, but cultural level; and in support of this he quotes the fact that not until Roman times[24] are the Hellenes spoken of as an *ethnos*, the term normally applied to such Greek people as the Boeotians or Arcadians, and even the bigger divisions like the Ionians and the Dorians. When in the *Laws* (III.692d–693a) Plato refers to the services rendered by Athens and Sparta to Hellas in resisting Xerxes, he reckons among the worst of the consequences of defeat the racial confusion which must have ensued. 'Virtually all the Greek stocks (τὰ τῶν Ἑλλήνων γένη)', he

---

[22] This summary is restricted to what seem the stronger of Stier's arguments. He brings forth many which are merely perverse; e.g. that ἑλληνίζειν meant primarily 'to speak correctly', and that there was no Greek language (as opposed to dialects). The absence of a standard literary Greek is irrelevant to the question of nationality; there are signs of German national consciousness as early as Walther von der Vogelweide, but no standard German till Luther created it in the fifteenth century.

[23] Cf. Hes. *Op.* 528; Archil. 52 (cf. Strabo VIII.6.6, c370); the date of both poets is uncertain; on Archilochus see A. A. Blakeway in *Greek poetry and life* (Oxford, 1936) 34–55; F. Jacoby in *CQ* 35 (1941) 97–109; H. Gundert in *Das neue Bild der Antike* 1 (1942) 130–52. A date *c.* 700 B.C. seems most probable. The word Πανέλληνες occurs in *Iliad* II.530 (the Catalogue) but this line is usually taken to be an interpolation; on the possible change in accentuation Ἑλλῆνες—Πανέλληνες—Ἕλληνες see W. Schulze, *SBBerlin* (1910) 806.

[24] An interesting passage in this connection is Polyb. XI.19.4; Hannibal kept together many men who were not only not ὁμοέθνεσιν [of the same *ethnos* or people] but not even ὁμοφύλοις [of the same *phyle* or race]. These included Libyans, Iberians, Ligurians, Celts, Phoenicians, Italians, and Hellenes. Stier, *op. cit.* (n. 5) 388 n. 113, dismisses this as Roman: but Polybius was Greek enough to get this sort of thing right. In fact, the passage does not contradict Stier's view; for Polybius distinguishes two types of grouping, ἔθνη [nations] and φυλαί [races], of which the latter are wider (οὐδ' ὁμοφύλοις [not of the same race]); the Hellenes may here be included as a distinct φυλή or race (containing various ἔθνη).

writes, 'would have been mixed up one with another, and barbarians with Greeks and Greeks with barbarians.' Clearly the Hellenes are not here being treated as a single racial and national stock, but rather as a cultural group comprising several nations.

This is not very convincing. The special case of Macedon, a somewhat remote and certainly mixed people containing Thracian and Illyrian as well as Greek-speaking elements, is not sufficient to destroy the general impression that in classical times the *Hellēnes* regarded themselves as a body of kin. An *ethnos* they may not be; a *genos* they certainly are,[25] and *genos* suggests kinship, not culture. This is supported by the early appearance in Hesiod of the eponymous Hellen,[26] the invented ancestor of the race; and when the Argead kings of Macedon were admitted to parity among the Greeks and to the Olympic games as a symbol of this, it was on genealogical grounds, *i.e.* those of kinship and race, not the grounds of culture, that their claims were made and accepted. It is to genealogy that Stier would attribute the many references to Hellenes as kinsmen and blood-relatives, συγγένεις and ὅμαιμοι.[27] But to minimise their importance on that account is to neglect the idea behind the invention of Hellen;[28] and those who argue that the *Hellēnes* form a cultural group over against the *barbaroi* would perhaps win more support for their thesis if they could point to an eponymous Barbar as ancestor to the *barbarophōnoi*. In view of these difficulties Stier cannot be said to have made out a case for thinking that 'Hellas' was originally a cultural rather than a racial or national concept; in this respect the orthodox view must continue to stand.

III

Let us pass to a further point. How, it may be asked, is the thesis of a Greek nation and a national consciousness in the minds of the Greeks to be reconciled with the geographically dispersed character of the Hellenic settlements? The expression 'Hellas' normally (though not invariably)[29] comprised all Greek cities, no matter where they

[25] *Cf.* Stier, *op. cit.* (n. 5) 99: 'stets begegnet ... der viel weitere Begriff γένος'.

[26] Tzetz. *ad Lycophron.* 284, fr. 7 Rzach. Hellen's three sons were Dorus, Xuthus, and Aeolus, *i.e.* the Dorians, Ionians, and Aeolians. 'This is not mythology, but early ethnological theory cast in the traditional mythological form of a genealogy' (H. J. Rose, *OCD s.v.* 'Hellen').

[27] See the passages from Isocrates, Aristophanes, Lysias, and Herodotus quoted by Stier, *op. cit.* (n. 5) 385 n. 78.

[28] Similarly the acceptance of the Dorians as part of the general stock of the Greeks is reflected in the story of the return of the Heracleidae.

[29] Hellas is used in a limited sense too, as for instance when Theopompus (*FGH* 15F 193) excludes Sicily, or Demosthenes limits it to central Greece: τίς ὁ συσκευάζεσθαι τὴν Ἑλλάδα

lay – on the shores of the Euxine, on the coastal plateau of Cyrenaica, or on the seaboard of Spain. Clearly there was never any question of uniting all these within a single nation – a geographical absurdity, unless one envisaged a vast empire like the Roman, embracing not merely the Greeks, but the whole of the provinces which their cities fringed. It was therefore virtually impossible for all the Greek cities to follow a common destiny. But for all that, there is something artificial[30] in seizing upon one group of cities on the Greek peninsula, and upon one great epoch in their common history, the Persian Wars, in order to establish a criterion of 'Greek' history that excludes western Greece and the scattered cities of the rest of the Mediterranean. For Sicily, no less than continental Greece, had its problem of unity against outside aggression, whether from barbarians like the Carthaginians or from the Athenians who were Greeks. In the speech advocating a general peace in Sicily in 424 B.C., which Thucydides (IV.64.3) puts in the mouth of Hermocrates of Syracuse, there is a vigour and capacity for thinking beyond the *polis* (if still ultimately in its interests) which is uncommon in Greece of the classical period. 'There is no disgrace', he asserts, 'in kinsmen (οἰκείους) giving way to one another, a Dorian to a Dorian, or a Chalcidian to his brethren; above and beyond this we are neighbours, live in the same country, are girt by the same sea, and go by the same name of Sicilians.' Here surely – it might be said – is a theme of Sicilian unity around which a history of the Sicilian Greeks might be written; it could tell of the Sicilian–Greek nation striving to achieve birth. But in fact, as Freeman saw,[31] there clearly was never any such thing. As far as nationality goes (and ruling out such sentiment as attached to the name of Ionian and Dorian) there was no essential difference between the attitude of the average Syracusan towards a Theban or a Corinthian, and his attitude towards a man of Messana or Leontini.

Despite such alliances of convenience as marked the Persian Wars in Greece proper, or the burst of pan-Sicilian self-interest in the face of Athenian ambitions which led to the Peace of Gela, the Greek cities everywhere remained separate and divided, each with its own laws, without rights of intermarriage, with different calendars and currencies, and (until some co-ordination was achieved about

καὶ Πελοπόννησον Φίλιππον βοῶν, ὑμᾶς δὲ καθεύδειν; ['who raised the cry that Philip was making preparations with Greece and the Peloponnese, while you were asleep?'] (19.303); *cf.* Ephorus, *FGH* 70F20. But a certain fluctuation is to be expected when the concept in question did not form a political unit.

[30] See above, n. 1.

[31] E. A. Freeman, *History of Sicily* 1 (Oxford, 1891) introduction: 'Sicily never was the home of any nation, but rather the meeting place of many.'

400 B.C.) with different scripts and alphabets. The vigour with which the member of the *polis* maintained his own political identity may be illustrated from the story of Plataea.[32] In 427, after a long siege, Plataea was obliged to surrender to the Spartans, its remaining inhabitants were massacred or enslaved, and a year later the city was razed to the ground by the Thebans.[33] Those Plataeans who had already escaped and so avoided this catastrophe were, as a very exceptional measure, granted Athenian naturalization. Nevertheless, twenty years later Aristophanes (*Frogs* 694) still refers to them as Plataeans; and during the early decades of the fourth century they keep making their appearance as a separate group. From the time of the King's Peace in 386 they once more resettle the ancestral site,[34] only to be expelled yet again in 373 by Thebes, the old enemy.[35] Finally in 338 after the battle of Chaeronea the remnants of the people came back to Plataea, this time to stay.[36]

Everything, as Martin points out, favoured the success of the amalgamation with Athens – the destruction of the old city, the lustre of the new, the solid advantages offered by the change; 'but national sentiment', he comments, 'resisted injuries and enticements alike, and survived all fortune's wreckage. The history of Plataea attests yet again the unparalleled tenacity with which that sentiment maintained its grip upon the Greek cities.' Faced with such an example one is tempted to doubt whether the Greeks were ever moved by ideals other than those of autonomy and freedom in their political life, by *autonomia* and *eleutheria* [freedom], the slogans of resistance to all bids for hegemony which might upset the balance of power in which their security rested.

IV

At this conclusion, however, one is brought up short. Granted that one may not treat Isocrates as the theorist of the League of Corinth, surely one may not dismiss entirely the current of panhellenism which runs through Aristophanes' *Lysistrata*, the Olympic orations of Gorgias and Lysias, to the long series of speeches or pamphlets in which Isocrates himself repeatedly flogged the theme of Greek concord. And what on the other hand of the many forms in which

[32] *Cf.* Martin, *op. cit.* (n. 16) 322–4.
[33] Thuc. III.52, 68.
[34] Paus. IX.1.4.
[35] Diod. XV.46.5.
[36] Paus. IX.1.8.

in practice Greeks joined together in leagues and alliances, to say nothing of the amphictyonies [leagues which regulated the affairs of a sanctuary] and the international festivals? All this, we are now assured, may be neglected. First the propaganda: analyse it, says Stier, and where do you find Greek national unity put forward as an ideal? Aristophanes' object is peace, an end of war, and amity between the cities, a policy which he claims to be in the common interest of all Greeks. But this is a very different matter from a national Greek state. Similarly Gorgias' Olympian speech of 392 and that of Lysias of 388 do not in essentials go beyond an anti-Persian crusade under Athenian or Spartan hegemony;[37] and though Isocrates turned to Athens, Thessaly, Syracuse, Sparta, and Macedon in succession in his search for the ideal leader, he too could not get beyond the same unreal context. How unreal it was became clear when finally he chose Philip II of Macedon to lead a pacified and single-minded Hellas against Persia; for if there is any practical trace of unity in fourth-century Greece, it was realised in the coalition which Demosthenes raised against Philip. For the next hundred and fifty years the one constant basis of common action in Greece is hostility towards Macedon. At the same time, we are not to imagine that Demosthenes was out to build a national state. He more than any man was anchored in the *polis*, and his alliance was always an instrument of Athenian freedom and hegemony, however ideal-istically conceived.

Isocrates remained a theorist. With Demosthenes we bridge the gap between theory and action. But if Demosthenes' league was in reality partial and particularist, so were all the other movements which various scholars have acclaimed as steps towards the realisa-tion of the nation; and this is not least because of the very character of a Greek *symmachia*,[38] which weighted it heavily against playing a role in the creation of a national state. A *symmachia* is primarily an alliance for the purpose of war. It is normally made for a limited period of time, and reflects a particular situation and a definite and essentially temporary balance of forces between its members. Frequently the problem of leading the combined forces is solved by formally conferring the hegemony on one state; thus Sparta was *hegemon* in the Peloponnesian League, and after Chaeronea the League of Corinth took the novel step of making an individual, Philip

---

[37] Gorgias: Aristotle, *Rhet.* iii.14, 1414b30ff. Lysias: Dion. Hal. *Lys.* 28.9; *cf.* Lysias 33. The date of Gorgias' speech is controversial; I follow A. Momigliano, *op. cit.* (n. 5) 184.

[38] On this topic see especially the excellent analysis of Martin, *op. cit.* (n. 16) 124ff.

II, *hegemon* – though many Greeks regarded this as a serious diminution of the rights of the *poleis* and something very like monarchy. The difficulty involved in transforming such a war-alliance into an instrument of political unification in time of peace has been acutely analysed by Martin, who points out that any attempt by the *hegemon* – the war-leader – to centralise political power was always felt by the rest to be an encroachment and an abuse. In the classic example of the fifth-century Delian League this feeling was behind a series of revolts, until finally it was only the Athenian navy which held the cities together, and Thucydides (II.63.2) makes Pericles candidly admit that the free association of cities had become like an Athenian tyranny. Isocrates also proposed to work through a *symmachia* and therefore, quite logically, he felt the need for an enemy – Persia – to serve as a *raison d'être*. But there was nothing in his programme which offered any hope that if Greece could have been allied under one of his prospective *hegemones*, and if the war against Persia could have been carried to a successful conclusion as a Greek (and not a Macedonian) enterprise, the coalition would have developed into a national state any more than the Athenian Confederacy against Salamis and Plataea.

Thus the Symmachies fell between two stools. Either they were based on a shared leadership, like the league against Sparta of 395, between Athens, Corinth, Argos, and Boeotia, in which case the balance was always delicate and usually shortlived; or one state enjoyed an acknowledged hegemony, and by the adoption of long-term aims tended to transform its military ascendancy into political superiority, and the alliance into an empire, which in turn caused the revulsion and stimulated the revolt of the subjects at the first opportunity. In these circumstances alliances could not develop into an instrument of panhellenic unity.

Finally, the Greeks themselves never felt such alliances to be more than combinations of sovereign states. War between Greek states was not normally thought of or spoken of as 'civil war'; nor was any political distinction drawn between Greeks from another city and any other foreigners. Both, for instance, were included equally in the Spartan expulsions of aliens. Such common feeling as existed between the Greeks as Greeks was of a cultural or religious character. The common religious centres and festivals were comparable with the international shrines and sports gatherings of the modern world; and such bodies as the Delphic Amphictyony were of the same character – religious, not political, and certainly not capable of developing into instruments of national unification.

V

I have given the thesis in outline only. Much of it is obviously exaggerated, though a good deal is true; and its adherents support it with a great many detailed arguments for which there is no room here. Many of the more dubious or paradoxical points – for instance, the assertion that there was no Greek language, but only a collection of Greek dialects, which are virtually separate languages – I have omitted, as I have the elaborate *tour de force* in which Stier marshals a set of impressive arguments for a possible thesis that Europe constitutes a single nation, a thesis which would of course be quite misleading. But I have not, I think, misrepresented the case, nor ignored any vital part of it. In criticism it will be useful first to consider a number of specific points.

First of all, as we have seen, the idea that Hellas is a purely cultural concept cannot be accepted, in view of the Greek stress on common ancestry and kinship. Consequently we ought not to neglect any evidence, scattered and scanty though it may be, which treats Hellas as something more than an international society of autonomous city-states. There are, for instance, several passages in which war between Hellenes is described as civil war. Granted, this is exceptional; granted, too, the term may be used in an extended sense. But for all that, these passages do presuppose in their readers a certain response, and for that reason they cannot be simply dismissed. Two writers use the word *stasis* to describe quarrels between Greek cities at the time of the Persian Wars. Theognis speaks of στάσις Ἑλλήνων λαοφόρος ['the civil strife of the Greeks which destroys the people'], and Herodotus tells[39] how the Athenians refused to press their claim to hegemony at Salamis lest Greece should thereby perish; for, he adds, 'civil war (στάσις ἔμφυλος) is as much worse than a war waged in concord as war is worse than peace'. Again Plato in the Republic (v.470) distinguishes between war and civil war, *polemos* and *stasis*, reserving the second title for wars within the Hellenic *genos*, which is of the same kin and family, οἰκεῖον καὶ σύγγενες.

This was certainly not the common politician's view. But it meant something, an idea in some men's minds, which was to find an echo increasingly in the next century. When for example in his *Panegyricus*[40] of 380 Isocrates wrote that the Athenians of old had regarded

---

[39] Theognis 781; Hdt. VIII.3; *cf.* H. Bengtson, *Einführung in die alte Geschichte* (Munich, 1949) 55.
[40] *Paneg.* 81. *Cf.* H. Berve, *Gnomon* 9 (1933) 302; Stier, *op. cit.* (n. 5) 118.

the cities of Greece as mere dwelling places, and Hellas as a common fatherland (κοινὴν πατρίδα τὴν Ἑλλάδα) he is undoubtedly rounding off a highly elaborate period with a striking formulation. Such a formulation may be concerned with propaganda rather than factual accuracy; but it must not be too far removed from the mental climate of the times and from the ideas current in the minds of the ordinary listeners. The fortunes of this particular formulation can, it so happens, be traced further. In the *Philippus* (127), written in 346, Isocrates, with the verbal economy of a publicist, used it again – with a difference; for now he admitted that the other potential leaders of Greece were too bound up in their own laws and constitutions; Philip alone could treat all Hellas as his *patris* [fatherland]. Once again, it may be objected, a metaphor and a fine phrase. But when, after the death of Alexander, the Athenians tried to stir up a last rally for freedom in the so-called Lamian War – the Hellenic War, as the ancient sources term it – they tacitly reverted to Isocrates' original use of the phrase by summoning the Greeks to resistance against Macedon with a reminder of how during their own former efforts against the Persians they had regarded Hellas as the 'common fatherland'.[41]

The point is not whether such expressions were sincere or even true: it is that they would not have been uttered had they not been calculated to have some effect; and the same is true of the panhellenic themes of the orators and the various references to common Greek action, such as Pericles' invitation to the Greek cities to send representatives to Athens to deliberate on peace and common action among the Hellenes, ἐπ' εἰρήνῃ καὶ κοινοπραγίᾳ τῶν Ἑλλήνων.[42] In this case, as Larsen argues,[43] it is no doubt true that Pericles was hoping to persuade the other cities to submit to the Athenian hegemony. What is significant is the panhellenic note which he thought it worth while to sound. Slight though this evidence may be when taken separately, or even when put into the balance against the tremendous weight of testimony for the attitude which made the separate *polis* the final criterion in all political decisions, it nevertheless points to the recognition of a concept of Hellas which was not simply a cultural union.

When on the report that Xerxes was at Sardes the Greek states resolved to appeal to Crete, Corcyra, and the Western cities, to come to the aid of Hellas,[44] their plea was made to cities with whom they

---

[41] Diod. XVIII.10.3.
[42] Plut. *Per.* 17; *cf.* V. Ehrenberg, *JHS* 70 (1950) 101.
[43] *CP* 39 (1944) 158.
[44] Hdt. VII.145.

felt themselves to be bound by ties of kinship. Within this group of states political relations were of a different character from those between Greeks and non-Greeks. For instance the conventions of warfare, which persisted from early times throughout the whole of Greek history, and which Berve,[45] who is in general sceptical about any idea of Greek nationality, counts among 'the few factors making for unity', laid down a standard of conduct in inter-Greek wars which was not observed or even expected to be observed in wars against barbarians.

The oath sworn by members of the Amphictyonic League[46] included an undertaking not to destroy any city belonging to a fellow member, not to reduce it to starvation, and not to cut off the supply of running water. Its date is uncertain, but it goes back to at least 590, at the end of the First Sacred War, and probably earlier. Historically the convention may well have arisen out of the perennial frontier raids between neighbouring cities, for the acquisition of land and booty, raids which the Greeks always distinguished from a major conflict offering a real threat to existence.[47] But by extension it served to humanise any wars between Greek cities, and tended towards the formulation of a whole series of νόμιμα πάσης Ἑλλάδος [customs of all Greece].[48] Since these conventions between Greeks go back to an early date, we may dismiss the idea that they rest on a recognition of merely cultural equality: they are a symbol of a consciousness of ties of real or pretended kinship.

This kinship is expressed more clearly than anywhere else in Herodotus who, in a famous passage,[49] records the reply of the Athenians after Salamis, when the Spartans were afraid lest they might make a separate peace with Xerxes. Such a course, they say, is

---

[45] *NJbb* (1938) 13.

[46] Aeschines 2.115, 3.109–11; for discussion of this controversial topic see F. Hampl, *Die griechischen Staatsverträge des 4. Jahrhunderts v. Chr. Geb.* (Leipzig, 1938) 4–6; Busolt-Swoboda, *Griechische Staatskunde* 2 (Munich, 1926) 1262, 1294; L. Robert, *Études épigraphiques et philologiques* (Paris, 1938) 293–316; D. W. Prakken, *AJP* 51 (1940) 62; G. Daux, *RA* (1941) 176; J. A. O. Larsen, *CP* 39 (1944) 145–7.

[47] Cf. Martin, *op. cit.* (n. 16) 332–40, quoting the wars between Tegea and Mantinea over the draining of the area, and the curious treaty of Thuc. v.46.2, by which Argos and Sparta agreed to make peace for fifty years, save any war waged for the possession of Cynuria: and for such a war the convention was carefully laid down.

[48] Eur. *Supplices* 311; cf. von Scala, *Studien des Polybios* 1 (Leipzig, 1890) 299–324, who collects a number of examples from Euripides (especially), Thucydides, Plato, Xenophon, Aristotle, and later writers. He shows that though the Peripatos in some cases transcended the limitation to Hellenes in applying these ideas, and though the Stoa ignored any criterion beyond the individual, in practice the conventions, as applied by the Greek states, continued to operate for Greeks only. There was a deterioration in practice after the third century, and especially after the coming of the Romans.

[49] Hdt. viii.144; cf. Stier, *op. cit.* (n. 5) 87ff., 100.

unthinkable, and that for many reasons. First there was the burning of the Athenian temples. 'Then', they continue, 'there is our common brotherhood with the Greeks: our common language, the altars and the sacrifices of which we all partake, the common character which we bear – did the Athenians betray all these, of a truth it would not be well.' These are clear, unambiguous words – common blood, common tongue, common religion, and a common way of life; they can scarcely be reconciled with the picture which we have just examined of an international community of completely independent national states.

VI

We must therefore frankly admit that the evidence is contradictory – so long as we insist on considering Greek history exclusively in terms of the *polis*. The field of reference must clearly be extended in order to discover some more flexible criterion. The root of the trouble in most discussion of nationality in Greece lies in too static an interpretation of the concept of a nation and in the attempt to establish too rigid a parallel with the modern world. In fact, as Eduard Meyer pointed out,[50] nations are a very advanced and complicated product of historical development, not something beyond history, as Stier suggests. 'Nations arise and nations decay', writes Bengston,[51] 'and this very process is the object of historical study.' In Greece, as elsewhere, all the political units were in a constant state of evolution which is liable to be obscured by the apparent rigidity of the *polis* itself. It is often said – not without justice – that Aristotle's political thought was rooted in the *polis*. But Aristotle recognised in the *ethnos* organised in villages, κατὰ κώμας, a traditional political unit alongside the city-state, self-sufficient as regards the bare necessities (αὐτάρκης ἐν τοῖς ἀναγκαίοις), though not adapted to pursue the good life.[52] Down to a late period peoples such as the Acarnanians, Aetolians and Arcadians were distributed among clans and cantons; in Arcadia, for instance, several such cantons were fused to form the cities of Tegea, Mantinea and Orchomenus during the sixth and fifth centuries, whereas Megalopolis was set up out of forty original

---

[50] *Op. cit.* (n. 7) 1.38ff.
[51] *Op. cit.* (n. 39) 46; *cf.* F. Schulz, *op. cit.* (n. 15) 109–39.
[52] Aristotle, *Politics* III.14, 1285b; IV (VII).4, 1326b. *Cf.* M. Gelzer, 'Das Problem des Klassischen und die Antike', *Acht Naumberger Vorträge*, published by W. Jaeger (Leipzig, 1931) 101 = *Kleine Schriften* 3 (Wiesbaden, 1962) 3–12; *cf.* Stier, *op. cit.* (n. 5) 392 n. 155. See especially Martin, *op. cit.* (n. 16) 32ff.

communities as a deliberate act of Theban policy after Leuctra. Hence it is possible to trace the dissolution of the old tribal units, the crystallisation into cities often harbouring the bitterest hostility towards each other, and finally the uneasy union of such cities in a new confederacy which restores the original ethnic unity on a higher plane.

The two stages of this process we know as synoecism and federalism; and where the first was carried through completely, as in Attica, the second never became necessary. But Attica was unique in the Greek world. The usual picture elsewhere is one of *ethne* and *poleis* at various stages of development, which often became involved in keen rivalries. Thus in Boeotia there was a constant tension between the unity of the *ethnos*, as expressed through the Boeotian League, and the typical claims to hegemony pressed by the most vigorous *polis*, Thebes. It is clear that the concept of 'nation' is of as little help in the comprehension of such rivalries and tensions as it would have been as a means of solving them.

Both synoecism and federalism continued to play an important role in Greece down to the latest days. As the areas where the *polis* predominated became tangled in the problems raised by the urge towards unlimited expansion and the resistance which it evoked – the problem of the Peloponnesian War, and the subsequent wars against Sparta and Thebes – the loose federations of the more backward or politically weaker areas came to play an increasingly important role.[53] It was from such districts as these, from Achaea, from Arcadia and from Aetolia, that the federal movement took its rise in the fourth and third centuries.

It may well be argued that federalism, like synoecism, has little to do with national unity. On the other hand, the federal state incorporates a principle of unification by consent, which enables it to grow larger without necessarily meeting the nemesis of the expanding hegemonic state. The Macedonian-controlled Leagues from 338 down to 224 were debarred from fostering unity in Greece precisely because they were Macedonian. Their political structure was often admirable. Both the League of Philip II and the League of Antigonus Doson have been praised as being among the most statesmanlike achievements of their kind in world history;[54] but both stood for outside domination, and though they may have had the support

[53] On this see Momigliano, *op. cit.* (n. 5) 65ff.
[54] For the League of Corinth see J. A. O. Larsen, *CP* 39 (1944) 160; for the Symmachy of Doson see A. Ferrabino, *La dissoluzione della libertà nella Grecia antica* (Padua–Milan, 1929) 84.

of one faction within the cities for reasons of party rivalry, they outraged the Greek feeling for freedom and autonomy. The Achaean Confederation on the contrary came within a very little of uniting the whole Peloponnese in a single state, and, what is more, of building up a genuine allegiance and feeling of being Achaean. One need only turn to the enthusiastic account of Polybius (II.37.7ff.) – an Arcadian – to realise this; under its control, he writes, 'the whole Peloponnese only falls short of being a single city in the fact of its inhabitants not being enclosed by one wall, all other things being, both as regards the whole and as regards each separate town, very nearly identical'. The architect of this remarkable structure was Aratus, a Dorian from Sicyon, who had advanced to a broader allegiance.

But the Achaean Confederation foundered; and the fault was not entirely with Aetolia or with Sparta, unable to forget its past and sink its identity. Quite apart from the social and economic unrest which played into the hands of Spartan kings advancing a revolutionary programme, one cannot ignore the fact that the bigger *poleis* of the Peloponnese were never wholly absorbed. A tendency to independent action in times of crisis and even outright differences in policy in such cities as Argos and Corinth set definite limits on the possibility of expansion. Whether there was ever an 'Achaean nation' is arguable: that the Confederacy was inescapable of developing into a 'Greek nation' is certain.

VII

Thus the story of federalism reveals the same fission and contrasts as the story of the fifth- and fourth-century *poleis*; and though it may demonstrate the inadequacy of the concept of the *polis* as nation for an understanding of Greek political development, it leaves enough of Stier's case intact to show how tenuous and feeble was the movement towards unity at all periods. The Greeks possessed enough of the components of a nation to conceive a national idea; but except in times of crisis, when this idea inspired them to common action and even to self-sacrifice, their violent political and patriotic feelings were expressed through the medium of smaller political units.

This formulation underlies certain general difficulties in the interpretation of Greek history. The view that Greek history is the struggle for the national state must be rejected. As Stier and Martin have shown, anything built around a concept so weakly felt and so ineffective in action must be quite false to the ideas and aims of the Greeks themselves, and for that reason stands condemned.

Furthermore, the story of Greece as the conflict of completely independent national states striving for freedom and autonomy is also
to be rejected, not because it would be a pointless story of failure, as
Ferrabino argues, but because such a formulation ignores various
positive values and achievements in the political field, including
the concept of a Greek nation, which must be given their full
value. Starting out from the second position, Jaeger has attempted to
interpret Greek history as *paideia*,[55] the unfolding record of Greek
thought directed towards the training of the human spirit. Jaeger has
given us a stimulating concept and a remarkable book; and though
it has been argued[56] that the interpretation of Greek history is not
to be built on the exposition of a culture which grew up primarily
in opposition to the main assumptions of Greek politics, this paradoxical criticism is not convincing. Many of the great names in the
history of Greek thought, it is true, were bitterly opposed to the idea
of liberty fundamental in Greek politics. But all accepted the framework of the *polis*. Socrates, for example, died rather than challenge
its claims by the flight that was open to him. Moreover there was
never a healthy intellectual development which did not involve a
strong element of friction against established society and its ideals.
In illustration of this one need look no further than the sequence
which ran from Sallust to Tacitus, and the attitude of protest to be
found in almost every writer under the early Roman Empire.

But if *paideia* withstands this criticism, it fails as a full interpretation of Greek history simply because it concentrates almost entirely
on what was thought and said to the exclusion of what was done and
experienced; and consequently it does not help us with our problem,
which is really one of a vital idea which appears to be at constant
variance with practical politics – the idea of the Greek nation.
Droysen, Beloch, Meyer, Stier – all in turn have brought different
criteria to the task of resolving this contradiction, and all have
reached different conclusions. It is therefore worth while considering
if the problem has been properly formulated. When a historian
defines the history of Greece in terms of a struggle for unity, or
describes the building of the 'United States of Greece' as 'the key
problem of Greek politics', what exactly does he mean?

---

[55] W. Jaeger, *Paideia* 1–3 (Oxford, 1939–45). A second edition of vol. 1 with notes was
published in 1946.
[56] Ferrabino, *op. cit.* (n. 54) 107ff.

VIII

I want to suggest that there is a permanent danger of over-simplifying the process of historical thinking, and that in approaching any period, or people, or problems, it is important that we should make certain conscious distinctions, and organise our ideas at several different levels.[57] Suppose, for example, we are concerned with Greek history between the battle of Mantinea and the Lamian War. First of all – and let us, for convenience of analysis and without prejudice, call this the lowest level – we should investigate the various policies and aims of Greek and non-Greek statesmen, the interests likely to influence them, the actions of the various states, and their outcome, in terms of the concepts and ideals and knowledge actually available to the people concerned. That is to say, we should try to read ourselves, for example, into Demosthenes' mind, and understand how it looked to him, and what he was hoping to do. We shall be preoccupied with particular incidents inside a general framework of ideals which are not our own: we shall be concerned with *eirēnē* [peace], *autonomia* [autonomy], *eleutheria* [freedom], *hēgemonia* [hegemony or leadership] – preferably kept in their Greek forms to connote Greek ideas. We shall try to assess just what a phrase like κοινὴ πατρίς [common fatherland] used of Hellas means to different people in this general context.

This or something like it, I take it, is what Collingwood meant by re-enacting past thoughts; it is an activity which lies at the very heart of historical study, and in it there is no room for moral judgements, but only for estimates of success and failure in the carrying out of various divergent aims. If we consider the period I have mentioned in these terms, we must I think agree that it is a record, very largely, of political failure. Freedom, autonomy, peace, hegemony – not one of these often contradictory aims was achieved for long at a time. If we stop here, the history of the fourth century in Greece must appear anything but satisfying.

However, it is essential that we should not stop here. In so far as the historian seeks to relive the past he deliberately restricts himself to the knowledge available at the time of which he writes. But he is also living in his own age, with all the advantages of knowing how the play ended; and he can see each act in relation to the whole. Now

---

[57] Indirectly the following section owers a good deal to Momigliano's *Filippo, op. cit.* (n. 5) *passim.*

because of what De Sanctis has called the 'creativity of history'[58] its process is not a mere series of permutations and combinations similar to that of shuffling cards or shaking dice. Out of the clash of deeds and policies, the genius or the malice of outstanding individuals, the unthinking obedience or the revulsion of the mass, the victories, defeats, migrations, conquests, and settlements, the social struggles, the shifting currents of trade, and all the infinite variety of a thousand and one other factors, something new is constantly coming to birth; and what is born in this way is neither a haphazard nor an arbitrary creation, but stands in a logical sequence to all that has preceded it. From the impasse of fourth-century politics, with the crisis of inter-state relations after Mantinea, the revival and impact of Macedon, and the social and economic problems of the Greek mainland, sprang Macedonian hegemony, the plan to conquer Persia, and the Hellenistic Age with its new values. The unravelling of this pattern is also the task of the historian.

At this stage he is no longer concerned with reliving the past. When Glotz brought the third-century temple accounts from Delos into relation with the fourth-century wage rates from Eleusis, he was able to tell a story about the standard of living among labourers in the Aegean area in the early Hellenistic period which had never existed before in anyone's mind:[59] it had been there objectively in the social relations of ordinary men, no doubt experienced by each one as domestic hardship and distress, but never reduced to the form and context in which Glotz now presented it. This kind of history is concerned with trends and currents; and because it must necessarily pass from the specific to the general, it is a perpetual invitation to discover schemes and patterns which transfer the motivation of events and the responsibility for their occurrence from the control of men to some mystical power or realm existing outside the process of events. Here, if he is not constantly on the alert, the historian will find logical and verbal abstractions, puffed up into metaphysical entities, waiting around every corner. But it is a risk he must run: for the full understanding of the past requires its interpretation not merely in the light of the past, but also in the light of the future – our past and present.

This distinction can help us, I think, in approaching the problem of Greek nationality. The idea of a Greek nation is alien to the

[58] *Op. cit.* (n. 1) 1.8: 'La storia infatti e eminentemente creatrice, vale a dire consiste nel perenne superamento di quel che in qualsiasi istante e dato.'
[59] *Journal des Savants* 11 (1913) 16, 206, 251; *cf.* W. W. Tarn in *The Hellenistic age* (Cambridge, 1923) 108ff.

thought of most Greeks at most periods throughout Greek history. Consequently when one tries to pin it down, it seems to dissolve, or reveals itself only in the sentiments of the exceptional person now and then; and its influence on action is negligible. Yet, when we analyse the course of Greek history in the light of after-knowledge, we can clearly trace a movement towards integration in larger units, arising out of the circumstances existing from time to time, taking various forms including synoecism and federalism, and possible because ultimately the Greeks felt themselves to be a single people, ὅμαιμόν τε καὶ ὁμόγλωσσον [of the same blood and of the same language]. In that sense Greek unity and even the Greek nation are concepts which can be studied and discussed without patent absurdity.

This trend towards integration was diverted into various channels and failed to complete itself – for reasons which have been emphasised repeatedly. From this failure what lesson is the historian to draw? Is he indeed to draw any lesson at all? 'Past events', wrote Polybius (XII.25e.6), 'make us pay particular attention to the future, if we really make thorough enquiry in each case into the past.' 'If my history be judged useful by those enquirers who desire an exact knowledge of the past as an aid to the interpretation of the future', wrote Thucydides (1.22.4), '... I shall be content.' To draw such lessons implies the passing of judgements on the past, and those judgements must be made *ex eventu*. To many historians this involves an illegitimate step, which they condemn as rank intellectual snobbery towards the past, with its assumption of 'We know better!' For example, in his inaugural lecture at Rome on the essence and characteristics of Greek history,[60] De Sanctis claimed that 'we ought not to do the actors in the drama of Greek history the injustice of closing with a *fabula docet*, and so pointing out to them what they ought to have done in place of what they actually did'. But is there really any injustice towards the past – which indeed lies beyond justice and injustice – in trying to judge its achievements in the light of knowledge which it never possessed – provided always that we keep this activity quite distinct from that of analysing the past in its own terms? In the days before we adopted sociology and psychology as our guides to action, men learnt their sociology and psychology from the salutary lessons of history. Some may feel that we should still be prepared to study those lessons and that a historian ought not to shrink from pointing them.

---

[60] *Op. cit.* (n. 9) 27.

For after all, though the historian is apt to believe that the subject he has chosen for study is one which he came to by chance, or because it seemed to have been neglected, or because it arose out of some earlier work, or for some other wholly personal reason, fifty years hence it will be quite obvious that the themes chosen by historians today, and the treatment accorded to them, were directly related to contemporary problems, or, to use De Sanctis' words,[61] to the spiritual needs of men and women living in the middle of the twentieth century. 'La vita è maestra della storia', he writes: life is the master of history – but conversely history is the master of life. Between the two there is a Heracleitean flux; and if it is the needs of our own time which determine our selection of historical themes, are we not then entitled to receive from our studies in exchange, not merely the enrichment of experience which comes from an added understanding of the integration of all that is past in the present – for this integrated essence is often subtle and remote – but also that wisdom which is the fruit of watching men partly like and partly unlike ourselves meeting, and either solving or failing to solve, problems that are partly like and partly unlike those which we ourselves have to face? If this is also one of the legitimate tasks of history, we can still turn with profit to the problem of Greek national unity.[62]

---

[61] *Op. cit.* (n. 1) 1.9–10; *cf.* Bengtson, *op. cit.* (n. 39) 2.
[62] This paper was read before the General Meeting of the Classical Association at Liverpool on 3 April 1951.

11 *Greeks and Others: From Antiquity to the Renaissance*†

ROBERT BROWNING

It is a commonplace both of sociological theory and of everyday experience that a human group often perceives and defines itself partly in terms of that which it is not – the Other. The Other is usually conceived not as a heterogeneous melange of different groups whose only common characteristic is that they are not Us. It is more often seen as a single group which is the antithesis of Us, marked by weakness where We display strength, by vice where We show virtue. In fact it may be a kind of mirror-image of ourselves rather than an entity belonging to the world of reality. The rhetoric of contemporary international relations illustrates the need to postulate an Other in order to define and legitimate what one is oneself.

Of course only individuals conceive or perceive. These words can be used only metaphorically of groups. But what individuals perceive or conceive is largely socially determined. The metaphor is one which usefully helps to describe reality. It is shared perceptions and commonly held conceptions which distinguish a community from a crowd.

An individual may today identify himself with different groups, and so postulate a different Other, for different purposes. Thus he may perceive himself as a citizen of his own city, as an inhabitant of a particular region, as a member of a particular linguistic or religious or professional group, as well as of a larger and more all-embracing group. In the world of today this larger group is usually a nation-state which in principle has sharply defined boundaries, both geographical and conceptual, and is intolerant of divided loyalties or 'grey areas'. This multiple self-perception, though it may create

---

† Originally published in Robert Browning, *History, Language and Literacy in the Byzantine World* (Variorum: Northampton, 1989), Ch. 2.

tension both within groups and in the minds of individuals, is not necessarily a mark of deviousness or dissidence, but reflects the complexity of the structure of human society. This was all the more true in earlier periods, where multiple self-perception was the rule rather than the exception. An obvious example in antiquity is St. Paul, who was a leading member of a Jewish community, a citizen of Tarsos in Cilicia – which was, as he remarked, 'no mean city' – a Roman citizen when he found himself in trouble with the local authorities, and a leader of the network of Christian communities which was beginning to form itself over large areas of the Roman Empire.

In the present paper I will try to examine the changing self-perception and self-identification within Greek society from classical antiquity till the fifteenth century, and the changing Other which helped the Greeks to define themselves. For a Greek of the fifth century B.C. – I do not wish here to discuss the archaic period, which poses different problems – the primary focus of a man's identity was his city. It was this which determined the dialect in which he spoke and thought, the religious observances in which he took part – though not his religious beliefs – the laws under which he lived, the wars in which he fought, the economic activities in which he engaged, whom he could marry, where his ancestors were buried, and the whole pattern and style of his life. A man was an Athenian, a Spartan, a Corinthian, an Argive, and he could neither change his city nor could he – except in a purely formal sense, should another city confer honorary citizenship on him – be a citizen of more than one city. For him the Other was a citizen of some other city, who was different from himself, and fundamentally different. He might be slightly ridiculous – one need recall only Aristophanes' Boeotians and Megarians – and he might often be menacing and hostile. The distinction between citizen and *xenos* [foreigner] was always of the utmost importance though it was a distinction between Greeks.[1] Thus the epitaph on the Athenian cavalrymen killed in a battle in the mid fifth century – perhaps the battle of Tanagra in 457 – addresses them as follows:

> Χαίρετ' ἀριστῆες πολέμου μέγα κῦδος ἔχοντες
> κοῦροι Ἀθηναίων, ἔξοχοι ἱπποσύνῃ
> οἵ ποτε καλλιχόρου περὶ πατρίδος ὠλέσαθ' ἥβην
> πλείστοις Ἑλλήνων ἀντία μαρνάμενοι.

---

[1] Cf. R. Sealey, *A History of the Greek City States 700–338 B.C.* (Berkeley–Los Angeles–London, 1976) 238; G.E.M. de Ste. Croix, *The Class Struggle in the Ancient Greek World* (London, 1981) 94–95.

[Greetings, you champions, you have the great glory of war, young men
of Athens, excellent in horsemanship, you who, for your fatherland of the
beautiful dances, have given your youth, fighting against the majority of the
Greeks.]

AP 7.254

The opposition between the κοῦροι Ἀθηναίων ['youths of the
Athenians'] and πλεῖστοι Ἑλλήνων ['the majority of the Greeks']
could not emerge more clearly.

But every Greek also shared a larger identity, as Greek opposed
to non-Greek or barbarian,[2] and he was usually in no doubt where
the boundaries of Greekness lay. Macedonian or Epirot royal houses
might occasionally cause problems – royal personages in many
societies are of ambiguous status – but otherwise there was usually
no doubt about whether an individual was Greek or not. What
were the defining characteristics of Greekness in the fifth century?
Herodotus tells us when he puts in the mouth of an anonymous
Athenian, whom a Macedonian king is trying to persuade not to
resist the Persians in 480, these words: αὖτις δὲ τὸ Ἑλληνικόν, ἐὸν
ὅμαιμόν τε καὶ ὁμόγλωσσον, καὶ θεῶν ἱδρύματά τε κοινὰ καὶ δυσίαι
ἤθεά τε ὁμότροπα, τῶν προδότας γενέσθαι Ἀθηναίους οὐκ ἂν εὖ
ἔχοι ['and then, the common Greek identity, our being of the same
blood and the same language, our common temples of the gods
and our sacrifices and our similar customs: it would be not well for
the Athenians to become betrayers of these things'] (Hdt 8.144.2).
So common descent, real or imagined, common language, common
religious institutions and observances, and a common way of life
were what marked a man as Greek. He who lacked any of these was
a barbarian, the Other. He might be threatening; or he might be
ridiculous, as is the King's Eye in Aristophanes' *Acharnians*. In the
years following the Persian wars he might be the object of a certain
gloating chauvinism, as are the Persians in Aeschylus' *Persae*, or even
of a contempt which had racist overtones, as are the Egyptians in the
same poet's *Suppliants*.[3] But he was always puzzlingly different and
more often than not somewhat menacing. As I illustrated the opposition between citizen and *xenos* by a public epitaph on soldiers killed
in battle, let me illustrate the solidarity between Greeks in the face of
non-Greeks by another such epitaph, that on the Athenians who fell
at Chaeronea in 338:

[2] On the complex and changing semantics of *barbaros* cf. Y.A. Dauge, *Le barbare:
Recherches sur la conception de la barbarie et de la civilisation* (Brussels, 1981); H. and R.
Kahane, 'On the meanings of Barbarus', Ἑλληνικά' (1986) 129–132.
[3] Cf. Martin Bernal, *Black Athena* (London–New Brunswick, 1987) 90.

Εἰ τὸ καλῶς θνήσκειν ἀρετῆς μέρος ἐστὶ μέγιστον,
ἡμῖν ἐκ πάντων τοῦτ' ἀπένειμε Τύχη
Ἑλλάδι γὰρ σπεύδοντες ἐλευθερίην περιθεῖναι
κείμεθ' ἀγηράτῳ χρώμενοι εὐλογίῃ.

[If to die well is the best part of courage, then to us above all others fortune has
granted this. For it is because we strove to give liberty to Greece that we lie here,
enjoying a glory that does not age.]

AP 7.253

Before we are carried away by over-simplified notions of patriotism,
let us remember that the enemy against whom these men were fighting, if the occasion of the inscription is as generally believed, was
Philip II of Macedonia, a barbarian in the eyes of many, but who
traced his ancestry back to Herakles, and whose forefathers had been
admitted to compete in the Olympic Games, an exclusively Hellenic
religious festival, more than a century and a half earlier. Philip's ambiguous status in the eyes of his contemporaries becomes clear when
we recall that at one and the same time Demosthenes in the 40s and
early 30s of the fourth century spoke of him contemptuously as
a barbarian from Pella,[4] while Isocrates was reminding him that
Ἄργος ἐστί σοι πατρίς ['Argos is your fatherland'] (Isocr., *Philip* 32).
The same Isocrates had observed as early as 380 that Athens had by
his time made the name of Hellene refer no longer to birth but to
culture: τὸ τῶν Ἑλλήνων ὄνομα πεποίηκεν μηκέτι τοῦ γένους, ἀλλὰ
τῆς διανοίας δοκεῖν εἶναι, καὶ μᾶλλον Ἕλληνας καλεῖσθαι τοὺς τῆς
παιδεύσεως τῆς ἡμετέρας ἢ τοὺς τῆς κοινῆς φύσεως μετέχοντας
['she has made it so that the name of the Greeks suggests no longer
a race (*genos*) but an intelligence, and that to be called "Greeks" is
given rather to those who share in our culture than to those who
share a common nature'] (Isocr., *Panegyricus* 50). Not all his contemporaries would have accepted this formulation without qualification.
Nevertheless it is clear that old distinctions were already becoming
blurred, and new ones were emerging in their place. These new distinctions reflected, if often vaguely and imperfectly, the new shape
which Greek society was gradually taking.

The Hellenistic kingdoms were too ephemeral and often too
nakedly exploitative to win true intellectual or emotional commitment, even when they engaged the political loyalty of their subjects.
No epitaphs commemorate soldiers who sacrificed their lives for the
Ptolemies of Egypt or the Seleucids of Syria. Many factors tended in

---

[4] Dem. 3.26, 18.68, with the revealing scholion on 3.16 in M.R. Dilts, *Scholia
Demosthenica*, 1 (Leipzig, 1983) 93, which reevaluates Philip as a Greek.

the early Hellenistic period to diminish the role of the city as a focus of identity and to increase that of the Greek community as a whole. In the first place there was massive emigration from the old Greek world to the new royal cities founded from the Nile to the Indus. It cannot be even approximately quantified, but it certainly led to the emergence of many Greek urban communities whose members had neither common descent nor common religious or political traditions. Secondly, Greeks travelled more frequently and farther than they had before, as mercenary soldiers, settlers, actors, doctors, athletes and others moved to and fro across the vastly extended Hellenistic world. Thirdly, the old epichoric Greek dialects were replaced for all public communication by the new *koine dialektos* [common dialect], which soon became the normal language of all Greek cities.† Fourthly, in the new Hellenistic kingdoms Greeks often formed a ruling elite among an alien majority. Hence arose an almost exaggerated emphasis on Greekness, the maintenance of which was fostered by exclusive social and educational institutions such as the gymnasium and the school, which took similar form throughout the Hellenistic world. Droysen's view that the Hellenistic period saw mutual Hellenisation of the east and orientalisation of Greek society has been long rejected in favour of more complex models. Alexander's vision of a fusion of Greek and Persian society was tacitly abandoned by his successors. Instead we find a more or less homogeneous Greek culture, which only later and only slowly began to absorb elements of the indigenous cultures of the subject peoples. It is typical that in Ai Khanum, on the left bank of the Oxus (Amu Darya), in northern Afghanistan, a column was set up in the third century inscribed with 140 moral maxims copied from a similar column in the sanctuary of Apollo in Delphi.[5] And when the great Mauryan king Asoka in the third century B.C. sought to promote Buddhism in the far north-western territories of his empire he set up in Kandahar an inscription outlining Buddhist moral teachings in Aramaic and Greek.[6]

These and other factors led to a change in the self-image of the Greeks. The distinction between Greek and barbarian overshadowed that between citizen and *xenos*. The Other par excellence was the barbarian, who was looked on with mingled contempt, curiosity, and occasionally disquiet.

---

† See here Ch. 6 (Morpurgo Davies).
[5] L. Robert, 'De Delphes à l'Oxus', *CRAI* 1968, 416–457.
[6] D. Schlumberger, 'Une nouvelle inscription grecque d'Açoka', *CRAI* 1964, 126–140.

Rome, when she first appeared on the eastern Mediterranean scene, was the object of disinterested scientific curiosity, but soon she became the object of crucial political decisions for the Hellenistic cities and states. How were the Romans to be fitted into traditional classifications, ethnic and political? Prima facie they belonged to the barbarian world. Plautus, in his brilliant adaptations of Greek New Comedy for the Roman stage, makes a joke of his fellow-countrymen being described as barbarians, as in the prologue to the *Trinummus* (probably authentic) 'Plautus vortit barbare' ['Plautus translated it into barbarian'] or *Miles Gloriosus* 211, where Naevius is called 'poeta barbarus' ['barbarian poet'] or *Stichus* 193 'ut mores barbaros discam' ['so I may learn barbarian customs']. His grave contemporary the elder Cato complains indignantly of the Greeks, 'nos quoque dictitant barbaros, et spurcius nos quam alios opicon appellatione foedant' ['they are always calling us barbarians and to dirty us more than others they give us the nickname of the Opici' (an Italian people)] (Pliny *NH* 29.7.15). Eratosthenes, who found the division of humanity into Hellenes and barbarians an unsatisfactory one, observes that that there are bad Greeks and good barbarians, such as the Romans and the Carthaginians, οὕτω θαυμαστῶς πολιτευομένους ['whose politics are arranged so marvellously'] (Strabo 1.4.9).

Perhaps mankind could be divided into three classes, Greeks, Romans and barbarians. This threefold division – which would have made Aristotle turn in his grave – turns up in both Greek and Latin writers. Examples are Philo, *De vita contemplativa* 48 τῆς Ἰταλικῆς πολυτελείας καὶ τρυφῆς, ἣν ἐζήλωσαν Ἕλληνές τε καὶ βάρβαροι ['the extravagance and luxury of Italy, envied by both Greeks and barbarians'] or Plutarch, *De fortuna Romanorum* 324B, ὁ δὲ Ῥωμαίων μέγας δαίμων ... παραμείνας βεβαίως ἐν γῇ καὶ θαλάττῃ καὶ πολέμοις καὶ εἰρήνῃ καὶ πρὸς Ἕλληνας καὶ πρὸς βαρβάρους ['The great guardian spirit of the Romans ... remained steadfast (by the city) both on land and sea, in war and in peace, against Greeks and against barbarians'] or Cicero, *De finibus* 2.49 'non solum Graecia et Italia sed etiam omnis barbaria' [not only Greece and Italy but even all of the barbarian land (lit.: all of 'Barbaria')]) or *De divinatione* 1.84 'si Graeci, si barbari, si maiores etiam nostri' ['Greeks, barbarians, even our own ancestors']. These testimonies date from the first century B.C. or later, but it is a reasonable assumption that the threefold classification originates much earlier.

A third possibility was that the Romans were really Greeks, albeit rather odd ones. Theories of the Greek origin of Rome abounded in Hellenistic times, since they satisfied the amour propre of both parties. They are reflected in Virgil's *Aeneid*, when Aeneas the Trojan finds the Arcadian Evander settled with his followers on the banks of the Tiber, on the future site of Rome. Several less familiar versions of the theory are to be found in the first book of Dionysius of Halicarnassus' *Roman Antiquities*, which was written expressly to demonstrate that the founders of Rome were Greek.

It has often been pointed out, and most recently and lucidly by Erich Gruen, that the Greeks of the Hellenistic age, even men as well-informed and perceptive as Polybios, generally failed to understand the structure and functioning of Roman society, and when they thought they did, they were more often than not disastrously wrong. 'There was no image of Rome in Greece, rather a succession of images coming in and out of focus. The westerner kept breaking patterns and frustrating attempts at configuration. To those who had to come to terms with it Roman behaviour was infuriatingly erratic, the combination of sluggishness and volatility unfathomable.'[7] How far this fatal misunderstanding was due to the dominance in Greek political and intellectual circles of the traditional antithesis of Greek and barbarian I leave to wiser heads than mine to decide. But it must have been disconcerting to tidy minds to be unable to determine whether the greatest military power in the Mediterranean world belonged to Us or to Them. Were the Romans really Greeks in fancy dress, or were they an inscrutable and menacing Other? In the meantime Rome proceeded to establish her domination over the Greek world.

Five centuries elapsed between the virtual end of Greek independence at the battle of Pydna in 168 B.C. and the foundation of Constantinople in 330 A.D. It is worth reminding ourselves that this is a period roughly equal to that which separates Christopher Columbus from Ronald Reagan, Ivan the Terrible from Mikhail Gorbachev, or Chaucer from Tennyson. Change was no doubt slower in general in the ancient world than it is today. Nevertheless these centuries saw a radical transformation in the Greeks' perception of themselves and others. The first few generations were marked by uncontrolled Roman exploitation of the new provinces – the names of Lucius Mummius and Gaius Verres remind us of some aspects of this exploitation – as well as by sporadic Greek resistance to Roman

---

[7] E.S. Gruen, *The Hellenistic World and the Coming of Rome* (Berkeley–Los Angeles–London, 1984), 1, 356. The whole of Chapter 10, 'The Greek View of Roman Expansion', pp. 316–357, provides a most illuminating treatment of this topic.

domination, culminating in the initial victories and final cataclysmic defeat of Mithradates IV, king of Pontos, in the first quarter of the first century B.C. Rome was then for most Greek communities – be they cities, confederations or kingdoms – the great Other, with whom one had either to seek accommodation or to risk an unequal confrontation.

With the stabilisation of Roman power, the end of the Roman civil wars, and the establishment of the Principate, accommodation becomes the rule on both sides. Yet there continued to be great tension and uncertainty in Greek communities. It was sometimes complicated by the Roman practice of granting citizenship to individuals in Hellenic cities. As early as 7 B.C. the inhabitants of Cyrene were divided into Greeks, Romans, and Greeks who also held Roman citizenship, and conflicts of interest existed between the groups. Such structures of democratic self-government as still existed in Greek cities were gradually dismantled or suppressed, usually with the warm approval and acquiescence of the upper classes of those cities.[8]

Individual cities became less dominant centres of identification than they had been in Hellenistic, let alone in classical times. Men might see themselves as belonging to a Roman province, which was itself sometimes the continuation of a much older ethnic or political unit. Or they might identify primarily with the larger world of Greek language, life and culture, for which Rome was the Other, powerful and unpredictable, intellectually and artistically inferior, but no longer positively hostile.

Even in the comfortable world of the Flavian emperors, of Hadrian, or the Antonines, with its relative prosperity, its common culture extending from the Clyde to the Euphrates, its flourishing trade, its lively Greek intellectual life – the age which Gibbon called 'the period in the history of the world during which the condition of the human race was most happy and prosperous' – even then we find too many expressions of unease about the situation of the Greek community within the Roman Empire to be lightly dismissed. Dio Chrysostom of Prusa, friend of three Roman emperors, reminds the citizens of Tarsos that 'leadership and power are vested in others' (*Or.* 34.48), and in another speech declares that 'nothing that goes on in the cities escapes the notice of the Roman authorities' – οὐ λανθάνει τῶν ἐν ταῖς πόλεσιν οὐδὲν τοὺς ἡγεμόνας· λέγω δὲ τοὺς

---

[8] See the evidence set out most fully by G.E.M. de Ste. Croix, *The Class Struggle in the Ancient Greek World* (London, 1981) 518–537.

μείζονας τῶν ἐνθάδε ['I speak of the more important ones in these parts'] (*Or.* 46.14). Plutarch, a Roman citizen, familiar with Roman history and institutions, and a man of eirenic disposition, when he offers advice to a young man recently elected to a magistracy in his city, warns him not to recall what Perikles said to himself – ἐλευθέρων ἄρχεις, Ἑλλήνων ἄρχεις, πολιτῶν Ἀθηναίων ['You are ruling free men, you are ruling Greeks, Athenian citizens']. Rather is he to remind himself that ἀρχόμενος ἄρχεις ὑποτεταγμένης πόλεως ἀνθυπάτοις, ἐπιτρόποις Καίσαρος ['You rule and are ruled, ruling a city that is controlled by proconsuls, the agents of Caesar']. He is not to τῷ στεφάνῳ πολὺ φρόνημα πιστεύειν, ὅρωντα τοὺς καλτίους ἐπάνω τῆς κεφαλῆς ['have great pride and trust in his crown, when you see the boots (of Roman soldiers) above your head']; higher than the crown of office is the senatorial boot (Latin *calceus*) of the Roman governor. He is to be like a skilled musician, and not παρεκβαίνειν τοὺς ῥυθμοὺς καὶ τὰ μέτρα της διδομένης ἐξουσίας ὑπο τῶν κρατούντων ['go beyond the degree of liberty in rhythms and metres permitted by those in authority']. Failure to do this will bring not συριγμός or χλευασμός ['hissing' or 'jeering']; upon many has fallen δεινὸς κολαστὴς πέλεκυς αυχένος τομεύς ['that terrible chastiser, the axe that cuts the neck'] – a line from a lost tragedy (Plutarch, *Praecepta gerundae reipublicae* 813e). Greek opinions on the emperor Nero throw an interesting light on Greek attitudes to Roman power. In general Nero had a bad press in antiquity. However the exhibitionistic Philhellenism which he displayed during his visit to Greece in 66/7 and in particular his proclamation of the 'freedom of the Greeks' in Corinth, were taken seriously by such level-headed witnesses as Plutarch and Dio Chrysostom. Cf. Plutarch, *De sera numinum vindicta* 22 (*Mor.* 567ff.) and Dio Chrysostom, *Or.* 21.9–10. A legend soon grew that Nero had not been killed, but was still alive and would return. Three false Neros appeared in the Greek-speaking regions of the Empire in the generation after his death, at least one of whom found general support among the Greek cities.[9]

There was, however, another way of looking at things. Lucian (ca. 120–180) was perhaps the first Greek to describe the whole Roman Empire as 'us'.[10] Aelius Aristides (ca. 120–ca. 190) illustrates both the conflict in the mind of self-conscious Greeks and the way in which that conflict was beginning to be resolved. On the one hand

[9] On the proclamation of freedom cf. F. Millar, *The Emperor in the Roman World* (London, 1971) 530ff.; on the false Neros cf. B.H. Warmington, *Nero: Reality and Legend* (London, 1969) 167–168.

[10] Cf. C.F. Jones, *Culture and Society in Lucian* (Harvard, 1986) 48–50, 89.

he displays an almost obsessive concern with the purity of the Greek language and with Greek culture and history, and praises Athens as the symbol of Greek culture and by implication of culture in general; these were common features of the ideology of the Second Sophistic. On the other hand he sees in Rome the great unifier, which enables both Greeks and others to transcend their Particularism. The Romans, he says, did not refuse to give their citizenship to others: 'on the contrary, you sought its extension as a worthy aim, and you have caused the word Roman to be the label, not of membership in a city, but of some common nationality, and this not just one among others, but one balancing all the rest. For the categories into which you now divide the world are not Hellenes and barbarians … The division which you have substituted is one into Romans and non-Romans … Many in every city are fellow-citizens of yours no less than of their own kinsmen, though some of them have not yet seen this city. There is no need of garrisons to hold their citadels, but the men of greatest standing and influence in every city guard their own fatherlands for you. And you have a double hold upon the cities, both from here and from your fellow-citizens in each.'[11] In other words many Greeks were now beginning to perceive themselves as Romans, without being any less Greeks at the same time. The same change emerges from the way in which Greek sophists no longer confine themselves to a local or regional role, but act as advisers to emperors and as a kind of lobby at the centre of imperial power. Greek notables begin, too, to play an active part in Roman administration and politics. A striking example from a slightly later period is Cassius Dio Cocceianus (ca. 150–ca. 235), both high Roman official and twice consul, and Greek man of letters. A less obvious testimony to this fusion of Greek and Roman identity is to be found in Gregory Thaumatourgos' (ca. 213–ca. 270) *Address to Origen*, in which the Cappadocian bishop expresses admiration for the perfection of Roman law and concludes by calling it συνελόντι εἰπεῖν Ἑλληνικώτατος ['in a word, most Greek'] (Greg. Thaumat. *Ad Origenem* 1, PG 10.1053A).

The period of Late Antiquity, from Constantine to Heraclius, saw three important developments which profoundly affected the perception by the Greeks of themselves and others. First of all Roman power in the Latin west declined and in many regions entirely collapsed. Personal and cultural links between the two halves of the

---

[11] Aelius Aristides, Εἰς Ῥώμην 63–64, trans. J.H. Oliver, *The Ruling Power* (Transactions of the American Philosophical Society 43 (1953) 902).

Empire gradually became fewer and looser. In the course of the fifth century Germanic kingdoms established themselves in Britain, Gaul, Spain, Africa, and finally in Italy itself. Their autonomy might sometimes be disguised under a fig-leaf of theoretical Roman authority. But in fact there was beginning in each of them the process of fusion of Roman and Germanic institutions and practices which underlay the formation of medieval western Europe. Greek and Roman began to coincide in a new way. The only real Romans left were now Greeks, and Romans they more and more called themselves, leaving 'Hellene' in its New Testament sense of 'pagan'.

Secondly, cities had largely lost what autonomy they had, and many of them in this period declined in size and importance. The ancient links between a city and its rural territory were often broken. A man's city no longer served as a primary focus of identity, men began to identify themselves by the province or region from which they came rather than by their native city, membership of which no longer brought any significant advantage. John the Cappadocian and John the Lydian are typical appellations in the age of Justinian. And just as men were identified by their province, so also were the all-pervading demons. When St. Theodore of Sykeon in Bithynia, around 600, encountered some demons of unusual character, they addressed him thus: οὐκ ἐσμὲν ἐκ τῆς συνοδίας ταύτης, ἀλλ' ἐκ τῶν μερῶν Καππαδοκίας πάρεσμεν ἐνθάδε ['We are not from this congregation, but we come here from the province of Cappadocia']. And being Cappadocian demons, they besought him in the name of St. George of Cappadocia to spare them.[12]

Last, and most important of all, was the complex of processes often lumped together under the heading of 'The Christianisation of the Roman Empire'. The outcome of these processes was the emergence in the late fourth and fifth century of Christianity as the dominant ideology – though not necessarily one entertained by the majority of its inhabitants – of what now became the Christian Roman Empire, a state which enjoyed a special metaphysical status and a supernatural legitimacy. Roman and Christian now became synonyms, as did pagan and barbarian. As well as the barbarian Other beyond the borders of the Empire, there was now also an internal Other, or rather several internal Others. Apart from such unassimilable groups as Jews and Manichaeans, there was the dwindling band of overt or covert pagans, who could easily be identified with the bearers of classical culture. These were from time to

---

[12] *La vie de Théodore de Sykéon*, ed. A.-J. Festugière (Brussels, 1970) 139.

time subjected to discrimination or persecution, as in 529, when inter alia the activity of the Academy at Athens was severely curtailed, if not terminated. 'Hellene' came to be more and more restricted to its New Testament sense of 'pagan', which it retained for centuries in Byzantine discourse. But classical culture was not generally rejected; it had been 'sanitised' by the fourth-century Fathers, and so formed part of the Hellenic-Christian amalgam which was the basis of Byzantine culture.

However, the most interesting Others were now members of sectarian Christian groups, who were excluded from the privileges of those whose beliefs had been authorised or confirmed by Church Councils – the 'true believers' or Orthodox – and whose very existence was regarded as a threat to the special status of the Empire. Among these sectarians there stood out the Monophysites. In the sixth century, from being a dissident group within the church, they became a counter-church, with its own hierarchy and its own theological literature. Its power base lay in Egypt, and to a lesser degree in Syria, both regions of predominantly non-Greek population. Book 1, Title 5 of Justinian's *Code* contains a long series of enactments limiting the legal rights and the personal freedom of dissident Christians and other internal Others. It is a dismal and depressing reminder of the strength of human intolerance.

The turbulent seventh and eighth centuries saw much loss of imperial territory. Palestine, Syria, Egypt and North Africa passed under the rule of the Muslim Arabs, while much of the Balkans lay open to invasion and settlement by Slavs, sometimes pushing southwards in tribal groups, sometimes organised and directed by Avar or Bulgar rulers. Virtual deurbanisation of many regions of the Empire and massive displacements of population undermined civic and regional identity. Roman, Greek (if not used in its sense of 'pagan') and Christian became synonymous terms, counterposed to 'foreigner', 'barbarian', 'infidel'. The citizens of the Empire, now predominantly of Greek ethnicity and language, were often called simply ὁ χριστώνυμος λαός ['the people who bear Christ's name']. War became the principal activity of the state, and it took on some of the characteristics of the Muslim *jihad*. The *Tactica* of Leo VI, which incorporates much earlier material, has a revealing section on the duties of καντάτορες [military musicians], whose task it was to elevate and maintain the morale of the soldiers. They were to remind them of the μισθὸν τῆς εἰς θεὸν πίστεως καὶ τὰς ἐκ βασιλέως εὐεργεσίας ['the reward for faith in God and the benefits that came from the king']. Their struggle was ὑπερ θεοῦ καὶ τῆς εἰς αὐτὸν ἀγάπης καὶ ὑπὲρ ὅλου τοῦ ἔθνους ['for God and their love for him and for the whole people']. It was κατὰ τῶν τοῦ θεοῦ ἐχθρῶν ['against the enemies of God']. The Romans τὸν θεὸν ἔχομεν φίλον τὸν ἔχοντα ἐξουσίαν τῆς ῥοπῆς τοῦ πολέμου ['have a beloved God with the power to turn the scales of war']. They were fighting for kinsmen and friends and country and ὑπὲρ ὅλου τοῦ ἔθνους ἡμῶν ['for the whole of our people']. They would win αἰωνία μνήμη ['eternal memory'] and rewards both from God and from the Emperor.[13] There is here a concatenation of old and new motifs – among the latter incidentally one of the earliest instances of the use of *ethnos* in its modern positive sense – which suggest an ideologically united and ethnically homogeneous community, preoccupied above all with the 'holy war' against the forces of Islam. The reality may have been less simple; this is after all a piece of official propaganda. However the confrontation with the Arabs was real enough. Yet at the same time there was a quite close contact between the two communities, with ambiguous loyalty in the border regions, institutionalised defection by individuals and groups, intermarriage and cultural exchange, all of which are mirrored in the epic of Digenis Akritas. As often happens, there was some discrepancy between the image which a group forms of itself and its real behaviour. With time, as the thrust of Muslim expansion was more and more directed eastwards, and as the Caliphate became weak and divided, the heat and passion went out of the confrontation with Islam – though it always remained a commonplace of Byzantine political and religious rhetoric – and more stable relations were established.

There had always been Christian communities beyond the borders of the Christian Roman Empire, in Armenia, Georgia, Nubia, Ethiopia, and above all in the Latin west. They were perceived, when they were perceived at all, as part of the χριστώνυμος λαός ['people who bear Christ's name']. That they were not also part of the Christian Empire was a mere temporary aberration. What posed in sharp form the problem of Christians who were not Romans and of Christian states which owed no allegiance to the Empire was the conversion of Bulgaria in 864/5, and to a lesser degree that of Kievan Rus' in 988. Before the conversion, Bulgaria clearly belonged to the Other. Which side of the divide was it on now? The dilemma was clear during the reign of Symeon. The patriarch and regent Nicholas Mysticus writes to him both as a fellow-Christian and as a sharer in Greek culture, both of which indeed he was. Yet at the same time

---

[13] *Leonis imperatoris tactica*, ed R. Vari (Budapest, 1922) Const. 12.71, pp. 60–62.

Symeon's army was besieging Constantinople, and a little later he had himself proclaimed Emperor of the Bulgarians and the Romans – βασιλεὺς τῶν Βουλγάρων καὶ τῶν Ῥωμαίων. It seems too that for a time he had influential adherents in Byzantine society. This may well reflect genuine uncertainty about where the boundary between Us and Them lay. A solution was found to the dilemma. Symeon died and with him the driving force of Bulgarian expansionism. His son and successor was married to a Byzantine princess, and Bulgaria became a member of the family of Christian nations, of which the emperor was the head. But this political solution clashed with the realities of power and of popular feeling in Byzantium – and probably in Bulgaria too. By the end of the tenth century Bulgaria, Christian though it was, had become the enemy who must be destroyed. The unexampled ferocity with which it was crushed is perhaps a measure of the acuity of the problem presented by powerful non-Roman Christian communities in conflict with the Byzantine Empire. The Rus' were farther away, and were only occasionally and briefly a threat to Byzantium after their conversion. They were not a permanent problem. Yet they could be, and from time to time were, perceived as part of the menacing Other. Michael Psellos writes of them that 'This barbarian nation had consistently cherished an insane hatred for the Roman Empire, and on every possible occasion, first on one imaginary pretext, then on another, they waged war against us' (Psellos, *Chronographia* 6.91). No mention here of the family of Christian nations; the Rus' are perceived as the archetypal Other.

What finally made the identity of Greek, Roman and Christian an untenable fiction was relations with the Latin west, both with secular rulers and with the Roman church. In the course of the eleventh and twelfth centuries confrontation at different levels became more and more frequent. There was religious antagonism. The Photian schism of the 860s was half forgotten, but the schism of 1054, though strictly speaking it concerned only a particular Pope and a particular patriarch, was symptomatic of the growing tension. Byzantine rulers and churchmen, and Byzantine society in general, were suspicious of papal claims to supremacy, in which they saw a challenge to the special status of church and state in the Byzantine Empire. Argument began over differences in doctrine and practice which had been ignored for centuries. There was military conflict, first with Norman attacks on Byzantine territory from the late eleventh century, then with the Crusades. These presented in the first place a threat to Byzantine internal security. Then their war aims were at variance with Byzantine foreign policy. The ambivalent status of the regimes which they set up, sometimes on territory which had been until recently Byzantine, and the overt anti-Byzantine declarations of some of their leaders, were seen as threatening the integrity of the Empire. There were economic contradictions too, as the privileges accorded to Venetian and Genoese traders appeared to threaten the Byzantine mercantile community, though in fact they may well have led to increased prosperity of Byzantine cities. There were increasingly abrasive personal contacts, as western colonies were established in Constantinople and elsewhere, and as westerners, often in origin mercenary soldiers, were appointed to high positions by the Comnenian emperors. All these factors made up a deadly witches' brew.

Greek identity became defined in contrast to western Christendom, which became in the twelfth century the Other par excellence. The westerners, from being fellow-Romans, became Franks or Latins, both of which were, and in Greek still are, pejorative terms. φραγγοστάφυλα ('Frankish grapes', i.e., blackcurrants) and φραγγόσυκα ('Frankish figs', i.e., prickly pears) are poor substitutes for real grapes and real figs. φραγγοπαναγία ('Frankish Madonna') is a somewhat offensive term denoting a simpering woman who pretends to be more virtuous than she is. There is a stereotype of the Latin. In Byzantine eyes he is arrogant, greedy, untrustworthy, cruel, he is perhaps not quite a real Christian. Niketas Choniates, a fair-minded man with wide experience of public office, characterises the Latins – without distinguishing between different western peoples – as follows:

> The most accursed Latins ... were filled with passionate longing for our blessings, they were ever ill-disposed towards our people, and remain forever workers of evil deeds. Though they may dissemble friendship, submitting to the needs of the time, yet they despise us as their bitterest enemies; and though their speech is affable and smoother than oil flowing noiselessly, yet are their words darts, and sharper than a two-edged sword. Between us and them the greatest gulf of disagreement has been fixed, and we are separated in purpose and diametrically opposed, even though we are closely associated and frequently share the same dwelling. Overweening in their pretentious display of straightforwardness, the Latins would stare up and down at us and behold with curiosity the gentleness and humility of our demeanour; and we, looking grimly upon their superciliousness, boastfulness and pomposity, with the drivel from their nose held in the air, are committed to this course and grit our teeth, secure in the power of Christ, who gives the faithful the power to tread on serpents and scorpions, and grants them protection from all harm and hurt. (Niketas Choniates, *History*, 301–302)

The westerner takes on the traditional characteristics of the barbarian – absence of order, boldness in attack but lack of staying power, brutality, and so on. Anna Comnena and later historians not infrequently call the western Christians *barbaroi*. In turn the westerners perceived the Greeks as devious, deceitful, cowardly, and corrupted by wealth.[14] There is even a physical stereotype of the westerner. He is tall and blond. He holds his head high. Why? Because, says the stereotype, he has chronic catarrh. Niketas Choniates and others speak of the *koryzos* [catarrh] of the Latins. A late twelfth-century churchman speaks of the κατακόρυζος φάρυγξ ['catarrh-filled throat'] of the *mixobarbaros* ['half-barbarian'] Pope Innocent III.[15]

The Byzantines are no longer the χριστώνυμος λαός ['people who bear Christ's name']. They are once again Romans – and in verse sometimes Ausones – and they are sometimes even Hellenes. There is a strong current of xenophobia in later twelfth-century Byzantium. Historians blame Manuel I for making Romans work for barbarians or foreigners. An orator congratulates Euphrosyne, the consort of Alexios III, on being a true Hellene. Riots are blamed on agitation by *xenoi* [foreigners]. In 1176 Venetians are expelled from every region of the Empire. In 1187 there is a massacre of Latins in Constantinople. In the 70s patriarch Michael of Anchialos – or possibly a contemporary pamphleteer writing in his name – advises Manuel I that subjection to the Muslims is to be preferred to rapprochment with the Latins.[16]

The disaster of the Fourth Crusade was traumatic, and its effects still colour Orthodox and post-Orthodox attitudes to the west, and not only in Greece. It confirmed the negative stereotypes on both sides. Niketas Choniates in his monody on the Frankish capture of Constantinople brings out with eloquence and passion all the traditional motifs of the Byzantine attitude to the Latin west, including the negative comparison of the westerners to the Muslims. His words are worth quoting in full:

> Such were the wrongs done by the armies from the west to Christ's chosen people. They showed no humanity to anyone, but stripped them of money and property, house and clothing, and left them nothing. These were the men of the brazen neck, the boastful spirit, the raised eyebrows, the youthful, shaven cheek, the bloodthirsty hand, the choleric nose, the lofty eye, the insatiable jaws, the unloving heart, the glib and piercing discourse that almost

---

[14] For western views of the Greeks in the age of the Crusades cf. the rich collection of material in B. Ebels-Hoving, *Byzantium in westerse ogen* (Assen, 1971).

[15] R. Browning, 'An Unpublished Address of Nicephorus Chrysoberges to Patriarch John X Kamateros of 1202', *Byzantine Studies/Etudes Byzantines* 5 (1978) 59–60.

[16] Chr. Loparev, 'Ob uniatstve Imperatora Manuila Komnina' *Viz. Vrem.* 14 (1907) 353.

danced upon their lips. These were the men who seemed to themselves understanding and wise, who kept their oath, loved truth and hated wickedness,
who were more pious and just than us Greeks, and kept more strictly Christ's
commandments, who bore the cross on their shoulders, and often swore by
it and by the Holy Scriptures to pass through Christian lands without shed-
ding blood, turning neither to left nor to right, to arm their hands against the
Saracens and to stain their swords with the blood of those who had sacked
Jerusalem, to offer no offence to women nor even to speak to them so long
as they wore the cross on their shoulders, for they had consecrated themselves to God and were marching in His army. ... The sons of Ishmael were
not so. They comported themselves humanely and gently towards the Latins'
fellow-countrymen when they captured Jerusalem. They did not fall like
neighing stallions on Latin women. They did not turn the empty tomb of
Christ into a cemetery, nor the path to the life-giving sepulchre into a road
to Hell. They did not turn life into death, nor resurrection into destruction.
They permitted all the Latins to withdraw against a moderate payment per
man, and left all the rest to its owner, though it might be as countless as the
sands of the sea. That is how the enemies of Christ treated the infidel Latins,
using neither sword nor fire nor hunger nor persecution nor nakedness
nor oppression, in all magnanimity. How different was the treatment we met
with from our fellow-Christians, though they had nothing to reproach us
with. (Niketas Choniates, *History* 762–763)

The Greeks had been humiliated, robbed and mishandled. Their
empire had been torn apart and divided among the victors without
a thought for its special status in the machinery of salvation or its
millennary history, and they themselves had been reduced to colonial
status in their own country. But they had something which the westerners lacked – an unbroken cultural tradition through the age of the
Church Fathers and the Roman empire back to classical antiquity.
Knowledge of the Greek language and familiarity with Greek literature gave their scholars and teachers direct access to the basic texts
of Christianity and to the wisdom of the ancients, in both of which
western society was beginning to be interested. So Hellenic identity
came to the fore in learned – and often in powerful – circles, though
no doubt most Greeks went on thinking of themselves as Romans, as
they have done up to the present century; to quote a famous Klephtic
ballad:

ἐγω Ῥωμιὸς γεννήθηκα, Ῥωμιὸς θενὰ πεθανω

[I was born a Roman; I will die a Roman.]

The Nicaean Empire was a more or less ethnically homogeneous
Greek state, which had shed many of the ecumenical pretensions of
the past. When Nikephoros Blemmydes speaks of τὰ σκῆπτρα τῶν
Ἑλλήνων ['the peoples of the Greeks'] instead of the traditional τὰ
σκῆπτρα τῶν Ῥωμαίων ['the peoples of the Romans'], he is thinking

not of the demographic composition of the empire but of its self-image. Indeed many Greeks saw in the recapture of Constantinople from the Latins in 1261 a calamity rather than a triumph, a return to a past which had played them false.

The first century of the revived – but pitifully diminished – empire saw an extraordinary emphasis on cultural identity and a flowering of scholarship, which has led historians to speak of the Second Byzantine Humanism. One need only recall the renaissance of classical studies and classical education due to Maximos Planudes, Manuel Moschopoulos, Thomas Magister, Demetrios Triklinios, and a host of lesser scholars, or the rigid Atticism prescribed by teachers and largely practised by men of letters, or the renewed interest in Greek mathematics and astronomy on the part of Michael Bryennios, Theodore Metochites, Gregory Chioniades and Nikephoros Gregoras. At the same time the early fourteenth century saw the birth of a new literature composed in an approximation to the spoken language. It is a mistake to regard these as opposing trends. Both the sometimes exaggeratedly finicky classicism and the interest in the vernacular as a vehicle of literature are assertions of Hellenic identity, an identity that was defined first and foremost in contrast to the Latins.[17]

Yet the crisis of late medieval Greek society could not be solved by dwelling nostalgically on its cultural heritage. A radical reexamination and reassessment of that heritage was called for. This is what George Gemistos Plethon did in the first half of the fifteenth century when he overtly advocated the establishment of a self-sufficient Greek state in the Peloponnese, and covertly championed the abandonment of Christianity in favour of a philosophical religion in classical guise. In effect what he was doing was to dismiss the Christian Roman Empire as an embarrassing irrelevance in the fifteenth century A.D. Momigliano once wrote an article on the disadvantages of monotheism for a universal state.[18] One of the prob-

---

[17] On Greco-Latin hostility in the fourteenth century cf. Barlaam of Calabria writing to Pope Benedict XII: 'A difference of dogma does not so much divide the hearts of the Greeks from you as the hatred of the Latins, which has entered their spirits as a result of the many and great evils which the Greeks have suffered from the Latins at various times, and are still suffering day by day.' *PL* 151.1336B). Greek resentment was often reciprocated in the west. Petrarch writes to the Doge of Genoa in 1352: 'As for the deceitful and futile Graeculi [little Greeks], who are incapable of any bold initiative ... I long to see that infamous empire, that seat of heresies, destroyed with our own hands' (V. Rossi, *Petrarca. Le familiari*, 3 (Florence, 1937) 120.85–88).

[18] A.D. Momigliano, 'The Disadvantage of Monotheism for a Universal State', *C.Ph.* 81 (1986) 285–297 (= *Ottavo Contributo alla Storia degli Studi classici e del Mondo Antico* (Rome, 1987) 313–328).

lems is what to do when God appears to have withdrawn his patronage. Plethon firmly grasped this nettle and sought to devise an alternative society with an alternative ideological support drawn from classical Greek philosophy. Not surprisingly he found few followers. Others continued to defend the privileged position of the Byzantine Empire in the universal scheme of things, in spite of its present troubles. Thus in 1394, when the empire was reduced to a handful of cities and was a tributary of the Ottoman Sultan, Patriarch Antony IV assured Grand Duke Vasilij Dimitrievich of Muscovy, who wished to abolish compulsory prayers for the emperor in Russian churches, that it was not possible for Christians to have a church but no emperor, since the imperial sovereignty and the church formed a single indivisible whole.

In fact they no longer did. Patriarchs exercised religious authority in regions which had never been subject to Byzantine rule, such as Moldavia, as well as in many others which had been lost to the empire. They also maintained relations with foreign sovereigns quite independently of the emperor in Constantinople. Already by the mid fourteenth century most Orthodox Greeks were no longer imperial subjects. The unity of state and church had been irreparably broken.

The growing Turkish threat forced the Byzantines to make approaches to the Latin west, so long perceived as the irreconcilable Other. The results of such approaches in general reflected little credit on either side. At the political level the search for military aid led only to ephemeral alliances and to expeditions which were too little and too late, though it did bring to England Manuel II, the first – and last – Roman emperor to set foot on British soil since Constantine. At the religious level attempts to come to terms with the west led only to humiliating and futile attempts at church union. It was in the intellectual domain that results were attained which have helped to shape the history of Europe. Men like Maximos Planudes at the end of the thirteenth century and the brothers Demetrios and Prochoros Kydones in the mid fourteenth recognised that the traditional Greek culture, of which they were themselves distinguished exponents, had become inadequate, and that the despised westerners had something to contribute. By their translations into Greek of works by Cicero, Augustine, Boethius, Thomas Aquinas and others they began to build a bridge across the gulf which history had created. They were met half-way by westerners who had begun to realise the fundamental value of the Greek heritage of culture. When in 1397 Manuel Chrysoloras, scholar, teacher and diplomat, and friend of the emperor Manuel II, accepted the invitation of chancellor Coluccio

Salutati to teach Greek in Florence, the bridge was completed. In the last generations of the Byzantine Empire ideas and individuals moved freely in both directions between Constantinople and Italy. It was too late to save Byzantine society, but in a sense the course of history was changed.

Others, perhaps in despair of political solutions, turned to the search for personal salvation, drawing not only on a rich tradition of Byzantine mysticism but also on Neoplatonist metaphysics. The uncreated light of Mount Tabor, which the Hesychasts [a contemplative monastic movement] strove by spiritual and physical exercises to glimpse, could almost as easily be interpreted as a Neoplatonist emanation from the One. The Hesychasts, who were mostly monks, may have been few in number, but their influence spread far and wide and reached the highest strata of society. In particular they had influential adherents among the higher clergy of Bulgaria, Serbia, Rumania and Russia, and so transcended Greek particularism. Metropolitan Kiprijan of Kiev and Moscow was a Bulgarian by birth, a Greek by education, and a Hesychast.[19] For all the distrust of the structures of authority which Hesychasts from time to time displayed, they were moving in the same direction as the other leaders of the Orthodox church, who found themselves more and more taking over the functions of social definition which they had previously shared with the state.

Bishops and monasteries alike had to make accommodations with reality, both in order to carry out their spiritual functions and to preserve their often extensive estates. God and Mammon gave the same counsel. Turkish conquest was often in Europe a stage-by-stage process. Ecclesiastical authorities, episcopal and monastic, often took steps to secure the recognition and protection which Islamic law offered to people of the book before they were fully incorporated into the Ottoman Empire. In this way they helped to create the *Rum milleti* [Greek Orthodox recognized minority], which long outlived the demise of the Byzantine Empire. In it religion, and not language, race or culture, determined a man's position in society and the laws to which he was subject. The Greeks belonged to the community of the Orthodox subjects of the Sultan. But within that larger unity they formed a self-conscious group marked off from their fellow Orthodox by language and culture and by a tradition of education

---

[19] On Kiprijan, a major figure in the history of the Russian church, cf. most recently D. Obolensky, *Six Byzantine Portraits* (Oxford, 1988) 173–200.

never entirely interrupted, which maintained their Greek identity.[20]

All these differing conceptions were, thanks to this educational tradition, present in the minds of those Greeks who, in the late eighteenth and early nineteenth centuries, had to redefine the community to which they belonged in a world of emergent nation-states. Theirs was a complex heritage, perhaps even a *damnosa hereditas* [fatal inheritance]. But it offered to the Greeks a depth of historical perspective and a range of choice which peoples with a shorter or less distinguished history might well envy.

---

[20] Cf. J. Irmscher, 'Les Grecs et l'idée de Rome après 1453', *La nozione di 'Romano' tra cittadinanza e universalità* [Da Roma alla terza Roma. Documenti e Studi, Studi II], (Rome, 1982) 385–390.

12 *The Construction of the 'Other'*†

WILFRIED NIPPEL

translated by Antonia Nevill

In ethnic groups, perception of one's own identity is for the most part accompanied by a delimitation with regard to an external world that is felt to be totally different from oneself. As Plato observed,[1] the idea that this external world is uniform derives simply from the fact that it differs, to a sometimes varying degree, from customary standards; this is linked, certainly in large kingdoms with strong state structures, with the tendency to consider one's own system as the only suitable one. It is enough to cite the Chinese view of foreigners[2] or the way in which the Egyptians understood themselves, recognising theirs as the kingdom of order in contrast with an external world characterised by chaos.[3] Less powerful ethnic groups can, in their turn, develop a feeling of affinity under the spur of an external threat.

Neither possibility arose immediately in the case of the Greeks. Thanks to the multiplicity of contacts with both highly developed and 'primitive' societies of various kinds, they were predisposed to perceive the external world in a different way.[4] It was only in the wake of contingent political developments that ethnocentric perspectives and stereotypes in the perception of foreignness evolved among them; the Greeks worked out, for the use of the whole of subsequent European history, both the models of an analysis of foreign cultures tending towards objectivity, and the *topoi* [commonplaces] with

---

† Originally published in S. Settis (ed.), *I Greci*, vol. 1, *Noi e I Greci* (Giulio Einaudi: Turin, 1996), 165–96.
[1] *Politics*, 262d–e.
[2] W. Franke, *China und das Abendland*, Göttingen 1962, pp. 21ff.
[3] W. Helck, 'Die Ägypter und die Fremden', *Saeculum*, XV (1964), pp. 103–14.
[4] H. Schwabl, 'Das Bild der fremden Welt bei den frühen Griechen', in *Grecs et Barbares*, Vandoeuvres–Geneva 1962, pp. 3–36; W. Speyer, 'Die Griechen und die Fremdvölker: Kulturebegegnungen und Wege zur gegenseitigen Verständigung', *Eos*, LXXVII (1989), pp. 17–29.

which to characterise those cultures (usable at will for very many types of society).

I GREEKS AND BARBARIANS

1 Cultural contacts and the sense of a common Greek identity

It is not possible here to run through the multitude of cultural and commercial relations in which the Greeks were engaged, from the protohistoric era, with the non-Greek world, especially the Near East and Egypt. It must only be stressed how those relations were not confined to influences upon Mycenaean civilisation, and that the most recent studies have rightly brought to the fore strong eastern influences on the religion, science, literature, art and material culture even of the Greeks in the archaic period.[5] Pirates, long-distance traders, mercenaries (chiefly in Egypt),[6] together with particularly mobile groups such as craftsmen, soothsayers, doctors and singers,[7] were the vehicles for such numerous contacts, whose repercussions went far beyond the adoption of Phoenician writing. These relations constituted no threat as long as the Greeks were not the object of hegemonic ambitions on the part of large kingdoms.[8]

The consciousness of a common Greek identity developed particularly during the period of colonisation, which brought the Greeks into contact with all the countries of the Mediterranean and the Black Sea. In a way, colonisation was determined by the fact that, after the collapse of the Mycenaean civilisation, no large-scale power structures were formed under a strong monarchy: the reconstruction of state structures proceeded, in fact, in conditions of restricted

---

[5] Cf. among others, T. J. Dunbabin, *The Greeks and their Eastern Neighbours: Studies in the Relations between Greece and the Countries of the Near East in the Eighth and Seventh Centuries B.C.*, ed. J. Boardman, London 1957; M. L. West, *Early Greek Philosophy and the Orient*, Oxford 1971; W. Burkert, 'Die orientalisierende Epoche in der griechischen Religion und Literatur', *Sitzungsberichte der Heidelberger Akademie des Wissenschaften, Philosophisch-historisch Klasse*, 1984, n. 1. [translated as *The Orientalizing Revolution*]; J. Boardman, *The Greeks Overseas: The Archaeology of their Early Colonies and Trade*, Harmondsworth 1964, pp. 56ff.; id., 'The Material Culture of Archaic Greece', in *CAH²*, III/3: *The Expansion of the Greek World, Eighth to Sixth Centuries B.C.*, Cambridge 1982, pp. 414–30; C. Roebuck, 'Trade', *ibid.*, pp. 446–60.

[6] T. F. R. G. Braun, 'The Greeks in Egypt', in *CAH²*, III/3 cit., pp. 32–56.

[7] *Odyssey*, 17. 383–5. Cf. W. Burkert, 'Itinerant Diviners and Magicians: A Neglected Element in Cultural Contacts', in R. Hägg (ed.), *The Greek Renaissance of the Eighth Century B.C.*, Stockholm 1983, pp. 116–22.

[8] A. Heuss, 'Die archaische Zeit Griechenlands als geschichtliche Epoche' (1946), in F. Gschnitzer (ed.), *Zur griechischen Staatskunde*, Darmstadt 1969, pp. 36–96, esp. pp. 39ff.; H. Schaeffer, 'Das Problem der griechischen Nationalität', in *id.*, *Probleme der alten Geschichte*, Göttingen 1963, pp. 269–306, esp. p. 271; C. Meier, 'Die vertrauten und die fremden Griechen', *Gymnasium*, XCVI (1989), pp. 287–316, esp. p. 296.

space, those of the city-state. At the time, the colonial movement contributed to the later consolidation of this form of political organisation,[9] not only by lightening the burden of its problems (demographic pressure first of all), but also by virtue of the fact that the foundation of new communities demanded a conscious reflection on the assumptions of one's own structures of government. In a world with hundreds of varied *poleis*, it is true that the first thing to assert itself was the sense of citizenship, but the fact that Greeks of disparate provenance lived together in the newly founded settlements must also have favoured an awareness of community, which found its echo in the emergence of a concept of panhellenism.[10] Conflict with the indigenous populations, in Sicily,[11] at Thasos[12] or Cyrene,[13] strengthened the feelings of solidarity among Greeks. Expansion in the northern regions, which were not culturally enticing but which were attractive for their material resources, was probably sometimes associated with the idea that the Greeks had, so to speak, civilised the surrounding world.[14] Too much importance must not be given to these experiences of conflict, above all if we contrast them with the numerous occasions on which sieges met with no resistance and were actually welcomed. However varied the forms assumed by relations with the non-Greek *milieu* may have been, it must be noted that, in general, the Greeks preserved their cultural identity, and it was their various neighbours, not themselves, who tended towards acculturation.[15] Awareness of community was expressed in the religious associations of the 'original stock' (Ionians, Dorians, Aeolians) on the Asia Minor coast[16] and at the *Hellenion* of Naucratis.[17] There was

---

[9] C. Meier, *Die Entstehung des Politischen bei den Griechen*, Frankfurt 1980, pp. 58ff. (It. trs. *La nascita della categoria del politico in Grecia*, Bologna 1988, pp. 61ff. [translated as *The Greek Discovery of Politics*]); A. Heuss, 'Vom Anfang und Ende "archaischer" Politik bei den Griechen', in *Gnomosyne: Menschliches Denken und Handeln in der frühgriechischen Literatur. Festschrift W. Marg zum 70. Geb.*, Munich 1981, pp. 1–29.

[10] Hesiod, *Works and Days*, 528; Strabo, 8.6.6 = C 370. Cf. F. W. Walbank, 'The Problem of Greek Nationality' (1951), in *id.*, *Selected Papers*, Cambridge 1985, pp. 1–19 [= Ch. 10, above]; M. I. Finley, 'The Ancient Greeks and their Nation', in *id.*, *The Use and Abuse of History*, London 1975, pp. 120–33.

[11] Thucydides, 6. 2–6.

[12] Archilochus, fr. 54 Diehl.

[13] Herodotus, 4.159.

[14] D. Timpe, 'Griechischer Handel nach dem nördlichen Barbaricum', in K. Düwel and Dietrich Claude (eds), 'Untersuchungen zu Handel und verkehr der vor- und frühgeschichtlichen Zeit in Mittel- und Nordeuropa', *Abhandlungen der Akademie der Wissenschaften in Göttingen. Phil.- hist. Klasse*, series 3, CXLIII (1985), pp. 181–213.

[15] A. J. Graham, 'The Colonial Expansion of Greece', in *CAH²*, III/3 cit., pp. 83–162, esp. p. 156.

[16] Herodotus, 1.142–49.

[17] *Ibid.*, 2.178.

a feeling of kinship from the point of view of origin,[18] language, religion and customs.[19] But neither religion nor ethnic derivation could unambiguously distinguish Greeks from non-Greeks; furthermore, there was constant awareness of how much of their own material and spiritual evolution was owed to the great eastern civilisations, chiefly Egypt, with its culture that was so much more ancient.[20] It is enough to cite the traditions about the adaptation of the names of deities and festivals,[21] or those about the travels in Egypt of Lycurgus, Solon, Pythagoras and Plato[22] (it is also true, however, that afterwards emphasis was placed on the fact that the models had been improved by adapting them to the Greeks' own requirements).[23] Language remained the best criterion of differentiation: originally, the concept of the Barbarian referred to those who did not speak Greek, but it was not necessarily connected with a sense of superiority.[24]

Accompanying the colonial movement, the mother-country saw the formation of institutions of a panhellenic nature which, at the same time, implied a delimitation in respect of non-Greeks: first of all the Olympic, Pythian, Isthmian and Nemean Games – open to Greeks only[25] – and the Delphic amphictyony [league which regulated the affairs of a sanctuary], with its restrictive rules for the conduct of war among Greeks.[26] The importance of Delphi resided in its inspired advice about the foundation of colonies and the fact that, in this way, the sanctuary became a place for the exchange of

---

[18] On the birth of the conviction concerning affinity of origins because of similarities in ways of life, cf. the chapter 'Ethnische Gemeinschaftsbeziehungen', in M. Weber, *Wirtschaft und Gesellschaft*, Tübingen 1976⁵, pp. 234ff. (It. trs. *Ecomonia e società*, Milan 1980, II, pp. 187ff. [translated as *Economy and Society*]).

[19] Cf. Herodotus, 8.144.2.

[20] Plato, *Timaeus*, 22b; Aristotle, *Politics*, 1329b33ff.

[21] Herodotus, 2.49–51 and *passim*. Cf. F. Hartog, 'Les grecs égyptologues', *Annales (ESC)*, XLI (1986), pp. 953–67 [translated above, Ch. 9].

[22] H. Dörrie, 'Platons Reisen zu fernen Völkern: Zur Geschichte eines Motivs der Platon-Legende und zu seiner Neuwendung durch Lactanz', in *Romanitas et Christianitas: Studia in honorem H. Waszink, Amsterdam* 1973, pp. 99–118.

[23] [Plato], *Epinomis*, 987d.

[24] J. Jüthner, *Hellenen und Barbaren: Aus der Geschichte des Nationalbewusstseins*, Leipzig 1923, pp. 1ff.; B. Funck, 'Studie zu der Bezeichnung "barbaros"', in E. C. Welskopf (ed.), *Soziale Typenbegriffe im alten Griechenland und ihr Fortleben in den Sprachen der Welt*, IV, Berlin 1981, pp. 26–51; E. Hall, *Inventing the Barbarian: Greek Self-definition through Tragedy*, Oxford 1989, p. 3ff.; J. Werner, 'Zur Fremdsprachenproblematik in der griechisch-romischen Antike', in C. W. Müller, K. Sier and J. Werner (eds), *Zum Umgang mit fremden Sprachen in der griechisch-romischen Antike*, Stuttgart 1992, pp. 1–20, esp. p. 6ff.

[25] Herodotus, 5.22. Cf. N. J Richardson, 'Panhellenic Cults and Panhellenic Poets', in *CAH²*, V. *The Fifth Century B.C.*, Cambridge 1992, pp. 223–44.

[26] Aeschines, 2.115.

information from all over the Greek world.[27] It was certainly no accident that such institutions arose in places which did not have at their
disposal the necessary potential for large-scale power structures.[28]
An aristocratic culture was predominant, embracing the entire Greek
world, and its elements (the games, symposia, relationships of marriage, friendship and proxenia)† were to characterise the perception
of life of the social elites right up to the late classical era.[29]

2 *Geography, ethnology and anthropology*

The expansion of the Greeks' geographical and cultural horizons
through colonisation and journeys of exploration led both to a
demand for ideas that were usable in practice, and to a strengthened
theoretical curiosity: these are reflected in the literature of coastal
voyages during the sixth and fifth centuries, culminating in the
geographical works of Hecataeus of Miletus.[30] From the middle of
the sixth century, the consolidation of the Achaemenid Empire
helped to broaden the picture the Greeks had of the world, as
is shown by the example of Scylax of Caryanda, who undertook
his voyage of exploration in Arabia and in India on orders from
Darius I.[31]

But from the very beginning, Greek reflections on foreign peoples,
fed by solid experience, practical demands and theoretical curiosity,
were also infiltrated by fictitious elements. The fringe zones of the
oikoumene [inhabited world] were suspected of being inhabited by
totally different and alien peoples. Accounts of imaginary creatures
like the Hyperboreans,[32] the Laestrygonians and cannibalistic

---

† The institution whereby a citizen represented the interests of another city within his
own.
[27] W. G. Forrest, 'Colonization and the Rise of Delphi', *Historia*, VI (1957), pp. 160–75;
Meier, *Die Entstehung* cit., pp. 73ff. (It. trs. pp. 76ff.).
[28] M. I. Finley, 'Foreword', in P. E. Easterling and J. V. Muir (eds), *Greek Religion and
Society*, Cambridge 1985, pp. xii–xx.
[29] O. Murray (ed.), *Sympotica: A Symposium on the Symposion*, Oxford 1990;
G. Herman, *Ritualised Friendship and the Greek City*, Cambridge 1987; E. Stein-Hölkeskamp,
*Adelskultur und Polisgesellschaft: Studien zum griechischen Adel in archaischer und Klassischer
Zeit*, Stuttgart 1989.
[30] K. Meister, *Die griechische Geschichtsschreibung: Von den Anfangen bis zu dem
Hellenismus*, Stuttgart 1990, pp. 15ff., 206ff., with full bibliography (It. trs. *La storiografia
greca: Dalle origini alla fine dell'Ellenismo*, Rome–Bari 1992); R. Werner, 'Zur Geschichte der
vorderorientalisch-phönikischen und mykenisch-griechischen Handels- und Kolonisations-
fahrten im Spiegel der Epos- und Periplus-Literatur', in *Orientalisch-ägäische Einflüsse in der
europäische Bronzezeit*, Bonn 1990, pp. 47–79.
[31] Herodotus, 4.44. Cf. A. Momigliano, 'Fattori orientali della storiografia ebraica post-
esilica e della storiografia greca' (1965), in *id., La storiografia greca*, Turin 1982, pp. 125–37.
[32] Herodotus, 4.13 (Aristeas), 4.32 (Hesiod and Epigoni); Pindar, *Pythian*, 10.30ff.; G. B.
Bianucci, 'La via iperborea', *Rivista di Filologia e di Istruzione Classica*, CI (1973), pp.

Cyclops,[33] the one-eyed Arimaspians,[34] the Pygmies[35] and the Amazons[36] were passed down from Homer to Aristeas (dated about 600),[37] up to the ethnographic and geographic works of the late sixth and early fifth century.

The opposition of Greeks and Persians in the fifth century decisively altered the relationships of the former with foreign cultures. On the one hand, empirical knowledge expanded to include a host of other peoples who were organised in a great variety of ways, as far as the heart of Asia: it helped, in fact, to create the conviction that it was necessary to strengthen theoretical reflection on the conditions and possibilities of socio-political structures. On the other, it produced a sense of superiority on the part of the Greeks which in its turn clashed with the capacity for drawing distinctions, of which they had however given remarkable proof.

Testifying to the growth in empirical knowledge and the effort to understand foreignness is the historiographical work of Herodotus. It made due allowance for the need to find one's bearings in a world where political upheavals had created a completely new measure of experience of the contingent;[38] as we know, Herodotus inserted into his *Histories* geographic and ethnographic digressions on the populations with which the Persian Empire had come into contact: in these sections a sharp interest is revealed in the multiplicity of potential social organisations.[39]

His exposition concentrates on religion, on customs – mainly in relation to the sexual sphere and funerary practices – and on ways of dressing and eating. As regards religion, it is worth noting that interest is focused on rituals that are sometimes describable.† Judge-

207–20; R. Dion, 'La notion d'Hyperboréens: ses vicissitudes au cours de l'antiquité', *Bulletin de l'Association G. Budé*, 1976, pp. 143–57; J. Romm, 'Herodotus and Mythic Geography. The Case of the Hyperboreans', *Transactions and Proceedings of the American Philological Association*, CXIX (1989), pp. 97–113; J. Gould, *Herodotus*, London 1989, pp. 90ff.

[33] *Odyssey*, 9.106ff., 10.81ff.

[34] Herodotus, 3.116, 4.13, 4.27.

[35] P. Janni, *Etnographia e mito: La storia dei Pigmei*, Rome 1978.

[36] J. Carlier, 'Voyage en Amazonie grecque', *Acta Antiqua Academiae Scientiarum Hungaricae*, XXVII (1979), pp. 381–405.

[37] J. D. P. Bolton, *Aristeas of Proconnesus*, Oxford 1962; W. Burkert, 'Herodot als Historiker fremder Religionen', in *Hérodote et les peuples non-Grecs*, Vandoeuvres–Geneva 1990, pp. 1–39, esp. p. 13.

[38] C. Meier, 'Die Entdeckung der Ereignisgeschichte bei Herodot', *Storia della storiografia*, X (1986), pp. 5–25.

[39] Gould, *Herodotus* cit., pp. 86–109; D. Lateiner, *The Historical Method of Herodotus*, Toronto 1989, pp. 145–62; W. Nippel, *Griechen, Barbaren und "Wilde": Alte Geschichte und Sozialanthropologie*, Frankfurt 1990, pp. 11–29.

† But see my comments above, introduction to Part II, and *Divinity and History*, pp. 220–2.

ments about truth and value are left on one side: however strange
they may appear, the various customs are respected as an expression
of the system currently in force among each people.[40] The fact that
some eat the bodies of their ancestors and would consider it impious
to cremate them, while exactly the opposite applies to others, proves
the universal validity of the principle of the νόμος βασιλεύς ['custom
is king'].[41] Herodotus' empiricism is also revealed in his omission
of, or deliberately sceptical reference to, a considerable part of the
elements of fantasy in earlier tradition. The effort to be objective
is reflected also in the constantly neutral use of the concept of the
Barbarian; noteworthy is the observation that the Egyptians define
as Barbarians all those who spoke a foreign language.[42]

At the same time, however, it is evident that even for Herodotus
the description of foreign cultures could not do without interpretative models shaped according to his own standards – which draws
attention to the general problem of the possibilities and limits of
knowledge of foreign cultures. Selection of what is deemed worth
mentioning is informed by his own idea of the 'normal case': whatever is atypical to the eyes of the observer appears as typical to the
society to which it refers, and all the more so if the description cites
only one or two characteristics. There is also the model of the 'opposite world', as, for example, with regard to Egyptian customs, which
appear in a list of 'upside-down versions'.[43] Herodotus makes use
also of models of polarisation: Egyptians and Scythians serve as
extreme cases, determined by their respective geographical-climatic
contexts;[44] the Egyptians are taken to be the most ancient people,[45]
the Scythians the newest,[46] but both have in common the refusal to
adopt foreign customs.[47]

If we look not at isolated cases but at all the phenomena described
by Herodotus, a highly differentiated typology of cultural forms

[40] S. C. Humphreys, 'Law, Custom and Culture in Herodotus', *Arethusa*, XX (1987), pp.
211–20; Burkert, 'Herodot' cit.
[41] Herodotus, 3.38.
[42] *Ibid.*, 2.158.5
[43] *Ibid.*, 2.35–36. This, however, does not define the whole of the description of Egypt. For
an appraisal of this, cf. the exhaustive treatment in A. B. Lloyd, *Herodotus Book II*, I–III,
Leiden 1975–88, and *id.*, 'Herodotus' Account of Pharaonic History', *Historia*, XXXVII
(1988), pp. 22–53.
[44] Herodotus, 4.28.
[45] *Ibid.*, 2.2.
[46] *Ibid*, 4.5.1.
[47] *Ibid*, 2.79.1, 2.91.1, 4.76.1, 4.80.5. S. Benardete, *Herodotean Inquiries*, The Hague
1969, p. 99; F. Hartog, *Le Miroir d'Hérodote: essai sur la representation de l'autre*, Paris 1980,
pp. 31ff. (It. trs. *Lo specchio di Erodoto*, Milan 1992, pp. 35ff. [translated as *The Mirror of
Herodotus*]).

is outlined. As far as the position of women is concerned, we are presented with, among others, the matrilinear naming of the Lycians,[48] equal rights for women and men among the Issedonians,[49] or even the military role played by the women of the Sarmatians[50] and of Libyan tribes.[51] With regard to sexual norms a distinction is made between an unbridled promiscuity that takes place publicly, as among some Caucasian and Indian tribes,[52] and various cultural norms that eliminate the brutishness of sexual relations in public:[53] such is the case among the Massagetae and the Nasamonians, where a man coupling with a woman must hang his quiver outside the wagon;[54] with the limitation of sexual activity at appointed phases of life, as for Thracian girls prior to marriage;[55] or still further with the prostitution of Lydian girls that is used to provide them with a dowry.[56]

Moreover, distinction is made between habitual cannibalism (among the 'Androphagi' ['Man-eaters']),[57] ritualised human sacrifice,[58] and feeding – given a cult meaning – on old and ill relatives.[59] There is a difference between the various primitive ways of life and food, according to whether people live on herbs, roots, berries or fruit, eat raw meat or fish, or dwell in the shelter of trees or caves.[60] At a higher level of civilisation, the nomadic livestock breeders are distinguished from the settled cultivators.[61]

Herodotus, however, does not reduce this broad typological range to an evolutionary outline. As regards the progress of civilisation, he knows only the model of the first invention (either on the part of a

[48] Herodotus, 1.173.

[49] *Ibid.*, 4.26.2.

[50] *Ibid.*, 4.116–17.

[51] *Ibid.*, 4.193. M. Rosellini and S. Saïd, 'Usages de femmes et autres nomoi chez les "sauvages" d'Hérodote', *Annali della Scuola Normale Superiore di Pisa, Classe di Lettere e Filosofia*, series 3, VII (1978), pp. 949–1005; S. Saïd, 'Usages de femmes et "sauvagerie" dans l'ethnographie grecque d'Hérodote à Diodore et Strabon', in *La femme dans le monde méditerranéen, I. Antiquité*, Lyon 1985, pp. 137–50.

[52] Herodotus, 1.203.2, 3.101.1.

[53] *Ibid.*, 4.180.5.

[54] *Ibid.*, 1.216.1, 4.172.2.

[55] *Ibid.*, 5.6.

[56] *Ibid.*, 1.93.4, 1.94.1.

[57] *Ibid.*, 4.106.

[58] *Ibid.*, 4.103.

[59] *Ibid.*, 1.216.2.

[60] A. Grassl, *Herodot als Ethnologe*, Diss. Munich 1904.

[61] Herodotus, 4.17ff., 4.186 with 4.91. B. D. Shaw, '"Eaters of Flesh, Drinkers of Milk": The Ancient Mediterranean Ideology of the Pastoral Nomad', *Ancient Society*, XIII–XIV (1982–83), pp. 5–31; P. Briant, *État et pasteurs au Moyen-Orient ancien*, Cambridge–Paris 1982, pp. 12ff.

certain person, or in a certain country) and its subsequent diffusion.[62]

Nevertheless, Herodotus' perception of foreign cultures is influenced *a priori* by contemporary theories about the repercussions of natural environment on social structure, or on the evolutionary course of civilisation. Here reference must be made to, among other ideas, the theory of climates, to be found in contemporary works on the environment in the Hippocratic *corpus*,[63] and the reflections on the development of man from animal which originated in part from the myth of Prometheus, but which were transformed by Protagoras[64] and Democritus into doctrines on the origin of civilisation.[65] Herodotus' proposal, according to which the Androphagi had neither law nor customs,[66] matches Protagoras' theory of law (δίκη) and mutual respect (αἰδώς) as preconditions for a stable human society.[67]

Similarly, we can clearly recognise how ethnographic discourse in the fifth and fourth centuries intersected with reflection on the beginnings of one's own social organisation and the development of theoretical alternatives. Attic tragedy explores the theme of the barely civilised or completely uncivilised woman, cruel and dominating.[68] Comedy (Aristophanes, *Ecclesiazusae*) jokes about the idea of women's political rule. Plato's[69] justification of the association of women and children, which would eliminate envy and discord, could reflect a statement by Herodotus[70] about the Agathyrsi, neighbours of the Thracians. Aristotle's[71] criticism, on the other hand, refers to the practice of the Libyan tribes, also attested by Herodotus,[72] by

[62] A. Kleingünther, '*Protos Heuretes*': *Untersuchungen zur Geschichte einer Fragestellung*, Leipzig 1933, pp. 46ff.; L. Edelstein, *The Idea of Progress in Classical Antiquity*, Baltimore 1967, p. 32; K. Thraede, under 'Erfinder' in *RAC*, V, coll. 1204ff.

[63] F. Heinimann, *Nomos und Physis: Herkunft und Bedeutung einer Antithese im griechischen Denken des 5. Jahrhunderts v. Chr.*, Basel 1945, pp. 13ff.; W. Backhaus, 'Der Hellenen–Barbaren-Gegensatz und die Hippokratische Schrift "peri aeron hydaton topon"', *Historia*, XXV (1976), pp. 170–85.

[64] On possible reciprocal influence, cf. A. Dihle, 'Herodot und die Sophistik', *Philologus*, CVI (1962), pp. 207–20; A. Corcella, *Erodoto e l'analogia*, Palermo 1984, pp. 239ff.; R. A. McNeal, 'Protagoras the Historian', *History and Theory: Studies in the Philosophy of History*, XXV (1986), pp. 299–318 [see now Thomas, *Herodotus in Context*].

[65] T. Cole, *Democritus and the Sources of Greek Anthropology*, Cleveland 1967.

[66] Herodotus, 4.106.

[67] Plato, *Protagoras*, 322c.

[68] J. Gould, 'Law, Custom and Myth: Aspects of the Social Position of Women in Classical Athens', *Journal of Hellenic Studies*, C (1980), pp. 38–59; C. Mossé, *La femme dans la Grèce antique*, Paris 1983, pp. 103ff.; C. Segal, 'Violence and the Other: Greek, Female and Barbarian in Euripides' *Hecuba*', *Transactions and Proceedings of the American Philological Association*, CXX (1990), pp. 109–31.

[69] *Republic*, 457cff.

[70] Herodotus, 4.104.

[71] *Politics*, 1262a16–24.

[72] Herodotus, 4.180.6.

which children were attributed to fathers on the basis of physical resemblance. The possibility of giving military training to women is demonstrated by Plato through the traditions of the Sarmatians.[73]

The *topoi* of ethnography, gathered together for the first time at the end of the fifth century by Hellanicus of Lesbos,[74] re-emerge in a range of fields of argument. Thus in the debate on the relativity of the law: the obligation of familial burial (Sophocles, *Antigone*) and the prohibition of incest are enumerated among fundamental 'unwritten' laws in that they are *a priori* a valid rule with respect to every positive law;[75] there are sophistic arguments on the relativity of the law (*Dissoi logoi*)† that refer to examples present in Herodotus. Later on, Aristotle in his school had the νόμιμα βαρβαρικά ['barbarian customs'] collected systematically[76] and emphasised the value of ethno-geographic literature for the purposes of just legislation,[77] while the Cynics and the first Stoics deduced from the whole collection of apparently absurd law, and the inherited ethnographic examples of incest, general promiscuity, sexual relations in public and cannibalism, that there were no such things as rules fixed by nature but only socially instituted conventions[78] (the Cynics' criticism of civilisation, on the other hand, also manifested itself in the shaping of the figure of the noble Barbarian, notably in the Scythian Anacharsis).[79]

According to fourth-century theories about the origin of civilisation, cannibalism or the eating of raw flesh bore witness to the brutish state of primitive man, a state from which the Barbarians living on the fringes of the civilised world had in practice not emerged.[80] Forms of sustenance were systematised by Aristotle[81] and refashioned by Dicearchus[82] into a system on several levels, ranging from gatherers and hunters to shepherds and farmers.[83] Theories

---

† The text of the *Dissoi Logoi* is Diels-Kranz, *Die Fragmente der Vorsokratiker*, no. 90.

[73] *Laws*, 804e.

[74] Eusebius, *Preparatio evangelica*, 10.3.16.

[75] Xenophon, *Memorabilia*, 4.4.22.

[76] Varro, *De lingua latina*, 7.70; Cicero, *De finibus*, 5.11.

[77] *Rhetoric*, 1360a33ff.

[78] Cicero, *Tusculanae disputationes*, i.108; A. O. Lovejoy and G. Boas, *Primitivism and Related Ideas in Antiquity*, Baltimore 1935, pp. 117ff., 260ff.; D Nörr, *Rechtskritik in der römischen Antike*, Munich 1974, pp. 44ff.

[79] E. Lévy, 'Les origines du mirage scythe', *Ktema*, VI (1981), pp. 57–68; J. F. Kindstrand, *Anacharsis: The Legend and the Apophthegmata*, Uppsala 1981.

[80] [Plato], *Epinomis*, 975a; Aristotle, *Nichomachean Ethics*, 1145a30ff., 1148b20ff.; Moschion, fr. 6 Nauck; Athenaeus, 660e–661c.

[81] *Politics*, 1256a30ff.

[82] fr. 48 Wehrli.

[83] K. E. Müller, *Geschichte der antiken Ethnographie und ethnologischen Theoriebildung*, I, Wiesbaden 1972, pp. 213ff.

about the origin of belief in the gods, of language, of the family and of property influenced doctrines on the birth of civilisation such as that of Epicurus. Crossing the boundaries of the area circumscribed by personal inspection and interrogation of witnesses, the historiography of the fourth century (Ephorus, Timaeus), as regards reconstruction of the most ancient eras, depends on conjectural generalisations on the origin of civilisation that are also reflected in aetiological legends.[84]

The connection between self-definition and observation of the foreigner is shown in the fact that the Barbarians were understood as the incarnation of a cultural stage through which the Greeks themselves had at one time passed. In his 'archaeology', Thucydides observes that the Greeks on the fringes and the Barbarians of his own time live in the same way as the ancient Hellenes had;[85] the Pelasgians were seen as survivors from a pre-Hellenic population.[86] In his own culture the existence of survivals from an earlier, semi-barbarian, cultural level, could be discovered.[87]

3 The politicisation of the Greek/Barbarian contrast

The resort to ethnographic material in the context of arguments about general social and political theory made clear the multiplicity of possible human organisations, but at the same time revealed the fact that the constitutions in force in the Greek *poleis*, for all their differences, nevertheless had the same valid foundation in that they relied on the consensus of the body of citizens, bound by a system of their own devising. This way of understanding themselves had been only reinforced, not initiated, by the Persian Wars, which implied that, despite the emphasis given to the differences in political culture of Greeks and Persians, the view of the reality of Persia was by no means entirely dominated by political antagonism:[88] Herodotus

[84] L. Pearson, 'Myth and archaeology in Italy and Sicily – Timaeus and his Predecessors', *Yale Classical Studies*, XXIV (1975), pp. 171–95; H. Strasburger, 'Umblick im Trümmerfeld der griechischen Geschischtsschreibung', *Historiographia Antiqua: Commentationes Lovanienses in honorem W. Peremans septuagenarii editae*, Leuven 1977, pp. 3–52; E. Gabba, 'True History and False History in Classical Antiquity', *Journal of Roman Studies*, CI (1981), pp. 50–62.

[85] Thucydides, 1.5–6.

[86] J. L. Myres, 'A History of the Pelasgian Theory', *Journal of Hellenic Studies*, XXVII (1907), pp. 170–225; R. A. McNeal, 'How Did Pelasgians Become Hellenes? Herodotus I. 56–58', *Illinois Classical Studies*, X (1985), pp. 11–21.

[87] Herodotus, 6.56–58; Plato, *Republic*, 452c; *id.*, *Cratylus*, 397c–d, 425e; *id.*, *Laws*, 680b; Aristotle, *Politics*, 1268b39ff., 1295a10ff.

[88] A. Momigliano, 'Persian Empire and Greek Freedom' (1979), in *id.*, *Settimo contributo alla storia degli studi classici e del mondo antico*, Rome 1984, pp. 61–75.

draws a picture of the richness of Persian customs that stemmed from a readiness to adopt elements from other cultures;[89] he points out the similarities of funeral customs for Persian and Spartan kings[90] and sets the 'debate on the constitution'[91] in a Persian *milieu*. These same Persian wars are looked at from various points of view.[92] Aeschylus (in the *Persians*, staged in 472) could represent the defeat of Xerxes on stage as a tragedy, just by assuming a sympathetic attitude.[93]† Herodotus, as he says in his preface, wanted to preserve the memory of the great and wonderful deeds of both Greeks and Barbarians. In his opinion the war had not been inevitable and, in particular, he showed scant sympathy for the Ionian rebellion that had unleashed this great disaster for the Greeks and Barbarians.[94] At the same time, however, even in these authors we find reflected the consciousness,[95] which had grown in the years following the great victories, of an irreconcilable opposition between Greek liberty and the despotic government of the Persians (or, rather, of the tyrants supported by them). As soon as this opposition was perceived as being rooted in the respective *nomoi* of the two sides, the *hybris* of Xerxes – embodied in the building of the bridge over the Hellespont – became precisely an attempt to abolish forever the boundary between them, with the desire to bring Greece too under his yoke.[96] The responsibility of the rulers, validity of the laws, freedom of speech and political equality of the Greeks was in stark contrast to Persia's despotic rule,[97] where the king could do as he pleased.[98] *Proskynesis*, demanded at the Persian court but intolerable for the Greeks, was the symbol of this difference.[99] The absence of liberty, on the other

---

† Contrast in particular now Harrison, *Emptiness of Asia*; see my comments, introduction to Part I.

[89] Herodotus, 1.131ff.

[90] *Ibid.*, 6.58–59.

[91] *Ibid.*, 3.80–82.

[92] For the portrayals of Persians as courageous warriors, cf. A. Bovon, 'La representation des guerriers perses et la notion de barbare dans la Ière moitié du Ve siècle', *Bulletin de Correspondance Hellénique*, LXXXVII (1963), pp. 575–602.

[93] C. Meier, *Die politische Kunst der griechischen Tragödie*, Munich 1988, pp. 76ff. [translated as *The Political Art of Greek Tragedy*].

[94] Herodotus, 5.97 [but see Harrison, *Divinity and History*, p. 242].

[95] K. Raaflaub, *Die Entdeckung der Freiheit: Zur historischen Semantik and Gesellschaftsgeschichte eines politischen Grundbegriffs der Griechen*, Munich 1985, pp. 71ff., 102ff.

[96] J. Jouanna, 'Les causes de la défaite des barbares chez Eschyle, Hérodote et Hippocrate', *Ktema*, VI (1981), pp. 3–15; Meier, *Die politische Kunst* cit., pp. 88ff.

[97] Aeschylus, *Persians*, 213, 584–97; Herodotus, 7.104.4.

[98] *Ibid.*, 3.31.4.

[99] Aeschylus, *Persians*, 587ff.; Euripides, *Orestes*, 1507; Herodotus, 7.136. Cf. A. Alföldi, 'Die Ausgestaltung des monarchischen Zeremoniells am römischen Kaiserhof' (1934), in *id.*, *Die Monarchische Repräsentation im römischen Kaiserreich*, Darmstadt 1970, pp. 9ff. [for *proskynesis*, see Introduction to Part II].

hand, was used to explain the surprising defeat of the Persians, whose soldiers were forced into battle by lashes of the whip.[100] Such a picture could be laden with what we might call 'ethnological' explanations. To the eyes of the Greeks, luxuriousness,[101] promiscuity and incest,[102] like the intrigues of the harem,[103] led to a gradual 'softening' of the Persians.[104] The epilogue of Xenophon's *Cyropaedia*[105] offers a collection of all those *topoi*, which by now have little to do with empirical observation[106] – the same process can be seen also in the projection of an ideal monarchy onto the earliest times of the Achaemenid Empire, a projection that determines the general character of the *Cyropaedia* and makes it the prototype of the *speculum principis* [a 'mirror to princes', a text offering advice to a ruler].[107] In the Hippocratic work on the environment (*Airs, Waters, Places, c.430*),[108] the un-warlike nature of the Asiatic is explained by either climatic conditions or the effects of the monarch's limitless power, although despotism is not univocally interpreted as the necessary consequence of the country's natural characteristics.[109]

The worsening of the image of the Persians came about chiefly in the Attic tragedy of the second half of the fifth century, and also later mirrored the Athenian demand for leadership of their empire based

[100] Herodotus, 7.56.1, 7.103.4, 7.223.3.

[101] *Ibid.*, 5.97.

[102] *Ibid.*, 3.31; Euripides, *Andromache*, 173ff.; Xanthus, in Clement of Alexandria, *Stromata*, 3.11.1 (= FGrHist, 756 F 31); Ctesias in Photius, *Bibliotheca*, 72 (=FGrHist, 688 F 15); *Dissoi Logoi*, 2.15; Antisthenes, in Athenaeus, 220c; Diogenes, according to Dio Chrysostom, 10.29ff.; Sextus Empiricus, *Outlines of Pyrrhonism*, 1.152.

[103] Cf. Herodotus and, above all, Ctesias. F. Jacoby, under 'Ktesias' in *RE*, XI, coll. 2032–73; A. Momigliano, 'Tradizione e invenzione in Ctesia' (1931), in *id.*, *Quarto contributo alla storia degli studi classici e del mondo antico*, Rome 1969, pp. 181–212; R. Drews, *The Greek Accounts of Eastern History*, Cambridge MA 1973, pp. 103ff.; H. Sancisi-Weerdenburg, 'Exit Atossa: Images of Women in Greek Historiography on Persia', in A. Cameron and A. Kuhrt (eds), *Images of Women in Antiquity*, London 1983, pp. 20–33; H. Sancisi-Weerdenburg, 'Decadence in the Empire or Decadence in the Sources? From Source to Synthesis: Ctesias', in *id.* (ed.), *Achaemenid History I: Sources, Structures and Synthesis*, Leiden 1987, pp. 33–46.

[104] Isocrates, 4.150ff.

[105] Xenophon, *Cyropaedia.*, 8.8.

[106] H. Sancisi-Weerdenburg, 'The Fifth Oriental Monarchy and Hellenocentrism: Cyropaedia VIII, 8 and its Influence', in H. Sancisi-Weerdenburg and A. Kuhrt (eds), *Achaemenid History* II: *The Greek Sources*, Leiden 1987, pp. 117–31. On the persistence of such a stereotype in ancient literature, cf. the material gathered in H. Haberkorn, *Beitrage zur Beurteilung der Perser in der griechischen Literatur*, Diss. Greifswald 1940.

[107] P. Hadot, under 'Fürstenspiegel', in *RAC*, VIII, coll. 577ff.; J. Tatum, *Xenophon's Imperial Fiction: On the 'Education of Cyrus'*, Princeton 1989.

[108] *Airs, Waters, Places*, 16, 23.

[109] On the link of the concept of the Barbarian with ecological and geographical factors in Chinese, Indian, Persian and Arabic sources, cf. R. I. Meserve, 'The Inhospitable Land of the Barbarians', *Journal of Asian History*, XVI (1982), pp. 51–89. [See further now Thomas, *Herodotus in Context*.]

on victories in the Persian wars.† This was at first accompanied by a tendency to generalisation:[110] instead of statements about the Persians, Thracians, Scythians and Egyptians, there appeared others on Barbarians understood as a uniform *genos* [race or family][111] to whom were attributed cumulatively determined models of behaviour.[112] At the same time, all this became increasingly laden with political undertones: there could be only hostility[113] between Greeks and Barbarians, just as within despotically governed Barbarian societies there could be no room for friendly relationships.[114] Moreover, the Barbarians allowed themselves to be ruled as if they were slaves.[115] The next step was to deduce from this that the Greeks ought to be in command over these slaves.[116] The identification of slaves with Barbarians was also made easier by the fact that the slaves present in Greece were for the most part non-Greeks.

The models of perception of the 'other' created in the fifth century were in part then heightened in the political theories of the fourth. The experience of the Peloponnesian War gave rise to the assumption according to which Greeks did not make use of the victor's absolute right with regard to other Greeks,[117] did not reduce them to slavery[118] and, more generally, should exercise moderation in inter-Greek warfare.[119] Such a principle found its counterpart in the theory of the Barbarians as natural enemies of the Greeks.[120] Referring also to Euripides,[121] Aristotle[122] identified the Barbarians – who allowed themselves to be ruled despotically – with the 'natural' slaves postulated by himself.[123] There were men who were so exclusively inclined

---

† Contrast Ch. 3 above (Saïd); Harrison, *Emptiness of Asia*, pp. 109–10.

[110] This is also valid in relation to the fact that, especially in depicted representations, battle against the Persians was placed in parallel with the mythical fights against the Amazons, Centaurs and Giants: cf. J. Boardman, 'Heracles, Theseus and Amazons', in D. Kurtz and B. Sparkes (eds), *The Eye of Greece: Studies in the Art of Athens*, Cambridge 1982, pp. 1–28; W. B. Tyrell, *Amazons: A Study in Athenian Mythmaking*, Baltimore 1984; Hall, *Inventing the Barbarian* cit., pp. 68ff.

[111] Euripides, *Hecuba*, 1199–201.

[112] Hall, *Inventing the Barbarian* cit., p. 161.

[113] Euripides, *Hecuba*, 1199–201.

[114] *Ibid.*, 328ff.

[115] *id.*, *Helen*, 276.

[116] *id.*, *Iphigenia in Aulis*, 1400; cf. *id.*, *Telephus*, fr. 719 Nauck; Thrasymachus, fr. 2 Diels.

[117] Xenophon, *Cyropaedia*, 7.5.73.

[118] *id.*, *Hellenica*, 1.6.15; *id.*, *Agesilaus*, 7.6.

[119] F. Kiechle, 'Zur Humanität in der Kriegführung der griechischen Staaten', *Historia*, VII (1958), pp. 129–56; on the practice, however, cf. R. Lonis, *Les usages de la guerre entre grecs et barbares des guerres médiques au milieu de IVe siècle av. J.-C.*, Paris 1969.

[120] Isocrates, 4.184, 12.163; Plato, *Republic*, 469b–471b; *id.*, *Menexenus*, 242d.

[121] *Iphigenia in Aulis*, 1400.

[122] *Politics*, 1252b7.

[123] *Ibid.*, 1254a15ff.

to use their physical strength, and endowed to such a limited extent with reason, that they should be assigned as slaves to a master for their own good: this would be as profitable for them as domestication is for animals. According to Aristotle, at all events, nature had not completely succeeded in its efforts to render the status of these natural slaves recognisable by their physical appearance; in antiquity, skin colour was not yet a matter for argument.[124] Aristotle tenaciously maintained the existence of natural slaves against anonymous adversaries who interpreted slavery only as the result of social conventions, in this instance the right of the victor in war[125] (which, however, did not imply in any cogent fashion that the abolition of the institution of slavery should be championed). Here we have also a resumption of the sophistic argument on the relationship between *nomos* and *physis*. However, it is not certain that sophists like Antiphon had truly developed the position according to which every type of slavery was contrary to nature. A declaration by Alcidamas[126] along those lines harked back to the liberation of Messenia after the battle of Leuctra (371), thus referring to a context within the Greek world. It is doubtful whether Aristotle really advised his pupil, Alexander, to reduce the Barbarians to slavery,[127] or whether this is rather the product of a later interpretation which required the rejection of the supposed piece of counsel on Alexander's part in order to represent a sovereign who saw himself as executing a cosmopolitan plan.[128] On the other hand, as far as we can see, Aristotle did not find immediate followers in antiquity for his peculiar justification of slavery. Roman jurists upheld the argument according to which all men were free by nature; slavery, however, would obtain its validity from the *ius gentium* [law of nations], which precisely diverged on this specific point from the *ius naturale* [natural law].[129]

But the theory of natural slavery conferred a particular effectiveness on the Aristotelian concept of despotism. In spite of some external resemblances, the despotism of the Barbarians differed from Greek tyranny by virtue of being a form of stable power, hereditary and firmly rooted in the *nomos* of society, which was based on the consensus of those who were dominated (who were by nature

[124] F. M. Snowden, *Before Color Prejudice: The Ancient View of Blacks*, Princeton 1983.
[125] *Politics*, 1253b20ff., 1255a5ff. Cf. H. Klees, *Herren und Sklaven*, Wiesbaden 1975; G. Cambiano, 'Aristotle and the Anonymous Opponents of Slavery', in M. I. Finley (ed.), *Classical Slavery*, London 1987, pp. 22–41.
[126] Scholium to Aristotle, *Rhetoric*, 1373b17.
[127] Plutarch, *Moralia* 329b–c; cf. Strabo, 1.4.9 = C 66ff.
[128] H. C. Baldry, *The Unity of Mankind in Greek Thought*, Cambridge 1965, pp. 113ff.
[129] *Digest*, 1.5.4 and *passim*.

servile). In the seventh book of the *Politics*,[130] Aristotle, by means of the application of the Hippocratic theory of climates, confines this nature to the peoples of Asia (otherwise intelligent and artistically endowed), and rules out the peoples who inhabit northern Europe, who, though incapable of instituting political communities, are characterised by military spirit (*thumos*); in this way he restricts despotism to the 'Asian Barbarians'. At the same time, however, Aristotle also mentions the possibility that, besides dominion over natural slaves, there might be a similar dominion over peoples, which would be exerted for the very good of the subjugated.[131] That implies the justification of rule by a people of advanced civilisation over other more backward peoples, who, however, could not be considered as natural slaves. This line of argument would later be developed by Cicero,[132] when he says that out of *humanitas* [humanity] it would be necessary to grant Barbarians a rule that met their interests (*utilitas*), or that Roman universal dominion should have effect as *patrocinium orbis terrarum* [the protection of the world].[133] The ambivalence of Aristotle's ensemble of theories had the effect that, on the one hand, the theory of natural slavery could be used for 'Barbarians' on a universal scale, and on the other that it was possible to restrict the concept of despotism to the confines of Asia (although there it could be transposed from the Persians to other peoples).

4 New horizons and old topoi

In the fourth century the *topoi*, by now consolidated, of the Greek/Barbarian contrast continued to be used – after the renewed subjection of the Greeks of Asia Minor to Persian sovereignty, which they felt as being reduced to slavery by the Barbarians[134] – by those who urged a campaign of vengeance and conquest against the Persian Empire. In Isocrates this took the form of a political emphasis on the separation, formerly understood only in a geographical sense, of Europe (which could mean only the Greek mainland or even just the Propontis region)[135] from Asia: this is explained by the orator's intent

---

[130] *Politics*, 1327b20ff.
[131] *Ibid.*, 1333b38ff.
[132] *Ad Quintum fratrem*, 1.1.27.
[133] *De officiis*, 2.27.
[134] Lysias, 2.59, 33.3.
[135] S. Mazzarino, 'L'image des parties du monde et les rapports entre l'Orient et la Grèce à l'époque classique', *Acta Antiqua Academiae Scientiarum Hungaricae*, VII (1959), pp. 85–101; L. Schumacher, 'Europa: vom Mythos zur geographischen Vorstellung', in *Kreta: Das Erwachen Europas*, Niederrheinisches Museum der Stadt Duisburg, Duisburg 1990, pp. 11–33.

to proclaim the role of the Macedonians (until then regarded as on the same level as semi-Barbarians) as champions of the panhellenic cause.[136] With the consolidation of Alexander's kingdom this specific variant of the Greek/Barbarian contrast became obsolete. It is true that, in Alexander's kingdom and the states of the Successors [the Seleucid, Ptolemaic and Antigonid kings], Macedonians and Greeks from a variety of points of origin came together into a uniform group that could be recognised in participation in gymnasia and religious associations, but an effective 'fusion' with groups of eastern populations did not occur.[137] Relations between Romans and Greeks were at first marked by the fact that the Greeks saw even the Romans as Barbarians and natural enemies;[138] but subsequently Roman universal dominion and the – unprecedented – acculturation of the Roman conquerors that took place thanks to Greek culture (which was later also reflected in the legends of the Romans' Greek origins) generated an awareness of a new cultural unity, which must have reached its height in the so-called Second Sophistic, that was distinct from pride in Greek culture and history and the contemporaneous self-identification with the Roman Empire; now it was the world outside the empire that came to be understood as that of the Barbarians.[139] And when the Germani penetrated the western part of the Empire, the self-definition 'Romans' used to distinguish themselves from the Germanic Barbarians passed to the eastern part, where it was maintained for the duration of the Byzantine Empire.[140]

The expansion of the area of experience through, first, Alexander's kingdom and then the Roman Empire[141] did not lead to an ethnography fed by empirical reality; rather, the exact opposite occurred.[142]

---

[136] A. Momigliano, 'L'Europa come concetto politico presso Isocrate e gli Isocratei' (1933), in *id.*, *Terzo contributo alla storia degli studi classici e del mondo antico*, Rome 1966, pp. 489–97; F. Chabod, *Storia dell'idea di Europa*, Bari 1961, Ch. 1; J. De Romilly, 'Isocrates and Europe', *Greece and Rome*, XXXIX (1992), pp. 2–13.

[137] A. B. Bosworth, 'Alexander and the Iranians', in *Journal of Hellenic Studies*, C (1980), pp. 1–21.

[138] Livy, 31.29.15.

[139] Y. A. Dauge, *Le barbare: recherches sur la conception romaine de la barbarie et de la civilisation*, Brussels 1981.

[140] K. Lechner, 'Byzanz und die Barbaren', *Saeculum*, VI (1955), pp. 292–306; R. Browning, 'Greeks and Others: From Antiquity to the Renaissance', in *History, Language and Literacy in the Byzantine World*, II, Northampton 1989, pp. 1–23 [= Ch. 11, above]; G. Lanata, 'Figure dell'altro nella legislazione giustinianea', *Materiali per una storia della cultura giuridica*, XXII (1992), pp. 3–26.

[141] Polybius, 3.57–59; Strabo, 1.2.1 = C 14.

[142] Cf. the material gathered by K. Trüdinger, *Studien zur Geschichte der griechisch-römischen Ethnographie*, Basle 1918, and, above all, K. E. Müller, *Geschichte der antiken Ethnographie und ethnologischen Theoriebildung*, I–II, Wiesbaden 1972–80. For an assessment, cf. D. Timpe, 'Ethnologische Begriffsbildung in der Antike', in H. Beck (ed.), *Germanenprobleme in heutiger Sicht*, Berlin–New York 1986, pp. 22–40.

The elements of fantasy in ancient tradition, which Herodotus had not known about or had deliberately eliminated, were revived.[143] Curiously, it was the totally uncritical historians of the fourth century who inveighed against the unreliability of such as Herodotus.[144] In the histories of the earliest times of Egypt and India, which have come down to us through the works of Diodorus and Arrian, who relied upon sources of the Hellenistic era, mythology, doctrines on the origins of civilisation, and ethnographic materials are all interwoven. Taking their inspiration from ecologico-climatic theories, historians of Alexander tried to include India on the basis of the Egyptian example of the country's dependence on a river.[145] India, moreover, was represented as a place where monsters and fantastic beings of all kinds[146] were rampant. At the same time, the accounts of the historians of Alexander and Megasthenes about the 'gymnosophists' – the 'naked wise men' of India – contributed to the traditions (later enriched by Jewish and Christian variants) about an eastern philosophy supposed to have been older than that of the Greeks.[147] In addition, there were travel novels and utopias – Hecataeus of Abdera on the Hyperboreans, Iambulus on the Island of the Sun.[148] Fictitious ethnography continued to prosper: there are sightings of Amazons (in Libya);[149] an inversion of the roles of the sexes is observed among various Barbarian tribes;[150] cannibalism and brutish promiscuity are discovered in the extremely primitive tribes on the fringes – ever more distant – of civilisation.[151] Ethnic stereo-

---

[143] A. Dihle, 'Arabien und Indien', in *Hérodote et les peuples non-Grecs* cit., pp. 41–68.

[144] A. Momigliano, 'The Place of Herodotus in the History of Historiography' (1958), in *id.*, *Secondo contributo alla storia degli studi classici*, Rome 1960, pp. 29–44; J. A. S. Evans, 'Father of History or Father of Lies: The Reputation of Herodotus', *Classical Journal*, LXIV (1968), pp. 11–17.

[145] A. Dihle, 'Zur hellenistischen Ethnographie', in *Grecs et Barbares* cit., pp. 205–32.

[146] Strabo, 2.1.9 = C 70.

[147] Diogenes Laertius, i pr. Cf. A. Dihle, 'Indische Philosophen bei Clemens Alexandrinus' (1964), in *id.*, *Antike und Orient: Gesammelte Aufsätze*, Heidelberg 1984, pp. 78–88; *id.*, 'The conception of India in Hellenistic and Roman literature', *Antike und Orient*, Heidelberg 1964, pp. 89–97; H. Dörrie, 'Die Wertung der Barbaren im Urteil der Griechen. Knechtnaturen? Oder Bewahrer und Künder heilbringender Weisheit?', in *Antike and Universalgeschichte: Festschrift Hans Erich Stier*, Munster 1972, pp. 146–75, esp. pp. 159ff.; W. Halbfass, *Indien und Europa: Perspektiven ihrer geistigen Begegnung*, Basle 1981, pp. 13ff.; K. Karttunen, 'The Country of Fabulous Beasts and Naked Philosophers: India in Classical and Medieval Literature', *Arctos*, XXI (1987), pp. 43–52; *id.*, 'Distant Lands in Classical Ethnography', *Grazer Beiträge: Zeitschrift für die klassische Altertumswissenschaft*, XVIII (1992), pp. 195–204 [see also Karttunen, *India in Early Greek Literature, India in the Hellenistic World*].

[148] Diodorus, 2.47, 2.55–60.

[149] *Ibid.*, 3.52–55.

[150] Strabo, 4.4.3 = C 197.

[151] Aristotle, *Nicomachaean Ethics*, 1148b19ff.; *id.*, *Politics*, 1338b19ff.; Diodorus, 3.15.2, 5.32.7; Strabo, 4.5.4, 16.4.17; Artemidorus, 1.8; on the enduring quality of these themes in late antiquity, cf. Dauge, *Le Barbare* cit., pp. 580ff.

types become *Wandermotive*, 'travelling' motifs: thus, for example, the Germani became the 'successors' to the Scythians.[152]

In the Roman era political exploitation of these *topoi* occasionally made a reappearance. The image of the eastern lord whose degeneracy stemmed from luxury and excesses found an echo in the civil war propaganda against Antony,[153] subsequently remaining as a motif in criticisms of tyrannical emperors.[154] As mentioned earlier, Roman conquests could also be interpreted as civilising missions: in their favour the material gains could be shown of transforming populations from a nomadic to settled existence[155] or the suppression of barbaric practices such as human sacrifice in Gaul and Britain.[156] Above all, the *topoi* on the cases of extreme barbarism found their way into the assertions of civil rivalries. Secret societies, sects and ethnic minorities were accused of cannibalism, human sacrifice and sexual excesses: the list goes from Bacchanalian worship, to Catiline's conspirators, to the Jews accused of ritual murders, even to the denunciation of the eucharist as a sexual orgy of Christian sisters and brothers.[157] The Christians took up the accusations, directing them against the Jews and Gnostic sects; the Fathers of the Church chiefly undertook to show the existence of such elements of barbarism in the religion or entertainments of the pagans. Diocletian's legislation against Manichaeism (identified with Persian customs) and incest is explained – against the background of a military quarrel with Persia – on the basis of traditions about Persian customs which, so it was said, authorised incest.[158]

II EUROPEANS, INDIANS AND ORIENTALS

The models for perceiving the 'other' developed in Antiquity now witnessed an admixture, in proportions that varied from instance to

[152] E. Norden, *Die germanische Urgeschichte in Tacitus Germania* (1921), repr. Darmstadt 1971.

[153] P. Zanker, *Augustus und die Macht der Bilder*, Munich 1987, pp. 65ff. (It. trs. *Augusto e il potere delle immagini*, Turin 1989, pp. 62ff. [translated as *The Power of Images in the Age of Augustus*].

[154] Alföldi, *Monarchische Repräsentation* cit., pp. 19ff.

[155] Pliny, *Natural History*, 16.4: Strabo, 4.1.5 = C 180.

[156] Caesar, *De bello Gallico*, 6.13ff.; Tacitus, *Annals*, 14.30; Pliny, *Natural History*, 30.13.

[157] W. Speyer, 'Zu den Vorwürfen der Heiden gegen die Christen', *Jahrbuch für Antike & Christentum*, VI (1963), pp. 129–35; A. Henrichs, 'Pagan Ritual and the Alleged Crimes of the Early Christians: A Reconsideration', in *Kyriakon: Festschrift Johannes Quasten*, I, Munster 1970, pp. 18–35.

[158] H. Chadwick, 'The Relativity of Moral Codes: Rome and Persia in Late Antiquity', in L. Schoedel and R. I. Wilken (eds), *Early Christian Literature and the Classical Intellectual Tradition: in honorem R. M. Grant*, Paris 1979, pp. 134–53.

instance, of empiricism and theory, personal autopsy and the transmission of literary *topoi*, efforts to understand foreign cultures and
ethnocentrism, justification of dominion over other civilisations and
admiration for high-level borrowings, self-reflection in the mirror of
the other and the projection of alternative social conceptions onto
the sphere of outsiders. In many ways these models influenced and
determined the type of relations that Europeans had with the rest of
the world and the picture they had of their own history. The structure of the concept of the Barbarian as 'a concept of asymmetrical
opposition'[159] justified and made possible its being reserved to define,
every time afresh, now pagans, now Muslims, now 'primitives'.[160]
Even the conceptual pairing of Europe/Asia could be employed
in differing situations: to repel Arabs, Mongols, Turks,[161] to justify
European colonialism, as well as to understand Europe's role in the
course of world history. The enormous variety in the interpretation
and adaptations of ancient ways of thinking can be followed here
only through a few selected examples. They will show how the traditions of Antiquity both defined in advance the image of newly
discovered worlds and determined the self-knowledge of the Europeans in the course of their global expansion.

1 Aristotle and the Indians

The observations and projections of ancient ethnography were
handed down to the Middle Ages chiefly through Pliny the Elder,
Solinus and Isidore of Seville; these were joined by the *Romance of
Alexander*, which enjoyed great popularity.[162] There was a recur-

---

[159] R. Kosselleck, 'Zur historischen-politischen Semantik asymmetrischer Gegenbegriffe', in
id., *Vergangene Zukunft: Zur Semantik geschichtlicher Zeiten*, Frankfurt 1979, pp. 211–59.

[160] V. Christides, 'Arabs as "Barbaroi" before the Rise of Islam', *Balkan Studies*, X (1969),
pp. 315–24; W. R. Jones, 'The Image of the Barbarian in Medieval Europe', *Comparative
Studies in Society and History*, XIII (1971), pp. 376–407; A. Borst, 'Barbaren, Geschichte eines
europäischen Schlagworts' (1972), in *Barbaren, Ketzer und Artisten*, Munich 1988, pp. 19–31.
The *topoi* of the Greek concept of the Barbarian (climatic theory, promiscuity, cannibalism,
Amazonism, etc.) can be found, referred by mirror image to the Europeans, in medieval Arab
ethnology: cf. A. Al-Azmeh, 'Barbarians in Arab Eyes', *Past and Present: A Journal of
Historical Studies*, CXXXIV (1992), pp. 3–18.

[161] Chabod, *Storia* cit.; J. Fischer, *Oriens-Occidens-Europa: Begriff und Gedanke 'Europa'
in der späten Antike und im frühen Mittelalter*, Wiesbaden 1957; D. Hay, *Europe: The
Emergence of an Idea*, Edinburgh 1968; M. Fuhrmann, *Europa – Zur Geschichte einer
kulturellen und politischen Idee*, Konstanz 1981; K. Leyser, 'Concepts of Europe in the Early
and High Middle Ages', *Past and Present: A Journal of Historical Studies*, CXXXVII (1992),
pp. 25–47.

[162] M. T. Hodgen, *Early Anthropology in the Sixteenth and Seventeenth Centuries*,
Philadelphia 1964; J. B. Friedman, *The Monstrous Races in Medieval Art and Thought*,
Cambridge MA 1981.

rence of the phenomenon by which literary themes were rediscovered in the reality of foreign cultures. The picture of India that had been formed by Hellenism continued to be reproduced;[163] and themes derived from ancient tradition were the ones that also determined the image of the Far East, starting from the Franciscan mission of the thirteenth century. The Mongols took the place of the Scythians,[164] and Marco Polo, although dismissing the Pygmies as a figment of imagination, could not avoid referring to the Amazons.[165] With the increasing European interest in Asia during the Middle Ages, elements of the traditional picture of India came to be applied to China as well.[166]

The image of the Far East thus formed also conditioned the European view of the New World. Columbus, who had searched in fact for the maritime route via the Indies, grasped the new reality with the help of categories that he had obtained from reading Marco Polo.[167] Integrated and confirmed during the Middle Ages, ancient tradition offered models for dealing with foreign cultures which enabled the New World to be understood according to familiar categories. Starting with Columbus' first accounts, then continuing with ethnographic works like those of Oviedo,[168] promiscuity, incest, human sacrifice and cannibalism were motifs that recurred whenever there was a need to bear witness to the primitive and violent nature of the savages, who were subdued by force. At the same time, obviously, other Indians were seen from the opposite angle, as peaceable

[163] R. Wittkower, 'Marvels of the East: A Study in the History of Monsters', *Journal of the Warburg and Courtauld Institute*, V (1942), pp. 159–97 (It. trs. 'Le meraviglie dell'Oriente: una ricerca sulla storia dei mostri', in *id.*, *Allegoria e migrazione dei simboli*, Turin 1987, pp. 84–152); H. Rau, 'The Image of India in European Antiquity and the Middle Ages', in J. Deppert (ed.), *India and the West: Proceedings of a Seminar Dedicated to the Memory of Hermann Goetz*, New Delhi 1983, pp. 197–208.

[164] C. W. Connell, 'Western Views on the Origins of the "Tartars": An Example of the Influence of Myth in the Second Half of the Thirteenth Century', in *Journal of Medieval & Renaissance Studies*, III (1973), pp. 115–37; J. Fried, 'Auf der Suche nach der Wirklichkeit: Die Mongolen und die europäische Erfahrungswissenschaft im 13. Jahrhundert', *Historische Zeitschrift*, CCXLIII (1986), pp. 287–332.

[165] Hodgen, *Early Anthropology* cit., p. 102. [For the suggestion, reminiscent of scholarship on Herodotus, that Marco Polo never travelled as far as he claims, see Wood, *Did Marco Polo Go to China?*.]

[166] F. Reichert, *Begegnungen mit China: Die Entdeckung Ostasiens im Mittelalter*, Sigmaringen 1992.

[167] *Id.*, 'Columbus und Marco Polo – Asien in Amerika. Zur Literaturgeschichte der Entdekkungen', in *Zeitschrift für Historische Forschung*, XV (1988), pp. 1–63; *id.*, *Begegnungen* cit., pp. 269ff.

[168] A. Gerbi, *La Natura delle Indie nove da Cristoforo Colombo a Gonzalo F. de Oviedo*, Milan–Naples 1975; B. Rech, 'Zum Nachleben der Antike im spanischen Überseeimperium, Der Einfluss antiker Schriftsteller auf die *Historia General y Natural de las Indias* des Gonzalo Fernandez de Oviedo (1478–1557), *Gesammelte Aufsätze zur Kulturgeschichte Spaniens*, XXXI (1984), pp. 181–244.

and innocent children. And not even in America could the Amazons be omitted.[169]

In the discussions in Spain on the legitimacy of colonial rule, the Aristotelian category of natural slavery acquired a specially explosive character.[170] This intellectual construct had become freshly available with the resumption of the study of Aristotle in the thirteenth century and was accepted by Thomas Aquinas and others; but the matter remained at the stage of theoretical study without immediate practical application.

The situation changed dramatically with the sixteenth-century controversies over the appropriate treatment of the Indians (who, despite the differences between cultures, were generically designated as Barbarians). The formula of natural slavery was applied for the first time to the Indians in 1510 by the theologian Johannes Maior, who was teaching in Paris: given that they lived like wild animals and that in their case the Aristotelian category of natural slave was valid, subjugation by Europeans was justified. Maior's argument was taken up again in Spain in 1512 when, provoked by the criticisms of the Dominicans, debate on colonial policy began. It was attractive because there was no need to rely on the authority of problematic legal reasons – like the *translatio imperii* [transferral of command] of the pope – but arguments could be put forward based on the characteristics peculiar to the dominated peoples themselves. At the same time, the *encomienda*, or system of forced labour, seemed to be justified as well.

Seeing that the theory of natural slavery had been authoritatively established by Aristotle, 'the philosopher', the burden of proof consisted solely in demonstrating the relevance of this category to the Indians. Since skin colour, which was attributed to climate, did not constitute an argument, physical characteristics could not be used to this end. The proof was therefore supplied at the level of institutions and customs. One of the strategies of reasoning established a link between the primitiveness of the Indians and the lack of private prop-

---

[169] F. Lestringant, 'De l'ubiquité des amazons au siècle des grandes découvertes', in *La Mythologie, clef de lecture du monde classique: Hommage à Raymond Chevalier*, Tours 1986, pp. 297–319.

[170] For full expositions of the Spanish colonial debate, cf., from the large amount of bibliography, above all J. Höffner, *Christentum und Menschenwürd: Das Anliegen der spanischen Kolonialethik im goldenen Zeitalter*, Trier 1947; L. Hanke, *Aristotle and the American Indians: A Study in Race Prejudice in the Modern World*, London 1959; A. Pagden, *The Fall of Natural Man: The American Indian and the Origins of Comparative Ethnology*, Cambridge 1982 (It. trs. *La caduta dell'uomo naturale: L'indiano d'America e le origini dell'etnologia comparata*, Turin 1989); J. Fisch, *Die europäische Expansion und das Völkerrecht*, Stuttgart 1984; Nippel, *Griechen* cit., Ch. 2 (with numerous bibliographical references).

erty, family and religion, or even their purely vegetarian diet: the ingenuous and peaceful savage would be placed for his own well-being under the protection of a master. The other variant concerned the aggressive savage, who supposedly practised human sacrifice, cannibalism, idolatry and sodomy, and was to be reduced to slavery because of this. The theory of natural slavery received further boosts after 1540, in connection with new controversies about the legislation of the system of forced labour. Argument culminated in the famous debate between Juan de Sepúlveda and Bartolemé de Las Casas before the Council of the Indies, at Valladolid, in 1550.[171] Sepúlveda, who had made a name for himself as a translator of Aristotle, qualified the Indians as natural slaves in the Aristotelian sense because of their scant capacity for reasoning; it was therefore a right, not to say a downright obligation, to exercise dominion over the Indians for their own good. Even though Sepúlveda's theory gained fame thanks to the opposition of Las Casas, nevertheless, as regards the repercussions on the history of international law, there is more significance in the arguments developed in the reflections of the theologians and jurists – something that cannot be set out in detail here: let it be stressed only that Francisco de Vitoria and his disciples at Salamanca saw the Indians essentially as subjects with equal dignity in international law, and considered that rule over them was justified only when it was the result of a just war originated by a violation on their part of the libertarian postulates of that law (*Relectiones de Indis*, 1539).

According to his concept, there was no right to a religious war of an offensive nature, which could also be used to punish the sins of the pagans. It is true, however, that even with Vitoria the customs, or rather, the sins, of the pagans come into play, and in a dual manner. First of all, he develops the following theme: if even Christians have no right to punish pagan transgressions of natural law, nevertheless, practices such as cannibalism and human sacrifice could legitimise a right to intervene in order to save the innocent – a right that would be based on the precept of loving one's neighbour. Here we find the origins of the principle that sanctions the right of humanitarian intervention.

Secondly, Vitoria observes that, in spite of everything, a certain backwardness does exist among the Indians at the level of civilis-

---

[171] L. Hanke, *All Mankind is One: A Study of the Disputation between Bartolomé de Las Casas and Juan Ginés de Sepúlveda in 1550 on the Intellectual and Religious Capacity of the American Indians*, De Kalb IL 1974; J. A. Fernándes-Santamaria, 'Juan Ginés de Sepúlveda on the Nature of the American Indians', in *Americans*, XXXI (1975), pp. 434–51.

ation, manifested in their primitive lifestyle, their absence of clothing, of cooked food, agriculture and urban culture, as well as in their cruel practices of human sacrifice and cannibalism. These defects spring from a lack, not of intellectual gifts, but rather of a suitable education. From this he infers the need for paternalistic assistance. Domination over the Indians can be justified in so far as it is exerted in their own interest. On this theme Vitoria harks back to Aristotle, who would not have postulated reduction to slavery but rather recourse to a solicitous authority such as is exercised over juveniles. The comparison implies that one day the Indians could be released from this relationship of guardianship.

It is not possible here to set out the successive developments in the doctrine of the rights of nations, nor the later fortunes of the concept of the 'slave by nature', which regained a particularly explosive quality in the North American debates on slavery,[172] after which in the eighteenth century, with the rise of a physical anthropology,[173] skin colour was for the first time brought into the argument.

2 Savages, Greeks and the development of civilisation

A third element exists, however, in the Spanish colonial debate that had considerable relevance for modern thinking about the Greeks and others, opening up new possibilities of cultural comparisons between the ancient world and the new.

To the argument about Indian customs even their defenders, first and foremost Bartolomé de Las Casas (*Apologética historia*, 1551), contributed: like all others, he too held the existence of cannibalism and human sacrifice among the Indians[174] to be a fact, however much he emphasises that the relevant accounts are based only on hearsay. But, in the context of his reasoning, Las Casas brings reference to antiquity into play in a new way.[175] He advocates a diversification of the concept of Barbarian, maintaining that this would in fact correspond with the positions of Aristotle and Thomas Aquinas. Las

[172] D. B. Davis, *The Problem of Slavery in Western Culture*, Ithaca NY 1966; M. Hartfield, 'New Thoughts on the Proslavery Natural Law Theory: The Importance of History and the Study of Ancient Slavery', *Southern Studies*, XXII (1983), pp. 244–59; J. D. Harrington, 'Classical Antiquity and the Proslavery Argument', *Slavery & Abolition*, X (1989), pp. 60–72.
[173] F. Lotter, 'Christoph Meiners und die Lehre von der unterschiedlichen Wertigkeit der Menschenrassen', in H. Boockmann and H. Wellenreuther (eds), *Geschichtswissenschaft in Göttingen*, Göttingen 1987, pp. 30–75; W. Demel, 'Wie die Chinesen gelb wurden: Ein Beitrag zur Frühgeschichte der Rassentheorien', *Historiche Zeitschrift*, CCLV (1992), pp. 625–66.
[174] A. Pagden, 'The Forbidden Food: Francisco de Vitoria and José de Acosta on Cannibalism', *Terrae Incognitae*, XIII (1981), pp. 17–30.
[175] *Id.*, *The Fall* cit., pp. 126ff. (It. trs. pp. 163ff.).

Casas therefore makes a distinction between four variants of the idea of the Barbarian. The first applies to all uncivilised, cruel men who lack self-control in given situations: in theory, this group may include men of every people, Scythians as well as Greeks or Romans; even Christians are not immune from relapse. The second variant concerns societies which have not reached a fixed level of civilisation, for instance those who have not developed a written culture: this is the case with Indians. The third category is formed by natural slaves in the Aristotelian sense, who would be incapable of any kind of organised community. However, it would be virtually impossible to find them in reality, and above all it could not be presumed that God had populated an entire continent with these unsuccessful products of nature. The fourth group comprises Barbarians in the sense of pagans. Their common characteristic is their persistent predisposition to vice, distinct from all material progress. That would be demonstrable in the case of the Romans, who on the one hand dominated all other peoples, and on the other were outstanding for their tremendous vices and horrible practices (such as sacrifices, bloody gladiatorial fights and obscene theatrical shows). In this regard, Las Casas can go back to the numerous testimonies present in the anti-pagan polemics of the Fathers of the Church, who had collected them specially in answer to the original accusations against the Christians.

As pagans, the Indians belong to the same category as the Greeks and Romans: that makes the indecency of their customs appear in a new light. After all, even ancient tradition has a large quantity of examples of cannibalism and human sacrifice, and not only among peripheral peoples – including the ancient 'Spaniards' – but also among the Greeks and Romans themselves, at least as regards the most ancient periods. Moreover, even then the distinction had been made between cannibalism and ritual sacrifice, not only by Plutarch but also by Christian writers like Clement, Eusebius and Lactantius. In this way Indian human sacrifice becomes evidence of a stage of religious evolution, which at the same time includes a disposition to pass on to Christianity.

Las Casas' reasoning is the beginning of a new debate about the Indians, intended to define their place in a general process of civilisation which all human peoples, however much distanced in time, would pass through, broadly speaking, in the same way. Nevertheless, from J. de Acosta (*Historia natural y moral de las Indias*, 1590) to Joseph-François Lafitau (*Moeurs des sauvages amériquains comparés aux moeurs des premiers temps*, 1724), who based his work empirically on the North American Iroquois, this discussion did not go beyond the context of the problem of the origin of the Indians and of locating them within a chronological scheme founded on the biblical image of the world, which laid down their line of descent from one of the sons of Noah.[176] But the fundamental starting point – that is, of placing the primitive peoples known though the 'discovery' of the 'New World' on an evolutionary rung preceding that of the Greeks and Romans – had to acquire a following. The theories of the French and Scottish Enlightenment took up this concept again in relation both to the stages of economic revolution and to those of marriage and the family.[177]

The theory of a succession of levels of economic attainment, to be found in Turgot and Adam Smith, and which later became the common heritage of the nineteenth-century national economy, could have resorted to corresponding schemes at several stages of Antiquity. Very different, on the other hand, seemed to be the case of the theories on the development of relations between the sexes: from John Millar to the nineteenth-century theorists – on one side, Bachofen, and on the other McLennan, Morgan (and Engels) plus various others – the principal objective consisted of reducing to an evolutionary scheme the data from the ethnographic literature of Antiquity, reflections on relations between the sexes in mythology and observations conducted on what were presumed to be recent 'savages' (notably the Iroquois of Lafitau and Morgan).[178] This meant that assertions passed down from ancient tradition were interpreted in the light of a 'nomological knowledge' – in other words, there was attributed to them a systematic value that they had not originally possessed: in this regard, there is a significance in the treatment given in the various theories, from John Millar to Morgan, to Herodotus' observations on the Lycians' matrilinear naming practice. The same critics of evolutionary theories – for example, among the historians of Antiquity, Eduard Meyer[179] – usually still used such information from ancient ethnographic tradition at face value, that is to say, on the same level as statements based on experience. From the late nineteenth century, the conviction began to grow of the existence in ancient ethnography of a record of cases of *topoi* linked to

---

[176] G. Gliozzi, *Adamo e il nuovo mondo: la nascita del'antropologia come ideologia coloniale: dale genealogie bibliche alle teorie razziali (1500–1700)*, Florence 1977; J.-P. Rubiés, 'Hugo Grotius' Dissertation on the Origin of the American Peoples and the Use of Comparative Methods', *Journal of the History of Ideas*, LII (1991), pp. 221–44.

[177] Nippel, *Griechen* cit., Ch. 3 (with bibliography).

[178] *Ibid.*, pp. 66ff., 102–17.

[179] *Id.*, 'Prolegomena zu Eduard Meyers Anthropologie', in W. M. Calder III and A. Demandt (eds), *Leben und Leistung eines Universalhistorikers*, Leiden 1990, pp. 311–28.

type; but nevertheless, even in the sciences of Antiquity it took a very long time before there was common agreement[180] on the need to look for the figure (in this case a variant of that of the 'world in reverse') underlying information – something which obliged people not to take testimonies of this kind as empirical observations.[181]

3 Oriental despotism and the Eurocentric image of history

With the revival of Aristotle, the idea of despotism was also resurrected.[182] The modern view of Asia taken by Europeans was decisively shaped. It is true, however, that from Bodin to Pufendorf to Montesquieu a discussion developed concerning despotism as a category subject to generalisation and universally employable in relation to powers based on the right of conquest. In the eighteenth-century French debate, this concept was directed polemically against absolutism itself and then, in like manner, against the Jacobin regime of Terror after the Revolution.[183]

In parallel, however, a discussion took place that focused the use of this category on various kingdoms of eastern origin: first the Ottoman Empire,[184] then Persia, India and China. Montesquieu (*Lettres persanes*, 1721; *Esprit des lois*, 1748), despite having introduced despotism as a universally applicable category, in actual fact always referred to oriental contexts, as known to him through contemporary travel literature.[185] This, in its turn, was influenced by preliminary pieces of knowledge drawn from ancient tradition. In

---

[180] S. Pembroke, 'Last of the Matriarchs: A Study in the Inscriptions of Lycia', *Journal of the Economic and Social History of the Orient*, VIII (1965), pp. 217–47; *id.*, 'Women in Charge: The Function of Alternatives in Early Greek Tradition and the Ancient Idea of Matriarchy', *Journal of the Warburg and Courtauld Institute*, XXX (1967), pp. 1–35; *id.*, 'The Early Human Family: Some Views 1770–1870', in R. R. Bolgar (ed.), *Classical Influences on Western Thought, A.D. 1650–1870*, Cambridge 1979, pp. 275–91; P. Vidal-Naquet, 'Esclavage et gynécocratie dans la tradition, le mythe et l'utopie', in C. Nicolet (ed.), *Recherches sur les structures sociales dans l'antiquité classique*, Paris 1970, pp. 63–80 (fuller English version in R. L. Gordon (ed.), *Myth, Religion and Society*, Cambridge–Paris 1981, pp. 187–200).

[181] B. Wagner-Hasel, 'Rationalitätskritik und Weiblichkeitkonzeptionen: Anmerkungen zur Matriarchatsdiskussion in der Altertumswissenschaft', in *id.* (ed.), *Matriarchatstheorien der Altertumswissenschaft*, Darmstadt 1992, pp. 295–373.

[182] R. Koebner, 'Despot and Despotism: Vicissitudes of a Political Term', *Journal of the Warburg and Courtauld Institute*, XIV (1951), pp. 275–302.

[183] M. Richter, under 'Despotism', in *Dictionary of the History of Ideas*, II, New York 1973, pp. 1–19.

[184] L. Valensi, 'The Making of a Political Paradigm: The Ottoman State and Oriental Despotism', in A. Grafton and E. Blair (eds), *The Transmission of Culture in Early Modern Europe*, Philadelphia 1990, pp. 173–203.

[185] F. Weil, 'Montesquieu et le despotisme', in *Actes du Congrès Montesquieu* (23–26 May 1955), Bordeaux 1956, pp. 191–215; D. Young, 'Montesquieu's View of Despotism and his

Montesquieu's sources, however, as in his own exposition, the *topoi* of the absolute power of the despot, slavery of his subjects, depravity of their customs and of a general spiritual inertia[186] are predominant. Using the natural and climatic conditions of Asia as the decisive cause,[187] it was also possible to explain why the situation remained constant over the centuries.[188] The absence of private land ownership was now thrown into particular relief. In similar vein, great consideration was given to Megasthenes' information that the whole land belonged to the king;[189] from this too, the deduction was made that the situation remained unchanged from one era to the next. The fact that the sovereign could dispose of everything as he pleased was held to be the effective foundation of despotism, especially of that of the Great Mogul in India, and was used to explain the country's backwardness.[190] N.-A. Boulanger (*Recherches sur l'origine du despotisme oriental*, 1761, posthumous) further emphasised the support provided to this power by the priestly caste. And A.-H. Anquetil-Duperron (*Législation orientale*, 1778) highlighted how these theories could also serve as justification for European colonial interests;[191] but his demonstrations of why the category of despotism was not accurate in the case of Turkey, Persia and India (given that in these countries private ownership existed and the rulers were restricted in the exercise of their power by traditions and laws) were widely ignored. Similarly, his edition of the *Zend-Avesta*, which opened a new path to an understanding of Zoroastrianism, had to contend with doubts about the authenticity of the work.[192] Not even

---

Use of Travel Literature', *Review of Politics*, XL (1978), pp. 392–405; A. Grosrichard, *Structures du sérail: La fiction du despotisme asiatique de l'occident classique*, Paris 1979.

[186] This model will also be predominant in Gibbon's description of the emperors of late antiquity: cf. only J. W. Burrow, *Gibbon*, Oxford 1985, pp. 46ff.

[187] R. Shackleton, 'The Evolution of Montesquieu's Theory of Climate', *Revue Internationale de Philosophie*, IX (1955), pp. 317–29, and, for the antecedents, M. J. Tooley, 'Bodin and the Medieval Theory of Climate', *Speculum*, XXVIII (1953), pp. 64–83.

[188] Cf. for instance, *Esprit des lois*, Book XIV, Ch. 4.

[189] Stabo, 15.1.40 = C 704; Diodorus, 2.40.2. Cf. B. Breloer, *Das Grundeigentum in Indien*, Diss. Bonn 1927, pp. 51ff.

[190] A. T. Embree, 'Oriental Despotism: A Note on the History of an Idea', *Societas: A Review of Social History*, I (1971), pp. 255–69; R. Minuti, 'Proprietà della terra e despotismo orientale: Aspetti di un dibattito sull'India nella seconda metà del Settecento', *Materiali per una storia della cultura giuridica*, VIII (1978), pp. 29–177; J. Fisch, 'Der märchenhafte Orient: Die Umwertung einer Tradition von Marco Polo bis Macaulay', *Saeculum*, XXXV (1984), pp. 246–66, esp. pp. 258ff. (on the exposition of François Bernier).

[191] F. Venturi, 'Despotismo orientale', *Rivista Storica Italiana*, LXXII (1960), pp. 117–26; S. Stelling-Michaud, 'Le mythe du despotisme oriental', *Schweiz: Beiträge zur allgemeinen Geschichte*, XVIII–XIX (1960–61), pp. 328–46; D. Metzler, 'A. H. Anquetil-Duperron (1731–1805) und das Konzept der Achsenzeit', in H. Sancisi-Weerdenburg and J. W. Drijvers (eds), *Achaemenid History, VII. Through Travellers' Eyes. European Travellers on the Iranian Monuments*, Leiden 1991, pp. 123–223.

Voltaire's protests (*Essai sur les moeurs et l'esprit des nations*, 1756) against China's being subsumed into the category of despotism prevented the persistence of the clichés.[192]

With Adam Smith (*Wealth of Nations*, 1776)[194] and the British discussion over the administration of India a new variant of climatic-ecological reasoning appeared, in which the development of the bureaucratic power apparatus (over village communities)[195] was explained by the need for irrigation and river regulation. Here too the arguments were later generalised, from both a temporal and spatial viewpoint, applying them potentially to all regimes in the Asian environment, from Antiquity to the modern era. On the one hand, this can be seen in the debate within socialism, where early comments by Marx and Engels concerning the English debate over India[196] also contributed to the Marxist category of 'the Asiatic mode of production' (*Vorwort zur Kritik der politischen Ökonomie*, 1859), suppressed for political reasons in the Soviet arguments of the thirties (about China) and later resumed only in the sixties.[197] On the other hand, there is Max Weber's universal-historic conception. Weber tried to explain the East's different development from the West's, chiefly in Antiquity, by the contrast between coastal and

[192] R. Schwab, *Anquetil-Duperron. Sa vie*, Paris 1934; J. Duchesne-Guillemin, *The Western Response to Zoroaster*, Oxford 1958, Ch. 1.

[193] E. W. Said, *Orientalism*, New York 1978; R. Kabbani, *Europe's Myths of Orient: Devise and Rule*, Basingstoke 1986; T. Hentsch, *L'Orient imaginaire: La vision politique occidentale de l'est mediterranéen*, Paris 1988.

[194] Book V, Ch. 1 and *passim*.

[195] For the debate on the 'Indian village community', cf. Nippel, *Griechen* cit., pp. 96ff. (with bibliography).

[196] For the sources of Marx, cf. W. Ruben, 'Karl Marx über indien und die Indienliteratur vor ihm', *Wissenschaftliche Zeitschrift der Humboldt-Universität Berlin*, III, 2 (1953–54), pp. 69–100. Newspaper articles written in 1853 for the *New York Daily Tribune* must, however, have become known only with their publication by D. Rjasanoff in *Unter dem Banner des Marxismus*, I (1925–26), pp. 370–402. The *Grundrisse der Kritik der politischen Ökonomie* (with the chapter 'Formen, die der kapitalischen Produktion vorhergehen') were not published until 1939–41, or 1953. Various statements on the relation between the irrigation system and despotic rule in India (by Marx in *Das Kapital*, I [1867], and Engels in the *Anti-Dühring* [1878]) were, however, known and had induced Karl Kautsky, among others, to discuss such a relation in general: 'Die moderne Nationalität', *Die Neue Zeit*, V (1887), pp. 392–405, 442–51.

[197] K. A. Wittfogel, *Oriental Despotism*, New York 1957 (with the extension of the theory to pre-Columbian societies and to Russia); G. Lichtheim, 'Oriental Despotism', in *id.*, *The Concept of Ideology and Other Essays*, New York 1967, pp. 62–93; D. Thorner, 'Marx on India and the Asiatic Mode of Production', *Contributions to Indian Sociology*, IX (1966), pp. 33–66; J. Pecirka, 'Die sowjetischen Diskussionen über die asiatische produktionsweise und über die Sklavenhalterformation', *Eirene*, III (1964), pp. 147–70; G. Sofri, *Il modo di produzione asiatico: Storia di una controversia marxista*, Turin 1969; S. P. Dunn, *The Fall and Rise of the Asiatic Mode of Production*, London 1982; R. Kössler, *Dritte Internationale und Bauernrevolution. Die Herausbildung des sowjetischen Marxismus in der Debatte um die 'asiatische' Produktionsweise*, Frankfurt 1982.

riverine civilisations (*Agrarverhältnisse im Altertum*, 1909);[198] he subsequently integrated this hypothesis with a theory of the sociology of religion, taking as his theme the religious assumptions of association in free urban communities in the West and the impediments to this form of 'fraternisation' in the East (*Die Stadt*; *Gesammelte Aufsätze zur Religionssoziologie*).[199]

The contrast between European dynamism and Asian stagnation, which lies at the root of these theoretical variants, must be seen against a broader background of universal historiography and philosophy of history. The reconstruction of the chronologies of the ancient Orient by Scaliger (1583) and new knowledge about Chinese traditions had cast doubt upon the chronology arranged in the perspective of the history of salvation and based on Eusebius. With this, the first foundations of biblical criticism were laid, on the one hand, and on the other a reassessment of Herodotus began.[200] The recurring attempts, right up to the late eighteenth century, to maintain the preconceived cornerstone of biblical chronology are proof of the extremely ambivalent effect of new knowledge about European historical consciousness. Universal-historic works, from the English *Universal History* (1736) up to those of the historians of Göttingen at the end of the eighteenth century,[201] allocated ample space to eastern civilisations but did not go beyond a resumé of the histories of the various peoples. German Romanticism (Herder, Friedrich and August Wilhelm Schlegel) cultivated an idealised picture of India, in which it appeared as the cradle of humanity and birthplace of religion, philosophy and poetry,[202] thus inspiring the study of Sanskrit and comparative mythology.[203] In the nineteenth century, the commitment to provide an interpretation of world history

[198] J. Deininger, 'Die politischen Strukturen des mittelmeerisch-vorderorientalischen Altertums bei Max Weber', in W. Schluchter (ed.), *Max Webers Sicht des antiken Christentums*, Frankfurt 1985, pp. 72–110; S. Breuer, 'Stromuferkultur und Küstenkultur: Geographische und ökologische Faktoren in Max Webers "ökonomischer Theorie der antiken Staatenwelt"', in *ibid.*, pp. 111–50.

[199] B. Nelson, 'On Orient and Occident in Max Weber', *Social Research*, XLIII (1976), pp. 114–29; W. Nippel, 'Max Weber's "The City" Revisited', in A. Molho, J. Emlen and K. A. Raaflaub (eds), *City-states in Classical Antiquity and Medieval Italy*, Stuttgart 1991, pp. 19–30.

[200] Nippel, *Griechen* cit., pp. 57ff. (with bibliography).

[201] H. W. Blanke, 'Verfassungen, die nicht rechtlich, sondern wirklich sind: A.H.L. Heeren und das Ende der Aufklärungshistorie', *Berichte zur Wissenschaftsgeschichte*, VI (1983), pp. 143–64.

[202] Halbfass, *Indien* cit., pp. 86ff.; U. Faust, *Mythologie und Religionen des Ostens bei Johann Gottfried Herder*, Münster 1977; A. Fuchs-Sumiyoshi, *Orientalismus in der deutschen Literatur: Untersuchungen zu Werken des 19. und 20. Jahrhunderts*, Hildesheim 1984.

[203] A. Momigliano, 'Friedrich Creuzer and Greek History' (1946), in *Contributo alla storia degli studi classici*, Rome 1955, pp. 233–48; W. Burkert, 'Griechische Mythologie und die

founded on a philosophy of history had the result, despite increased knowledge about oriental civilisations, that a Eurocentric view of history regained importance. Hegel (*Vorlesungen über die Philosophie der Geschichte; Grundlinien der Philosophie des Rechts*),[204] using both ancient tradition and modern travel literature on China, India and Persia, had inserted and arranged these countries in a history of the 'progress of the awareness of liberty': among the Orientals only one man – that is the theocratic sovereign – was free; the decisive breaks arose from the Greek victories in the Persian wars and with the advent of Christianity.[205] Droysen saw in the fusion of Greek and oriental cultural elements the roots of this victory of Christianity in world history and on this based his new conception of the Hellenistic era as a historically decisive period.[206] Ranke eliminated the 'eternally immobile'[207] oriental peoples from his *Weltgeschichte* (1880), which concentrated exclusively on the causal relations that had led to modern Europe.[208] The task of the *Griechische Kulturgeschichte* (1898–1902, posthumous) by Jacob Burckhardt was to try to determine the 'place of the Greek spirit in world history between East and West': in the 'agonistic spirit of the Greeks' he saw the characteristic that clearly distinguished them from eastern civilisations.[209]

Scientific and extra-scientific reasons, especially in nineteenth-century German studies, caused the problem of the confines within which the new *Altertumswissenschaft* [science of antiquity] should take account of oriental as well as Graeco-Roman Antiquity to remain a subject of controversy. From the end of the eighteenth

---

Geistesgeschichte der Moderne', in *Les études classiques aux XIXe et XXe siècles: leur place dans l'histoire des idées*, Vandoeuvres-Geneva 1980, pp. 159–207; F. Graf, *Griechische Mythologie*, Munich 1985.

[204] 354ff.

[205] E. Schulin, *Die weltgeschichtliche Erfassung des Orients bei Hegel und Ranke*, Göttingen 1958; D.-Y. Song, *Die Bedeutung der asiatischen Welt bei Hegel, Marx und Max Weber*, Diss. Frankfurt 1972.

[206] A. Momigliano, 'Per il centenario dell'Alessandro Magno di J. G. Droysen' (1933), in *Contributo* cit., pp. 263–73; *id.*, 'Introduzione all'Ellenismo' (1970), in *Quinto contributo alla storia degli studi classici e del mondo antico*, Rome 1975, pp. 267–91; *id.*, 'J. G. Droysen: Between Greeks and Jews' (1970), in *ibid.*, pp. 109–26; B. Bravo, *Philologie, histoire, philosophie de l'histoire: Etude sur J. G. Droysen, Historien de l'antiquité*, Wrocław 1968; R. Bichler, *'Hellenismus': Geschichte und Problematik eines Epochenbegriffs*, Darmstadt 1983.

[207] For this *topos* in eighteenth- and nineteenth-century European literature cf. R. Dawson, *The Chinese Chameleon: An Analysis of European Conceptions of Chinese Civilization*, London 1967, pp. 65ff.

[208] E. Kessel, 'Rankes Idee der Universalhistorie', *Historische Zeitschrift*, CLXXVIII (1954), pp. 269–308.

[209] A. Momigliano, 'Introduzione alla "Griechische Kulturgeschichte" di Jacob Burckhardt' (1955), in *Secondo contributo* cit., pp. 283–98; I. Weiler, *Der Sport bei den Völkern der Alten Welt*, Darmstadt 1981, pp. 1ff., 53ff.

century, the Germans defined themselves as a *Kulturnation* [nation based on common culture] by virtue of reference to the timeless values of Greek culture:[210] with that, from the time of Wilhelm von Humboldt and Friedrich August Wolf, the foundations had been laid for the preference accorded in universities and high schools to the study of Graeco-Roman rather than oriental Antiquity.[211] With the ever increasing prominence of the national question, an approach to Antiquity also developed in the form of national histories which made the old conception of universal history appear obsolete.[212] The development of Indo-Germanic linguistics contributed to a self-restriction with regard to eastern civilisations into which anti-Semitic undertones soon penetrated.[213] At the same time, however, there was no lack of pleas like that of Boeckh, in favour of an *Altertums-wissenschaft* that would embrace the entire Near Eastern and Mediterranean world.[214] But by now the scientific approach was making its mark for its critical treatment of the sources. With the decipherment of hieroglyphics and cuneiform script and the consolidation of the orientalist's specialist disciplines, finally realised despite considerable opposition, demands increased until they assumed almost unreal proportions. That became clearly apparent with Eduard Meyer, who did not manage to complete his vast *Geschichte des Altertums* (1885–1930), a history based on the sources. Students of the 'classic' *Altertumswissenschaft* continued to look upon the Near East, for preference from the point of view of the Greek sources:[215] that encouraged the persistence of clichés even in works claiming to be scientifically specialised, as also in philosophical-

[210] The German picture of Greece had no need for personal inspection; accounts of journeys and descriptions of ancient monuments were chiefly the domain of the English: cf. R. Jenkyns, *The Victorians and Ancient Greece*, Oxford 1980; D. Constantine, *Early Greek Travellers and the Hellenic Ideal*, Cambridge 1985; *id.*, 'The City and its People: The Recovery of the Classical Past', *Publications of the English Goethe Society*, n.s., LVIII (1989), pp. 27–42.

[211] Cf. the introduction in W. Nippel (ed.), *Über das Studium der Alten Geschichte*, Munich 1993 (with bibliographic references).

[212] Thus already in Niebuhr's review to Heeren (1813), in *Kleine historische und philologische Schriften*, 2 Sammlung (Berlin, 1843), pp. 107–58.

[213] L. Poliakov, *Le mythe aryen*, Brussels 1971; Burkert, *Die orientalisierende Epoche* cit., pp. 8ff.; J. Wiesehöfer, 'Zur Geschichte der Begriffe "Arier" und "Arisch" in der deutschen Sprachwissenschaft und Althistorie des 19. und der ersten Halfte des 20. Jahrhunderts', in H. Sancisi-Weerdenburg and J. W. Drijvers (eds), *Achaemenid History, V. The Roots of the European Tradition*, Leiden 1990, pp. 149–65.

[214] A. Boeckh, 'Rede z. Eröffnung der elften Versammlung deutscher Philologen, Schulmänner u. Orientalisten ... 1850', in *id.*, *Gesammelte Kleine Schriften, II. Reden*, Leipzig 1859, pp. 183–99, republished in Nippel, *Über das Studium* cit., pp. 148–60.

[215] Cf. A. Momigliano, *The Classical Foundations of Modern Historiography*, Berkley CA 1990, pp. 5ff. (It. trs. *Le radici classiche della storiografia moderna*, Florence 1992, p. 12): in one's youth it was customary to say that one had to master Greek for oriental history and German for Greek history.

historical depictions à la Spengler and Toynbee. How intensely the preconstituted images of the differences and similarities between the Greeks on the one side and the orientals and 'savages' on the other influenced and determined the subjects of research and interpretations of the sciences of Antiquity, starting in the nineteenth century, and what part was played by the differences between national scholarly traditions, are questions which are still awaiting a systematic analysis.

Intellectual Chronology

BC

*c.*570	François vase
*c.*560–546	Croesus king of Lydia
499–494	Ionian revolt against Persian rule
490–479	Persian Wars
472	Aeschylus' *Persians* performed in Athens
431–404	Peloponnesian War
420s	Herodotus' *Histories* 'published'
415	Euripides, *Trojan Women* performed
413	Euripides, *Iphigenia in Tauris*
408/6	Euripides, *Bacchae* and *Iphigenia in Aulis*
401	Xenophon and 'Ten Thousand' at battle of Cunaxa
392	Gorgias' Olympian oration
388	Lysias' Olympian oration
380	Isocrates, *Panegyricus*
346	Isocrates, *Philip*
334–323	Alexander's conquest of Asia
322	Aristotle dies
mid-2nd c.	Polybius, *History*; Plautus adopts Greek description of fellow Romans as barbarians
168	Roman subjugation of Greece at battle of Pydna
late 1st c.	Diodorus Siculus, *Universal History*; Strabo, *Geography*; Dionysius of Halicarnassus (in his *Roman Antiquities*) develops idea of Greek origins of the Romans

AD

*c.*50–120	Plutarch
mid-2nd c.	Pausanias, *Description of Greece*
*c.*60–230	The rise of a cultural 'hellenism' in the so-called 'Second Sophistic'
330	Foundation of eastern capital of Roman empire, Constantinople
527–65	Reign of emperor Justinian, responsible for attempted 're-

	conquest' of western Roman empire; his troops mocked as 'Graeci'
866–912	Emperor Leo VI
12th c.	Gregory of Corinth, grammarian
1148	Anna Comnena's *Alexiad* completed
1170s	Emperor Manuel I advised that Muslims are better masters than 'Latins' (in 1176 Venetians expelled from Byzantine empire)
1204	Sack of Constantinople in Fourth Crusade
1271–95	'Travels' of Marco Polo
mid-14th c.	Latin works of e.g. Cicero, Augustine, Boethius, Aquinas translated into Greek
1510	Johannes Maior ascribes an Aristotelian 'natural slavery' to Indians
1551	Bartolomé de Las Casas, *Apologetica Historia*
1590	J. de Acosta, *Historia natural y moral de las Indias*
1724	J.-F. Lafitau, *Moeurs des sauvages amériquaines comparés aux moeurs des premiers temps*
18th c.	Physical anthropology distinguishes between 'races'
1833	Johann Gustav Droysen, *History of Hellenism*
1861	J. J. Bachofen develops theory of 'matriarchy' among barbarian peoples
1912–27	K. J. Beloch, *Griechische Geschichte*
1951	F. W. Walbank, 'The problem of Greek nationality'
1980	François Hartog, *Le miroir d'Hérodote*
1987	Martin Bernal, *Black Athena*
1989	Edith Hall, *Inventing the Barbarian*

Guide to Further Reading

The general introduction and the introductions to parts provide ample references to further reading on all of the themes and sources discussed in this book. I limit myself here to the most accessible editions of ancient texts, and to recent books on the Greek representation of foreign peoples.

There is a wide choice of translations of Herodotus: the folksy version of David Grene (University of Chicago Press), with, however, a less than full introduction and set of notes; the rather grey version of Robin Waterfield (Oxford University Press), with superlative introduction and notes by Carolyn Dewald; or the excellent revision of Aubrey de Sélincourt's Penguin translation by John Marincola. A splendid introduction to Herodotus is John Gould's *Herodotus*, newly reissued by Bristol Classical Press. In addition to Redfield's piece above (Ch. 1), see especially François Hartog's *Mirror of Herodotus*; Leslie Kurke's *tour de force, Coins, Bodies, Games and Gold* (Princeton, 1999) came to my notice too late for me to make reference to it elsewhere in this volume.

Aeschylus' *Persians* is best approached through the (parallel Greek and English) edition by Edith Hall (Aris and Phillips). (The Loeb translation is scarcely readable; the Penguin and University of Chicago editions provide cheaper alternatives). The plays of Euripides are currently being translated afresh by John Davie (Penguin) and James Morwood (Oxford University Press); in both cases, translations are prefaced by clear, if brief, introductions to modern scholarship; in addition to these, David Kovacs is producing an excellent series of editions and translations of Euripides in the Loeb Classical Library series (again including both Greek and English texts in parallel). A series of short *Companions* to individual ancient tragedies and to their performance histories is now forthcoming from Duckworth. For barbarians in tragedy, see especially Edith Hall's *Inventing the Barbarian*; for a reading of Aeschylus' *Persians* against the backdrop of Herodotus' *Histories*, see Harrison, *The Emptiness of Asia*.

Isocrates and Xenophon are accessible through old Loeb Classical Library editions (and through some Penguin translations). For the definition of Greek identity through myth or language, see Jonathan Hall, *Ethnic Identity in Greek Antiquity*. For contacts between Greece and the Near East, see M. L. West, *The East Face of Helicon*, Ch. 12, D. M. Lewis, *Sparta and Persia*, and Margaret Miller, *Athens and Persia in the Fifth Century* BC.

Bibliography

Anderson, B., *Imagined Communities: Reflections on the Origin and Spread of Nationalism* (revised edn, London: Verso, 1991)

Andrewes, A., 'Thucydides and the Persians', *Historia* 10 (1961), 1–18

Arafat, K., and C. Morgan, 'Athens, Etruria and the Heuneburg: mutual misconceptions in the study of Greek-barbarian relations', in I. Morris (ed.), *Classical Greece: Ancient Histories and Modern Archaeologies* (Cambridge: Cambridge University Press, 1994), 108–34

Archibald, Z. H., *The Odrysian Kingdom of Thrace: Orpheus Unveiled* (Oxford: Oxford University Press, 1998)

Armayor, O. K., 'Herodotus' catalogue of the Persian Empire', *TAPA* 108 (1978), 1–9

Asheri, D., 'Fra Ellenismo e Iranismo. Studi sulla società e cultura di Xanthos nella età achemenide', in *Modes de Contacts et Processus de transformation dans les sociétés anciennes* (Pisa/Rome: École Française de Rome, 1983), 485–502

——, 'Herodotus on Thrace and Thracian society', in W. Burkert et al., *Hérodote et les peuples non-Grecs* (Geneva: Fondation Hardt Entretiens 35, 1990), 131–69

Auberger, J., *Ctésias: histoires de l'Orient* (Paris: Belles Lettres, 1991)

Austin, M. M., *Greece and Egypt in the Archaic Age*, PCPS Suppl. 2 (Cambridge, 1970)

——, 'Greek tyrants and the Persians 546–479 BC', *CQ* 40 (1990), 289–306

Backhaus, W., 'Der Hellenen-Barbaren-Gegensatz und die Hippokratische Schrift *peri aeron hydaton topon*', *Historia* 25 (1976), 170–85

Bacon, H., *Barbarians in Greek Tragedy* (New Haven: Yale University Press, 1961)

Badian, E., 'The deification of Alexander the Great', in H. J. Dell (ed.), *Ancient Macedonian Studies in Honor of Charles F. Edson* (Thessaloniki: Institute for Balkan Studies 158, 1981), 27–71

Balcer, J. M., 'The Greeks and the Persians: the processes of acculturation', *Historia* 32 (1983), 257–67

——, 'Fifth century BC Ionia: a frontier redefined', *REA* 87 (1985), 31–42

Baslez, M.-F., 'Présence et traditions iraniennes dans les cités de l'Égée',

REA 87 (1985), 137–55

——, 'Les communautés d'Orientaux dans la cité grecque: formes de sociabilité et modèles associatifs', in R. Lonis (ed.), *L'Étranger dans le Monde Grec* (Nancy: Presses Universitaires de Nancy, 1988), 139–58

Bengtson, H., *The Greeks and the Persians: From the Sixth to the Fourth Centuries*, tr. J. Conway (London: Weidenfeld and Nicolson, 1969)

Berlinerbau, J., *Heresy in the University: The 'Black Athena' Controversy and the Responsibilities of American Intellectuals* (New Brunswick: Rutgers University Press, 1999)

Berlin, I., *The Hedgehog and the Fox: An Essay on Tolstoy's View of History* (London: Weidenfeld and Nicolson, 1953)

Bernal, M., *Black Athena. The Afroasiatic Roots of Western Civilization*, 2 vols (London: Free Association, 1987–91)

Bickermann, E. J., 'Origines Gentium', *CPh* 47 (1952), 65–81

——, 'À propos d'un passage de Charès de Mytilène', *PP* 18 (1963), 241–55

Bigwood, J. M., 'Ctesias as historian of the Persian wars', *Phoenix* 32 (1978), 19–41

Boedeker, D., 'Protesilaos and the end of Herodotus' *Histories*', *CSCA* 7 (1988), 30–48

Bosworth, A. B., *Conquest and Empire: The Reign of Alexander the Great* (Cambridge: Cambridge University Press, 1988)

Bovon, A., 'La représentation des guerriers perses et la notion de barbare dans la première moitié de Ve siècle', *BCH* 87 (1963), 579–602

Boyce, M., *A History of Zoroastrianism* (Leiden: Brill, 1975–91)

Braun, T. F. R. G., 'The Greeks in the Near East', *CAH* III^2 pt 3 (1982), 1–31

——, 'The Greeks in Egypt', *CAH* III^2 pt 3 (1982), 32–56

Briant, P., *Histoire de l'empire Perse de Cyrus à Alexandre* (Paris: Fayard, 1996)

Brixhe, C., 'La langue d'étranger non-Grec chez Aristophane', in R. Lonis (ed.), *L'Étranger dans le Monde Grec* (Nancy: Press Universitaires de Nancy, 1988), 113–38

Brosius, M., *Women in Ancient Persia (559–331 BC)* (Oxford: Oxford University Press, 1996)

Brown, P., *The Making of Late Antiquity* (Cambridge MA: Harvard University Press, 1978)

Burkert, W., 'Herodot als Historiker fremder Religionen', in W. Burkert et al., *Hérodote et les peuples non-Grecs* (Geneva: Fondation Hardt Entretiens 35, 1990), 1–39

——, *The Orientalizing Revolution*, tr. M. E. Pinder and W. Burkert (Cambridge MA: Harvard University Press, 1992)

——, et al., *Hérodote et les peuples non-Grecs* (Geneva: Fondation Hardt Entretiens 35, 1990)

Burstein, S., 'Greek contact with Egypt and the Levant: ca. 1600–500 BC', *Ancient World* 27 (1996), 20–28

——, 'The Hellenistic age', in S. M. Burstein, R. MacMullen, K. A. Raaflaub and A. M. Ward (eds), *Ancient History: Recent Work and New Directions* (Claremont CA: Regina, 1997), 17–54

Buxton, R., *Imaginary Greece: The Contexts of Mythology* (Cambridge: Cambridge University Press, 1994)

Cartledge, P., 'Herodotus and the "Other": a meditation on empire', *Echos du Monde Classique* 34 (1990), 27–40

——, *The Greeks* (Oxford: Oxford University Press, 1993, rev. edn 1997)

——, 'The machismo of the Athenian empire – or the reign of the phaulus', in L. Foxhall and J. Salmon (eds), *When Men were Men: Masculinity, Power and Identity in Classical Antiquity* (London: Routledge, 1998), 54–67

Castriota, D., *Myth, Ethos and Actuality: Official Art in Fifth-Century BC Athens* (Madison: University of Wisconsin Press, 1992)

Clarke, K., *Between Geography and History: Hellenistic Constructions of the Roman World* (Oxford: Oxford University Press, 1999)

Clogg, R., *A Concise History of Greece* (Cambridge: Cambridge University Press, 1992)

Cohen, B. (ed.), *Not the Classical Ideal: Athens and the Construction of the Other in Greek Art* (Leiden: Brill, 2000)

Coleman, J. E., and C. A. Walz (eds), *Greeks and Barbarians: Essays on the interactions between Greeks and Non-Greeks in Antiquity and the Consequences for Eurocentrism* (Bethesda MD: CDL Press, 1997)

Colledge, M., 'Greek and non-Greek interaction in the art and architecture of the Hellenistic East', in A. Kuhrt and S. Sherwin-White (eds), *Hellenism in the East: The Interaction of Greek and Non-Greek Civilizations from Syria to Central Asia after Alexander* (London: Duckworth, 1987), 134–62

Colley, L., *Britons: Forging the Nation 1707–1837* (New Haven: Yale University Press, 1992)

Colvin, S. C., *Dialect in Aristophanes* (Oxford: Oxford University Press, 1999)

Daumas, M., 'Aristophane et les Perses', *REA* 87 (1985), 289–305

Davidson, J., *Courtesans and Fishcakes: The Consuming Passions of Classical Athens* (London: HarperCollins, 1997)

Dench, E., *From Barbarians to New Men: Greek, Roman and Modern Perceptions of Peoples from the Central Apennines* (Oxford: Oxford University Press, 1995)

Derrida, J., *Dissemination*, tr. B. Johnson (London: Athlone Press, 1981)

Descoeudres, J.-P. (ed.), *Greek Colonists and Native Populations* (Oxford: Oxford University Press, 1990)

Detienne, M., *The Creation of Mythology*, tr. Margaret Cook (Chicago: University of Chicago Press, 1986)

——, and J.-P. Vernant, *The Cuisine of Sacrifice among the Greeks*, tr. Paula Wissing (Chicago: University of Chicago Press, 1989)

Dewald, C., review of F. Hartog, *The Mirror of Herodotus*, *CPh* 85

(1990), 217–24

——, 'Wanton kings, pickled heroes and gnomic founding fathers: strategies of meaning at the end of Herodotus' *Histories*', in D. H. Roberts, F. M. Dunn and D. Fowler (eds), *Classical Closure* (Princeton NJ: Princeton University Press, 1997), 62–82

Dihle, A., *Die Griechen und die Fremden* (Munich: C. H. Beck, 1994)

Diller, A., *Race Mixture among the Greeks before Alexander* (Urbana: University of Illinois, 1937)

Diller, H., 'Die Hellenen–Barbaren-Antithese im Zeitalter der Perserkriege', in H. Schwabl et al., *Grecs et Barbares* (Geneva: Fondation Hardt Entretiens 8, 1961), 37–82

Dillery, J., *Xenophon and the History of his Times* (London: Routledge, 1995)

Donadoni, S. F., 'Gli Egiziani e le lingue degli altri', in his *Cultura dell' antico Egitto* (Rome: Dipartimento di Scienze Storiche Archeologiche e Antropologiche dell' Antichità, 1986), 193–206

Dörrie, H.,'Die Wertung der Barbaren im Urteil der Griechen. Knechts-naturen? Oder Bewahrer und Künder heilbringender Weisheit?', in *Antike und Universalgeschichte: Festschrift H. Stier* (Münster: Aschendorff, 1974), 146–75

Dougherty, C., *The Poetics of Colonisation: From City to Text in Archaic Greece* (Oxford: Oxford University Press, 1993)

Dover, K. J., *Greek Homosexuality* (London: Duckworth, 1978)

Drews, R., 'The first tyrants in Greece', *Historia* 21 (1972), 129–44

——, *The Greek Accounts of Eastern History* (Cambridge MA: Center for Hellenic Studies and Harvard University Press, 1973)

duBois, P., *Centaurs and Amazons* (Ann Arbor: University of Michigan Press, 1982)

Dubuisson, M., 'Remarques sur le vocabulaire grec de l'acculturation', *Revue Belge de Philologie et d'Histoire* 60 (1982), 5–32

Due, B., *The Cyropaedia: Xenophon's Aims and Methods* (Aarhus: Aarhus University Press, 1989)

Erskine, A., 'Money-loving Romans', *Papers of the Leeds International Latin Seminar* 9 (1996), 1–11

——, *Troy between Greece and Rome* (Oxford: Oxford University Press, 2001)

Ferrari Pinney, G., 'For the heroes are at hand', *JHS* 104 (1984), 181–3

Finley, M. I., 'The Ancient Greeks and their nation', in his *The Use and Abuse of History* (London: Hogarth, 1986), 120–33

Flower, M. A., *Theopompus of Chios: History and Rhetoric in the Fourth Century* BC (Oxford: Oxford University Press, 1997)

Fol, A., and I. Mazarow, *Thrace and the Thracians* (London: Cassell, 1977)

Fol, A., B. Nikolov and R. F. Hoddinott, *The New Thracian Treasure from Rogozen, Bulgaria* (London: British Museum Publications, 1986)

Fornara, C. W., *Herodotus: An Interpretative Essay* (Oxford: Oxford

University Press, 1971)

Foucault, M., *A History of Sexuality*, vol. 3, tr. R. Hurley (London: Penguin, 1990)

Fowler, R. L., 'Herodotus and his contemporaries', *JHS* 116 (1996), 62–87

Francis, E. D., 'Greeks and Persians: the art of hazard and triumph', in D. Schmandt-Bessarat (ed.), *Ancient Persia: The Art of an Empire* (Malibu: Undena, 1980), 53–86

Fraser, P. M., *Ptolemaic Alexandria*, 3 vols (Oxford: Oxford University Press, 1971)

Froidefrond, C., *Le mirage égyptien dans la littérature grecque d'Homère à Aristote* (Paris: Ophrys, 1971)

Geddes, A. G., 'Rags and riches: the costume of Athenian men in the fifth century', *CQ* 37 (1987), 307–31

Georges, P., *Barbarian Asia and the Greek Experience* (Baltimore: Johns Hopkins University Press, 1994)

Gera, D. L., *Xenophon's Cyropaedia: Style, Genre and Literary Technique* (Oxford: Oxford University Press, 1993)

Gianotti, G., 'Ordine e simmetria nella rappresentazione del mondo: Erodoto e il paradosso del Nilo', *Quaderni della Storia* 27 (1988), 51–92

Gittings, C. E., *Imperialism and Gender: Constructions of Masculinity* (New Lambton, NSW: Dangaroo, 1996)

Goldhill, S. D., *Reading Greek Tragedy* (Cambridge: Cambridge University Press, 1986)

——, 'The Great Dionysia and civic ideology', *JHS* 107 (1987), 58–76, reprinted in J. J. Winkler and F. I. Zeitlin (eds), *Nothing to Do with Dionysos? Athenian Drama in its Social Context* (Princeton NJ: Princeton University Press, 1990), 97–129

Goody, J., *The East in the West* (Cambridge: Cambridge University Press, 1996)

Gordon, R. L., 'The real and the imaginary: production and religion in the Graeco-Roman world', *Art History* 2 (1979), 5–34

Gould, J., 'On understanding Greek religion', in P. E. Easterling and J. V. Muir (eds), *Greek Religion and Society* (Cambridge: Cambridge University Press, 1985), 1–33

——, *Herodotus* (London: Weidenfeld and Nicolson, 1989)

——, 'Herodotus and religion', in S. Hornblower (ed.), *Greek Historiography* (Oxford: Oxford University Press, 1994), 91–106

Graf, D., 'Medism: the origin and significance of the term', *JHS* 104 (1984), 15–30

Gray, V., 'Herodotus and the rhetoric of otherness', *AJP* 116 (1995), 185–211

Green, P., *The Greco-Persian Wars* (Berkeley CA: University of California Press, 1996)

Griffith, M., 'The King and Eye: the rule of the father in Greek tragedy', *PCPS* 44 (1998), 20–84

Haider, P. W., 'Griechen im Vorderen Orient und in Ägypten bis ca. 590 v. Chr.', in C. Ulf (ed.), *Wege zur Genese griechische Identität: Die Bedeutung der früharchaischen Zeit* (Berlin: Akademie Verlag, 1996), 59–115

Hall, C., *White, Male and Middle Class: Explorations in Feminism and History* (Cambridge: Polity, 1992)

——, *Civilizing Subjects* (Oxford: Polity Press, forthcoming)

Hall, E., *Inventing the Barbarian: Greek Self-Definition through Tragedy* (Oxford: Oxford University Press, 1989)

——, 'The archer scene in Aristophanes' *Thesmophoriazousae*', *Philologus* 133 (1989), 38–54

——, 'Asia unmanned: images of victory in classical Athens', in J. Rich and G. Shipley (eds), *War and Society in the Greek World* (London: Routledge, 1993), 107–33

——, *Aeschylus*, Persians (Warminster: Aris and Phillips, 1996)

Hall, J. M., *Ethnic Identity in Greek Antiquity* (Cambridge: Cambridge University Press, 1997)

Halliwell, F. S., 'The sounds of the voice in old comedy', in E. M. Craik (ed.), *'Owls to Athens'* (Oxford: Oxford University Press, 1990), 69–79

——, *The Laughter of Dionysus* (forthcoming)

Harrison, E. B., 'Hellenic identity and Athenian identity in the fifth century BC', in S. J. Barnes and W. S. Melion (eds), *Cultural Differentiation and Cultural Identity in the Visual Arts* (Studies in the History of Art 27, Hanover and London: University Press of New England, 1989), 41–61

Harrison, T., 'Herodotus and the ancient Greek idea of rape', in S. Deacy and K. Pierce (eds), *Rape in Antiquity* (London: Duckworth, 1997), 185–208

——, 'Herodotus' conception of foreign languages', *Histos* 2 (1998), www.dur.ac.uk/Classics/Histos

——, *Divinity and History: The Religion of Herodotus* (Oxford: Oxford University Press, 2000)

——, *The Emptiness of Asia: Aeschylus'* Persians *and the History of the Fifth Century* (London: Duckworth, 2000)

——, 'Sicily in the Athenian imagination: Thucydides on the Persian wars', in C. Smith and J. Serrati (eds), *Ancient Sicily from Aeneas to Cicero* (Edinburgh: Edinburgh University Press, 2000), 84–96, 199–201

——, 'The Persian invasions', in E. Bakker, I. De Jong and H. van Wees (eds), *A Companion to Herodotus* (Leiden: Brill, forthcoming)

——, 'Persian dress and Greek freedom: the representation of eastern decadence in Greek historiography from Hecataeus to Alexander' (forthcoming)

Hartog, François, *The Mirror of Herodotus*, tr. J. Lloyd (Berkeley CA: University of California Press, 1988)

——, 'Fondements grecs de l'idée d'Europe', *Quaderni della Storia* 43 (1996), 5–17

——, *Memories of Odysseus*, tr. J. Lloyd (Edinburgh: Edinburgh University Press, 2001)

Heather, P., *Goths and Romans 332–489* (Oxford: Oxford University Press, 1991)

Henderson, J., '*Timeo Danaos*: Amazons in early Greek art and pottery', in S. Goldhill and R. Osborne (eds), *Art and Text in Ancient Greek Culture* (Cambridge: Cambridge University Press, 1994), 85–137

Herzfeld, M., *Ours Once More: Folklore, Ideology and the Making of Modern Greece* (Austin: University of Texas Press, 1982)

Hirsch, S. W., *The Friendship of the Barbarians: Xenophon and the Persian Empire* (Hanover and London: University Press of New England, 1985)

Hobsbawm, E., *Nations and Nationalism* (2nd edn, Cambridge: Cambridge University Press, 1992)

Hornblower, S., *Mausolus* (Oxford: Oxford University Press, 1982)

——, 'Persia', *CAH* VI² (1994), 45–96

Horrocks, G., *Greek: A History of the Language and its Speakers* (London: Longman, 1997)

Hunter, V. J., *Policing Athens: Social Control in the Attic Lawsuits, 420–320 BC* (Princeton NJ: Princeton University Press, 1994)

Jannsens, E., 'Les étrangers comme élement comique dans les comédies d'Aristophane', *Mélanges Georges Smets* (Bruxelles: Éditions de la librairie encyclopédique, 1952), 455–60

Jones, C. P., *Kinship Diplomacy in the Ancient World* (Cambridge MA: Harvard University Press, 1999)

Jouanna, J., 'Les causes de la défaite des Barbares chez Eschyle, Hérodote et Hippocrate', *Ktema* 6 (1981), 3–15

——, 'Collaboration ou résistance au barbare: Artémise d'Halicarnasse et Cadmos de Cos chez Hérodote et Hippocrate', *Ktema* 9 (1984), 15–26

Jüthner, J., *Hellenen und Barbaren: Aus der Geschichte des National-bewusstseins* (Leipzig: Dieterich' sche Verlagsbuchhandlung, 1923)

Karttunen, K., *India in Early Greek Literature* (Helsinki: Finnish Oriental Society, 1989)

——, *India in the Hellenistic World* (Helsinki: Finnish Oriental Society, 1997)

Kopce, G., and I. Tokumaru (eds), *Greece between East and West: 10th–8th Centuries BC* (Mainz am Rhein: Philipp von Zabern, 1992)

Kuhrt, A., and S. Sherwin-White (eds), *Hellenism in the East: The Interaction of Greek and Non-Greek Civilizations from Syria to Central Asia after Alexander* (London: Duckworth, 1987)

——, 'Xerxes' destruction of Babylonian temples', in H. Sancisi-Weerdenburg and A. Kuhrt (eds), *Achaemenid History II: The Greek Sources* (Leiden: Nederlands Instituut voor het Nabije Oosten, 1987), 69–78

Kurke, L., 'The politics of *habrosyne* in archaic Greece', *ClAnt* 11 (1992), 91–120

Lattimore, R., 'The wise adviser in Herodotus', *CPh* 34 (1939), 24–35

——, 'Herodotus and the names of the Egyptian gods', *CPh* 35 (1940), 357–65

Laurot, B., 'Idéaux grecs et barbarie chez Hérodote', *Ktema* 6 (1981), 57–68

Lavelle, B. M., *The Sorrow and the Pity: Prolegomena to a History of Athens under the Peisistratids c.560–510 BC* (Stuttgart: Historia Einzelschriften 80, 1993)

Lefkowitz, M., *Not Out of Africa: How Afrocentrism Became an Excuse to Teach Myth as History* (New York: Basic Books, 1996)

——, and G. Rogers, *Black Athena Revisited* (Chapel Hill: University of North Carolina Press, 1996)

Lenfant, D., 'Ctésias et Hérodote ou les réécritures de l'histoire dans la Perse achéménide', *REG* 109 (1996), 348–80

Levine, M. M., and J. Peradotto (eds), *The Challenge of Black Athena*, special issue, *Arethusa* 22 (1989)

Lévy, E., 'Les origines du mirage scythe', *Ktema* 6 (1981), 57–68

——, 'Naissance du concept de barbare', *Ktema* 9 (1984), 5–14

——, 'Hérodote *philobarbaros* ou la vision du barbare chez Hérodote', in R. Lonis (ed.), *L'Étranger dans le monde grec*, vol. 2 (Nancy: Presses Universitaires de Nancy, 1992), 193–244

Lewis, D. M., *Sparta and Persia* (Leiden: Brill, 1977)

——, 'Persians in Herodotus', in M. H. Jameson (ed.), *The Greek Historians: Papers Presented to A. E. Raubitschek* (Palo Alto: ANMA, 1985), 89–105, reprinted in his *Selected Papers in Greek and Near Eastern History*, ed. P. J. Rhodes (Cambridge: Cambridge University Press), 345–61

——, 'The Persepolis tablets: speech, seal and script', in A. K. Bowman and G. Woolf (eds), *Literacy and Power in the Ancient World* (Cambridge: Cambridge University Press, 1994), 17–32, 218–20

Lissarrague, F., 'Être Scythe à Athènes', in F. Lissarrague (ed.), *L'Autre guerrier* (Paris: Découverte, 1990), 125–49

Lissarrague F., *The Aesthetics of the Greek Banquet: Images of Wine and Ritual,* tr. A. Szegedy-Maszak (Princeton: Princeton University Press, 1990)

Lloyd, A. B., 'Herodotus on Egyptians and Libyans', in W. Burkert et al., *Hérodote et les peuples non-Grecs* (Geneva: Fondation Hardt Entretiens 35, 1990), 215–53

Lloyd, G. E. R., *Polarity and Analogy: Two Types of Argumentation in Early Greek Thought* (Cambridge: Cambridge University Press, 1966)

Lombardo, M., '"*Habrosyne* e *habra*" nel mondo Greco arcaico', in *Forme di Contatto e Processi di Trasformazione nelle Società anticha* (Pisa/Rome: École Française de Rome, 1983), 1077–103

Long, T., *Barbarians in Greek Comedy* (Corbendale: University of Illinois Press, 1986)

Loraux, N., *L'invention d'Athènes: Histoire de l'oraison funèbre dans la 'cité classique'* (Paris: Mouton, 1981), tr. A. Sheridan as *The Invention of Athens: The Funeral Oration in the Classical City* (Cambridge MA: Harvard University Press, 1986)

Luraghi, N., 'Der Erdbebenaufstand und die Entstehung der messenischen Identität', in V.-M. Strocka and D. Papenfuss (eds), *Gab es das griechische Wunder?* (Akten des 16. Fachsymposium der Alexander von Humbold Stiftung, forthcoming)

McDonald, M., *'We Are Not French!' Language, Culture and Identity in Brittany* (London: Routledge, 1989)

McInerney, J., *The Folds of Parnassos: Land and Ethnicity in Ancient Phokis* (Austin: University of Texas Press, 1999)

Mackie, Hilary, *Talking Trojan: Speech and Community in the Iliad* (New York: Rowman and Littlefield, 1996)

Malkin, I., *The Returns of Odysseus: Colonization and Ethnicity* (Berkeley CA: University of California Press, 1998)

Martorelli, A., 'Storia persiana in Erodoto: echi di versioni ufficiali', *Rendiconti dell'Istituto Lombardo* 111 (1977), 115–25

Meier, C., *The Greek Discovery of Politics*, tr. D. MacLintock (Cambridge MA: Harvard University Press, 1990)

——, *The Political Art of Greek Tragedy*, tr. A. Webber (Cambridge: Polity, 1993)

Mikalson, J. D., *Honor Thy Gods: Popular Religion in Greek Tragedy* (Chapel Hill: University of North Carolina Press, 1991)

Miller, M. C., 'Midas as the Great King in Attic fifth-century vase painting', *Antike Kunst* 31 (1988), 79–89

——, 'Persians: the Oriental Other', *Source: Notes in the History of Art* (1995), 38–44

——, *Athens and Persia in the Fifth Century* BC: *A Study in Cultural Receptivity* (Cambridge: Cambridge University Press, 1997)

Mills, S., *Theseus, Tragedy and the Athenian Empire* (Oxford: Oxford University Press, 1997)

Missiou, A., '*DOULOS TOU BASILEÔS*: the politics of translation', *CQ* 43 (1993), 377–91

Mitchell, L. G., *Greeks Bearing Gifts: The Public Use of Private Relationships in the Greek World 435–323* BC (Cambridge: Cambridge University Press, 1997)

Moles, J., 'Herodotus warns the Athenians', *Papers of the Leeds International Latin Seminar* 9 (1996), 259–84

Momigliano, A., 'George Grote and the study of Greek history', in his *Contributo alla storia degli studi classici* (Rome: Edizioni di Storia e Letteratura, 1955), 213–31

——, 'L'Europa come concetto politico presso Isocrate e gli Isocratei', in his *Terzo contributo alla storia degli studi classici e del mondo antico* (Rome: Edizioni di Storia e Letteratura, 1966)

——, 'Tradizione e invenzione in Ctesia', in his *Quarto contributo* (Rome: Edizioni di Storia e Letteratura, 1969), 181–212

——, *Alien Wisdom* (Cambridge: Cambridge University Press, 1975)

Morris, S., *Daidalos and the Origins of Greek Art* (Princeton NJ: Princeton University Press, 1992)

——, 'Homer and the Near East', in I. Morris and B. Powell (eds), *A New Companion to Homer* (Leiden: Brill, 1997), 599–623

Mosley, D. J., 'Greeks, barbarians, language and contact', *Ancient Society* 2 (1971), 1–6

——, *Envoys and Diplomacy in Ancient Greece* (Wiesbaden: Historia Einzelschriften 22, 1973)

Munson, R. V., 'Three aspects of Spartan kingship in Herodotus', in R. M. Rosen and J. Farrell (eds), *Nomodeiktes: Greek Studies in Honour of Martin Ostwald* (Ann Arbor: University of Michigan Press, 1993), 39–54

Murray, G., *Aeschylus: The Creator of Tragedy* (Oxford: Oxford University Press, 1940)

Murray, O., 'Herodotus and oral history', in H. Sancisi-Weerdenburg and A. Kuhrt (eds), *Achaemenid History II: The Greek Sources* (Leiden: Nederlands Instituut voor het Nabije Oosten, 1987), 93–115, reprinted in N. Luraghi (ed.), *Herodotus in Context* (Oxford: Oxford University Press, forthcoming)

—— (ed.), *Sympotica: A Symposium on the Symposion* (Oxford: Oxford University Press, 1990)

——, 'History and reason in the ancient city', *Papers of the British School at Rome* 59 (1991), 1–13

Murray, P., 'What is a *muthos* for Plato?', in R. Buxton (ed.), *From Myth to Reason? Studies in the Development of Greek Thought* (Oxford: Oxford University Press, 1999), 251–62

Nippel, W., *Griechen, Barbaren und 'Wilde': Alte Geschichte und Sozialanthropologie* (Frankfurt: Fischer, 1990)

Nylander, C., *Ionians in Pasargadae* (Uppsala: Almkvist and Wiksell, 1970)

Ober, J., *Political Dissent in Democratic Athens: Intellectual Critics of Popular Rule* (Princeton NJ: Princeton University Press, 1999)

Osborne, R., 'Early Greek colonisation? The nature of Greek settlement in the West', in N. Fisher and H. van Wees (eds), *Archaic Greece: New Approaches and New Evidence* (London: Duckworth, 1998), 251–69

Parker, R., *Athenian Religion: A History* (Oxford: Oxford University Press, 1996)

——, *Cleomenes on the Acropolis: An Inaugural Lecture Delivered before the University of Oxford on 12 May 1997* (Oxford: Oxford University Press, 1998)

Pascal, P., *Les Îles Nomades. Conquérir et résister dans l'Enquête d'Hérodote* (Paris: Éditions de l'école des hautes études en sciences sociales, 1997)

Pelling, C., 'Aesehylus' *Persae* and history', in C. Pelling (ed.), *Greek*

Tragedy and the Historian (Oxford: Oxford University Press, 1997), 1–19

Pembroke, S., 'Women in charge: the function of alternatives in early Greek tradition and the ancient idea of matriarchy', *Journal of the Warburg and Courtald Institutes* 30 (1967), 1–35

Peremans, W., 'Egyptiens et étrangers dans l'Egypte ptolémaïque', in H. Schwabl et al., *Grecs et Barbares* (Geneva: Fondation Hardt Entretiens 8, 1961), 121–66

Perlman, S., 'Isocrates' *Philippus* and Panhellenism', *Historia* 18 (1969), 370–4

——, 'Panhellenism, the polis and imperialism', *Historia* 25 (1976), 1–30

Pickstock, C., *After Writing: On the Liturgical Consummation of Philosophy* (Oxford: Blackwell, 1998)

Planinc, Z., *Plato's Political Philosophy: Prudence in the Republic and the Laws* (London: Duckworth, 1991)

Powell, B. B., *Homer and the Origin of the Greek Alphabet* (Cambridge: Cambridge University Press, 1991)

Pretagostini, R., 'Aristofane "etnologo": il mondo persiano nella falsa ambasceria del prologo degli *Acarnesi*', *Seminari Romani* 1.1 (1998), 41–56

Preus, A., 'Greek philosophy in Egypt: from Solon to the Arab conquest', in J. E. Coleman and C. A. Walz (eds), *Greeks and Barbarians: Essays on the Interactions between Greeks and Non-Greeks in Antiquity and the Consequences for Eurocentrism* (Bethesda MD: CDL Press, 1997), 155–74

Pryke, S., 'Nationalism and sexuality: what are the issues?', *Nations and Nationalism* 4 (1998), 529–46

Pugliese Carratelli, G., 'Le guerre mediche ed il sorgere della solidarità ellenica', in *La Persia e il Mondo Greco-Romano* (Rome: Accademia Nazionale dei Lincei 76, 1966), 147–56

Raeck, W., *Zum Barbarenbild in der Kunst Athens im 6. Und 5. Jahrhundert v. Chr.* (Bonn: Rudolf Habelt, 1981)

Reverdin, O., 'Crise spirituelle et évasion', in H. Schwabl et al., *Grecs et Barbares* (Geneva: Fondation Hardt Entretiens 8, 1961), 85–120

Ridgway, D., *The First Western Greeks* (Cambridge: Cambridge University Press, 1992)

Rochette, B., 'Grecs et Latins face aux langues étrangères', *Revue Belge de Philologie et d'Histoire* 73 (1995), 5–16

Romilly, J. de, 'Isocrates and Europe', *Greece and Rome* 39 (1992), 2–13

Romm, J., 'Herodotus and mythic geography: the case of the Hyperboreans', *TAPA* 119 (1989), 97–113

——, *The Edges of the Earth in Ancient Thought: Geography, Exploration and Fiction* (Princeton NJ: Princeton University Press, 1992)

Rood, T. C. B., 'Thucydides' Persian Wars', in C. Kraus (ed.), *The Limits of Historiography* (Leiden: Brill, 1999), 141–68

Root, M. C., *The King and Kingship in Achaemenid Art* (Leiden: Brill, 1979)

——, 'From the heart: powerful Persianisms in the art of the western empire', in H. Sancisi-Weerdenburg and A. Kuhrt (eds), *Achaemenid History VI: Asia Minor and Egypt: Old Cultures in a New Empire* (Leiden: Nederlands Instituut voor het Nabije Oosten, 1991), 1–29

Rosellini, M., and S. Saïd, 'Usages de femmes et autres *nomoi* chez les "sauvages d'Hérodote"', *ASNP* ser. 3, 8 (1978), 949–1005

Rudhardt, J., *Notions fondamentales de la pensée religieuse et actes constitutifs du culte dans la Grèce classique* (2nd edn, Paris: Picard, 1992)

Runciman, W. G., 'Doomed to extinction: the *polis* as an evolutionary dead-end', in O. Murray and S. Price (eds), *The Greek City from Homer to Alexander* (Oxford: Oxford University Press, 1990), 347–67

Said, E. W., *Orientalism* (New York: Pantheon, 1978)

——, *Culture and Imperialism* (London: Chatto and Windus, 1993)

Saïd, S., 'Darius et Xerxes dans les *Perses* d'Eschyle', *Ktema* 6 (1981), 17–38

——, (ed.), *Hellenismos: Quelques jalons pour une histoire de l'identité grecque* (Leiden: Brill, 1991)

Sancisi-Weerdenburg, H., 'Exit Atossa: images of women in Greek historiography on Persia', in A. Cameron and A. Kuhrt (eds), *Images of Women in Antiquity* (London: Routledge, 1983), 20–33

——, 'The death of Cyrus: Xenophon's *Cyropaedia* as a source for Iranian history', in *Papers in honour of Professor Mary Boyce, Acta Iranica: Hommages et Opera Minora X–XI*, vol. II (Leiden: Brill, 1985), 459–71

——, 'Decadence in the empire or decadence in the sources? From sources to synthesis: Ctesias', in H. Sancisi-Weerdenburg (ed.), *Achaemenid History I: Sources, Structures and Synthesis* (Leiden: Nederlands Instituut voor het Nabije Oosten, 1987), 33–45

——, 'The fifth oriental monarchy and hellenocentrism: Cyropaedia VIII viii and its influence', in H. Sancisi-Weerdenburg and A. Kuhrt (eds), *Achaemenid History II: The Greek Sources* (Leiden: Nederlands Instituut voor het Nabije Oosten, 1987), 117–31

——, 'The orality of Herodotus' *Medikos Logos* or: the Median empire revisited', in H. Sancisi-Weerdenburg, A. Kuhrt and M. C. Root (eds), *Achaemenid History VIII: Continuity and Change* (Leiden: Nederlands Instituut voor het Nabije Oosten, 1994), 39–55

Schwabl, H., 'Das Bild der fremden Welt bei den frühen Griechen', in H. Schwabl et al., *Grecs et Barbares* (Geneva: Fondation Hardt Entretiens 8, 1961), 1–36

Sherwin-White, S., 'Seleucid Babylonia: a case study for the installation and development of Greek rule', in A. Kuhrt and S. Sherwin-White (eds), *Hellenism in the East* (London: Duckworth, 1987), 1–31

——, and A. Kuhrt, *From Samarkand to Sardis: A New Approach to the Seleucid Empire* (London: Duckworth, 1993)

Shipley, G., *The Greek World after Alexander 323–30 BC* (London: Routledge, 2000)

Snowden, F. M., *Before Color Prejudice: The Ancient View of Blacks* (Cambridge MA: Harvard University Press, 1983)

——, 'Greeks and Ethiopians', in J. E. Coleman and C. A. Walz (eds), *Greeks and Barbarians: Essays on the Interactions between Greeks and Non-Greeks in Antiquity and the Consequences for Eurocentrism* (Bethesda MD: CDL Press, 1997), 103–26

Sordi, M., *L'Europa nel mondo antico, Contributi dell' Istituto di storia antica* 12 (Milan: Vita e Pensiero, 1986)

Sourvinou-Inwood, C., 'Tragedy and religion: constructs and readings', in C. Pelling (ed.), *Greek Tragedy and the Historian* (Oxford: Oxford University Press, 1997), 161–86

Southern, R. W., 'England's first entry into Europe', in his *Medieval Humanism and Other Studies* (Oxford: Blackwell, 1970), 135–57

Stadter, P., 'Herodotus and the Athenian *arche*', ASNP 22.3–4 (1992), 781–809

Starr, C. G., 'Greeks and Persians in the 4th Century BC', *Iranica Antiqua* 11 (1975), 39–99, 12 (1977), 49–115

Swain, S., *Hellenism and Empire: Language, Classicism, and Power in the Greek World* AD 50–250 (Oxford: Oxford University Press, 1996)

Tanner, J., 'Shifting paradigms in classical art history', *Antiquity* 68 (1994), 650–5

Tatum, J., *Xenophon's Imperial Fiction: On* The Education of Cyrus (Princeton NJ: Princeton University Press, 1989)

Thomas, R., *Literacy and Orality in Ancient Greece* (Cambridge: Cambridge University Press, 1992)

——, *Herodotus in Context: Ethnography, Science and the Art of Persuasion* (Cambridge: Cambridge University Press, 2000)

Thompson, D., *Memphis under the Ptolemies* (Princeton NJ: Princeton University Press, 1988)

Thomson, J. A. K., *Greeks and Barbarians* (London, New York: George Allen and Unwin, 1921)

Tsetskhladze, G. R., *The Greek Colonisation of the Black Sea Area: Historical Interpretation of Archaeology* (Stuttgart: Historia Einzelschriften 121, 1998)

Tsteskhladze, G. R., and F. de Angelis (eds), *The Archaeology of Greek Colonisation: Essays Dedicated to Sir John Boardman* (Oxford: Oxford University Committee for Archaeology, Monograph 40, 1994)

Tuplin, C. J., 'Persians as Medes', in H. Sancisi-Weerdenburg, A. Kuhrt and M. C. Root (eds), *Achaemenid History VIII: Continuity and Change* (Leiden: Nederlands Instituut voor het Nabije Oosten, 1994), 235–56

——, *Achaemenid Studies* (Stuttgart: Historia Einzelschriften 99, 1996)

Tyrrell, W. B., *Amazons: A Study in Athenian Mythmaking* (Baltimore: Johns Hopkins University Press, 1984)

Ulf., C., 'Griechische Ethnogenese versus Wanderungen von Stämmen und

Stammstaaten', in C. Ulf (ed.), *Wege zur Genese griechische Identität: Die Bedeutung der früharchaischen Zeit* (Berlin: Akademie Verlag, 1996), 240–80

Vickers, M., 'Interactions between Greeks and Persians', in H. Sancisi-Weerdenburg and A. Kuhrt (eds), *Achaemenid History IV: Centre and Periphery* (Leiden: Nederlands Instituut voor het Nabije Oosten, 1990), 253–62

Vidal-Naquet, P., *The Black Hunter: Forms of Thought and Forms of Society in the Greek World*, tr. P. Szegedy-Maszak (Baltimore: Johns Hopkins University Press, 1986)

——, 'The place and status of foreigners in Athenian tragedy', in C. Pelling (ed.), *Greek Tragedy and the Historian* (Oxford: Oxford University Press, 1997), 109–19

Walbank, F. W., 'Monarchy and monarchic ideas', *CAH* VII² pt 1, 62–100

Weber, Max, *Economy and Society: An Outline of Interpretative Sociology* (Berkeley CA: University of California Press, 1979)

Weiler, I., 'The Greek and non-Greek world in the archaic period', *GRBS* 9 (1986), 21–9

——, 'Soziogenese und soziale Mobilität im archaischer Griechenland', in C. Ulf (ed.), *Wege zur Genese griechische Identität: Die Bedeutung der früharchaischen Zeit* (Berlin: Akademie Verlag, 1996), 211–39

West, M. L., *The East Face of Helicon: West Asiatic Elements in Greek Poetry and Myth* (Oxford: Oxford University Press, 1997)

West, W. C., 'Saviors of Greece', *GRBS* 11 (1970), 271–82

Wiesehöfer, J., *Ancient Persia from 550 BC to 650 AD*, tr. A. Azodi (London: I. B. Tauris, 1996)

Wood, F., *Did Marco Polo Go to China?* (Boulder CO: Westview Press, 1998)

Woodard, R., *Greek Writing from Knossos to Homer* (New York: Oxford University Press, 1997)

Zanker, Paul, *The Power of Images in the Age of Augustus*, tr. A. Shapiro (Ann Arbor: University of Michigan Press, 1988)

Index